along these lines

third canadian edition

writing paragraphs and essays

John Sheridan Biays
Broward Community College

Carol Wershoven
Palm Beach Community College

Lara Sauer
George Brown College

Pearson Canada
Toronto

To Mom and Dad—with love and thanks.

—L.S.

ADVANCE COPY

ISBN-13: 978-0-13-701894-9
ISBN-10: 0-13-701894-9

Vice-President, Editorial Director: Gary Bennett
Editor-in-Chief: Ky Pruesse
Acquisitions Editor: Chris Helsby
Supervising Developmental Editor: Suzanne Schaan
Developmental Editor: Rachel Stuckey
Marketing Manager: Loula March
Production Editor: Claire Horsnell
Copy Editor: Lenore Latta
Proofreaders: Lisa LaFramboise, Nancy Mucklow
Production Coordinator: Janis Raisen
Composition: Integra
Art Director: Julia Hall
Cover Design: Jennifer Stimson
Cover Image: Arctic-Images/Getty Images

1 2 3 4 5   13 12 11 10 09

Printed and bound in the United States of America.

ALONG THESE LINES/Pearson Education Canada

WRITIN *roach*

GRAMMAR FOR WRITERS: The Bottom Line

ALONG THESE LINES/Pearson Education Canada

CONTENTS

ALONG THESE LINES/Pearson Education Canada

ALONG THESE LINES/Pearson Education Canada

ALONG THESE LINES/Pearson Education Canada

PREFACE

The third Canadian edition of *Along These Lines: Writing Paragraphs and Essays*, has been refined and expanded in response to the encouraging reactions and practical suggestions from careful and generous reviewers. This edition also includes many of the practical changes from the most recent U.S. edition by John Sheridan Biays and Carol Wershoven.

THE WRITING CHAPTERS

We have retained what you liked most: the meticulous and intensive coverage of the writing process. This step-by-step coverage traces the stages of writing, from generating ideas, to planning and focusing, to drafting and revising, to final proofreading. The word *lines* in the title refers to these stages, which are called **Thought Lines, Outlines, Rough Lines,** and **Final Lines,** and serve as convenient prompts for each stage. Every writing chapter covering a rhetorical pattern takes the students through all the stages of writing, in detail.

These chapters are filled with exercises and activities, both individual and collaborative, because we believe that basic writers are more motivated and learn more easily when they are *actively* involved with individual or collaborative tasks. In keeping with these beliefs and with the emphasis on process, this edition of *Along These Lines* offers instructors more choices than ever.

New Features

In response to the suggestions of colleagues and reviewers, this edition contains these significant changes and refinements:

- Learning objectives and relevant quotations at the beginning of each writing chapter give students an idea of what to expect in the chapter.
- A new discussion of paraphrasing, including exercises, has been added to Chapter 2.
- The discussion of plagiarism has been updated and dealt with in more depth.
- A new **Communication at Work** feature, which demonstrates the relevance of all forms of communication in the workplace, is included in every writing chapter.
- Many of the writing chapters now contains new Canadian readings dealing with up-to-date topics relevant to today's student.

- The newly added research appendix, which includes documentation for both the MLA and APA formats, includes a progressive essay clearly demonstrating how to incorporate research into a student paper. The section on MLA documentation, and the text as a whole, has been thoroughly updated to reflect the new seventh edition of the *MLA Handbook for Writers of Research Papers*, published in 2009.

Additional Features

Along These Lines continues to include these distinctive features:

- A lively, conversational tone, including question-and-answer formats and dialogues
- Not much "talk" about writing; no more than two pages of print in a row without a chart, a box, a list, an example, or an exercise
- Small, simple clusters of information surrounded by white space rather than intimidating expanses of small print
- Boxed examples of the outline, draft, and final version of the writing assignment in each chapter
- Exercises throughout each chapter—not merely at the end—so each concept is reinforced as soon as it is introduced
- Exercises that are not merely fill-in-the-blanks, but collaborative assignments that have students writing with peers, interviewing classmates, reacting to others' suggestions, and building on others' ideas
- Numerous writing topics and activities in each chapter, providing more flexibility for the instructor
- A separate and detailed chapter on "Writing from Reading," explaining and illustrating the steps of prereading, reading, annotating, summarizing, and reacting (in writing) to another's ideas
- Vocabulary definitions for each reading selection
- Grouping of selections by rhetorical pattern
- Readings selected to appeal to working students, returning students, and students who are parents and spouses
- Selections on topics such as getting an education, understanding generational divisions and definitions, fitting in, or feeling left out
- Readings that are accessible and of particular interest to this student audience—many of the selections thus come from popular periodicals
- Topics for writing sparked by the content of the reading and designed to elicit thinking, not rote replication of a model

THE GRAMMAR CHAPTERS

Updated, more challenging, and sophisticated exercises have been added to each chapter, and the second part of the text maintains the following features:

- Emphasis on the most important skills for college readiness
- Grammar concepts taught step-by-step, as in "Two Steps to Check for Fragments"
- Numerous exercises, including practice, editing, and collaborative exercises
- Paragraph-editing exercises at the end of each grammar chapter to connect the grammar principles to writing assignments
- An ESL appendix

Instructors will find *Along These Lines* easy to use for several reasons:

- It has so many exercises, activities, assignments, and readings that teachers can select strategies they prefer and adapt them to the needs of different class sections.
- The exercises serve as an instant lesson plan for any class period or as individualized work for students in a writing lab.

Along These Lines will appeal to instructors, but more importantly it will work for students. The basic premise of this book is that an effective text should respect students' individuality and their innate desire to learn and succeed. We hope it helps your students flourish by providing them with a foundation of respect, encouragement, and ongoing collaboration as they work through the writing process.

SUPPLEMENTS

Exercise Booklet (978-0-13-207149-9). This student supplement is available for purchase and contains additional exercises for all parts of *Along These Lines*: rhetoric, reading, and grammar.

Instructor's Resource Manual. This manual offers a number of valuable instructor resources, including information on syllabus planning, chapter outlines, collaborative exercises, and answers to text exercises. The Instructor's Resource Manual is available for downloading from a password-protected section of Pearson Education Canada's online catalogue (**www.pearsoned.ca/highered**). Navigate to your book's catalogue page to view a list of those supplements that are available. See your local sales representative for details and access.

CourseSmart. CourseSmart is a new way for instructors and students to access textbooks online anytime from anywhere. With thousands of titles across hundreds of courses, CourseSmart helps instructors choose the best textbook for their class and give their students a new option for buying the assigned textbook as a lower cost eTextbook. For more information, visit www.coursesmart.com.

ACKNOWLEDGMENTS

I thank the following people at Pearson Education Canada who contributed to the realization of this book: Chris Helsby, acquisitions editor; Rachel Stuckey, developmental editor; Claire Horsnell, production editor; and Lenore Latta, copy editor.

Thanks are due to the instructors who provided reviews for the second Canadian edition: Francis Aleba, MacEwan College; Leonne Beebe, University College of the Fraser Valley; Jane Barley, Thompson Rivers University; Monica Ekvall, Lethbridge College; Vladis Gislason, NAIT; Enid Gossin, Seneca College; Debbie Hlady, Camosun College; Neil Hudson, Saint Mary's University; Ingrid Hutchinson, Fanshawe College; Jill Jackson, University of Windsor; Jen Lowery, SAIT; Jean Mills, Conestoga College; Alan Orr, George Brown College; John Patterson, Vancouver Community College; and Guy Wilkinson, Langara College. Their feedback offered valuable guidance for this revision.

Lastly, I would like to thank my family: Deon, Daniel, and most of all, Mom and Dad, whose support has helped me more than they know.

Lara Sauer

WRITING IN STEPS:

The Process Approach

INTRODUCTION

Learning by Doing

Writing is a skill, and, like any skill, it improves with practice. This book gives you the opportunity to improve your writing through a number of activities. Some activities can be done alone; some require you to work with a partner or with a group. Some you can do in the classroom; some you can do at home. The important thing to remember is that *good writing takes practice*; you can learn to write well by writing.

Steps Make Writing Easier

Writing is easier if you *do not try to do everything at once*. Producing a piece of effective writing demands that you think, plan, focus, draft, re-think, focus, revise, edit, and proofread. You can become frustrated if you try to do all these things at the same time.

To make the task of writing easier, *Along These Lines* breaks the process into four major parts:

THOUGHT LINES

In this stage, you *think* about your topic, and you gather ideas. You *react* to your own ideas and add more ideas to your first thoughts. Or you *react* to other people's ideas as a way of generating your own writing material. This is often called *prewriting*.

OUT LINES

In this stage, you begin to *plan* your writing. You examine your ideas and begin to *focus* them around one main idea. Planning involves combining, dividing, and even discarding the ideas you started with. It involves more thinking about the point you want to make and the order of details that can best express your point.

ROUGH LINES

In this stage, the thinking and planning begin to shape themselves into a piece of writing. You complete a *draft* of your work, a rough version of the finished product. And then you think again, as you examine the draft and check it. Checking it begins the process of *revision*, "fixing" the draft so that it takes the shape you want and expresses your ideas clearly.

FINAL LINES

In this stage, the final version of your writing gets one last, careful *review*. When you prepare the final copy of your work, you *proofread* to identify and correcting any mistakes in spelling, mechanics, or punctuation you may have overlooked. This step is the *final check* of your work to make sure your writing is the best that it can be.

These four stages in the writing process—*thought lines*, *outlines*, *rough lines*, and *final lines*—may overlap. You may be changing your plan (the *outlines* stage) even as you work on the *rough lines* of your paper. And no rule prevents you from moving back to an earlier step when necessary. Thinking of writing as a series of steps helps you to see the process as a *manageable task*. You can avoid doing everything at once and becoming overwhelmed by the challenge.

Throughout the chapters of this text, you will have many opportunities to become familiar with the four stages of effective writing. Working individually and with your classmates, you can become a better writer along *all* lines.

ALONG THESE LINES/Pearson Education Canada

CHAPTER 1
Writing a Paragraph

LEARNING OBJECTIVES

After you have read this chapter and completed its exercises and assignments, you should be able to

- generate ideas for a writing topic
- narrow the range of your ideas
- distinguish appropriate topic sentences from those that are too broad or too narrow
- write an appropriate topic sentence for a paragraph
- organize and plan your paragraph
- generate supporting details for your paragraph
- draft and edit your paragraph

"A word after a word after a word is power."

~ MARGARET ATWOOD

▼ MARGARET ATWOOD IS A CANADIAN POET, NOVELIST, AND LITERARY THEORIST.

WHAT IS A PARAGRAPH?

Usually, students write because they have an assignment requiring them to write on some topic or choice of topics, and the writing is due by a certain day. Assume that you get such an assignment and it calls for one paragraph. You might wonder, "Why a paragraph? Why not something large, like a two- or three-page paper? After all, many classes will ask for papers, not just paragraphs."

For one thing, an essay is really just a series of paragraphs. If you can write one good paragraph, you can write more than one. The **paragraph** is the basic building block of any essay. It is a group of sentences focusing on one idea or one point. Keep this concept in mind: one idea to a paragraph. Focusing on one idea or one point gives a paragraph **unity**. If you have a new point, start a new paragraph.

You may ask, "Doesn't this mean a paragraph will be short? How long should a paragraph be, anyway?" To convince a reader of one main point, you need to make the point, support it, develop it, explain it, and describe it. There will be shorter and longer paragraphs, but for now, you can assume your paragraph will be somewhere between seven and twelve sentences long.

ALONG THESE LINES/Pearson Education Canada

This chapter will guide you through each stage of the writing process:

- **Thought Lines**—how to generate and develop ideas for your paragraph
- **Outlines**—how to organize your ideas
- **Rough Lines**—how to make and revise rough drafts
- **Final Lines**—how to edit and refine your ideas

We give extra emphasis to the thought lines in this chapter to give you that extra help in getting started.

WRITING THE PARAGRAPH IN STEPS

THOUGHT LINES   ### GATHERING IDEAS FOR A PARAGRAPH

Suppose your instructor asks you to write a paragraph about your favourite city or town. You already know your **purpose**—to write a paragraph that makes some point about your favourite city or town. You have an **audience** since you are writing this paragraph for your instructor and classmates. Knowing your audience and purpose is important for writing effectively. Often, your purpose is to write a specific kind of paper for a class. But sometimes you may have to write for a different purpose or audience, such as writing instructions for a new employee at your workplace, or a letter of complaint to a manufacturer, or a short biographical essay for a scholarship application.

communication at work

The following excerpt is from the article "Good (and Bad) Writing Skills Stand Out on the Job" (2005) by Michael Kinsman:

> [A] survey of 120 human resources directors* found that two-thirds of salaried workers depend upon their writing skills, and an inability to write can severely limit workers as they try to climb into supervisory and management jobs.... 'It's a skill you need to learn early and develop every step along the way through your education ... employers want it because they know good writing requires good thinking.'

Participating members included those from Ford Motor Company, DaimlerChrysler, GM, Bristol-Myers, Dow Chemical, Eastman Kodak, IBM, Lockheed Martin, McGraw-Hill, and Motorola.

Freewriting, Brainstorming, Keeping a Journal

Once you have identified your audience and purpose, you can begin by finding some way to *think on paper*. To gather ideas, you can use the techniques of freewriting, brainstorming, or keeping a journal.

Freewriting Give yourself fifteen minutes to write whatever comes into your mind on your subject. If your mind is a blank, write, "My mind's a blank. My mind's a blank," over and over until you think of something else. The main goal here is to *write without stopping*. Do not stop to tell yourself, "This is stupid," or "I can't use any of this in a paper." Do not stop to correct your spelling or punctuation. Just write. Let your ideas flow. Write *freely*. Here is an example:

ALONG THESE LINES/Pearson Education Canada

Freewriting about a Favourite City or Town

Favourite city or town. City? I like Montreal. It's so big and exciting. Haven't been there much, though. Only once. My home town. I like it. It's just another town but comfortable and friendly. Maybe Thunder Bay. Lots of fun visits there. Grandparents there. Hard to pick a favourite. Different places are good for different reasons.

Brainstorming **Brainstorming** is like freewriting because you write whatever comes into your head, but it is a little different because you can pause to *ask yourself questions* that will lead to new ideas. When you brainstorm alone, you "interview" yourself about a subject. You can also brainstorm and ask questions within a group. Here's an example:

Brainstorming about a Favourite City or Town

Favourite place.

City or town.

What's the difference between a city and a town?

Doesn't matter. Just pick one. Cities bigger.

How is city life different from town life?

Cities are bigger. More crowded, like Toronto.

Which do you like better, a city or a town?

Sometimes I like cities.

Why?

There is more to do.

So, what city do you like?

I like Montreal, Thunder Bay.

Is Thunder Bay a city?

Yes. A small one.

Do you like towns?

I loved this little town in Nova Scotia.

If you feel as though you are running out of ideas in brainstorming, try to form a question out of what you've just written. Go where your questions and answers lead you. For example, if you write, "There is more to do in cities," you could form these questions:

What is there to do? Sports? Entertainment? Outdoor exercise? Meeting people?

You could also make a list of your brainstorming ideas, but remember to *do only one step at a time.*

Keeping a Journal A **journal** is a notebook of your personal writing, a notebook in which you write *regularly* and *often*. It is not a diary, but it is a place to record your experiences, reactions, and observations. In it, you can write about what you have done, heard, seen, read, or remembered. You can include sayings that you would like to remember, news clippings, snapshots—anything that you would like to recall or consider. A journal provides an enjoyable way to practise your writing, and it is a great source of ideas for writing.

> ### Journal Entry about a Favourite City or Town
>
> I'm not going north to see my grandparents this summer. They're coming here instead of me going to Thunder Bay. I'd really like to go there. I like the cool weather. It's better than months of heat, humidity, and smog here in Toronto. I'll miss going there. I've been so many times that it's like a second home. Thunder Bay is great around Christmas time.

Finding Specific Ideas

Whether you freewrite, brainstorm, or consult your journal, you end up with something on paper. Follow those first ideas; see where they can take you. You are looking for specific ideas, each of which can focus the general one you started with. At this point, you do not have to decide which specific idea you want to write about. You just want to *narrow your range* of ideas.

You might think, "Why should I narrow my ideas? Won't I have more to say if I keep my topic big?" But remember that a paragraph has one idea; you want to state it clearly and with convincing details for support. If you try to write one paragraph on the broad topic of city life versus town life, for example, you will probably make so many general statements that you will either say very little or bore your reader with big, sweeping statements. General ideas are big, broad ones. Specific ideas are smaller, narrower ones. If you scanned the freewriting example on a favourite city or town, you might underline several specific ideas as possible topics:

> Favourite city or town. City? I like <u>Montreal</u>. It's so big and exciting. Haven't been there much, though. Only once. <u>My home town</u>. I like it. It's just another town but comfortable and friendly. Maybe <u>Thunder Bay</u>. Lots of fun visits there. Grandparents there. Hard to pick a favourite. Different places are good for different reasons.

Consider the underlined terms. They are specific places. You could write a paragraph about any one of these places, or you could underline specific places in your brainstorming questions and answers:

> Favourite place.
>
> City or town.
>
> **What's the difference between a city and a town?**
>
> Doesn't matter. Just pick one. Cities bigger.
>
> **How is city life different from town life?**
>
> Cities are bigger. More crowded, like <u>Toronto</u>.

Which do you like better, a city or a town?

Sometimes I like cities.

Why?

There is more to do.

So, what city do you like?

I like <u>Montreal, Thunder Bay</u>.

Is Thunder Bay a city?

Yes. A small one.

Do you like towns?

I loved this <u>little town in Nova Scotia</u>.

Each of these specific places could be a topic for your paragraph.

If you reviewed the journal entry on a favourite city or town, you would also be able to underline specific places:

I'm not going north to see my grandparents this summer. They're coming here instead of me going to <u>Thunder Bay</u>. I'd really like to go there. I like the cool weather. It's better than months of heat, humidity, and smog here in <u>Toronto</u>. I'll miss going there. I've been so many times that it's like a second home. Thunder Bay is great around Christmas time.

Remember that if you follow the steps, they can lead you to specific ideas.

Selecting One Topic

Once you have a list of specific ideas that can lead you to a specific topic, you can pick one topic. Let's say you decided to work with the list of places you gathered through brainstorming:

Toronto

Montreal

Thunder Bay

a little town in Nova Scotia

Looking at this list, you decide you want to write about Thunder Bay as your favourite city.

EXERCISE **1**	**CREATING QUESTIONS FOR BRAINSTORMING**

Below are several topics. For each one, brainstorm by writing at least six questions related to the topic that could lead you to further ideas. The first topic is done for you:

1. **topic:** careers

Question 1: <u>What are the current job prospects in my field?</u>

Question 2: <u>What can I do with a liberal arts degree?</u>

Question 3: <u>Why do people move from job to job these days?</u>

Question 4:   What are the best career websites?

Question 5:   Should I consider an apprenticeship?

Question 6:   Should I go to college or university ?

2. **topic:** driving

Question 1:   _____

Question 2:   _____

Question 3:   _____

Question 4:   _____

Question 5:   _____

Question 6:   _____

3. **topic:** complaining

Question 1:   _____

Question 2:   _____

Question 3:   _____

Question 4:   _____

Question 5:   _____

Question 6:   _____

4. **topic:** bargains

Question 1:   _____

Question 2:   _____

Question 3:   _____

Question 4:   _____

Question 5:   _____

Question 6:   _____

EXERCISE 2

FINDING SPECIFIC DETAILS IN FREEWRITING

Below are two samples of freewriting. Each is a written response to a different topic. Read each sample, and then underline any words and phrases that could become the focus of a paragraph.

Freewriting Reaction to the Topic of Travel

I like to travel. But I'd rather drive than fly. When I drive, I can decide when to stop and go. When you fly, you can get stuck on the runway for hours and never take off. Then when you're in the air, you can't get out until it's over.

ALONG THESE LINES/Pearson Education Canada

Plus, think of airline food. Disgusting soggy sandwiches or tiny bags of pretzels. And there is no leg room. I can drive and find a nice truck stop restaurant.

Freewriting Reaction to the Topic of Pollution

Pollution. Save the planet. Smoke pollutes. Big smokestacks at the edge of the city belch smoke all the time. And even smokers pollute, especially indoors. No-smoking rules are controversial. I used to smoke and never thought about pollution. Noise pollution is a pain, too. People who live next to a highway must hear noise all the time.

EXERCISE 3

FINDING SPECIFIC DETAILS IN A LIST

Below are several lists of words or phrases. In each list, one item is a general term; the others are more specific. Underline the words or phrases that are more specific. The first list is done for you.

1. <u>The Winnipeg Free Press</u>
   newspapers
   <u>Vancouver Sun</u>
   <u>The Globe and Mail</u>
   <u>Le Devoir</u>

2. annoying TV jingles
   late-night infomercials
   psychic hotlines
   home financing commercials
   television commercials

3. stock car racing
   sports
   cheerleaders
   stadium ticket prices
   soccer
   coaches out of control

4. coffee
   decaffeinated
   brewed
   latte
   cappucino
   espresso

5. Norooz
   Christmas
   holidays
   Diwali
   Ramadan
   Kwanzaa

6. student services
   financial aid
   career counselling
   peer tutoring
   housing placement
   health services

EXERCISE 4

FINDING TOPICS THROUGH FREEWRITING

The following exercise must be completed with a partner or a group. Below are several topics. Pick one and freewrite on it for ten minutes. Then read your freewriting to your partner or group. Ask your listener(s) to jot down any words or phrases from your writing that could lead to a specific topic for a paragraph.

Your listener(s) should read to you the jotted-down words or phrases. You will be hearing a collection of specific ideas that came from *your* writing. As you listen, underline the words in your freewriting.

Freewriting topics (pick one):

1. a happy occasion
2. a hated chore
3. a special childhood memory

Freewriting on (name of topic chosen):

_____

_____

_____

_____

_____

_____

Adding Details to a Specific Topic

You can develop the specific topic you picked in a number of ways:

1. *Check your list* for other ideas that seem to fit with the specific topic you've picked.
2. *Brainstorm*—ask yourself more questions about your topic, and use the answers as detail.
3. *List* any new ideas you have that may be connected to your topic.

One way to add details is to go back and check your brainstorming for other ideas about Thunder Bay:

I like Thunder Bay.

a small city

Now you can brainstorm some questions that will lead you to more details. The questions do not have to be connected to each other; they are just questions that could lead you to ideas and details:

What's a small city?

It doesn't have skyscrapers or freeways or millions of people.

So, what makes it a city?

Hundreds of visitors come there every day.

What's so great about Thunder Bay?

You're never more than ten minutes away from the bush or the lake.

Is the lake clean?

Sure. And the water is a clear blue.

What else can you do in Thunder Bay?

There are lots of things to do outdoors.

Like what?

Fishing and camping. Cross-country and downhill skiing.

ALONG THESE LINES/Pearson Education Canada

Another way to add details is to list any ideas that may be connected to your topic. The list might give you more specific details:

grandparents live there	grandparents feed me
cool in summer	I use their car

If you had tried all three ways of adding detail, you would end up with this list of details connected to the topic of a favourite city or town:

a small city	clear blue water
no freeways	outdoor activities
no skyscrapers	fishing and camping
not millions of people	cross-country and downhill skiing
hundreds of visitors daily	grandparents live there
can always visit family for free	cool in summer
bush and lake nearby	grandparents feed me
clean lake	I use their car

INFOBOX | **GATHERING IDEAS: A SUMMARY**

The thought lines stage of writing a paragraph enables you to gather ideas. This process begins with several steps:

1. *Think on paper and write down any ideas that you have about a topic.* You can do this by freewriting, by brainstorming, or by keeping a journal.
2. *Scan your writing for specific ideas that have come from your first efforts.* List these specific ideas.
3. *Pick one specific idea.* Then, by reviewing your early writing, by questioning, and by thinking further, you can add details to the one specific idea.

This process may seem long, but once you have worked through it several times it will become nearly automatic. When you think about ideas before you try to shape them into a paragraph, you are off to a good start. Confidence comes from having something to say, and once you have a specific idea, you will be ready to begin shaping and developing details that support your idea.

EXERCISE
5

ADDING DETAILS TO A TOPIC BY BRAINSTORMING

Below are two topics. Each is followed by two or three details. Brainstorm more questions, based on the existing details, that can add more details.

1. **topic:** advantages of going to college part-time

   details: saves money
   less stressful

   Question 1: How much money can you save? _____

   Question 2: What expenses can you cut? _____

   Question 3: What stresses can be reduced? _____

   Question 4: _____

ALONG THESE LINES/Pearson Education Canada

Question 5: _____

Question 6: _____

2. **topic:** losing a wallet

   details: frightening experience
   leads to time-consuming tasks
   identity is stolen

Question 1: What is frightening about the experience? _____

Question 2: What are the tasks? _____

Question 3: _____

Question 4: _____

Question 5: _____

Question 6: _____

ADDING DETAILS BY LISTING

Below are four topics for paragraphs. For each topic, list details that seem to fit the topic.

1. **topic:** government benefits
   details:

   a. _____

   b. _____

   c. _____

   d. _____

2. **topic:** copyright infringement
   details:

   a. _____

   b. _____

   c. _____

   d. _____

3. **topic:** unusual jobs
   details:

   a. _____

   b. _____

   c. _____

   d. _____

4. **topic:** good neighbours
   details:
   a. _____
   b. _____
   c. _____
   d. _____

FOCUSING IDEAS FOR A PARAGRAPH

The next step of writing is to *focus your ideas around some point.* Your ideas will begin to take a focus if you re-examine them, looking for related ideas. Two techniques that you can use are

- marking a list of related ideas
- mapping related ideas

Listing Related Ideas

To develop a marked list, take another look at the list we developed under the topic of a favourite city or town. The same list is shown below, but you will notice some of the items have been marked with symbols that show related ideas:

N marks ideas about Thunder Bay's **natural** good points

O marks ideas about Thunder Bay's **outdoor activities**

F marks ideas about **family** in Thunder Bay

Here is the marked list of ideas related to the topic of a favourite city or town:

a small city

no freeways

no skyscrapers

not millions of people

hundreds of visitors daily

F can always visit family for free

N bush and lake nearby

N clean lake

N clear blue water

O outdoor activities

O fishing and camping

O cross-country and downhill skiing

F grandparents live there

N cool in summer

F grandparents feed me

F I use their car

You have no doubt noticed that some items are not marked: a small city, no freeways, no skyscrapers, not millions of people, hundreds of visitors daily.

Perhaps you can come back to them later, or you may decide you do not need them in your paragraph.

To make it easier to see what ideas you have and how they are related, try *grouping related ideas*, giving each list a title, such as the following:

Natural Good Points of Thunder Bay

bush and lake nearby

clean lake

clear blue water

cool in summer

Outdoor Activities in Thunder Bay

fishing and camping

cross-country and downhill skiing

Family in Thunder Bay

can always visit family for free

grandparents live there

grandparents feed me

I use their car

Mapping

Another way to focus your ideas is to mark your first list of ideas and then cluster the related ideas into separate lists. You can **map** your ideas like this:

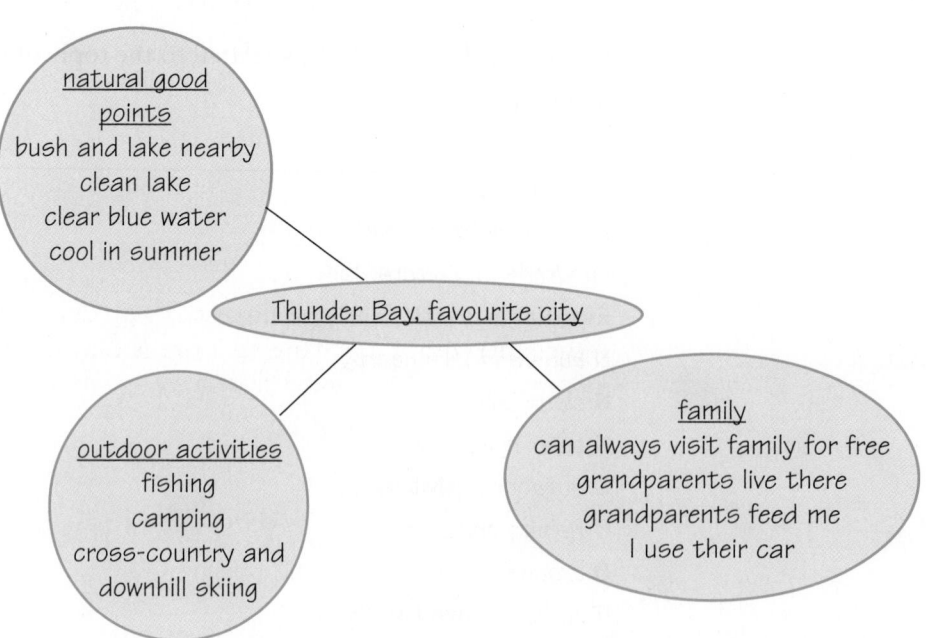

Whatever way you choose to examine and group your detail, you are working toward a focus, a point. You are asking and beginning to answer the question, "Where do the details lead?" The answer will be the topic sentence of your paragraph. It will be the *main idea* of your paragraph.

Forming a Topic Sentence

To form a topic sentence, you can do the following:

1. Review your details and see if you can form some general idea that summarizes the details.
2. Write that general idea as one sentence.

Your sentence that summarizes the details is the **topic sentence**. It makes a general point, and the specific details that you have gathered will support this point.

To form a topic sentence about your favourite city, Thunder Bay, follow the steps. First, there are many details about Thunder Bay. It is time to ask questions about the details. You could ask yourself, "What kind of details do I have? Can I summarize them?" You might then write the summary as the topic sentence:

I love Thunder Bay because it has forests and lakes, outdoor life, and family.

Check the sentence against your details. Does it cover your "natural good points" of Thunder Bay? Yes. The topic sentence sums them up as *forests and lakes.* Does it cover outdoor activities and family? Yes. The topic sentence says the place has *outdoor life and family.*

Writing Good Topic Sentences

Be careful. Topics are not the same as topic sentences. *Topics* are the subjects you will write about. A *topic sentence* states the main idea you have developed on a topic. Consider the differences between the topics and the topic sentences below:

topic:	Why courtesy is important
topic sentence:	Courtesy takes the conflict out of unpleasant encounters.
topic:	Violence on television
topic sentence:	Violence on television promotes violence in our youth.

Topic sentences do not announce; they make a point. Look at the sentences below, and notice the differences between the sentences that announce and the topic sentences:

announcement:	I will discuss the process of changing a tire.
topic sentence:	Changing a tire is easy if you have the right tools and follow a simple process.
announcement:	An analysis of why recycling paper is important will be the subject of this paper.
topic sentence:	Recycling paper is important because it saves trees, money, and even certain animals.

Topic sentences can be too big to develop in one paragraph. A topic sentence that is *too broad* may take many paragraphs, even pages of writing, to develop. Look at the very broad sentences below, and then notice how they can be narrowed:

too broad:	Athletes get paid too much money. (This sentence is too broad because the term "athletes" could mean anything from professional boxers to college

football players to neighbourhood softball teams; "too much money" could mean any fee that basketball players receive for endorsing products to bonuses that professional football players get if they make it to the Super Bowl. The sentence could also refer to all athletes in the world at any time in history.)

a narrower, better topic sentence: Last year, several professional baseball players negotiated high but fair salaries.

too broad: I changed a great deal in my last year of high school. (The phrase "changed a great deal" could refer to physical changes, intellectual changes, or emotional changes or to changes in attitude, changes in goals, or changes in just about any other aspect you can think of.)

a narrower, better topic sentence: In my last year of high school, I overcame my shyness.

Topic sentences can be too small to develop in one paragraph. A topic sentence that is *too narrow* cannot be supported by detail. It may be a fact that cannot be developed. A topic sentence that is too narrow leaves you with nothing more to say:

too narrow: I hate reality television shows.
an expanded topic sentence: I hate reality television shows for two reasons.

too narrow: It takes twenty minutes to get out of the airport parking lot.
an expanded topic sentence: Congestion at the airport parking lot is causing problems for travellers.

The thought lines stage begins with free, unstructured thinking and writing. As you work through the thought lines process, your thinking and writing will become more focused.

INFOBOX   FOCUSING IDEAS: A SUMMARY

The thought lines stage of writing a paragraph enables you to develop an idea into a topic sentence and related details. You can focus your thinking by working in steps:

1. Mark a list of related details, or try mapping to group your ideas.
2. Write a topic sentence that summarizes your details.
3. Check that your topic sentence is a sentence, not a topic. Make sure that it is not too broad or too narrow, and that it is not an announcement. Check that it makes a point and focuses the details you have developed.

| EXERCISE 7 | GROUPING RELATED ITEMS IN LISTS OF DETAILS |

Below are lists of details. In each list, circle the items that seem to fit into one group; then, underline the items that seem to belong to a second group. Some items may not belong in either group. The first list is done for you.

1. topic: **shopping**
   (leaves little money for savings)
   (time consuming)
   time with friends
   supports the economy
   keep up with trends
   (crowded malls)
   lots of advertisements
   get some exercise
   (encourages materialism)
   buy things you like

   Facebook
   blogs
   wikis
   plasma TVs
   iPod

2. topic: **technology**
   cellphones
   Blu-ray
   laptops
   digital cameras
   YouTube

3. topic: **falling in love**
   romantic moments
   shared thoughts
   jealousy
   Valentine's Day
   mutual respect
   emotional security
   petty arguments
   shared dreams
   fear of commitment
   possessiveness

| EXERCISE 8 | WRITING TOPIC SENTENCES FOR LISTS OF DETAILS |

Below are lists of details that have no topic sentence. Write an appropriate topic sentence for each list.

1. topic sentence: _____
   People do not have to be in great shape to take walks.
   Walking burns calories.
   It is good for the heart.
   It is good for the bones and muscles.
   It doesn't cost anything to walk.
   Walking is convenient.
   It requires no exercise equipment or gym membership.
   It can be done almost anywhere.

2. topic sentence: _____
   Tamara spoke clearly in speech class.
   Her presentations were well organized.
   She critiqued classmates' speeches tactfully.
   She volunteered to be a speech team leader.
   In communicating, she maintained her sense of humour.
   She motivated others to complete their speech research.

3. **topic sentence:** _____

Cecilia was the fastest swimmer on the team.
She encouraged all the new team members.
She was a friend to all the old members.
She worked well with the coaches.
She never missed a practice.
She was never late for a meet.
She cheered for all her teammates.

4. **topic sentence:** _____

Carlos worked twenty hours a week at a service station.
He never missed work.
He took four classes at college.
He was always studying in the student centre.
He had two sons, Daniel, four, and Tyler, one.
He and his wife, Shondra, loved their boys.
He was working and studying to make a better life for his family.

EXERCISE 9

TURNING TOPICS INTO TOPIC SENTENCES

Below is a list. Some of the items in the list are topic sentences, but some are topics. Put an X by the items that are topics. In the lines below the list, rewrite the topics into topic sentences.

1. _____ Three reasons to learn a second language.
2. _____ Breaking a habit takes willpower.
3. _____ The most rewarding experience of my life.
4. _____ Buying books is a good way to spend your money.
5. _____ How I learned to cook.
6. _____ My brother discovered his talents on his first job.
7. _____ High-school friendships can be lasting ones.
8. _____ Why driving is stressful.
9. _____ I got a B in history because I studied and reviewed.
10. _____ My greatest disappointment was missing my sister's wedding.

Rewrite the topics. Make each one into a topic sentence:

_____

_____

_____

_____

_____

_____

ALONG THESE LINES/Pearson Education Canada

EXERCISE **10**	REVISING TOPIC SENTENCES THAT ARE TOO BROAD

Below is a list of topic sentences. Some of them are too broad to support in one paragraph. Put an X by the ones that are too broad. Then, on the lines below the list, rewrite those sentences, focusing on a limited idea, a topic sentence that could be supported in one paragraph.

1. _____ Working is extremely unpleasant.
2. _____ The most challenging aspect of babysitting was getting the children to go to bed.
3. _____ Taxes are not fair to many people.
4. _____ Camille's honesty makes her a trustworthy friend.
5. _____ Two speeding tickets set my finances back for months.
6. _____ Leon believes in the Canadian way of life and wants it for his children.
7. _____ People should leave their neighbours alone when it comes to little things.
8. _____ Teresa hopes her children will be educated and thoughtful voters.
9. _____ Violence is ruining Canada.
10. _____ My parents fought to keep us out of a gang.

Rewrite the broad sentences. Make each one more limited.

_____

_____

_____

_____

_____

_____

EXERCISE **11**	MAKING ANNOUNCEMENTS INTO TOPIC SENTENCES

Below is a list of sentences. Some are topic sentences. Some are announcements. Put an X by the announcements. Then, on the lines below the list, rewrite the announcements to make them into topic sentences.

1. _____ Lying to a spouse is a destructive habit.
2. _____ The consequences of driving with bald tires will be the subject of this paper.
3. _____ The need for a new recreation centre will be explained.
4. _____ Moving to a new city can be a chance for a fresh start.
5. _____ Ridgefield deserves better cable television service.
6. _____ More benches throughout the city would make it more attractive to pedestrians.
7. _____ Why clearer road signs are needed in this town is the area to be discussed.

8. _____ This essay concerns the growing number of bike thefts on campus.

9. _____ A ban on smoking in public parks would protect people who rely on the parks for a natural retreat.

10. _____ This paper will be about running a marathon.

Rewrite the announcements. Make each one a topic sentence.

_____

_____

_____

_____

_____

_____

EXERCISE 12

REVISING TOPIC SENTENCES THAT ARE TOO NARROW

Below is a list of topic sentences. Some of them are topics that are too narrow; they cannot be developed with details. Put an X by the ones that are too narrow. Then, on the lines below, rewrite those sentences as broader topic sentences that could be developed in one paragraph.

1. _____ It snowed when I drove to Canmore.

2. _____ On rainy days, I have to pay careful attention to the way I drive.

3. _____ My apartment has only one room.

4. _____ Denzel missed the plane because his car broke down on the freeway.

5. _____ Buy-Low is a discount store.

6. _____ Clever use of space made my tiny office look larger.

7. _____ Nilsa drives a Chevrolet.

8. _____ My old Corolla was a great car for long trips.

9. _____ Chris takes six vitamins every morning.

10. _____ Dr. Chan studied at Dalhousie.

Rewrite the narrow sentences. Make each one broader.

_____

_____

_____

_____

_____

_____

 ## DEVISING A PLAN FOR A PARAGRAPH

Checking Your Details

Once you have a topic sentence, you can begin working on an **outline** for your paragraph. The outline is a plan that helps you stay focused in your writing. The outline begins to form when you write your topic sentence and write your list of details beneath the topic sentence. You can now look at your list and ask yourself an important question: "Do I have *enough details* to support my topic sentence?" Remember, your goal is to write a paragraph of seven to twelve sentences.

Consider this topic sentence and list of details:

topic sentence:	People can be very rude when they shop in supermarkets.
details:	push in line
	express lane
	too many items

Does the list contain enough details for a paragraph of seven to twelve sentences? Probably not.

Adding Details When There Are Not Enough

To add detail, try brainstorming. Ask yourself some questions like these:

Where else in supermarkets are people rude?
Are they rude in other lanes besides the express lane?
Are they rude in the aisles? How?
Is there crowding anywhere? Where?

By brainstorming, you might come up with this list of details:

topic sentence:	People can be very rude when they shop in supermarkets.
details:	push in line
	express lane
	too many items
	hit my cart with theirs in aisles
	block aisles while they decide
	push ahead in deli area
	will not take a number
	argue with cashier over prices
	yell at the bag boy

Keep brainstorming until you feel you have enough details for a seven- to twelve-sentence paragraph. Remember that it is better to have too many details than too few, for you can always delete the extra details later.

If you try brainstorming and still do not have many details, you can refer to your original ideas—your freewriting or journal—for other details.

Eliminating Details That Do Not Relate to the Topic Sentence

Sometimes, what you thought were good details do not relate to the topic sentence because they do not fit or support your point. Eliminate details that do not relate to the topic sentence. For example, the following list contains details that really do not relate to the topic sentence. Those details are crossed out.

ALONG THESE LINES/Pearson Education Canada

topic sentence: Waiters have to be very patient in dealing with their customers.

details: customers take a long time ordering
~~waiter's salary is low~~
waiters have to explain specials twice
customers send orders back
customers blame waiters for any delays
customers want food instantly
waiters can't react to sarcasm of customers
waiters can't get angry if customer does
~~waiters work long shifts~~
customers change their mind after ordering

From List to Outline

Take another look at the topic sentence and list of details on a favourite city or town:

topic sentence: I love Thunder Bay because it has forests and lakes, outdoor life, and family.

details: a small city

no freeways

no skyscrapers

not millions of people

hundreds of visitors daily

can always visit family for free

bush and lake nearby

clean lake

clear blue water

outdoor activities

fishing and camping

cross-country and downhill skiing

grandparents live there

cool in summer

grandparents feed me

I use their car

After you scan that list, you are ready to develop the outline of the paragraph.

An outline is a plan for writing, and it can be a type of draft in list form. It sketches what you want to write and the order in which you want to present it. An organized, logical list will make your writing *unified* since each item on the list will relate to your topic sentence.

When you plan, keep your topic sentence in mind:

I love Thunder Bay because it has <u>forests and lakes</u>, <u>outdoor life</u>, and <u>family</u>.

ALONG THESE LINES/Pearson Education Canada

Notice the underlined key words, which lead to three key parts of your outline:

forests and lakes

outdoor life

family

You can put the details on your list together so that they connect to one of these parts:

forests and lakes

—bush and lake nearby, clean lake, clear blue water, cool in summer

outdoor life

—fishing and camping, cross-country and downhill skiing

family

—can always visit family for free, grandparents live there, grandparents feed me, I drive their car

With this kind of grouping, you have a clearer idea of how to organize a paragraph.

Now that you have grouped your ideas with key words and details, you can write an outline.

As you can see, the outline combined some of the details from the list. Even with these combinations, the details are very rough. As you reread the list of details, you will notice places that need more combination, places where ideas need more explaining, and places that are repetitive. Keep in mind that an outline is merely a very rough organization of your paragraph.

INFOBOX   **AN OUTLINE FOR A PARAGRAPH**

topic sentence: I love Thunder Bay because it has forests and lakes, outdoor life, and family.

details: **forests and lakes**
It is cool in the summer.
The bush and the lake are nearby.
The lake is clean.
The water is clear blue.
outdoor life
It has lots of outdoor activities.
I can fish and camp.
I can cross-country and downhill ski.
family
My grandparents live in Thunder Bay.
I stay at their house.
They feed me.
I use their car.

As you work through the steps of designing an outline, you can check for the following:

Coherence: Putting Your Details in Proper Order

Check the sample outline again, and you will notice that the details are grouped in the same order as the topic sentence: first, details about forests and lakes; next, details about outdoor life; and then, details about family in Thunder Bay. Putting the details in an order that matches the topic sentence is a logical order for this paragraph.

Putting the details in logical order makes the ideas in your paragraph easy to follow. The most logical order for a paragraph depends on the subject of the paragraph. If you are writing about an event, you might use **time order** (such as telling what happened first, second, and so forth); if you are arguing some point, you might use **emphatic order** (such as saving your most convincing idea for last); if you are describing a room, you might use **space order** (such as from left to right or from top to bottom).

The format of the outline helps to organize your ideas. The topic sentence is written above the list of details. This position helps you to remember that the topic sentence is the main idea, and the details that support it are written under it. The topic sentence is the most important sentence of the paragraph. You can easily check the items on your list, one by one, against your main idea. You can also develop the **unity** (relevance) and **coherence** (logical order) of your details.

When you actually write a paragraph, the topic sentence does not necessarily have to be the first sentence in the paragraph. Read the paragraphs below, and notice where each topic sentence is placed.

Topic Sentence at the Beginning of the Paragraph

<u>Watching a horror movie on the late show can keep me up all night.</u> The movie itself scares me to death, especially if it involves a creepy character sneaking up on someone in the dark. After the movie, I'm afraid to turn out all the lights and be alone in the dark. Then every little noise seems like the sound of a sinister intruder. Strange shapes seem to appear in the shadows. My closet becomes a place where someone could be hiding. There might even be a creature under the bed! And if I go to sleep, these strange invaders might appear from under the bed or in the closet.

Topic Sentence in the Middle of the Paragraph

The kitchen counters gleamed. In the spice rack, every jar was organized neatly. The sink was polished, and not one spot marred its surface. The stove burners were surrounded by dazzling stainless steel rings. <u>The chef kept an immaculate kitchen.</u> There were no finger marks on the refrigerator door. No sticky spots dirtied the floor. No crumbs hid behind the toaster.

Topic Sentence at the End of the Paragraph

On long summer evenings, we would play softball in the street. Sometimes we'd play until it was so dark we could barely see the ball.

ALONG THESE LINES/Pearson Education Canada

Then our mothers would come to the front steps of the row houses and call us in, telling us to stop our play. But we'd pretend we couldn't hear them. If they insisted, we'd beg for a few minutes more, or for just one more game. It was so good to be outdoors with our friends. It was warm, and we knew we had weeks of summer vacation ahead. There was no school in the morning; there would be more games to play. <u>We loved those street games on summer nights.</u>

Since many of your paragraph assignments will require a clear topic sentence, be sure you follow your instructor's directions about placement of the topic sentence.

✓ **CHECKLIST**   **FOR AN OUTLINE**

✓ **Unity:** Do all the details relate to the topic sentence? If they do, the paragraph will be unified.

✓ **Support:** Do you have enough supporting ideas? Can you add to these ideas with even more specific details?

✓ **Coherence:** Are the details listed in the right order? If the order of points is logical, the paragraph will be coherent.

EXERCISE 13   **ADDING DETAILS TO SUPPORT A TOPIC SENTENCE**

The topic sentences below have some—but not enough—detail. Write sentences to add details to the list below each topic sentence.

1. **topic sentence:** My habit of being late has hurt me several times.

   a. <u>When I am late for class, I often miss the announcement of a test for the next class meeting.</u>

   b. <u>I was so late that I missed the chance to buy tickets for a sold-out game.</u>

   c. <u>If I'm late, I drive too fast and sometimes get tickets.</u>

   d. _____

   e. _____

   f. _____

   g. _____

2. **topic sentence:** Raising a baby is expensive.

   a. <u>Babies need medicine.</u>

   b. _____

   c. _____

   d. _____

e. _____

f. _____

g. _____

3. **topic sentence:** A parent can show his or her love without spending a great deal of money.

    a. <u>Attending a child's school events shows interest.</u> _____

    b. _____

    c. _____

    d. _____

    e. _____

    f. _____

    g. _____

4. **topic sentence:** The first day of college can be confusing and tense.

    a. <u>A student may not know how to find the classroom for his or her first</u> <u>class.</u> _____

    b. _____

    c. _____

    d. _____

    e. _____

    f. _____

    g. _____

EXERCISE 14

ELIMINATING DETAILS THAT DO NOT FIT

Below are topic sentences and lists of supporting details. Cross out the details that do not fit the topic sentence.

1. **topic sentence:** Computers can limit or harm a small child's growth.

    details: Some children spend too much time indoors on their computers when they could be outdoors.
    They may lose out on the health benefits of exercise.
    They may rely on the computer as a substitute for interacting with real friends.
    In some cases, a child who spends too much time in cyberspace can become very uncomfortable around others.
    As a child, I always had several friends at my house.
    Computers can expose children to questionable pictures or photographs.
    All children should be encouraged to read.

2. **topic sentence:** Everywhere I look, I see how music influences fashion.

   details: Music celebrities wear a certain style.

   Soon, the style becomes a fad.

   One diva will be famous for her hairstyle.

   Then her fans want their hair styled the same way.

   Another celebrity is photographed in trendy clothing.

   He creates a line of clothing named after him, crossing into the fashion industry.

   Many stars in the music world have to look good.

   If a popular musician wears a certain kind of jewellery, like a necklace or bracelet, many fans want the same jewellery.

   Music is a universal language.

3. **topic sentence:** People give many reasons for not buckling their safety belts.

   details: Some people say they are in a hurry.

   Others say they are only driving around the block.

   Police officers get very upset when parents do not buckle up their children.

   Some people say they have a right not to buckle up if they don't want to.

   A few say they don't want to be buckled in if they drive into a lake.

   Many say they were about to buckle up, in a minute.

   Some say they just forgot.

   Air bags are a useful addition to auto safety devices.

EXERCISE 15

COHERENCE: PUTTING DETAILS IN THE RIGHT ORDER

These outlines have details that are in the wrong order. In the space provided, number the sentences in the right order: 1 would be the number for the first sentence, and so on.

1. **topic sentence:** Our garage sale was a disaster from start to finish.

   _____ By noon, we had nothing left to sell, and people were still coming.

   _____ People began to arrive at 8:30, before we had put out all the merchandise.

   _____ These early arrivals grabbed all the best bargains, even before we had a chance to put on price tags.

   _____ We started setting up at 8:15, thinking we had plenty of time.

   _____ At mid-morning, our yard was full of people, most of them complaining because we had so little left to sell.

   _____ The latest arrivals left, complaining because they had made a trip for nothing.

   _____ We were up at 7:30 a.m., putting Garage Sale signs around the neighbourhood.

   _____ We spent the afternoon cleaning up.

   _____ That evening, we swore our next sale would start earlier and include more merchandise.

2. **topic sentence:** A parent's job is never done.

_____ At work I have to keep an eye on the clock to make sure I leave in time to pick up my son from school.

_____ After dinner, it's time for his bath.

_____ Then there is the daily scramble to make the school bus.

_____ We have dinner together.

_____ The first order of the day is to wake up my son.

_____ The race is on to pick him up on time.

_____ Breakfast usually consists of cereal for him and a large cup of coffee for me.

_____ We read a story before he gets into bed.

_____ Only after he's in bed do I realize I still have to put away all his toys.

3. **topic sentence:** Losing my car keys was a stressful experience.

_____ I rushed out the door, grabbing for my car keys on the counter, where I always left them.

_____ I grabbed some keys, but they were my brother's house keys.

_____ I was late for work, as usual, so I hurried out of the apartment.

_____ When I had done a thorough search of the counter, I panicked.

_____ Trying to be calm, I looked more closely at the counter, searching for my car keys under a pile of mail, behind a stack of magazines, next to the spice rack.

_____ My next step was a frantic search of my entire apartment and the car.

_____ Unable to find my keys anywhere, I called my boss to tell him I would be late.

_____ Then I called a friend, who gave me a ride to work.

ROUGH LINES **DRAFTING AND REVISING A PARAGRAPH**

Drafting a Paragraph

The outline is a draft in list form. You are now ready to write the list in paragraph form, to "rough out" a draft of your assignment. This stage of writing is the time to draft, revise, edit, and draft again. You may write several drafts in this stage, but don't think of this as an unnecessary chore or a punishment. It is a way of taking the pressure off yourself. By revising in steps, you are reminding yourself that the first try does not have to be perfect.

Review the outline on a favourite city or town on page 23. You can create a first draft of this outline in the form of a paragraph. (Remember that the first line of each paragraph is indented.) In the draft of the paragraph below, the first sentence of the paragraph is the topic sentence.

> ### A First Draft of a Paragraph
>
> I love Thunder Bay because it has forests and lakes, outdoor life, and family. Thunder Bay is cool in the summer. The bush and the lake are nearby. The lake is clean. The water is clear blue. Thunder Bay has lots of outdoor activities. I can fish and camp. I can cross-country and downhill ski. I can always visit my family for free. My grandparents live in Thunder Bay. They feed me. I use their car.

Revising

Once you have a first draft, you can begin to think about revising and editing it. **Revising** means rewriting the draft by making changes in the order of the sentences (coherence) and in the content (unity). **Editing** includes making changes in the choice of words and in the length, pattern, and kinds of sentences (style), in the selection of details (support), and in sentence structure and punctuation (grammar). It may also include adding **transitions**, which are words, phrases, or sentences that link ideas.

One way to begin revising and editing is to read your work aloud to yourself. Listen to your words, and consider the questions in the following checklist.

CHECKLIST | **FOR REVISING THE DRAFT OF A PARAGRAPH**

- ✓ Am I staying on my point?
- ✓ Should I take out any ideas that do not relate?
- ✓ Do I have enough to say about my point?
- ✓ Should I add any details?
- ✓ Should I change the order of my sentences?
- ✓ Is my choice of words appropriate?
- ✓ Is my choice of words repetitive?
- ✓ Are my sentences too long? Too short?
- ✓ Should I combine any sentences?
- ✓ Am I running sentences together?
- ✓ Am I writing complete sentences?
- ✓ Can I link my ideas more smoothly?

If you apply the checklist to the first draft of the paragraph on a favourite city or town, you will probably find these rough spots:

- The sentences are very short and choppy.
- Some sentences could be combined.
- Some words are repeated often.
- Some ideas would be more effective if they were supported by more detail.
- The paragraph could use a few transitions.

Consider the following revised draft of the paragraph, and notice the changes, underlined, that have been made in the draft. You'll also notice some errors that will need to be corrected at the proofreading stage.

> ### A Revised Draft of a Paragraph
>
> I love Thunder Bay, <u>ON,</u> because it has forests and lakes, outdoor life, and family. <u>Thunder Bay is cool in the summer, and the bush and the lake are nearby.</u> <u>The lake is clean with clear blue water.</u> <u>In adition,</u> Thunder Bay has lots of outdoor activities. I can fish and camp <u>in the cool Summer</u> months, or I can cross-country and downhill ski <u>all winter long. Best of all,</u> my grandparents live in Thunder Bay. <u>They are my favourite relatives, and they make me fell very welcome.</u> <u>When I am in Thunder Bay, I stay with them, enjoy their food, and use their car.</u>

topic sentence: detail added

sentences combined

transition added

details added

details added

transition added

sentences combined

ALONG THESE LINES/Pearson Education Canada

When you are revising your own paragraph, you can use the checklist to help you. Read the checklist several times; then reread your draft, looking for answers to the questions on the list. If your instructor agrees, you can work with your classmates. You can read your draft to a partner or a group. Your listener(s) can react to your draft by applying the questions on the checklist and by making notes about your draft as you read. When you are finished reading aloud, your partner(s) can discuss the notes about your work.

EXERCISE **16**	**REVISING A DRAFT BY COMBINING SENTENCES**

The paragraph below has many short, choppy sentences. The short, choppy sentences are underlined. Wherever you see two or more underlined sentences clustered next to each other, combine the clustered sentences into one clear, smooth sentence. Write your revised version of the paragraph in the spaces above the lines.

Paragraph to Be Revised

My brother is a baseball fanatic. He wakes up in the morning thinking about the game. He reaches for the newspaper. He checks out all the baseball scores. He talks about baseball during breakfast. He can't stop talking and thinking about baseball during work. He talks about his favourite teams during his break. He has baseball conversations during lunch. With customers, he argues about the sport. My brother's clothes reflect his obsession. He has seven baseball caps. There are three baseball jackets in his closet. He owns at least twelve shirts marked with team insignia. For him, it's always basebal season.

EXERCISE **17** 	**ADDING DETAILS TO A DRAFT**

Complete this exercise with a partner or a group. The paragraph below lacks the kind of details that would make it more interesting. Working with a partner or a group, add the details to the blank spaces provided. When you are finished with the additions, read the revised paragraph to the class.

Paragraph to Be Revised

Popular movies come in a variety of forms. Some offer exciting action sequences. The action may involve war, in a movie like _____, or a dramatic chase, in films such as _____ and _____. Other popular movies feature tragic love stories. _____ is this kind of film. Every year, one kind of film especially popular with children is the blockbuster animated feature, like _____ or _____. Equally popular are the outrageous comedies that appeal to teens or college students. Movies such as _____ and _____ are perfect examples of these comedies. Clearly, there are films to suit all tastes and ages.

 FINAL LINES   ## PROOFREADING AND POLISHING A PARAGRAPH

The final version of your paragraph is the result of careful thinking, planning, and revising. After you've written as many drafts as you need, you then read to polish and proofread. You can avoid too many last-minute corrections if you check your last draft carefully. Check that draft for the following:

- spelling errors
- punctuation errors
- grammar errors
- word choice
- a final statement

Take a look at an earlier draft of the paragraph on a favourite city or town. Corrections are written directly above the crossed-out material. At the end of the paragraph, you will notice a concluding sentence has been added to unify the paragraph.

> ### Correcting the Last Draft of a Paragraph
>
>   Ontario
> I love Thunder Bay, ~~ON~~, because it has forests and lakes, outdoor life, and family. Thunder Bay is cool in the summer, and the bush and the lake are
> nearby. The lake is clean with clear blue water. In ~~adition~~^{addition}, Thunder Bay has lots
> of outdoor activities. I can fish and camp in the cool ~~Summer~~^{summer} months, or I can cross-country and downhill ski all winter long. Best of all, my grandparents live
> in Thunder Bay. They are my favourite relatives, and they make me ~~foll~~^{feel} very welcome. When I am in Thunder Bay, I stay with them, enjoy their food, and use
> their car. Thunder Bay has the perfect natural advantages, outdoor lifestyle, and family ~~connection~~^{connections} to make it my ~~favorite~~^{favourite} city.

Giving Your Paragraph a Title

When you prepare the final version of your paragraph, you may be asked to give it a title. The title should be short and should fit the subject of the paragraph. For example, an appropriate title for the paragraph on a favourite city or town could be "My Favourite City," or "The City I Love." Check with your instructor to see if your paragraph needs a title. In this book, the paragraphs do not have titles.

The Final Version of a Paragraph

Below is the final version of the paragraph on a favourite city or town. As you read it, you will notice a few more changes. Even though the paragraph went through several drafts and many revisions, the final copy still reflects some additional polishing: some details have been added, some have been made more specific, and some words have been changed. These changes were made as the final version was prepared. (They are underlined for your reference.)

> ### A Final Version of a Paragraph (*changes from the previous draft are underlined*)
>
> I love Thunder Bay, Ontario, because it has forests and lakes, outdoor life, and family. Thunder Bay is <u>comfortably</u> cool in the summer, and the bush and <u>Lake Superior</u> are <u>only ten minutes away.</u> The lake is clean with clear blue water. In addition, Thunder Bay <u>offers many</u> outdoor activities. <u>In the nearby forests,</u> I can fish and camp in the cool summer months, or I can cross-country and downhill ski all winter long. Best of all, my grandparents live in Thunder Bay. They are my favourite relatives, and they make me feel very welcome. When I am in Thunder Bay, I stay with them, enjoy their <u>delicious Ukrainian</u> food, and use their car. Thunder Bay has the perfect natural advantages, outdoor lifestyle, and family connections to make it my favourite city.

Reviewing the Writing Process

This chapter has taken you through four important stages in writing. As you become more comfortable with them, you will be able to work through them more quickly. For now, try to remember the four stages.

INFOBOX	THE STAGES OF THE WRITING PROCESS

Thought Lines: gathering and developing ideas, thinking on paper through freewriting, brainstorming, mapping, or keeping a journal.
Outlines: planning the paragraph by combining and dividing details, focusing the details with a topic sentence, listing the supporting details in proper order, and devising an outline.
Rough Lines: writing a rough draft of the paragraph, then revising and editing it several times.
Final Lines: preparing the final version of the paragraph, with one last proofreading check for errors in preparation, punctuation, and mechanics.

EXERCISE **18**	PROOFREADING TO PREPARE THE FINAL VERSION

Following are two illustration paragraphs with the kind of errors it is easy to overlook when you prepare the final version of an assignment. Correct the errors by writing above the lines. There are eleven errors in the first paragraph and eight errors in the second paragraph.

ALONG THESE LINES/Pearson Education Canada

1.   Every time I am on the telephone and I need to write something down, I am caught in a terible dilemma. First of all, their is never any paper nearby. Even thou I live in an apartment full of schoolbooks notebooks pads, and typing paper, they're is never any papper near the telephone. I wind up desperately looking for anything I can write on. Sometimes i write on coupons my mother has saved in the kitchen, but coupons are shiny and don't take writing well. If I do manage to find some better paper, I can't find a pen or pencil! Our home is full of pen's and pencil's, but I can never find even a stubbby old pencil or a leaky old ballpoint when I need it. In emergencies, I have taken telephone messages with a crayon and a lipstick.

2.   Insufficient parking is a serious prolem for student's at Carlyle College. Very often, students are forced to drive around the filled rows for ten or twenty minutes, looking for a solitary space. if they find one, it is at the end of a long row. And by the time they find it and have walked the long way to there class-room, they are late for class. They run the risk of missing a quiz or being penalize in some other way. For those who cannot find a space, there are even more risky alternatives. Some students parks in a faculty spot or in a fire Lane. These students risk getting a ticket and a fine, but they must weigh this risk against missing class. Carlyle College administrators need to reconize students' parking dilemmas and provide more parking spaces for students who just want to get to class on time.

Lines of Detail: A Walk-Through Assignment

This assignment involves working within a group to write a paragraph.

Step 1: Read the three sentences below. Pick the one sentence you prefer as a possible topic sentence for a paragraph. Fill in the blank, if necessary, for the sentence you chose.

Pick one sentence and fill in the blank (if necessary):

a. Holding down a part-time job while at school can be challenging for a college or university student.

b. If money were no problem, the car I'd buy is _____ (fill in the name of the car).

c. _____ was the most stressful period in my life (fill in the time in your life).

Step 2: Join a group composed of other students who picked the same topic sentence you picked. In your class, you'll have "job" people, "car" people, and "stress" people. Brainstorm in a group. Discuss questions that could be used to get ideas for your paragraph.

For the job topic, sample questions could include, "What are the most challenging aspects of working and studying?" or "How does this challenge affect other areas or aspects of a student's life?" For the car topic, sample questions could include, "Have you ever driven this kind of car?" or "Do you know anyone who has one?" For the food topic, sample questions could include, "Why was it so stressful?" or "How did you overcome the stress?"

As you discuss, write the questions, not the answers, below. Keep the questions flowing. Do not stop to say, "That's silly" or "I can't answer that." Try to devise at least ten questions.

Ten Brainstorming Questions

1. _____

2. _____

3. _____

4. _____

5. _____

6. _____

7. _____

8. _____

9. _____

10. _____

Step 3: Split up. Alone, begin to think on paper. Answer as many questions as you can, or add more questions and answers, or freewrite.

Step 4: Draft an outline of the paragraph. You will probably have to change the topic sentence to fit the detail you have gathered. For example, your new topic sentence might be something like:

Holding down a part-time job while at school can be challenging because of _____, _____, and _____.

ALONG THESE LINES/Pearson Education Canada

or

If money were no problem, I would buy a _____ for its performance, _____, and _____.

or

_____ was the most stressful period in my life because _____.

Remember to look at your details to see where they lead you. The details will help you to refine your topic sentence.

Step 5: Prepare the first draft of the paragraph.

Step 6: Read the draft aloud to your writing group, the same people who met to brainstorm. Ask each member of your group to make at least one positive comment and one suggestion for revision.

Step 7: Revise and edit your draft, considering the group's ideas and your own ideas for improvement.

Step 8: Prepare a final version of the paragraph.

Writing Your Own Paragraph

When you write on any of these topics, follow the four basic stages of the writing process in preparing your paragraph.

1. Begin this assignment with a partner. The assignment requires an interview. Your final goal is to write a paragraph that will introduce a class member, your partner, to the rest of the class. In the final paragraph, you may design your own topic sentence or use one of the topic sentences below, filling in the blanks with the material you have discovered:

There are several things you should know about _____ (fill in your partner's name).

or

Three unusual events have happened to _____ (fill in your partner's name).

Before you write the paragraph, follow these steps:

Step 1: Prepare to interview a classmate. Make a list of six questions you might want to ask. They can be questions like, "Where are you from?" or "Have you ever done anything unusual?" Write *at least six questions* before you start the interview. List the questions on the following interview form, leaving room to fill in short answers later.

Interview Form

Question 1: _____

Answer: _____

Question 2: _____

Answer: _____

ALONG THESE LINES/Pearson Education Canada

Question 3: _____

Answer: _____

Question 4: _____

Answer: _____

Question 5: _____

Answer: _____

Question 6: _____

Answer: _____

Additional questions and answers:_____

_____

_____

Step 2: Meet and interview your partner. Ask the questions on your list. Jot down brief answers. Ask any other questions you think of as you are talking; write down the answers on the additional lines at the end of the interview form.

Step 3: Change places. Let your partner interview you.

Step 4: Split up. Use the list of questions and answers about your partner as the thought lines part of your assignment. Work on the outline and draft steps.

Step 5: Ask your partner to read the draft version of your paragraph, to write any comments or suggestions for improvement below the paragraph, and to mark any spelling or grammar errors in the paragraph itself.

Step 6: When you have completed a final version of the paragraph, read the paragraph to the class.

2. Below are some topic sentences. Select one and use it to write a paragraph.

It is difficult to find time for myself these days.

My daily life provides several irritations.

I love/hate reality TV shows.

College is a good place to _____ and _____.

3. Write a paragraph on one of the topics below. Create your own topic sentence; explain and support it with specific details.

a favourite activity	the best gift
a dreaded chore	one stress-buster
a sad occasion	the best time of day
a challenging class	the ugliest car
my biggest regret	my most prized possession
an exciting sport	a proud moment

CHAPTER 2
Writing from Reading

LEARNING OBJECTIVES

After you have read this chapter and completed its exercises and assignments, you should be able to

- read a piece of writing and identify its thesis and main ideas
- make notes of the main ideas in a piece of writing
- write a summary and a paraphrase of a piece of writing
- avoid plagiarizing a piece of writing
- respond to a piece of writing
- write an essay test effectively and efficiently

"Say all you have to say in the fewest possible words, or your reader will be sure to skip them; and in the plainest possible words or he will certainly misunderstand them."

~ JOHN RUSKIN

▼
JOHN RUSKIN, BORN IN THE NINETEENTH CENTURY, WAS KNOWN FOR HIS ART AND SOCIAL CRITICISM.

WHAT IS WRITING FROM READING?

One way to find topics for writing is to draw from your ideas, memories, and observations. Another way is to write from reading that you've done. You can *react* to it; you can *agree* or *disagree* with something you've read. In fact, many college assignments ask you to write about an assigned reading: an essay, a chapter in a textbook, an article in a journal. This kind of writing requires an active, involved attitude toward your reading. Such reading is done in steps:

1. preread
2. read
3. reread with a pen or pencil

After you've completed these three steps, you can write from your reading. You can write about what you've read or you can react to what you've read.

AN APPROACH TO WRITING FROM READING

Attitude

Before you begin the first step of this reading process, you have to have a certain **attitude**. That attitude involves thinking of what you read as half of a conversation. The writer has opinions and ideas; he or she makes points just as you do when you write or speak. The writer supports his or her points with specific details. If the writer were speaking to you in a conversation, you would respond to his or her opinions or ideas. You would agree, disagree, or question. You would jump into the conversation, linking or contrasting your ideas with those of the other speaker.

The right attitude toward reading demands that you read the same way you converse: you *become involved*. In doing this, you "talk back" as you read, and later you react in your own writing. Reacting as you read will keep you focused on what you are reading. If you are focused, you'll remember more of what you read. With an active, involved attitude, you can begin the step of prereading.

Prereading

Before you actually read an assigned essay, a chapter in a textbook, or an article in a journal, magazine, or newspaper, take a few minutes to **preread** it: look it over, and be ready to answer the questions in the prereading checklist below.

CHECKLIST   FOR PREREADING

- ✓ How long is this reading?
- ✓ Will I be able to read it in one sitting, or will I have to schedule several time periods to finish it?
- ✓ Are there any subheadings in the reading? Do they give any hints about the reading?
- ✓ Are there any charts? Graphs? Boxes of information?
- ✓ Are there any photographs or illustrations with captions? Do the photos or captions give me any hints about the reading?
- ✓ Is there any introductory material about the reading or its author? Does the introductory material give me any hints about the reading?
- ✓ What is the title of the reading? Does the title hint at the point of the reading?
- ✓ Are any parts of the reading underlined, italicized, or emphasized in some other way? Do the emphasized parts hint at the point of the reading?

Why Preread?

Prereading takes very little time, but it helps you immensely. Some students believe it's a waste of time to scan an assignment; they think they should jump right in and get the reading over with. However, spending just a few minutes on preliminaries can save hours later. And, most important, prereading helps you to become a *focused reader*.

ALONG THESE LINES/Pearson Education Canada

If you scan the length of an assignment, you can pace yourself. And if you know how long a reading is, you can alert yourself to its plan. A short reading, for example, has to come to its point fairly soon. A longer essay may take more time to develop its point and may use more details and examples.

Subheadings, charts, graphs, illustrations, and boxed or other highlighted materials are important enough that the author wants to emphasize them. Looking over that material *before* you read gives you an overview of the important points that the reading will contain.

Introductory material or introductory questions will also help you to know what to look for as you read. Background on the author or on the subject may hint at ideas that will come up in the reading. Sometimes even the title of the reading will give you the main idea.

You should preread so that you can start reading the entire assignment with as much *knowledge* about the writer and the subject as you can get. When you then read the entire assignment, you will be reading *actively,* for more knowledge.

Forming Questions before You Read

If you want to read with a focus, it helps to ask questions before you read. Form questions by using the information you gain from prereading.

Start by noting the title and turning it into a question. If the title of your assigned reading is "Reasons for the War Measures Act," you can ask the question, "What were the reasons for the War Measures Act?"

You can turn subheadings into questions. If you are reading an article on beach erosion, and one subheading is "Artificial Reefs," you can ask, "How are artificial reefs connected to beach erosion?"

You can also form questions from graphs and illustrations. If a chapter in your history book includes a photograph of a Gothic cathedral, you could ask, "How are Gothic cathedrals connected to this period in history?" or "Why are Gothic cathedrals important?" or "What is Gothic architecture?"

You can write down these questions, but it's not necessary. Just forming questions and keeping them in the back of your mind helps you read actively and stay focused.

An Example of the Prereading Step

Take a look at the article that follows. Don't read it; *preread* it.

A Ridiculous Addiction
Gwinn Owens

Gwinn Owens, a retired editor and columnist for the Baltimore Evening Sun, *writes this essay about his experience in parking lots, noting that the search for a good parking space "transcends logic and common sense."*

Let us follow my friend Frank Bogley as, on the way home from work, he swings into the shopping mall to pick up a liter of Johnny Walker, on sale at the Bottle and Cork. In the vast, herringboned parking area there are, literally, hundreds of empty spaces, but some are perhaps as much as a 40-second walk from the door of the liquor store. So Bogley, a typical American motorist, feels compelled to park as close as possible.

He eases down between the rows of parked cars until he notices a blue-haired matron getting into her Mercedes. This is a prime location, not more than 25 steps from the Bottle and Cork. Bogley stops to await her departure so as to slip quickly into the vacated slot. She shuts the door of her car as Bogley's engine surges nervously. But she does not move. She is, in fact, **preening** her hair and **perusing** a magazine she just bought.

preening: primping, making yourself appear elegant

perusing: reading

stymied: hindered, blocked, defeated

The **stymied** Bogley is now tying up traffic in that lane. Two more cars with impatient drivers assemble behind him. One driver hits his horn lightly, then angrily. Bogley opens his window and gives him the finger, but reluctantly realizes that the Mercedes isn't about to leave. His arteries harden a little more as, exasperated, he gives up and starts circling the lot in search of another space, passing scores of empty ones which he deems too far from his destination. Predictably, he slips into the space for the handicapped. "Just for a moment," he says to his conscience.

The elapsed time of Bogley's search for a convenient parking space is seven minutes. Had he chosen one of the abundant spaces only a few steps farther away, he could have accomplished his mission in less than two minutes, without frazzled nerves or skyrocketing blood pressure—his as well as those who were backed up behind him. He could have enjoyed a little healthful walking to reduce the paunch that is gestating in his middle.

addiction: a compulsive habit

Frank Bogley suffers an acute case of parking **addiction**, which afflicts more Americans than the common cold. We are obsessed with the idea that it is our constitutional right not to have to park more than 10 steps from our destination.

transcends: rises above, goes beyond the limits of

Like all addictions, this quest for the coveted spot **transcends** logic and common sense. Motorists will pursue it without concern over the time it takes, as if a close-in parking space were its own sweet fulfillment. They will park in the fire lane, in the handicapped space or leave the car at the curb, where space is reserved for loading.

atavistically: primitively

The quest **atavistically** transcends politeness and civility. My local paper recently carried a story about two motorists who, seeing a third car about to exit a spot, both lusted for the vacancy. As soon as the departing vehicle was gone, one of the stand-bys was a little faster and grabbed the coveted prize. The defeated motorist leaped from his car, threw open his rival's door and punched him in the snoot. He was charged with assault. Hell hath no fury like a motorist who loses the battle for a close-in parking space.

coveted: desired, eagerly wished for

acrimonious: bitter, harsh

The daily obsession to possess the **coveted** slot probably shortens the life of most Americans by at least 4.2 years. This **acrimonious** jockeying, waiting, backing, maneuvering for the holy grail of nearness jangles the nerves, constricts the arteries and turns puppylike personalities into snarling mad dogs.

I know a few Americans who have actually kicked the habit, and they are extraordinarily happy people. I am one, and I owe my cure to my friend Lou, who is the antithesis of Frank Bogley. One day I recognized Lou's red Escort in the wallflower space of the parking lot at our local supermarket. There was not another vehicle within 80 feet.

ALONG THESE LINES/Pearson Education Canada

ensconced: securely sheltered

In the store I asked him why he had **ensconced** his car in lonely splendor. His answer made perfect sense: "I pull in and out quickly, nobody else's doors scratch my paint and I get a short walk, which I need." Lou, I might point out, is in his 60s and is built like 25—lean and fit.

idiocy: foolish behaviour

These days, I do as Lou does, and a great weight has been lifted. Free of the hassle, I am suddenly aware of the collective **idiocy** of the parking obsession—angry people battling for what is utterly without value. I acquire what does have value: saving of time, fresh air, peace of mind, healthful exercise.

The only time I feel the stress now is when I am a passenger with a driver who has not yet taken the cure. On one recent occasion I accepted a ride with my friend Andy to a large banquet at which I was a head-table guest. The banquet hall had its own commodious parking lot, but Andy is another Frank Bogley.

He insisted on trying to park near the door "because it is late." He was right, it *was* late, and there being no slots near the door, he then proceeded to thread his way through the labyrinth of the close-in lot, as I pleaded that I didn't mind walking from out where there was plenty of space. He finally used five minutes jockeying his big Lincoln into a Honda-size niche. Thanks to Andy's addiction, I walked late into the banquet hall and stumbled into my conspicuous seat in the midst of the solemn

contempt: scorn, lack of respect

convocation. My attitude toward him was a mixture of pity and **contempt**, like a recovering alcoholic must feel toward an incipient drunk.

These silly parking duels, fought over the right not to walk 15 more steps, can be found almost anywhere in the 50 states. They reach their ultimate absurdity, however, at my local racquet and fitness club. The battle to park close to the door of the ath-

emporium: store

letic **emporium** is fought as aggressively as at the shopping mall. Everyone who parks there is intending to engage in tennis, squash, aerobic dancing, muscle building or some other kind of athletic constitutional. But to have to exercise ahead of time by walking from the lot to the door is clearly regarded by most Americans as unconstitutional.

The Results of Prereading

By *prereading* the article, you might notice the following:

> The title is "A Ridiculous Addiction."
> The author is a retired newspaper writer from Baltimore.
> There are many vocabulary words you may need to know.
> The essay is about parking lots.
> The introductory material says that the American habit of searching for a desirable parking space goes beyond the limits of common sense.

You might begin reading the article with these questions in mind:

> What is the addiction?
> How can an addiction be ridiculous? An addiction is usually considered something very serious, like an addiction to drugs.
> What do parking spaces have to do with addiction?
> What's so illogical about looking for a good parking space?

ALONG THESE LINES/Pearson Education Canada

Reading

The first time you read, try to get a sense of the whole piece you are reading. Reading with questions in mind can help you to do this. If you find that you are confused by a certain part of the reading selection, go back and reread that part. If you do not know the meaning of a word, look in the margin to see if the word is defined for you. If it is not defined for you, try to figure out the meaning from the way the word is used in the sentence.

If you find that you have to read more slowly than you usually do, don't worry. People vary their reading speed according to what they read and why they are reading it. If you are reading for entertainment, for example, you can read quickly; if you are reading a chapter in a textbook, you must read more slowly. The more complicated the reading selection, the more slowly you will read it.

An Example of the Reading Step

Now *read* "A Ridiculous Addiction." When you've completed your first reading, your answers to the prereading questions that you formed will probably be like those below:

Answers to Prereading Questions

> The author says that the ridiculous addiction is the need to find the best parking space.
> He means it's ridiculous because it makes parking a serious issue, and because people do silly things to get good parking spots.
> People are illogical about getting parking spaces because they'll even be late for an event in order to get a good one. Or they often get upset.

Rereading with Pen or Pencil

The second reading is the crucial one. At this point, you begin to *think on paper*, as you read. In this step, you make notes or write about what you read. Some students are reluctant to do this, for they are not sure *what* to note or write. Think of making these notes as a way of learning, thinking, reviewing, and reacting. Reading with a pen or pencil in your hand keeps you alert. With that pen or pencil, you can do the following:

> Mark the main point of the reading.
> Mark other points.
> Circle words you don't know and define them in the margin.
> Question parts of the reading you're not sure of.
> Evaluate the writer's ideas.
> React to the writer's opinions or examples.
> Add ideas, opinions, or examples of your own.

It's easiest to do this right on the book, although if you're reading a library book or a book that doesn't belong to you, you can use sticky notes or make notes on a separate sheet. There is no single system for marking or writing as you read. Some readers like to underline the main idea with two lines and to underline other important ideas with one line. Some students like to put an asterisk (a star) next to important ideas, while others like to circle key words.

Some people use the margins to write comments like, "I agree!" or "Not true!" or "That's happened to me." Sometimes readers put questions in the margin; sometimes they summarize a point in the margin, next to its location in the essay. Some people make notes in the white space above the reading and list important points, while others use the space at the end of the reading. Every reader who writes as he or she reads has a personal system; what these systems share is an attitude. If you *write as you read*, you concentrate on the reading selection, get to know the writer's ideas, and develop ideas of your own.

As you reread and write notes, don't worry too much about noticing the "right" ideas. Think of rereading as the time to jump into a conversation with the writer.

An Example of Rereading with Pen or Pencil

For "A Ridiculous Addiction," your marked article might look like the following:

A Ridiculous Addiction

by Gwinn Owens

Let us follow my friend Frank Bogley as, on the way home from work, he swings into the shopping mall to pick up a liter of Johnny

zigzagged ← Walker, on sale at the Bottle and Cork. In the vast, (herringboned) parking area there are, literally, hundreds of empty spaces, but some are perhaps as much as a 40-second walk from the door of the liquor store. So Bogley,

the bad habit a typical American motorist, <u>feels compelled to park as close as possible.</u>

He eases down between the rows of parked cars until he notices a blue-haired matron getting into her Mercedes. This is a prime location, not more than 25 steps from the Bottle and Cork. Bogley stops to await her departure so as to slip quickly into the vacated slot. She shuts the door of her car as Bogley's engine surges nervously. But she does not move. She is, in fact, preening her hair and perusing a magazine she just bought.

The stymied Bogley is now tying up traffic in that lane. Two more cars with impatient drivers assemble behind him. One driver hits his horn lightly, then angrily. Bogley opens his window and gives him the finger, but reluctantly realizes that the Mercedes isn't about to leave. His arteries harden a little more as, exasperated, he gives up and starts circling the lot

considers ← in search of another space, passing scores of empty ones which he (deems)

I hate this! too far from his destination. <u>Predictably, he slips into the space for the handicapped.</u> "Just for a moment," he says to his conscience.

<u>The elapsed time of Bogley's search for a convenient parking space is</u>

wasted time <u>seven minutes.</u> Had he chosen one of the abundant spaces only a few steps farther away, <u>he could have accomplished his mission in less than two</u> <u>minutes,</u> without <u>frazzled nerves</u> or <u>skyrocketing blood pressure</u>—<u>his as</u> <u>well as those who were backed up behind him.</u> He could have enjoyed a

irritation

developing ← little healthful walking to reduce the paunch that is (gestating) in his middle.

Frank Bogley suffers an acute case of parking addiction, which afflicts more Americans than the common cold. <u>We are obsessed with</u> <u>the idea that it is our constitutional right not to have to park more than</u> <u>10 steps from our destination.</u>

<u>Like all addictions, this quest for the coveted spot transcends logic</u> <u>and common sense.</u> Motorists will pursue it without concern over <u>the time</u> <u>it takes,</u> as if a close-in parking space were its own sweet fulfillment. They will <u>park in the fire lane, in the handicapped space</u> or <u>leave the car at the</u> <u>curb, where space is reserved for loading.</u>

The quest atavistically <u>transcends politeness and civility.</u> My local paper

example

recently carried a story about two motorists who, seeing a third car about to exit a spot, both lusted for the vacancy. As soon as the departing vehicle was gone, one of the standbys was a little faster and grabbed the coveted prize. The defeated motorist leaped from his car, threw open his rival's door and punched him in the snoot. He was charged with <u>assault.</u> Hell hath no fury like a motorist who loses the battle for a close-in parking space.

The daily obsession to possess the coveted slot probably shortens the life of most Americans by at least 4.2 years. This acrimonious jockeying,

valued object won ← waiting, backing, maneuvering for the (holy grail) of nearness <u>jangles the</u>
after heroic effort   <u>nerves, constricts the arteries</u> and <u>turns puppylike personalities into</u> <u>snarling mad dogs.</u>

I know a few Americans who have actually kicked the habit, and they are extraordinarily happy people. I am one, and I owe my cure to my

opposite ← friend Lou, who is the (antithesis) of Frank Bogley. One day I recognized Lou's red Escort in the wallflower space of the parking lot of our local supermarket. There was not another vehicle within 80 feet.

In the store I asked him why he had ensconced his car in lonely splendor. His answer made perfect sense: <u>"I pull in and out quickly, nobody</u>
breaking the habit: advantages
<u>else's doors scratch my paint and I get a short walk, which I need."</u> Lou, I might point out, is in his 60s and is built like 25—lean and fit.

These days, I do as Lou does, and a great weight has been lifted. Free of the hassle, I am suddenly aware of the collective idiocy of the

ALONG THESE LINES/Pearson Education Canada

parking obsession—angry people battling for what is utterly without

value. I acquire what does have value: <u>saving of time, fresh air, peace of</u>
more advantages
<u>mind, healthful exercise.</u>

The only time I feel the stress now is when I am a passenger with
back to bad habit
a driver who has not yet taken the cure. On one recent occasion

I accepted a ride with my friend Andy to a large banquet at which I was
spacious ←———
a head-table guest. The banquet hall had its own (commodious) parking

lot, but Andy is another Frank Bogley.

He insisted on trying to park near the door "because it is late." He

was right, it was late, and there being no slots near the door, he then pro-
maze, puzzle ←———
ceeded to thread his way through the (labyrinth) of the close-in lot, as I

pleaded that I didn't mind walking from out where there was plenty of

space. He finally <u>used five minutes jockeying his big Lincoln into a</u>
How true!
<u>Honda-size niche.</u> Thanks to Andy's addiction, I walked late into the ban-

quet hall and stumbled into my conspicuous seat in the midst of the

solemn convocation. My attitude toward him was a mixture of pity and
beginning ←———
contempt, like a recovering alcoholic must feel toward an (incipient) drunk.

<u>These silly parking duels, fought over the right not to walk more</u>
more on bad habit
<u>than 15 steps, can be found almost anywhere in the 50 states.</u> They reach

their ultimate absurdity, however, at my local racquet and fitness club.

The battle to park close to the door of the athletic emporium is fought as

aggressively as at the shopping mall. Everyone who parks there is intend-

ing to engage in tennis, squash, aerobic dancing, muscle building or some

other kind of athletic constitutional. But to have to exercise ahead of time

by walking from the lot to the door is clearly regarded by most Americans

as unconstitutional.

What the Notes Mean

In the sample above, the underlining indicates sentences or phrases that seem
important. The words written between the lines or in the margin are often summaries of what is underlined. The words *wasted time, irritation,* and *advantages,*
for instance, are like subtitles or labels added by the reader. The asterisks refer
to very important ideas.

Some words in the margin are reactions. When Owens describes a man
who parked illegally in a handicapped spot, the reader notes, "I hate this!"
When the writer talks about a Lincoln trying to fit into a Honda-sized spot, the
reader writes, "How true!" Several words in the margin are definitions. For
example, the word *herringboned* in the selection is defined as *zigzagged* in
the margin.

ALONG THESE LINES/Pearson Education Canada

The marked-up article is a flexible tool. You can go back and mark it further. You may change your mind about your notes and comments and find other better or more important points in the article.

You write as you read to involve yourself in the reading process. Marking what you read can help you in other ways, too. If you are to be tested on the reading selection or asked to discuss it, you can scan your markings and notations at a later time for a quick review.

| EXERCISE 1 | **READING AND MAKING NOTES** |

Below is the last paragraph of "A Ridiculous Addiction." First, read it. Then reread it and make notes on the following:

1. Underline the sentence that begins the long example in the paragraph.
2. Circle a word you don't know and define it in the margin.
3. In the margin, add your own example of a place where people fight for parking spaces.
4. At the end of the paragraph, summarize the point of the paragraph.

Paragraph from "A Ridiculous Addiction"

These silly parking duels, fought over the right not to walk more than 15 steps, can be found almost anywhere in the 50 states. They reach their ultimate absurdity, however, at my local racquet and fitness club. The battle to park close to the door of the athletic emporium is fought as aggressively as at the shopping mall. Everyone who parks there is intending to engage in tennis, squash, aerobic dancing, muscle building, or some other kind of athletic constitutional. But to have to exercise ahead of time by walking from the lot to the door is clearly regarded by most Americans as unconstitutional.

Main point of the paragraph: _____

_____

_____

WRITING A SUMMARY OF A READING

There are a number of ways you can write about what you've read. You may be asked for a summary or paraphrase of an article or chapter, or for a reaction to it, or to write about it on an essay test. For each of these, this chapter will give you guidelines so that you can follow the stages of the writing process.

A **summary** of a reading tells the important ideas in brief form in your own words. It includes (1) the writer's main idea, (2) the ideas used to explain the main idea, and (3) some examples used to support the ideas.

When you preread, read, and make notes on the reading selection, you have already begun the thought lines stage for a summary. You can think further, on paper, by *listing the points* (words, phrases, sentences) you've already marked on the reading selection.

ALONG THESE LINES/Pearson Education Canada

THOUGHT LINES   ## GATHERING IDEAS: SUMMARY

Marking a List of Ideas

To find the main idea for your summary and the ideas and examples connected to the main idea, you can mark related items on your list. For example, the expanded list below was made from "A Ridiculous Addiction." Four symbols are used:

k	the **kinds** of close spots people will take
×	all **examples** of what can happen when people want a good spot
–	the **negative** effects of the close-parking habit
+	the **advantages** of breaking the habit

A List of Ideas for a Summary of "A Ridiculous Addiction"

k no close spots, takes handicapped

× seven minutes looking for close spot

– wasted time, could have found another in two minutes

× got mad

× made others wait

× they got angry

Americans obsessed with right to good spot

transcends logic

no common sense

k park in fire lane

k leave car at curb

k loading zone

– impolite

× an assault over a spot

– jangles nerves, constricts arteries, makes people act like mad dogs

kicking the habit

+ get in and out fast

+ no scratched car doors

+ good exercise

+ saving time

+ fresh air

+ peace of mind

+ healthful exercise

× late for big dinner

× fitness clubs the silliest—won't walk

The marked list could be reorganized, like this:

kinds of close spots people will take

handicapped

fire lane

curb

loading zone

examples of what can happen when people want a good spot

seven minutes of wasted time

others, waiting behind, get mad

an assault over a spot

late for a big dinner

members of the fitness club won't walk

negative effects of the close-parking habit

wasted time

impolite

jangles nerves, constricts arteries

makes people mad dogs

advantages of breaking the habit

get in and out fast

no scratched car doors

good exercise

saving time

fresh air

peace of mind

healthful exercise

Selecting a Main Idea

The next step in the process is to select the idea you think is the writer's main point. If you look again at the list of ideas, you'll note a cluster of ideas that are unmarked:

1. Americans obsessed with the right to a good spot
2. transcends logic
3. no common sense

You might guess that they are unmarked because they are more general than the other ideas. In fact, these ideas are connected to the title of the essay: "A Ridiculous Addiction," and they are connected to some of the questions in the prereading step of reading: "What's the addiction?" and "How can an addiction be ridiculous?"

Linking the ideas may lead you to a *main idea* for the summary of the reading selection:

Americans' obsession with finding a good parking spot makes no sense.

Once you have a main idea, check it to see if it fits with the other ideas in your organized list. Do the ideas in the list connect to the main idea? *Yes*. "Kinds of close spots people take" explains how silly it is to break the law. "Examples of what can happen" and "negative effects" show why the habit makes no sense, and "advantages of breaking the habit" shows the reasons to conquer the addiction.

Once you have a main point that fits an organized list, you can move to the *outlines stage* of a summary.

ALONG THESE LINES/Pearson Education Canada

EXERCISE 2

MARKING A LIST OF IDEAS AND FINDING THE MAIN IDEA FOR A SUMMARY

Below is a list of ideas from an article called "How to Ride Ups, Downs of Learning New Skills." Read the list, and then mark it with one of these symbols:

> **X = examples** of different learning styles
> **S = steps** in learning
> **A = advice** from successful people

After you've marked all the ideas, survey them, and think of one main idea. Try to focus on an idea that connects to the title, "How to Ride Ups, Downs of Learning New Skills."

List of Ideas

_____ Kids tend to learn by trial and error and are ready to learn from their mistakes.

_____ Excitement and confidence replace fear and confusion as the learner can say, "I know this."

_____ If you want to increase your success rate, double your failure rate.

_____ Confidence and comfort levels are highest when the course begins.

_____ Another student prefers to study alone to avoid distractions.

_____ Focus all your energy on improving, learning, and achieving your goals.

_____ Utter confusion, frustration, and discomfort make the learner feel lost.

_____ Some adults view change with suspicion and uncertainty and are uncomfortable moving into new situations.

_____ One student enjoys studying with a group to exchange ideas and bolster her confidence.

Main idea: _____

_____

_____

_____

 **DEVISING A PLAN: SUMMARY**

Below is a sample of the kind of outline you could do for a summary of "A Ridiculous Addiction." As you read it, you'll notice that the main idea of the thought lines stage has become the topic sentence of the outline, and the other ideas have become the details.

> Outline for a Summary of "A Ridiculous Addiction"

topic sentence: Americans' obsession with finding a good parking spot makes no sense.

details:

examples

Many bad or silly things can happen when people try for a good spot.

One person wasted seven minutes.

He made other drivers angry.

Someone else got involved in an assault.

Someone else was late for a big dinner.

Silly people, on their way to a fitness club, will avoid the walk in the fitness club parking lot.

negative effects

Looking for a close spot can make people impolite or make them act like mad dogs.

It can jangle drivers' nerves or constrict arteries.

Some people will even break the law and take handicapped spots or park in a fire lane or loading zone.

advantages of kicking the habit

If people can give up the habit, they can gain advantages.

A far-away spot is not popular, so they can get in and out of it fast.

Their cars won't be scratched.

They get exercise and fresh air by walking.

In the preceding outline, some ideas from the original list have been left out (they were repetitive) and the order of some points has been rearranged. That kind of selecting and rearranging is what you do in the outlines stage of writing a summary.

 **DRAFTING AND REVISING: SUMMARY**

Attributing Ideas in a Summary

The first draft of your summary paragraph is the place where you combine all the material into one paragraph. This draft is much like the draft of any other paragraph, with one exception: When you summarize another person's ideas, be sure to say whose ideas you are writing. That is, *attribute* the ideas to the writer. Let the reader of your paragraph know

1. the author of the selection you are summarizing, and
2. the title of the selection you are summarizing.

You may wish to do this by giving your summary paragraph a *title*, such as

A Summary of "A Ridiculous Addiction," by Gwinn Owens

(Note that you put the title of Owens' essay in quotation marks.)

Or you may want to put the title and author into the paragraph itself. Below is a draft summary of "A Ridiculous Addiction" with the title and author incorporated into the paragraph.

A Draft for a Summary of "A Ridiculous Addiction"

"A Ridiculous Addiction" by Gwinn Owens says that Americans' obsession with finding a good parking spot makes no sense. Many bad or silly things can happen when people try for a good spot. One person wasted seven minutes. He made other drivers angry. Someone else got involved in an assault. Someone else was late for a big dinner. Silly people, on their way to a fitness club, will avoid the walk in the fitness parking lot. Looking for a close spot can make people impolite or make them act like mad dogs. It can be stressful. Some people even break the law and take handicapped spots or park in a fire lane or loading zone. If people can give up the habit, they can gain advantages. A far-away spot is not popular, so they can get in and out of it fast. Their cars won't be scratched. They get exercise and fresh air by walking.

When you look this draft over and read it aloud, you may notice a few problems:

1. It is wordy.
2. In some places, the word choice could be better.
3. Some of the sentences are choppy.
4. It might be a good idea to mention that the examples in the summary were given by Gwinn Owens.

Revising the draft would mean rewriting to eliminate some of the wordiness, to combine sentences or smooth out ideas, and to insert the point that the author, Gwinn Owens, gave the examples used in the summary. When you state that Owens created the examples, you are clearly giving the author credit for his ideas. Giving credit is a way of attributing ideas to the author.

Note: When you refer to an author in something that you write, use the author's first and last name the first time you make a reference. For example, you would write "Gwinn Owens" the first time you refer to this author. Later in the paragraph, if you want to refer to the same author, use only his or her last name. Thus, a second reference would be to "Owens."

 ## PROOFREADING AND POLISHING: SUMMARY

Look carefully at the final version of the summary. Notice how the sentences have been changed, and words added or taken out. "Owens" is used to show that the examples given came from the essay.

> ## A Final Version of a Summary of "A Ridiculous Addiction"

"A Ridiculous Addiction" by Gwinn Owens says that Americans' obsession with finding a good parking spot makes no sense. Owens gives many examples of the unpleasant or silly things that can happen when people try for a good spot. One person wasted seven minutes and made the other drivers angry. Someone else got involved in an assault; another person was late for an important dinner. At fitness club parking lots, people coming to exercise are missing out on the exercise of walking through the parking lot. Looking for a good spot can turn polite people into impolite ones or even make them act like mad dogs. The search is not only stressful; it can also lead people to break the law by taking handicapped, fire lane, or loading zone spots. If people broke the habit and took spots farther away from buildings, they would have several advantages. No one wants the far-away spots, so drivers can get in and out fast, without any scratches on their cars. In addition, people who break the habit get exercise and fresh air.

Writing summaries is good writing practice, and it also helps you to develop your reading skills. Even if your instructor does not require you to turn in a polished summary of an assigned reading, you may find it helpful to summarize what you have read. In many classes, midterms or other exams cover many assigned readings. If you make short summaries of each reading as it is assigned, you will have a helpful collection of focused, organized material to review.

WRITING A PARAPHRASE OF A READING

A **paraphrase** is like a summary: you use your own words to express the ideas found in a reading in the same order. However, a paraphrase is usually as long or longer than the original because its purpose is to restate the entire content in different words rather than stating the main ideas as in a summary. Because of its length, you generally won't be asked to write a paraphrase of anything longer than a paragraph or so.

Let's see how it works. Ever heard "A bird in the hand is worth two in the bush?" or "The early bird catches the worm?" These statements are *proverbs*, frequently used sayings that express common truths. However, proverbs can be difficult to understand if you haven't heard them all your life. How would you explain "The early bird catches the worm" to a recent newcomer to Canada?

You might say, "Well, 'the early bird catches the worm' means that people who wake up early benefit more than people who don't." You have just *paraphrased* the proverb.

EXERCISE **3**	**PARAPHRASING**

Paraphrase the following proverbs, working individually or in a group.

1. You are what you eat.
2. When the cat's away, the mice will play.
3. A rolling stone gathers no moss.

ALONG THESE LINES/Pearson Education Canada

4. Too many cooks spoil the broth.
5. Once bitten, twice shy.
6. A penny saved is a penny earned.
7. Many hands make light work.
8. A chain is only as strong as its weakest link.
9. A friend in need is a friend indeed.
10. Least said, soonest mended.

Paraphrasing a Paragraph

Paraphrasing is very similar to summarizing, only you don't have to distill as much information; remember that a paraphrase is usually as long or even longer than the original. So, in keeping with the summary-writing steps, follow these paraphrasing steps:

Step 1: Read the passage three times. The first time, read to understand the passage; the second, read to define any terms you don't understand. Lastly, read the passage looking at paragraph structure and the order in which the ideas are presented.

Step 2: Start to translate the ideas into your own words, maintaining the same order in which they were presented in the original passage. When reading the paraphrase, the reader should hear *your* voice, not the original author's.

Step 3: Revise your paraphrase for unity and coherence; does it contain all the important ideas? Do the sentences flow together?

Step 4: Edit your paraphrase for spelling and grammar.

communication at work

Employers demand good communication skills, both spoken and written. Read the following paragraph, taken from an article entitled "Employers Complain about Communication Skills," by Jim McKay (2005), and consider its paraphrases:

> Communication skills often top the list of qualities employers seek not just for entry-level jobs but for executive and blue-collar positions as well. But the qualities persistently are at the bottom of what potential recruits bring to an interview. When the National Association of Colleges and Employers recently asked employers what skill was most lacking in college job candidates, good communication skills was first.

An unacceptable paraphrase:

> Communication skills are the most important qualities employers look for, not only for entry-level jobs, but other positions as well. However, recruits don't often bring these qualities to interviews. The National Association of Colleges and Employers said good communication skills were most lacking in college job candidates.

This paraphrase is unacceptable because much of it has been copied from the original (see italics); changing a few words here and there and changing the sentence structure (see underlining) don't mean you have paraphrased.

(continued)

ALONG THESE LINES/Pearson Education Canada

An acceptable paraphrase:

> Employers often say that communication skills are the most important qualities they look for, for virtually any position. However, they also say that these qualities are among those they see the least in job interviews. Employers told the National Association of Colleges and Employers that they found communication skills were the most deficient quality in recent college graduates.

EXERCISE 4

PARAPHRASING A PARAGRAPH

The following passage is from a *Toronto Star* article entitled "Mass Collaboration: Harnessing the Power of Global Ideas" by Sharda Prashad (2007). Write a paraphrase of the passage.

> Mass collaboration, a large number of people and companies coming together on the Web to innovate and create value, is evidenced in the operating system Linux, the online encyclopaedia Wikipedia, and the virtual communities of YouTube and MySpace. While owners of traditional bricks-and-mortar businesses might be quick to dismiss mass collaboration as a new-fangled notion that won't reap profit, in *Wikinomics* the authors emphasize that profits and mass collaboration go hand-in-hand.

_____

_____

_____

_____

_____

_____

_____

A Note on Plagiarism

"Borrowed thoughts, like borrowed money, only show the poverty of the borrower."

~ LADY MARGUERITE BLESSINGTON, COUNTESS OF BLESSINGTON

Plagiarism is the act of copying someone else's words or ideas and passing them off as your own, even if done inadvertently. It is a serious academic offence, one which usually incurs some sort of academic penalty; check the academic policy of your college or university to find out what its stand is on plagiarism, and consult with your instructor if you have any questions or concerns about your own work.

Keep in mind that you do *not*, necessarily, have to copy from the original word-for-word for your summary to be considered plagiarized. Similar sentence structure and phrasing are also signs of plagiarism.

The following excerpt is from an article by Maura Welch (2006), originally published in the *Boston Globe*, and ironically about online plagiarism:

> Beth gets more than 500 hits per day at her blog, Cursed to First, which serves as a very personal homage to the Red Sox and the Patriots, so she knew that spicy entries like "Chicks dig the long ball" were being read. She didn't realize until recently that they were also being ripped off.
>
> Last month, an alert reader informed Beth that her blog was being plagiarized. Dozens of Beth's blog entries had been stolen, word-for-word, over six months. Names of people in her life were changed to the names of people whom the plagiarist apparently knew, creating the impression that she had lived Beth's experiences and had thought her thoughts.

On the same day this was published, the following was published on an e-business website:

> Beth's blog got more than 500 hits per day, mostly from Red Sox and New England Patriots fans, not an unusual occurrence since she lives in Boston.
>
> But one of Beth's regular readers told her that her blog was being plagiarized on a regular basis, word-for-word over the past six months. The thief simply changed the names of Beth's friends in her post to those in the thief's post (which was, of course, actually Beth's).

This was considered plagiarism, and the article on the e-business website was removed.

EXERCISE **5**	**IDENTIFYING PLAGIARISM**

With a partner or in a small group, discuss the excerpt from the *Boston Globe* (above) and the excerpt from the e-business website. Why is the second considered plagiarism?

_____

_____

_____

_____

_____

_____

WRITING A REACTION TO A READING

A summary or a paraphrase is one kind of writing you can do after reading, but there are other kinds. You can write a **reaction** to a reading by writing on a topic related to the reading or by agreeing or disagreeing with some idea within the reading.

Writing on a Related Idea

Your instructor might ask you to react by writing about some idea you got from your reading. If you read "A Ridiculous Addiction," for example, your instructor might have asked you to react to it by writing about some practice or habit that irritates you. You can begin to gather ideas by freewriting.

THOUGHT LINES   ## GATHERING IDEAS: REACTION

Freewriting

You can freewrite in a reading journal, if you wish. To freewrite, you can

- write key points made by the author
- write about whatever you remember from the reading selection
- write down any of the author's ideas that you think you might want to write about someday
- list questions raised by what you've read
- connect the reading selection to other things you've read, heard, or experienced
- write any of the author's exact words that you might like to remember, putting them in quotation marks

A freewriting that reacts to "A Ridiculous Addiction" might look like this:

> ### Freewriting for a Reaction to a Reading
>
> **"A Ridiculous Addiction"—Gwinn Owens**
>
> People are silly in fighting for parking spaces. Owens says these are "silly parking duels." They get mean. Take handicapped spots. Angry. They fight over spots. Get angry when people sit in their cars and don't pull out of a spot. They jam big cars in small spaces, cars get damaged. They're "angry people battling for what is utterly without value." Why? To make a quick getaway?

Freewriting helps you review what you've read, and it can give you topics for a paragraph that is different from a summary.

Brainstorming

After you freewrite, you can brainstorm. You can ask yourself questions to lead you toward a topic for your own paragraph. For instance, brainstorming on the idea "angry people battling for what is utterly without value" could look like this:

> ### Brainstorming after Freewriting
>
> Owens says people fighting for spaces are "battling for what is utterly without value." **So why do they do it? Is there any other time drivers battle for what has no value?**

ALONG THESE LINES/Pearson Education Canada

Sure. On the highway. All the time.

How?

They weave in and out. They cut me off. They tailgate. They speed.

What are they fighting for?

They want to gain a few minutes. They want to get ahead. Driving is some kind of contest for them.

Then, don't they get some kind of satisfaction from the battle?

Not really. I often see them at the same red light I've stopped at. And their driving is very stressful for them. It raises their blood pressure, makes them angry and unhappy. They can't really win.

Could you write a paragraph on drivers who think of driving as a contest? If so, your brainstorming, based on your reading, might lead you to a topic.

Developing Points of Agreement or Disagreement

Another way to use a reading selection to lead you to a topic is to review the selection and jot down any statements that provoke a strong reaction in you. You are looking for sentences with which you can agree or disagree. If you already marked "A Ridiculous Addiction" as you read, you might list these statements as points of agreement or disagreement:

> ### Points of Agreement or Disagreement from a Reading
>
> "Hell hath no fury like a motorist who loses the battle for a close-in parking space." —agree
>
> "This quest for the coveted spot transcends logic and common sense." —disagree

Then you might pick one of the statements and agree or disagree with it, in writing. If you disagreed with the second statement that "this quest for the coveted spot transcends logic and common sense," you might develop the thought lines part of writing by listing your own ideas. You might focus on why a close parking space is important to you. With a focus and a list of reasons, you could move to the outlines part of writing from reading.

OUT LINES **DEVISING A PLAN: AGREE OR DISAGREE**

An outline might look like the one below. As you read it, notice that the topic sentence and ideas are your opinions, not the ideas of the author of "A Ridiculous Addiction." You used his ideas to come up with your own thoughts.

An Outline for an Agree or a Disagree Paragraph

topic sentence: Sometimes a close parking spot is important.

details:

convenience   {   I may have heavy bags to carry from the store.
                        Cars can be vandalized.

car safety   {   Vandalism and burglary are more likely if the car is
                        parked at a distance.

personal safety   {   I can be attacked in a parking lot.
                        Attacks are more likely at night.
                        Muggings are more likely if I am parked far away.

DRAFTING AND REVISING: AGREE OR DISAGREE

If your outline gives you enough good points to develop, you are on your way to a paragraph. If you began with the ideas above, for example, you could develop them into a paragraph like this:

> ### A Draft for an Agree or a Disagree Paragraph
>
> Sometimes a close parking spot is important. The short distance to a store can make a difference if I have heavy bags or boxes to carry from the store to my car. Convenience is one reason for parking close. A more important reason is safety. In my neighbourhood, cars are often vandalized. Sometimes, cars get broken into. Cars are more likely to get vandalized or burglarized if they are parked far from stores. Most of all, I am afraid to park far from stores or restaurants because I am afraid of being attacked in a parking lot, especially at night. If I am far away from buildings and other people, I am more likely to be mugged.

POLISHING AND PROOFREADING: AGREE OR DISAGREE

When you read the previous paragraph, you probably noticed some places where it could be revised:

- It could use more specific details.
- It should attribute the original idea about parking to Gwinn Owens, probably in the beginning.
- Some sentences could be combined.

Below is the final version of the same paragraph. As you read it, notice how a new beginning, added details, and combined sentences make it a smoother, clearer, and more developed paragraph.

> ### Final Version for an Agree or a Disagree Paragraph
>
> In his essay "A Ridiculous Addiction," Gwinn Owens says that people who look for close parking spaces are foolish, but I think that sometimes a close parking spot is important. The short distance to a store can make a difference if I have

ALONG THESE LINES/Pearson Education Canada

heavy bags or boxes to carry from the store to my car. Convenience is one reason for parking close, but the more important reason is safety. In my neighbourhood, cars are often vandalized. Antennas get broken off; paint gets deliberately scratched. Sometimes, cars get broken into. Radios and CD players are stolen. Cars are more likely to get vandalized or burglarized if they are parked far from stores. Most of all, I am afraid to park far from stores or restaurants because I am afraid of being attacked in a parking lot, especially at night. If I am far away from buildings or other people, I am more likely to be mugged.

Reading can give you many ideas for your own writing. Developing those ideas into a polished paragraph requires the same writing process as any good writing, a process that takes you through the steps of thinking, planning, drafting, revising, editing, and proofreading.

WRITING FOR AN ESSAY TEST

Most essay questions require a form of writing from reading. That is, your instructor asks you to write about an assigned reading. Usually, an **essay test** requires you to write from memory, not from an open book or notes. Such writing can be stressful, but breaking the task into steps can eliminate much of the stress.

Before the Test: The Steps of Reading

If you work through the steps of reading several days before the test, you are halfway to your goal. Prereading helps to keep you focused, and your first reading will give you a sense of the whole selection. The third step, rereading with a pen or pencil, can be particularly helpful when you are preparing for a test. Most essay questions will ask you to summarize a reading selection or to react to it. In either case, you must be familiar with the reading's main idea, supporting ideas, examples, and details. If you note these by marking the selection, you are teaching yourself about the main point, supporting ideas, and structure of the reading selection.

Shortly before the test, review the marked reading assignment. Your notes will help you to focus on the main point and the supporting ideas.

During the Test: The Stages of Writing

Answering an essay question for a test may seem very different from writing at home. After all, on a test, you must rely on your memory and write within a time limit, and these restrictions can make you feel anxious. However, by following the stages of the writing process, you can meet that challenge calmly and confidently.

- **Thought lines:** Before you begin to write, think about the question: Is the instructor asking for a summary of a reading selection? Or is he or she asking you to react to a specific idea in the reading by describing or developing the idea with examples or by agreeing or disagreeing? For example, in an essay question about "A Ridiculous Addiction," you might be asked (1) to explain what Gwinn Owens thinks are the advantages and disadvantages of seeking a close parking space (a summary); (2) to explain what he means when he says that fighting for parking turns drivers into mad dogs (a reaction, where you develop and explain one part of the reading);

or (3) to agree or disagree that close spaces are utterly without value (a reaction, so you have to be aware of what Owens said on this point).

Once you've thought about the question, list or freewrite your first ideas about the question. At this time, don't worry about how "right" or "wrong" your writing is; just write your first thoughts.

- **Outlines:** Your writing will be clear if you follow a plan. Remember that your audience for this writing is your instructor and that he or she will be evaluating how well you stick to the subject, make a point, and support it. Your plan for making a point about the subject and supporting that point can be written in a brief outline.

  First, reread the question. Next, survey your list of freewriting. Does it contain a main point that answers the question? Does it contain supporting ideas and details?

  Next, write a main point and then list supporting ideas and details under the main point. Your main point will be the topic sentence of your answer. If you need more support, try brainstorming.

- **Rough lines:** Write your point and supporting ideas in paragraph form. Remember to use effective transitions and to combine short sentences.

- **Final lines:** You will probably not have time to copy your answer, but you can review it, proofread it, and correct any errors in spelling, punctuation, and word choice. This final check can produce a more polished answer.

Organize Your Time

Some students skip steps; they immediately begin writing their answer to an essay question, without thinking or planning. Sometimes they find themselves stuck in the middle of a paragraph, panicked because they have no more ideas. At other times, they find themselves writing in a circle, repeating the same point over and over. Occasionally, they even forget to include a main idea.

You can avoid these hazards by spending time on each of the stages. Planning is as important as writing. For example, if you have half an hour to write an essay, you can divide your time like this:

- 5 minutes: thinking, freewriting, listing
- 10 minutes: planning, outlining
- 10 minutes: drafting
- 5 minutes: reviewing and proofreading

Focusing on one stage at a time can make you more confident and your task more manageable.

Lines of Detail: A Walk-Through Assignment

Here are two ideas from "A Ridiculous Addiction":

1. The typical driver has a compulsion about finding a convenient parking space.
2. People who search for good parking spots become mean and nasty.

Pick one of these ideas, with which you agree or disagree. Write a paragraph explaining why you agree or disagree. To write your paragraph, follow these steps:

Step 1: Begin by listing at least two reasons why you agree or disagree. Use your own experience with parking lots to come up with your reasons. For example, for statement 1, you could ask yourself these questions: Are all drivers concerned with parking spaces? How do you know? Is it a compulsion or just practical behaviour? For statement 2, you might ask questions like these: Have you ever seen nastiness in parking lots? Have you ever experienced it? What actions were mean? Answering such questions can help you come up with your reasons for agreement or disagreement.

Step 2: Read your list to a partner or to a group. With the help of your listener(s), you can add reasons or details to explain the reasons.

Step 3: Once you have enough ideas, transform the statement you agreed or disagreed with into a topic sentence.

Step 4: Write an outline by listing your reasons and details below the topic sentence. Check that your list is in a clear and logical order.

Step 5: Write a draft of your paragraph. Check that you have attributed Gwinn Owens' statement, that you have enough details, and that you have combined any choppy sentences. Revise your draft until the paragraph is smooth and clear.

Step 6: Before you prepare the final copy, check your last draft for errors in spelling, punctuation, and word choice.

Writing Your Own Paragraph on "A Ridiculous Addiction"

When you write on one of these topics, be sure to work through the stages of the writing process in preparing your paragraph.

1. Gwinn Owens writes about Americans' addiction to the close parking space. Write about another addiction that we Canadians also share with Americans. Instead of writing about a topic like drug or alcohol addiction, follow Owens' example and write about a social habit that is hard to break. You might, for instance, write about these habits:

driving while talking on a cellphone	tailgating
	speeding
weaving in and out of traffic	pushing in line
driving too slowly	littering
running yellow traffic lights	arriving late
talking during a movie	

Once you've chosen a habit, brainstorm, alone or with a partner, for details. Think about details that could fit these categories:

why the habit is foolish	when and where people act this way
why the habit is dangerous	advantages of breaking the habit

Ask yourself questions, answer them, and let the answers lead to more questions. Once you've collected some good details, work through the stages of writing a paragraph.

2. Gwinn Owens writes about a great invention, the car, and about the parking problems caused by cars. Below are several other recent inventions that can cause problems. Your goal is to write a paragraph about the problems one of these inventions can cause.

To start, pick two of the following inventions. Alone, or with a partner or a group, brainstorm both topics: ask questions, answer them, and add details, so that each topic can lead you to enough ideas for a paragraph.

After you've brainstormed, pick the topic you like better and work through the stages of preparing a paragraph.

Topics to brainstorm: problems that could be caused by online banking, portable storage devices (i.e. USB drives), wireless internet access, cellphones, telecommuting, MP3 players, or email.

WRITING FROM READING: THE WRITING PROCESS

To practise the skills you've learned in this chapter, follow the steps of prereading, reading, and rereading with a pen or pencil as you read the following selection.

They Hoot, He Scores
Frank Hayes

Frank Hayes, a former publisher, works in advertising and is a freelance writer. He lives with his wife in Kingston, Ontario.

Before you read this selection, consider these questions:

> *When you were growing up, what sports did you play?*
>
> *Did you train with a team? On your own?*
>
> *How important is peer approval to teenagers?*
>
> *Have you ever been "centred out" at school? How did you feel?*

I've probably played in more than 500 hockey games in my life, but one game sticks out in my mind, its image chiselled upon my memory.

venerable: worthy of deep respect

My school was entered in a high school tournament, and for the first time, we were going to play in the Montreal Forum—that **venerable** hockey shrine where some of the greatest hockey players in the world have appeared. We young teenagers were awestruck but we were also **intimidated** and frightened, a sell-out crowd adding to our nervousness.

intimidated: threatened

cavernous: huge, deep, like a cave

In the locker room, we put on our uniforms and waited in a daze for the call announcing the start of the game. When it came, we self-consciously filed into the **cavernous** arena. Then, for the first time, we saw and heard the boisterous, mostly teenaged crowd. They were waving school banners of every conceivable colour and creating such a thunderous noise, we could feel the sound waves.

adrenaline: hormone affecting muscular action

unceremoniously: lacking form, in an undignified manner

I decided to overcome my nervousness by leaping over the boards onto the newly surfaced ice. Once the other players left the bench, I took a few steps and jumped. With **adrenaline** surging through me, I cleared the boards by 10 inches. A good start. Then disaster struck. I landed at a bad angle, fell on my backside and began to slide **unceremoniously** out to centre ice.

ALONG THESE LINES/Pearson Education Canada

clamour: confused noise

perimeter: outer boundary

taunts: scornful, mocking remarks

exhilarated: inspired, animated
alleviate: relieve

obscurity: lack of fame

When I first fell, the crowd noise was a constant **clamour**. It gradually increased to a deafening roar as I neared the face-off circle. Once there, alone, I was encircled by the two teams, who were warming up, skating around the **perimeter** of the rink. Unhurt physically but wrecked emotionally, I quickly got up, planning to lose myself in the group of players looping the rink. But to my astonishment, with the crowd's approval, the other players were skating toward me in a diminishing oval, laughing and applauding me with embarrassing enthusiasm.

I went immediately to our bench and sat hunched over the boards, my face in my arms, trying not to hear the **taunts** and jeers from the spectators around me.

Then the game started. In a few minutes, with the incident seemingly forgotten by the fans, I began to enjoy the occasion.

Before the start of the second period, we began warming up by slowly gliding around the rink. I was feeling **exhilarated** and needed to **alleviate** the pent-up energy inside me. So faster and faster I skated as I dodged around the slower skaters. Soon, I was in a trance and in full flight.

But, hurtling around the corner of the rink, I saw, too late, a door open onto the ice surface—directly in my path. I couldn't stop and rammed into it at warp speed. There was a dull thud when I hit the door, followed by a loud echoing crash when it slammed shut. The fans, reminded anew of the first occurrence, responded with the ear-piercing sounds that only a crowd of teenagers could produce, while I was wishing for a way to vanish from the arena.

Fortunately, the gods were looking on me favourably that night. With only five minutes left in a tied game, some universal law kicked in to even things up. In a scramble in front of the opposing net, I banged in the winning goal. I accepted it as a fair trade-off: several minutes of mind-numbing embarrassment for a glorious moment of victory. After that game, I survived to play another 20 years of—uneventful—amateur hockey, in complete **obscurity**.

UNDERSTANDING "THEY HOOT, HE SCORES"

1. The author, Frank Hayes, uses specialized hockey terms. Explain to the non–hockey fan what each term means:

   the boards _____

   _____

   centre ice _____

   _____

   face-off circle _____

   _____

   second period _____

   _____

2. Throughout the article, from the call announcing the game to the final winning goal, the crowd plays an important role. Locate the two instances when the crowd humiliates the author and describe its behaviour.

_____

_____

_____

_____

3. Was the last sentence of this article what you expected? How does this sentence change the feeling of the piece?

_____

_____

_____

_____

WRITING FROM READING "THEY HOOT, HE SCORES"

When you write on any of the following topics, be sure to work through the stages of the writing process in preparing your paragraph.

1. Using the ideas and examples you gathered in the previous exercise, write a summary paragraph of Hayes' article.

2. While team sports can build the spirit of co-operation, the hockey player in this article does not experience support from either his team-mates or the fans. Write about a time when you felt left out or over-looked in a sports situation.

3. Here are two ideas from "They Hoot, He Scores":

   a. The purposes of team sports in high school are to have fun, to promote healthy bodies, and to develop co-operation skills.
   b. The purposes of team sports in high school are to win, to build your school's reputation, and to provide elite athletes with competitive challenge.

   Pick one of the ideas with which you agree or disagree. Write a paragraph explaining why you agree or disagree.

4. The author continued to play hockey long past his high-school years. If your instructor permits, interview several people in your class to find out in what exercise activities or sports they participate.

   Plan a paragraph with this topic sentence:

   Today, adults participate in many exercise activities and sports.

   In your group, have each member support the topic sentence by talk-ing about himself or herself. You might mention age, type of exercise activ-ity or sport, previous experience in school or community sports, special talents, and so forth. As each member describes himself or herself, write down the details. Ask follow-up questions and write down the answers. After you have gathered enough specific examples, write your paragraph.

ALONG THESE LINES/Pearson Education Canada

CHAPTER 3
Illustration

LEARNING OBJECTIVES

After you have read this chapter and completed its exercises and assignments, you should be able to

- distinguish between broad statements and specific examples
- add specific examples to broad statements and topic sentences
- generate ideas for an illustration paragraph
- write an appropriate topic sentence for an illustration paragraph
- draft and edit an effective illustration paragraph

"Example is not the main thing in influencing others. It is the only thing."

~ ALBERT SCHWEITZER

▼

ALBERT SCHWEITZER WAS A THEOLOGIAN, PHILOSOPHER, AND DOCTOR WHO WON THE 1952 NOBEL PEACE PRIZE FOR HIS WORK IN AFRICA.

WHAT IS ILLUSTRATION?

Illustration uses specific examples to support a general point. In your writing, you frequently use illustration when you want to explain to your friends why the iPod is (or isn't) the best MP3 player around, or why your college is (or isn't) the best, for example.

communication at work

Have you ever looked at job postings? Most job postings will say something like "The ideal candidate must have . . . ," followed by a list of skills or experience expected of the candidate. For example, you might see a posting like this:

The ideal candidate must have:

- a B.N. degree from a recognized institution
- 2–3 years' experience in the health care industry
- excellent communication skills, both spoken and written
- excellent teamwork skills

The list above, as specific *examples* of the skills required, is an example of illustration at work. How would you describe your dream job?

Hints for Writing an Illustration Paragraph

Knowing What Is Specific and What Is General A general statement is a broad point. The following statements are general:

> Traffic can be bad on Hamilton Boulevard.
> Car insurance costs more today than it did last year.
> My part-time job makes me miss out on many after-school gatherings.

You can support a general statement with specific examples:

general statement:	Traffic can be bad on Hamilton Boulevard.
specific examples:	During the morning rush hour, the exit to King Street is jammed.
	If there is an accident, cars can be backed up for a kilometre.

general statement:	Car insurance costs more today than it did last year.
specific examples:	Last year I paid $150 a month; this year I pay $200 a month.
	My mother, who has never had a traffic ticket, has seen her insurance premium rise fifty percent.

general statement:	It is difficult to meet people at my college.
specific examples:	After class, most students rush to their jobs.
	There are very few places to sit and talk between classes.

When you write an illustration paragraph, be careful to support a general statement with specific examples, not with more general statements:

not this:

general statement:	College is harder than I thought it would be.
more general statements:	~~It is tough to be a college student. Studying takes a lot of my time.~~

but this:

general statement:	College is harder than I thought it would be.
specific examples:	I cannot afford to miss any classes.
	I have to study at least two hours a day.

If you remember to illustrate a broad statement with specific examples, you will have the key to this kind of paragraph.

EXERCISE 1	**RECOGNIZING BROAD STATEMENTS**

Each list below contains one broad statement and three specific examples. Underline the broad statement.

1. Montréal's Arcade Fire is considered one of the best bands in independent music.
   Canadian bands are receiving more international recognition.

ALONG THESE LINES/Pearson Education Canada

The New Pornographers' album *Twin Cinema* was #7 on *Spin*
magazine's "40 Best Albums of 2005" list.
Alexisonfire has had major tours in Japan, Australia, and the United States.

2. My two-year-old son is into everything.
   He climbs onto the kitchen table.
   I have found him sitting in the laundry basket.
   He loves to explore the hall closet.

3. A stranger stopped to help me with my flat tire yesterday.
   Random acts of kindness are frequent in our community.
   A woman at the market offered to carry an elderly man's groceries
   to his car.
   Somebody knocked on my mother's door to tell her she had left her
   car lights on.

4. The office printer ran out of ink just before an important deadline.
   A sudden power failure caused the loss of an expensive program.
   An important backup disk turned out to be blank.
   Even computer technology is not always reliable.

5. Many working parents struggle to spend time with their children.
   Students do their class work and work full- or part-time jobs, too.
   Everybody seems to be short of free time these days.
   People work overtime because they need the extra money even if they
   lose their free time.

EXERCISE 2

DISTINGUISHING THE GENERAL STATEMENT FROM THE SPECIFIC EXAMPLE

Each of the following statements is supported by three items of support. Two of
these items are specific examples; one is too general to be effective. Underline
the one that is too general.

1. **general statement:** High technology is not necessarily the best technology.
   support: Computers' CPUs are getting faster all the time.
   Blackberries and cellphones can make us available to work at
   any time, increasing stress levels.
   Some studies show that the frequencies emitted by cellphones
   may be dangerous.

2. **general statement:** A positive attitude is a great asset.
   support: Looking on the bright side is a good thing.
   Smiling can actually improve a person's mood.
   Most people like to be around an optimist, so a positive attitude
   can lead to more friends.

3. **general statement:** Colleges and universities try to create a welcoming
   environment for new students.
   support: Students are given tours of the campus.
   I certainly did feel welcome on my first day.
   Free T-shirts foster a feeling of belonging.

4. **general statement:** The local coffeehouse is becoming the preferred
    meeting place for today's youth.
    support: More and more coffeehouses are remodelling to include free
    WiFi access.
    Coffeehouses offer a more welcoming, relaxed atmosphere
    than the local mall.
    Everyone meets there.

5. **general statement:** Most bookstores sell more than books.
    support: Many sell CDs.
    They sell lots of things.
    Most sell a variety of magazines.

EXERCISE

3

ADDING SPECIFIC EXAMPLES TO A GENERAL STATEMENT

With a partner or group, add four specific examples to each general statement
below.

1. **general statement:** Many demands are made on a college student's finances.

    examples: _____

    _____

    _____

    _____

2. **general statement:** Poor customer service is more common than good
    customer service.

    examples: _____

    _____

    _____

    _____

3. **general statement:** With just a few changes, people can lead healthier,
    less stressful lives.

    examples: _____

    _____

    _____

4. **general statement:** Online course supplements such as WebCT and
    Blackboard are a boon to students.

    examples: _____

    _____

ALONG THESE LINES/Pearson Education Canada

_____

_____

5. **general statement:** There are several places on campus where students can meet and socialize.

examples: _____

_____

_____

_____

WRITING THE ILLUSTRATION PARAGRAPH IN STEPS

THOUGHT LINES

GATHERING IDEAS: ILLUSTRATION

Suppose your instructor asks you to write a paragraph about some aspect of cars. You can begin by listing ideas about your subject to gather ideas and to find a focus for your paragraph. Your first list might look like the following:

Listing Ideas about Cars

cars in my neighbourhood	cars in the college parking lot
my brother's car	parking at college
car prices	car insurance
drag racing	

This list includes many specific ideas about cars. You could write a paragraph about one item or about two related items on the list. Reviewing the list, you decide to write your paragraph on cars in the college parking lot.

Adding Details to an Idea

Now that you have a narrowed topic for your paragraph, you decide to write a list of ideas about cars in the college parking lot:

Cars in the College Parking Lot: Some Ideas

vans	older people's cars, Volvos and Cadillacs
cars with strollers and car seats	racing cars, modified, brightly tinted
beat-up old cars, some with no bumpers	elaborate sound systems
few new sports cars, gifts from rich parents	bumper stickers
some SUVs	some stickers have a message
	some brag

Creating a Topic Sentence

If you examine this list, looking for *related ideas*, you can create a topic sentence. The ideas on the list include (1) details about the kinds of cars, (2) details about what is inside the cars, and (3) details about the bumper stickers. Not all the details fit into these three categories, but many do.

Grouping the related ideas into the three categories can help you focus your ideas into a topic sentence.

Kinds of Cars

beat-up old cars, some with no bumpers	some SUVs
vans	older people's cars, Volvos and Cadillacs
few new sports cars, gifts from rich parents	racing cars, modified, brightly tinted

Inside the Cars

elaborate sound systems	strollers and car seats

Bumper Stickers

some stickers have a message	some brag

You can summarize these related ideas in a topic sentence:

Cars in the college parking lot reflect the diversity of people at the school.

Check the sentence against your detail. Does it cover the topic? *Yes.* The topic sentence begins with "Cars in the college parking lot." Does it make some point about the cars? *Yes.* It says the cars "reflect the diversity of people at the school."

Since your details are about old and new cars, what is inside the cars and on the bumper stickers, you have many details about differences in cars and some hints about the people who drive them. The word "diversity" in your topic sentence will cover all of these details.

EXERCISE 4

FINDING SPECIFIC IDEAS IN FREEWRITING

Below are two samples of freewriting. Each is a response to a broad topic. Read each sample, and then underline any words that could become a more specific topic for a paragraph.

Freewriting Reaction to the Topic of Food

What comes to my mind when I think about food? I'm hungry right now. Can't bring food into class though. Three o'clock in the afternoon is the worst: between classes and so long after lunch, I need either chocolate or coffee. Can't afford to buy food every day though. Must remember to make a lunch for tomorrow. Food on campus is so expensive! $7 for a burger and fries. Hot dogs from the cart outside are much cheaper though. I wish this city had more interesting street food. Samosas, burritos, noodles would all be tastier than hot dogs.

ALONG THESE LINES/Pearson Education Canada

Freewriting Reaction to the Topic of Health

I'm healthy. Health class? I have to take a health class next term. I think it's about nutrition, vitamins, exercise. Health is a hard subject to write about. I just take it for granted that I'll be healthy. I've never really been sick. Just childhood things like chicken pox. One bad case of strep throat. That was awful. Then there was that time last year when I had to go to the emergency room. A three-hour wait! The doctor's office is not that much better though.

| EXERCISE **5** | FINDING SPECIFIC IDEAS IN LISTS |

Below are two lists. Each is a response to a broad topic. Read each list, and then underline any words that could become a more specific topic for a paragraph.

Topic: Technology in Daily Life

lots of technology	YouTube
scanners at the supermarket	Skype
cyberspace	new breakthroughs
voice mail	drive-through banking
blogs	surveillance cameras

Topic: Music

different kinds of music	music around the world
legendary rappers	my favourite songs
the best radio station	the year's most popular
people and music	downloads
country music	advertising jingles

| EXERCISE **6** | GROUPING RELATED IDEAS IN LISTS OF DETAILS |

Below are lists of details. In each list, circle the items that seem to fit into one group; then underline the items that seem to fit into a second group. (For an example, see Chapter 1, Exercise 7.) Some items may not fit into either group.

1. topic: losses

lost credit card	lost self-esteem
lost moral standards	lost wallet
lost keys	lost in the woods
lost in the final period	lost notebook
lost sense of purpose	lost innocence

2. **topic: studying for a test**
   cramming at 4:00 a.m.   essay test
   calmly reviewing the text   notes from class
   frantically reading the book   budgeting time to study
   trying to memorize it all   getting a good night's sleep
   staying up all night   connecting key ideas and terms

3. **topic: birthday gifts**
   a CD by your favourite group   a Lexus SUV
   gifts from parents   a romantic gift
   airline tickets to Jamaica   new shirts
   a special, framed photo   a giant birthday cake
   aftershave or cologne   a complete entertainment unit

4. **topic: travelling to college by bus**
   can study on the bus   saves gas money
   bus can be late   you can be late and miss it
   waiting for bus in the rain   walk from bus to school
   no parking hassles   variety of bus riders
   traffic congestion   bus drivers

EXERCISE 7

WRITING TOPIC SENTENCES FOR LISTS OF DETAILS

Below are lists of details that have no topic sentences. Write an appropriate topic sentence for each one.

1. topic sentence: _____

   _____

   The house has a beautiful hardwood floor.
   It also has high ceilings.
   There is a small but cozy fireplace in the living room.
   The entrance hall is spacious.
   The kitchen needs a new sink and refrigerator.
   There is a leak in the roof over the big bedroom.
   Several of the window frames are rotted.
   The bathroom tile needs to be replaced.

2. topic sentence: _____

   _____

   Alicia's boyfriend Keith teases her about her weight.
   He is also critical of her intelligence, her personality, and her style.
   He even criticizes her friends.
   Keith is often late or fails to show up for a date with Alicia.
   He gets angry if she questions him about his absence.
   He tells her she is too controlling.
   He never apologizes for his bad behaviour.

3. topic sentence: _____

_____

Alex was once stopped by a police officer.
The officer said Alex had a broken tail light.
He wanted to give Alex a ticket.
Alex started his usual line of jokes and stories.
Soon the officer let Alex off with a warning.
Another time, Alex fell during a soccer game.
He broke a bone in his foot and was rushed to the emergency room.
Instead of complaining about the pain, Alex tried to look on the funny side.
He talked about his "superfoot" and soon had the doctor and nurses laughing.

4. topic sentence: _____

_____

Sharing a room with two sisters, there is always a lack of privacy.
As I was growing up, I always had to wear hand-me-down clothes and shoes.
We always have big family dinners where we sit down and share our news.
Whenever I need advice or a shoulder to cry on, there is always someone to talk to.
My sisters and I have always been very competitive, fighting for everything from our parents' attention to the last piece of cake.
I have never felt lonely in my family.
It costs a lot of money to feed a family of five.
Everyone from my grandparents to my nephews helps out when there is work to be done.
We have only one car, so it is always very crowded whenever we have to go somewhere.

5. topic sentence: _____

_____

When I took my first airplane trip, a stranger helped me to find my connecting flight.
Some good person mailed my wallet (and all its contents) back to me when I lost it.
An elderly customer at the restaurant where I work gave me a ride home when my car wouldn't start.
One day when I was holding my crying baby, a man let me cut ahead in the supermarket line.
The crossing guard on my block always says, "Hi, how are you doing?" when I walk by, even though I don't know him.
A boy in the city went two blocks out of his way to show me the way to the court buildings.

EXERCISE 8

CHOOSING THE BETTER TOPIC SENTENCE

Below are lists of detail. Each list has two possible topic sentences. Underline the better topic sentence for each list.

1. possible topic sentences:

   a. Canadians eat many different foods.

   b. Typical Canadian food includes food from many countries.

   People of many heritages enjoy Chinese food.
   Tofu and fried rice are available everywhere.
   Pho, a Vietnamese soup with noodles, makes for a cheap yet flavourful lunch.
   Pasta is a favourite dish for many people.
   Caribbean jerk chicken and pastries are sold at the local college cafeteria.
   My neighbour introduced me to Chelo-Kabab, a famous Iranian dish.
   My personal choices are Indian curries and papadums.

2. possible topic sentences:

   a. In a crisis, it is good to have friends.

   b. A crisis can reveal a person's true friends.

   I had plenty of friends in high school.
   Dave was my basketball buddy; we played every Thursday afternoon.
   Jiwon and I used to make jokes in our math class.
   I had known Eddie since he had moved into my neighbourhood when we were both eight years old.
   Harry and I worked together at the movie theatre.
   I ran into Carlos at parties, and we became friends.
   Then I was seriously hurt in a bad car accident.
   Dave came to see me in the hospital, once.
   Jiwon sent me a funny card.
   Eddie called and said he hadn't had a chance to come to the hospital.
   I never saw Carlos again.
   Only Harry came to see me all through my months of rehabilitation.

3. possible topic sentences:

   a. Humour can hide a person's dark side.

   b. The ability to make people laugh is a true talent.

   Sean was always the joker in our group.
   He was lively, cheerful, and quick with a witty comment.
   He could make me break into laughter during the most serious movie.
   When I got scolded for laughing, Sean would sit, looking very serious.
   His expression made me laugh even more.
   Sean was always the centre of fun and good times.
   Then one day I saw him sitting alone in our college cafeteria.
   He didn't know anyone was looking at him.
   His expression was sad and lonely.

ALONG THESE LINES/Pearson Education Canada

 **DEVISING A PLAN: ILLUSTRATION**

When you plan your outline, keep your topic sentence in mind:

> Cars in the college parking lot reflect the diversity of people at the school.

Remember the three categories of related details:

> kinds of cars
>
> inside the cars
>
> bumper stickers

These three categories can give you an idea for how to organize the outline.

Below is an outline for a paragraph on cars in the college parking lot. As you read the outline, you will notice that details about the insides of the cars and about bumper stickers have been added. Adding details can be part of the outlining stage.

An Outline for an Illustration Paragraph

topic sentence: Cars in the college parking lot reflect the diversity of people at the school.

details:

kinds of cars:

There are beat-up old cars.

Some have no bumpers.

There are vans.

There are a few new sports cars.

Maybe these are gifts from rich parents.

There are some SUVs.

Older people's cars, like Volvos and Cadillacs, are there.

There are a few racing cars, modified and heavily tinted.

inside the cars:

Some cars have elaborate sound systems.

Some have a baby stroller or car seat.

Some have empty paper cups and food wrappers.

bumper stickers:

Some have stickers for a club.

There are stickers with a message.

There are stickers that brag.

As you can see, the outline used the details from the list and included other details. You can add more details, combine some details to eliminate repetition, or even eliminate some details as you draft your paragraph.

EXERCISE 9

ADDING DETAILS TO AN OUTLINE

Below are three partial outlines. Each has a topic sentence and some details. Working with a partner or group, add more details that support the topic sentence.

1. **topic sentence:** Most teenagers have the same worries.

    a. They are concerned about their appearance. _____

    b. They obsess about finding the right person to love. _____

    c. They worry about fitting in. _____

    d. _____

    e. _____

    f. _____

    g. _____

2. **topic sentence:** Pets are good for their owners' well-being.

    a. You can get healthy exercise by walking a dog. _____

    b. Widows and widowers with pets tend to live longer. _____

    c. An aquarium populated with fish adds tranquility to any room. _____

    d. _____

    e. _____

    f. _____

    g. _____

3. **topic sentence:** Even if you don't have air-conditioning, there are ways to keep cool in the summer heat.

    a. Find a big shady tree and sit under it. _____

    b. Wear loose cotton clothing. _____

    c. Buy a fan. _____

    d. _____

    e. _____

    f. _____

    g. _____

EXERCISE 10

ELIMINATING DETAILS THAT ARE REPETITIVE

In the following outlines, some details use different words to repeat an example given earlier in the list. Cross out the repetitive details.

1. **topic sentence:** Everybody has some advice for fighting a cold.

    My mother thinks vitamin C tablets will help.
    My grandmother believes in chicken soup with a good dash of pepper.

My uncle says the only way to shake a cold is to go to bed and
sleep it off.
"Drink plenty of liquids," says my neighbour.
My roommate urges bed rest.
My sister, who is interested in alternative medicine, urges me to try
an herbal tea.
My boss says there is an old saying, "Feed a cold and starve a fever,"
which means that I should make sure I eat enough.
At school, my instructor told me to take lots of fluids.

2. **topic sentence:** After many mistakes, I've learned to think before I act.

I bought the first car I saw.
It was overpriced and full of hidden mechanical problems.
I chose my college major because everyone else was majoring in
business and I was in a hurry to register.
I am not interested in my business courses.
A friend of mine insulted me, and I was so angry that I hit him.
I barely avoided being arrested.
I didn't shop around before I got my car.
My mother asked me for a favour, and I blurted out the first excuse
I could think of.
I hurt my mother's feelings.
I'm stuck in business classes that bore me.
My temper got me into trouble with a friend and the law.

3. **topic sentence:** The cheapest product is not always the best to buy.

I bought cheap toothpaste, but it felt gritty on my teeth.
Cheap dishwashing liquid is weaker than the more expensive,
concentrated kind.
My $1.99 umbrella lasted through only one rainy day.
Using gritty toothpaste is like brushing my teeth with sand.
Big bags of cookies can taste dry and stale.
I bought a pack of sale-priced ballpoint pens and they leaked all over
my backpack.
I loved my $2.99 shirt, but it fell apart after one washing.
What good is a bargain umbrella that turns inside out when the
wind starts to pick up?

 ## DRAFTING AND REVISING: ILLUSTRATION

Review the outline on cars in the college parking lot on page 75. You can create a
first draft of this outline in the form of a paragraph. At this point, you can combine
some of the short, choppy sentences of the outline, add details, and add transitions
to link your ideas. You can revise your draft using the checklist on the next page.

Transitions

As you revise your illustration paragraph, you may find places where one idea
ends and another begins abruptly. This problem occurs when you forget to add
transitions, which are words, phrases, or sentences that connect one idea to
another. Using transitions effectively will make your writing clear and smooth.

When you write an illustration paragraph, you will need some transitions that link one example to another and other transitions to link one section of your paragraph to another section. Here are some transitions you may want to use in writing an illustration paragraph.

INFOBOX	TRANSITIONS FOR AN ILLUSTRATION PARAGRAPH

for example	for instance
one example	one instance
a second example	the first instance
another example	another instance
other examples	in addition
in the case of	to illustrate
like	other kinds
such as	once

CHECKLIST	CHECKLIST FOR REVISING AN ILLUSTRATION PARAGRAPH

✓ Should some of the sentences be combined?
✓ Do I need more or better transitions?
✓ Should I add more details to support my points?
✓ Should some of the details be more specific?

Look carefully at the following draft of the paragraph on cars in the college parking lot, and note how it combines sentences, add details, and uses transitions to transform the outline into a clear and developed paragraph.

A Draft of an Illustration Paragraph

topic sentence

detail added

detail added

transition added

transition added

detail added

detail added

detail added

details added

details added

Cars in the college parking lot reflect the diversity of people at the school. There are beat-up old cars, some with no bumpers, near several vans. There are one or two new sports cars, like BMWs; they might belong to the few lucky students with rich and generous parents. Other kinds include SUVs and older people's cars such as Volvos and Cadillacs. In addition, the parking lot holds a few racing cars, modified and highly tinted. Some cars have elaborate sound systems for music lovers. Others must belong to parents because they have a baby stroller or car seat inside. Many are filled with empty paper cups or food wrappers since busy students have to eat on the run. Many cars also have bumper stickers; some are for clubs, like the Charlottetown Athletic Club, while others have a message such as "Give Blood: Save Lives" or "Save the Whales." Some stickers brag that the driver is the "Proud Parent of an Honour Roll Student," and some may warn other drivers, "If you can read this, you're driving too closely!"

EXERCISE 11 — REVISING A DRAFT BY COMBINING SENTENCES

The paragraph below has many short, choppy sentences, which are underlined. Wherever you see two or more underlined sentences clustered next to each other, combine them into one clear, smooth sentence. Write your revised version of the paragraph in the spaces above the lines.

Mr. Gonsalves, my high-school English teacher, had a whole bag of tricks for keeping the class awake and alert. Sometimes a student would fall asleep. The student would be in the back of the classroom. Mr. Gonsalves would stand beside the sleeping student's desk and stare silently. The rest of the class would begin to laugh. The laughing woke up the student. At other times, when Mr. Gonsalves was teaching a grammar lesson, the class would become bored. Mr. Gonsalves would startle everyone by suddenly singing loudly. He was such a terrible singer that we all jumped to attention. Once Mr. Gonsalves really went to extremes. He made the whole class sing. The song was one he had written. It was a song about punctuation. In every class, Mr. Gonsalves' students had to be prepared for surprises.

EXERCISE 12 — REVISING A DRAFT BY ADDING TRANSITIONS

The paragraph below needs some transitions. Add appropriate transitions (words or phrases) to the blanks.

My girlfriend Elise has some annoying habits. _____, she never lets me finish a sentence. Whenever I start to say something, Elise jumps in with her own idea or with what she thinks I am about to say. _____, she likes to plan too far ahead. On Monday, she wants to know exactly what we'll be doing on Saturday night. I'm more spontaneous and like to wait until Friday or Saturday to decide. _____, she worries too much. _____, she worries when I am late for school. She also worries when I have a cold. She is afraid it may turn into pneumonia. Elise is clearly a talker, a planner, and a worrier, but these are all minor flaws. She isn't perfect, but she is perfect for me.

EXERCISE 13

ADDING DETAILS TO A DRAFT

The paragraph below lacks the kind of details that would make it more interesting. Working with a partner or group, add details to the blank spaces provided. When you are finished, read the revised paragraph to the class.

The clothes people wear to work depend on their positions. The average college student who works in a restaurant is likely to wear _____ or _____ on the job. Men who work behind the counter of an expensive men's clothing store may be required to dress in _____, while women who sell makeup in department stores often have to wear _____ and perfect makeup. If a person works as a teller in a bank, he or she cannot come to work in _____. Instead, appropriate dress is _____ and _____. Executives in financial corporations are often expected to dress in _____, _____, and _____. On the other hand, people in creative fields such as music or film production can wear almost anything from _____ to _____ when they work.

FINAL LINES

PROOFREADING AND POLISHING: ILLUSTRATION

As you prepare the final version of your illustration paragraph, make any changes in word choice or transitions that can refine your writing. Below is the final version of the paragraph on cars in the college parking lot. As you read it, you will notice a few more changes:

- Some details have been added
- Several long transitions have been added. The paragraph needed to signal the shift in subject from the kinds of cars to what was inside the cars; then it needed to signal the shift from the interior of the cars to bumper stickers.
- A concluding sentence has been added to reinforce the point of the topic sentence: A diverse college population is reflected in its cars.

> ### A Final Version of a Paragraph (*changes from the last draft are underlined*)

Cars in the college parking lot reflect the diversity of the people at the school. There are beat-up old cars, some with no bumpers, near several vans. There are one or two new sports cars, like BMWs; they might belong to the few lucky students with rich and generous parents. Other kinds include SUVs and older people's cars such as Volvos and Cadillacs. In addition, the parking lot holds a few racing cars, modified and highly tinted. <u>What is inside the cars is as revealing as the cars themselves.</u> Some cars have elaborate sound systems for music lovers <u>or for those who just like everyone to know they're coming</u>. Others must belong to parents because they have a baby stroller or car seat inside. Many are filled with empty paper cups or food wrappers since busy students have to eat on the run. <u>Bumper stickers also tell a story.</u> Many cars also have bumper stickers; some are for clubs, like the Charlottetown Athletic Club, while others have a message such as "Give Blood: Save Lives" or "Save the Whales." Some stickers brag that the driver is the "Proud Parent of an Honour Roll Student," and some may warn other drivers, "If you can read this, you're driving too closely!" <u>A walk through the parking lot hints that this college is a place for all ages, backgrounds, and interests.</u>

Before you prepare the final version of your illustration paragraph, check your latest draft for errors in spelling or punctuation and for any errors made in typing and copying.

| EXERCISE **14** | **PROOFREADING TO PREPARE THE FINAL VERSION** |

Below are two illustration paragraphs with the kinds of errors it is easy to overlook when you prepare the final version of an assignment. Correct the errors by writing above the lines. There are eleven errors in the first paragraph and nine errors in the second paragraph.

1.   Today, when people say they want a drink of water, they could be axsing for a number of drinks. Of coarse, there is water right from the faucet, but many people drink bottle water. There are dozens of brans of bottled water and there are also to basic kind of water in bottles. One kind is fizzy, and one kind is flat. In edition, there are many new types of water, such as water with vitamins, water with caffeine, and Flavoured water. These days, a whole row in the supermarket can be filled with ten or twenty variety of water, and restaurants may offer a choice of water, from free tap water to expensive kins of bottled water. As a result a person who asks for a glass of water has to be very specific.

2.   Every member of my family has a peculiar driving habit. My Father, for example, always drives with the windows open even if it is freezing. Riding with him, I have saw ice crystles forming on the car seats. My mother also has a strange driving habit, but her's is more dangerous. She never looks into her rear-view mirror. Instead, she just changes lane's whenever she feels like it. I always say my prayers when I get into a car with her. Unlike my mother, my brother is a very cautious driver. He was in an accident, and it scared him so much that he drives very slowly and does'nt change lanes unless he has to. I am too impatient to ride with him. Finally, my habit is quiet dramatic I blast the radio so that it can be heard a block away. My parents wont even ride with me because they are afraid they will burst their eardrums. In our family, every driver, because of some personal driving weirdness, tends to drive alone.

Lines of Detail: A Walk-Through Assignment

Your assignment is to write an illustration paragraph about music.

Step 1: Freewrite or brainstorm on this broad topic for ten minutes.

Step 2: Review your freewriting or brainstorming. Underline any parts that are a specific idea related to the broad topic, music.

Step 3: List all the specific ideas. Choose one as the narrowed topic for your paragraph.

Step 4: Add related ideas to your chosen, narrowed topic. Do this by reviewing your list for related ideas and by brainstorming for more related ideas.

Step 5: List all your related ideas and review their connection to your narrowed topic. Then write a topic sentence for your paragraph.

Step 6: Write a first draft of your paragraph.

Step 7: Revise your first draft. Be sure it has enough details and clear transitions. Combine any choppy sentences.

Step 8: After a final check for any errors in punctuation, spelling, and word choice, prepare the final version of the paragraph.

Writing Your Own Illustration Paragraph

When you write on any of these topics, follow the four basic stages of the writing process in preparing your illustration paragraph.

1. Begin this assignment with a partner or group. Together, write down as many old sayings as you can. (Old sayings include such statements as "It's not whether you win or lose; it's how you play the game," or "Money can't buy happiness.") If anyone in your group speaks a second language, ask him or her to translate and explain any old sayings from that language.

   Once you have a long list of sayings, split up. Pick one saying, then write a paragraph on that saying. Your paragraph should give several examples that prove the truth of the saying.

2. Below are some topic sentences. Select one and use it to write a paragraph in which you give examples of the topic sentence.

   I think of my friend _____ when I hear people talk of "running the rat race."

   Online course supplements such as WebCT and Blackboard are a boon to students.

   Technology is making us lazy.

   Ergonomics (designing office furniture and office space so that workplace injuries and fatigue are minimized) is being considered more and more in today's offices.

   A trade is an excellent career choice.

   Women's health issues are at the forefront of the medical community's concerns.

   _____ is an example of a world-class city.

3. Select one of the topics listed below. Write a paragraph on some narrowed part of the topic. If you choose the topic of jobs, for example, you might narrow the topic to your experiences working at a supermarket.

jobs	fears	dreams	mistakes
stress	money	television	technology
computers	children	celebrities	surprises
fashion	challenges	memories	holidays

WRITING FROM READING: THE WRITING PROCESS

Sticky Stuff
Kendall Hamilton and Tessa Namuth

This article is a tribute to three modern products that hold our lives together. One got its start when its creator was walking his dog, another changed its original purpose, and the third was the result of a boring sermon.

Before you read this selection, consider these questions:

> *What is the difference between an* invention *and an* innovation?
> *Do you agree with this statement? "There is always an easier way to do a job."*
> *Do most new technologies help or harm us?*

Never before in the history of humankind has it been so easy to attach one thing to another. Over the past century, inventive minds have brought us a **bounty** of products designed to keep our daily lives—and who knows, maybe even the universe—together. The paper clip, for instance, is not only an **ingenious amalgam** of form and function, but it's also a powerful force for order. Below are a few more of the finest products.

Anybody who's ever struggled with a stuck zipper or stubborn button owes a debt of gratitude to Georges de Mestral, the Swiss engineer who gave us all an alternative. After a walk in the woods with his dog one day in 1948, de Mestral **marvelled** at the ability of **burrs** to fasten themselves to his dog's coat and to his own wool clothing. De Mestral shoved a bit of burr under a microscope and saw that its barbed, hooklike seed pods meshed beautifully with the looped fibres in his clothes. Realizing that his discovery could **spawn** a fastening system to compete with, if not replace, the zipper, he devised a way to reproduce the hooks in woven nylon, and **dubbed** the result Velcro, from the French words *velours* and *crochet*. Today Velcro-brand hook-and-loop fasteners (which is how trademark attorneys insist we refer to the stuff) not only save the **arthritic,** fumble-fingered, or just plain lazy among us untold aggravation with our clothing, they secure gear—and astronauts—aboard the space shuttle, speed diaper changes, and help turn the machine-gun turrets in the M1A1 tank. Velcro U.S.A., Inc., engineers have even used the product to assemble an automobile. Try doing that with zippers.

bounty: a generous number

ingenious: clever
amalgam: combination

marvelled: wondered

burrs: the rough, prickly case around the seeds of certain plants

spawn: produce

dubbed: named

velours: velvet
crochet: small hook

arthritic: people with arthritis, an inflammation of the joints

ALONG THESE LINES/Pearson Education Canada

Some theorize that the world is held together by Scotch tape. If that's not true, it could be: 3M, the company behind the brand, makes enough tape each day to circle the earth almost three times. This was certainly not foreseen by a young 3M engineer named Richard Drew when he invented the tape in 1930. Drew, who'd come up with the first masking tape after overhearing a burst of frustrated **invective** in an auto-body painting shop, **sought** to create a product to seal the cellophane that food producers were starting to use to wrap everything from bread to candy. Why not coat strips of cellophane itself with adhesive, Drew wondered, and Scotch tape was born. It was also soon **rendered obsolete** for its original purpose, as a process to heat-seal cellophane packaging **debuted. Ironically,** the **Great Depression** came to the rescue: consumers took to the tape as a dollar-stretcher to keep worn items in service. Ever since, it's just kind of stuck.

The Post-it note not only keeps information right where we want it, but it may also be the best thing ever to come out of a dull sermon. Art Fry, a chemical engineer for 3M who was active in his church choir, was suffering through just such a sermon one day back in 1974 when he got to thinking about a problem he'd been having with **improvised** bookmarks falling out of his **hymnal.** "I realized what I really needed was a bookmark that would attach and detach lightly, wouldn't fall off, and wouldn't hurt the hymnal," recalls Fry, now 66 and retired from 3M. Fry called to mind a weak adhesive developed by his **colleague,** Spencer Silver. Fry slathered a little of the adhesive on the edge of a piece of paper, and *voila*! He wrote a report about his invention and forwarded it to his boss, also jotting a question on one of his new bookmarks and pressing it down in the middle of one page. His boss scribbled an answer on the note and sent it back to Fry, attached to some other paperwork. Later, over coffee, the two men realized Fry had invented a new communications tool. Today Post-its are **ubiquitous**—available in eighteen colours, twenty-seven sizes, and fifty-six shapes. Some even contain fragrances that smell like pizza, pickles, or chocolate. Soon, perhaps, we'll have our notes and eat them, too.

invective: angry, abusive language
sought: searched

rendered: became
obsolete: out of date, no longer useful
debuted: was introduced
ironically: opposite of what is expected
Great Depression: a period in Canada and the United States, beginning in 1929 and continuing through the 1930s, when business, employment, and stock-market values were low and poverty was widespread
improvised: created on the spot, without planning
hymnal: a book of hymns, religious songs
colleague: a fellow worker
voila!: French for "there it was!"

ubiquitous: everywhere

UNDERSTANDING "STICKY STUFF"

1. Complete the following table:

Name of the Inventor	Innovative Product	Year

2. The article discusses three products that we use daily. What do these products have in common?

_____

_____

ALONG THESE LINES/Pearson Education Canada

3. Choose one of the men mentioned in the article. Describe how he came up with his innovative idea. Where was he? What was he doing at the moment of insight? Why did he think that his idea would be successful?

_____

_____

_____

_____

_____

_____

WRITING FROM READING: "STICKY STUFF"

When you write on any of the following topics, work through the stages of the writing process in preparing your paragraph.

1. Write a paragraph about one item in modern technology you just cannot live without. In your paragraph, explain why this invention is essential in your daily life.

2. "Sticky Stuff" is about three inventions that hold things together. In a paragraph, select one such item (for instance, Scotch tape, duct tape, masking tape, paper clips, or superglue), and describe ways to use it creatively or in an emergency. Use this topic sentence:

   _____ (name of the item) has several creative and emergency uses.

   If your instructor agrees, you might want to brainstorm about one or two items and their uses as a way of getting started.

3. Think of some item that many children take for granted today but that you did not have when you were growing up. (For example, you could write about portable CD players, DVDs, or cable or satellite television.) In a paragraph, describe the item, what it does, and how children take it for granted. Then explain how you amused yourself without this item.

4. Post-it notes are such a small convenience that people may not notice how useful they are. Write a paragraph about one other small convenience (in the office, the car, or the kitchen) that is extremely useful. Explain how it works, and consider how people coped before this item was created.

5. Look around your classroom for five minutes and ask yourself this question: What could be designed better? For instance, how could the desks be improved so that the writing surface is larger? How could the chairs be more comfortable? Are many students loaded with heavy book bags? How could these bags be improved? Are there bulletin boards? Are they effective? Focus on one item in the classroom and write a paragraph about how it could be improved, redesigned, or reinvented.

CHAPTER 4
Description

LEARNING OBJECTIVES

After you have read this chapter and completed its exercises and assignments, you should be able to

- generate ideas for a descriptive paragraph
- distinguish between general and more effective, specific words and phrases for your descriptive paragraph
- use effective sense words and phrases in your descriptive paragraph
- create a dominant impression for your descriptive paragraph
- organize your ideas in a logical order
- draft and edit an effective descriptive paragraph

"Don't tell me the light is shining; show me the glint of light on broken glass."

~ ANTON CHEKHOV

ANTON CHEKHOV WAS AN EARLY TWENTIETH-CENTURY RUSSIAN PLAYWRIGHT.

WHAT IS DESCRIPTION?

Description shows a reader what a person, place, thing, or situation is like. When you write description, you try to *show* something, not *tell*, about it; Chekhov was referring to this in his quotation above. An effective description puts the reader in that place, helps the reader understand that person, and gives the reader a feeling for that situation.

Hints for Writing a Descriptive Paragraph

Using Specific Words or Phrases The reader will see what you are describing if you use specific words and phrases. When a word or phrase is *specific*, it is exact and precise. The opposite of specific language is *general* language, which is vague or fuzzy. Think of the difference between specific and general in this way:

Imagine that you are browsing through a used-car lot. A salesman approaches you.

"Can I help you?" the salesman asks.
"I'm looking for a good, reliable car," you say.
"Well, what kind of car did you have in mind?" asks the salesman.

"Not too old," you say.
"A sports car?" asks the salesman.
"Maybe," you say.

The conversation could go on and on. You are being general in saying that you want a "good, reliable" car. The salesman, however, is looking for specific details: How old a car do you want? What model of car?

In writing, if you use words like "good" or "nice" or "bad" or "interesting," you will have neither a specific description nor an effective piece of writing. Whenever you can, try to use the more precise word instead of the general term. To find a more precise term, ask yourself such questions as "What type?" or "How?" The examples below show how a general term can be replaced by a more specific one.

general word:　　　　　　light (Ask "What kind?")
more specific words:　incandescent, fluorescent, early morning, dappled

general word:　　　　　　novel (Ask "What genre [type]?")
more specific words:　science fiction, literary, romance, graphic, mystery

general word:　　　　　　ran (Ask "How?")
more specific words:　raced, sprinted, loped

general word:　　　　　　nice (Ask "How?")
more specific words:　friendly, outgoing, courteous

EXERCISE 1 — IDENTIFYING GENERAL AND SPECIFIC WORDS

Below are lists of words. Put an X by the most general term in each list. The first one is done for you.

List 1

____ waiter
_X_ restaurant employee
____ cook
____ cashier
____ dishwasher

List 2

____ government
____ federal
____ municipal
____ provincial

List 3

____ community college
____ university
____ preschool
____ educational institution
____ secondary school

List 4

____ spring
____ mineralized
____ flavoured
____ water
____ sparkling

List 5

____ convenience
____ department
____ store
____ pet
____ specialty

List 6

____ mathematics
____ algebra
____ calculus
____ geometry
____ statistics

EXERCISE 2 — RANKING GENERAL AND SPECIFIC ITEMS

Below are lists of items. In each list, rank the items from the most general (1) to the most specific (4).

List 1

_____ health care provider
_____ surgeon
_____ physician
_____ brain surgeon

List 2

_____ *Singin' in the Rain*
_____ musical romantic comedy
_____ romantic comedy
_____ funny movie

List 3

_____ college services
_____ academic help
_____ help for students
_____ tutoring

List 4

_____ first-person shooter game
_____ video game
_____ shooter game
_____ *Halo 3*

EXERCISE 3 — INTERVIEWING FOR SPECIFIC ANSWERS

To practise being specific, interview a partner. Ask your partner to answer the questions below. Write his or her answers in the spaces provided. When you have finished, change places. In both interviews, your goal is to find specific answers, so you should both be as explicit as you can in your answers.

Interview Questions

1. How did you get to school this morning?

   _____

2. What sound do you think is the most irritating?

   _____

3. What is your favourite sport?

   _____

4. What TV personality do you most dislike?

   _____

5. Name three objects that are in your wallet or purse right now.

   _____

6. What food reminds you of your childhood?

   _____

7. What would you say is the one defining moment in your life?

   _____

8. What is the most enjoyable part of your day?

   _____

9. What do you like most about your school, college, or university?

_____

10. What would you do if you won ten million dollars?

_____

EXERCISE **4**	FINDING SPECIFIC WORDS OR PHRASES

List four specific words or phrases beneath each general one. You may use brand names where they are appropriate. The first word on List 1 is done for you.

List 1

    general word: bad
    specific word or phrase: annoying

_____

_____

_____

List 2

    general word: said
    specific word or phrase:

_____

_____

_____

_____

List 3

    general word: room
    specific word or phrase:

_____

_____

_____

_____

List 4

    general word: angry
    specific word or phrase:

_____

_____

_____

_____

List 5

general word: good-looking
specific word or phrase:

_____

_____

_____

_____

communication at work

Tourism plays an important role in Canada's economy. In the following paragraph, the Parks Canada website describes the beauty of British Columbia and Alberta's National Parks:

> The grizzly bear stops and looks toward the sound. Sniffing the air, he searches the dim, early-morning horizon. That sweet smell of spring pervades the cool Rocky Mountain air. In the distance, Mount Victoria and Mount Lefroy mark the Continental Divide. Soon, newly-sprouted wildflowers will greet the hikers who pass this way.

Note the use of specific descriptive words such as *dim, early-morning, pervades, and newly sprouted.* Think of a place that has special meaning for you. How would you describe it?

EXERCISE 5

IDENTIFYING SENTENCES THAT ARE TOO GENERAL

Below are lists of sentences. Put an X by one sentence in each group that is general and vague.

1. a. _____ Jose is an easygoing person.

    b. _____ Jose always has a new joke.

    c. _____ Jose makes faces at me in class.

2. a. _____ She criticized anyone who tried to help her at her work.

    b. _____ She expected the worst out of her job.

    c. _____ She had a bad attitude.

3. a. _____ It was a sweltering day.

    b. _____ It was 40 degrees C in the shade.

    c. _____ The news warned people of the risk of heatstroke.

4. a. _____ Often I have to deal with irate customers.

    b. _____ For six hours I have to lift boxes weighing more than fifty pounds each.

    c. _____ My job isn't easy.

5. **a.** ____ I want to live life to the fullest.

   b. ____ I want to travel to India and study my heritage.

   c. ____ I want to get married and raise a family.

Using Sense Words in Your Descriptions One way to make your description specific and vivid is to use **sense words**. As you plan a description, ask yourself:

What does it *look* like?
What does it *sound* like?
What does it *smell* like?
What does it *taste* like?
What does it *feel* like?

Sense details make a description vivid. Remember, you are trying to *show*, not *tell*, so try to include details about the five senses in your descriptions. Often you can brainstorm sense details more easily if you focus your thinking.

INFOBOX	DEVISING SENSE DETAIL

For the sense of	Think about
sight	colours, light and dark, shadows, or brightness.
hearing	noise, silence, or the kinds of sounds you hear.
smell	fragrance, odours, scents, aromas, or perfume.
taste	bitter, sour, or sweet, or compare the taste of one thing with another.
touch	the feel of things: texture, hardness, softness, roughness, smoothness.

EXERCISE 6

BRAINSTORMING SENSE DETAIL FOR A DESCRIPTIVE PARAGRAPH

With a partner or a group, brainstorm the following ideas for a paragraph. That is, for each topic, list at least six questions and answers that could help you create sense details. Be prepared to read your completed exercise to another group or to the class.

1. **topic:** Public transit becomes dirtier and dirtier every day.

Brainstorm questions and answers: _____

_____

_____

_____

_____

_____

_____

2. **topic:** Riding the subway during rush hour makes me nauseous.

   Brainstorm questions and answers: _____

   _____

   _____

   _____

   _____

3. **topic:** The fireworks celebration dazzled the children.

   Brainstorm questions and answers: _____

   _____

   _____

   _____

   _____

   _____

EXERCISE 7

WRITING SENSE WORDS

Write sense descriptions for the following items.

a. Write four words or phrases to describe the texture of beach sand:

   _____

   _____

b. Write four words or phrases to describe how the sofa in the student lounge looks:

   _____

   _____

c. Write four words or phrases to describe the sounds of a traffic jam:

   _____

   _____

d. Write four words or phrases to describe the taste of chocolate ice cream:

   _____

   _____

WRITING THE DESCRIPTIVE PARAGRAPH IN STEPS

THOUGHT LINES   GATHERING IDEAS: DESCRIPTION

Writing a descriptive paragraph begins with thinking on paper and looking for specific details and sense descriptions. You can think by brainstorming, freewriting, or writing in a journal. For example, you might decide to write about your brother's bedroom. Brainstorming might lead you to something like the following list of ideas:

A Brainstorming List for a Descriptive Paragraph

older brother Michael—got a big bedroom

I shared with my little brother

stars pasted on the ceiling

took a long time to fix it up the way he wanted it

lots of books about science fiction in two bookcases

movie posters of *AI: Artificial Intelligence* and *The Matrix*

DVDs of old movies like *Raiders of the Lost Ark* in the bookcases

his bed had no headboard, made to look like a couch

Star Trek pillows on the bed

The Dominant Impression

When you think you have enough details, you can begin to think about focusing them. Look over these details and consider where they are taking you. If you were to look at the list above, you might identify ideas that keep appearing in the details:

stars pasted on the ceiling

lots of books about science fiction in two bookcases

movie posters of *AI: Artificial Intelligence* and *The Matrix*

DVDs of old movies like *Raiders of the Lost Ark* in the bookcases

Star Trek pillows on the bed

Reading over this list, you realize that all the specific titles of films or television shows are related to fantasy or science fiction. Therefore, one main idea about your brother's bedroom relates to his interest in fantasy or science fiction. This idea is the **dominant impression,** or the main point of the description. It is the topic sentence of the description paragraph. For example, it could be the following:

My brother's bedroom reflected his fascination with fantasy and

science fiction.

Once you have a dominant impression, you are ready to add more ideas to explain and support it. You should try to make the added details specific by using sense description where appropriate.

EXERCISE

8

ADDING DETAILS TO A DOMINANT IMPRESSION

Below are sentences that could be used as a dominant impression in a descriptive paragraph. Add more details. Some details, to explain and support the dominant impression, are already given.

1. **dominant impression:** My friend John had obviously pulled an all-nighter.

   details:

   a. He spoke incoherently. _____

   b. He had bags under his eyes. _____

   c. _____

   d. _____

   e. _____

2. **dominant impression:** My closet was crammed with ten years of accumulated junk.

   details:

   a. Boxes piled on the top shelf threatened to fall. _____

   b. A suspect odour wafted up from the floor. _____

   c. _____

   d. _____

   e. _____

3. **dominant impression:** You could feel the tension in the school library the week before exams.

   details:

   a. No one dared utter a sound. _____

   b. Some students had sat for hours, without moving and with heads bowed toward their books.

   c. _____

   d. _____

   e. _____

4. **dominant impression:** Nothing compares to the atmosphere at an important soccer game.

   details:

   a. Tens of thousands of fans packed the stands. _____

   b. The fans roared their approval and stomped their feet at every goal.

   c. _____

   d. _____

   e. _____

EXERCISE **9**	**CREATING A DOMINANT IMPRESSION FROM A LIST OF DETAILS**

Below are lists of details. For each list, write one sentence that could be used as the dominant impression created by the details.

1. dominant impression: _____

_____

_____

_____

   details: People on beach towels sat elbow to elbow.
   A beach volleyball game took up the remaining space.
   The lifeguard could barely be seen above the players and sun bathers.
   At the shore line, parents watched small children build sand castles and wade in shallow water.
   Meanwhile, the deep water was filled with swimmers and people on floats.
   CD players and radios blasted above the laughter of children, the shouts of the swimmers, and the victory cries of the volleyball teams.

2. dominant impression: _____

_____

_____

_____

   details: The thunder roared while the lightning crashed and crackled, coming closer and closer.
   Rain gushed into the streets.
   The wind became stronger.
   Leaves and tree branches flew in the air.
   Doors blew shut and windows flew open.
   Cars pulled over to the side of the road.
   Pedestrians ran for cover.

3. dominant impression: _____

_____

_____

_____

   details: The jury returned to their seats, looking down at the floor.
   They would not look at the defendant or the lawyers.
   No one spoke.
   The only sound in the courtroom was the swish of the judge's robes as she returned to her chair.
   The defendant turned pale; he clenched his knuckles.

The jury chairperson clenched the verdict in his hand, but his fingers were shaking.

The reporters leaned forward in their seats, waiting for the verdict to be read.

4. **dominant impression:** _____

_____

_____

_____

details: The man in the dentist's waiting room had sweat trickling down his face.

His jaw was clenched.

He sat on the edge of his chair.

He kept looking at the clock.

His eyes were full of misery.

His hands trembled as he tried to flip through a magazine.

When the nurse called his name, he jumped.

OUT LINES   ## DEVISING A PLAN: DESCRIPTION

You can use your dominant impression as the topic sentence of your outline. Beneath the topic sentence, list the details you have collected. Once you have this rough list, check the details, and ask:

Do all the details relate to the topic sentence?
Are the details in logical order?

Below are the topic sentence and a list of details for the paragraph describing a bedroom. The details that are crossed out *don't fit* the topic sentence.

topic sentence: My brother's bedroom reflected his fascination with fantasy and science fiction.

details: ~~older brother Michael—got a big bedroom~~

~~I shared with my little brother~~

stars pasted on the ceiling

~~took a long time to fix it up the way he wanted it~~

lots of books about science fiction in two bookcases

movie posters of *AI: Artificial Intelligence* and *The Matrix*

DVDs of old movies like *Raiders of the Lost Ark* in the bookcases

~~his bed had no headboard, made to look like a couch~~

Star Trek pillows on the bed

Notice what is crossed out. The details about the size of Michael's bedroom, the other brother's bedroom, the time it took Michael to fix up his bedroom, and the bed that looked like a couch do not really have much to do with the topic sentence. The topic sentence is about Michael's fascination with science fiction and fantasy. It is about how his bedroom revealed that fascination.

Remember that, as you write and revise, you may decide to eliminate other ideas, or to re-insert ideas you once rejected, or to add new ideas. Changing your mind is a natural part of revising.

Once you've decided on your list of details, check their *order*. Remember, when you write a description, you are trying to make the reader *see*. It will be easier for the reader to imagine what you see if you put your description in a simple, logical order. You might want to put descriptions in order by *time order* (first to last) or by *space order* (top to bottom, or right to left). You might also group by *similar types* or categories (for example, all about the flowers in a park, then all about the trees).

If you are describing a house, for instance, you may want to start with the outside of the house and then describe the inside. You don't want the details to shift back and forth, from outside to inside and back to outside. If you are describing a person, you might want to group together all the details about his or her face before you describe the body. You might describe a meal from first course to dessert.

Look again at the details of the outline describing the bedroom. It is logical to use three categories to create a simple order: from the ceiling to the walls and then to the furniture. Now look at the following outline and notice how this order works.

> ## An Outline for a Descriptive Paragraph

topic sentence: My brother's bedroom reflected his fascination with fantasy and science fiction.

details:

ceiling

Stars were pasted on the ceiling.

At night, they glowed in the dark.

The room appeared to be covered by a starry sky.

walls

Movie posters covered the walls.

There was a poster of Steven Spielberg's film, *AI: Artificial Intelligence.*

Another poster, of *The Matrix*, was framed.

furniture

There were lots of books about science fiction in two bookcases.

I remember *Fahrenheit 451* and *The War of the Worlds.*

DVDs of old movies like *Raiders of the Lost Ark* were also stacked on the bookshelves.

The bed was piled high with *Star Trek* pillows.

You have probably noticed that the outline has more details than the original list. These details help to make the descriptions more specific. You can add them to the outline and to the drafts of your paragraph.

Once you have a list of details that are focused on the topic sentence and arranged in some logical order, you can begin the stage of writing the descriptive paragraph.

EXERCISE 10

FINDING DETAILS THAT DO NOT RELATE

Survey the following lists. Each list includes a topic sentence and several details. In each list cross out the details that do not relate to the topic sentence.

1. **topic sentence:** The pond was a tranquil retreat.

   details: Few people knew of this small place.
   It was hidden from the road by a thick wall of trees.
   The road was two bumpy lanes.
   The trees encircled a shady shore of pebbles and greenery.
   Yellow wildflowers bloomed on the edges of the pond.
   The water was lightly ruffled by the breeze.
   I could hear the soft wind in the trees.
   I could hear the buzz of small summer insects.
   I was alone with my own thoughts and dreams.
   Someday I would come back and bring a picnic.

2. **topic sentence:** My Uncle Oscar was a wonderful playmate.

   details: He always had a joke for his nieces and nephews.
   When he ran out of jokes, he had a plan for a new adventure.
   Uncle Oscar died last year.
   Sometimes he would take us exploring in the neighbourhood.
   Whenever he came over, he would arrive on time.
   He would push us on the swings for hours.
   Uncle Oscar was the one who pleaded with our parents to let us stay up longer and play another game.
   He was my mother's brother.

3. **topic sentence:** Levar was a very spoiled child.

   details: He would interrupt his mother when she was talking to people.
   He'd pull at her sleeve or the hem of her dress.
   He'd whine, "Mom, Mom, I want to go now," or "Mom, can I have a dollar?"
   He had about a hundred toys.
   Whenever he broke a toy, he got a new one right away.
   Levar wore designer clothes, even to play in.
   Levar had no set bedtime; he was allowed to stay up as long as he wanted.
   Levar had a little sister, Denise.
   Levar had big, black eyes with long, soft lashes.

EXERCISE 11

PUTTING DETAILS IN ORDER

Below are lists that start with a topic sentence. The details under each topic sentence are not in the right order. Put each detail in logical order by labelling it, with 1 being the first detail, 2 the second, and so forth, after the topic sentence.

ALONG THESE LINES/Pearson Education Canada

1. **topic sentence:** The plane trip went very smoothly. (Arrange the details in time order.)

   details: _____ Our plane departed on time.
   _____ We had no turbulent weather in the air.
   _____ We arrived at the airport in plenty of time to get good seats.
   _____ When we went to claim our luggage, all of it was there.
   _____ Our plane arrived on time.

2. **topic sentence:** The restaurant was dirty and unappealing. (Arrange the details according to space order, from outside to inside.)

   details: _____ Soot smeared the sign that said, "Burgers and Shakes."
   _____ Finger smudges covered the glass front door.
   _____ The chrome edges of the counter were caked with food.
   _____ Inside the entrance, we smelled the rancid odour of grease.
   _____ We approached a counter covered with crumbs.

3. **topic sentence:** The man showed off his money. (Arrange the details according to spatial position, from head to foot.)

   details: _____ His shoes were a glossy, soft leather.
   _____ His hair was elaborately styled.
   _____ Two diamond earrings shone in his left ear.
   _____ His wrist boasted a platinum Rolex.
   _____ His shirt was silk.

EXERCISE **12**	CREATING DETAIL USING A LOGICAL ORDER

The following lists include a topic sentence and indicate a required order for the details. Write five sentences of detail in the required order.

1. **topic sentence:** The medicine cabinet in my bathroom is full of everything except medicine.
   (Describe the contents of the cabinet from top shelf to bottom shelf.)

   a. _____

   b. _____

   c. _____

   d. _____

   e. _____

2. **topic sentence:** The day was full of surprises.
   (Describe the day from beginning to end.)

   a. _____

   b. _____

c. _____

d. _____

e. _____

3. **topic sentence:** The scene after the blizzard showed people at their best. (First describe the scene; then describe the people's behaviour.)

a. _____

b. _____

c. _____

d. _____

e. _____

4. **topic sentence:** The bodyguard was a frightening person. (Describe him from head to foot.)

a. _____

b. _____

c. _____

d. _____

e. _____

ROUGH LINES

DRAFTING AND REVISING: DESCRIPTION

After you have an outline, the next step is creating a first rough draft of the paragraph. At this point, you can begin combining some of the ideas in your outline, making two or more short sentences into one longer one. Or you can write your first draft in short sentences and combine the sentences later. Your goal is simply to put your ideas into paragraph form. Then you can see how they look and check them to see what needs to be improved.

The first draft of a paragraph will not be perfect. If it were perfect, it wouldn't be a first draft. Once you have the first draft, check it, using the following checklist.

✓

CHECKLIST   FOR REVISING A DESCRIPTIVE PARAGRAPH

✓ Are there enough details?

✓ Are the details specific?

✓ Do the details use sense words?

✓ Are the details in order?

✓ Is there a dominant impression?

✓ Do the details connect to the dominant impression?

✓ Have I made my point?

A common problem in writing description is creating a fuzzy, vague description. Take a look at the following fuzzy description:

> The football fans were rowdy and excited. They shouted when their team scored. Some people jumped up. The fans showed their support by cheering and stomping. They were enjoying every minute of the game.

The description could be revised so that it is more specific and vivid:

> The football fans were rowdy and excited. When their team scored, they yelled, "Way to go!" or "Stomp 'em! Crush 'em!" until they were hoarse. Three fans, wearing the team colours of blue and white on their shirts, shorts, and socks, jumped up, spilling their drinks on the teenagers seated below them. During timeouts, the fans chanted rhythmically, and throughout the game they stomped their feet in a steady beat against the wooden bleachers. The atmosphere was electric. As people chanted, whooped, and woofed, they turned to grin at each other and thrust their clenched fists into the air.

The vivid description meets the requirements of the checklist. It has sufficient specific details. The details use sense words to describe what the fans looked and sounded like, give a *feel* for the place, and also support a dominant impression of rowdy, excited fans. The vivid, specific details make the point; they create an atmosphere and *put* the reader in the stadium.

EXERCISE 13

REVISING A PARAGRAPH BY FINDING IRRELEVANT SENTENCES

Below are two descriptive paragraphs. In each, there are sentences that are irrelevant, meaning that they don't have anything to do with the first sentence, the topic sentence. Cross out the irrelevant sentences in the following paragraphs.

1.   Leo looked and sounded as if he were trying to control his anger. I know what that's like because I've been furious and had to suppress my feelings. Leo's face was nearly purple with rage, and his eyes were blazing. He spoke very slowly and quietly, but his tone implied that he was holding himself back from an outburst. His jaw was tight, showing his stress. I could hear his shallow breathing as he tried to calm down. Breathing can be the key to changing your frame of mind; it's an important part of meditation.

2.   The garage was crammed with junk and dirt. Empty cardboard boxes, collapsing into each other, lined one wall. Other boxes were filled with newspapers and smaller boxes. A workbench against one wall held rusty screwdrivers and an assortment of loose nails and hooks. Above the bench, a pegboard was covered by dangling hammers, clippers, and cords, some of them covered by rags

ALONG THESE LINES/Pearson Education Canada

and gardening gloves. My father keeps all his gardening tools in a shed in the yard. A large bag of dog food had spilled its contents across one end of the garage. To avoid this kind of mess, dog food can be stored in large plastic containers. The place was so full of debris that there was hardly room for the one car parked on the oil-stained floor.

| EXERCISE **14** | REVISING A PARAGRAPH FOR MORE SPECIFIC DETAILS |

In the following paragraphs, the details that are underlined are not specific. Change the underlined sentences to a more specific description. Write the changes in the lines below each paragraph.

1.   The Caribbean Festival ended with a delicious island dinner. To begin, banana bread and spicy conch fritters were served. The main course included snapper marinated in lime juice and broiled golden on the outside and tender on the inside. Crispy coconut shrimp, pigeon peas and rice, and mango relish completed this course. <u>The meal ended with a great dessert.</u>

revisions: _____

_____

2.   The classroom was a dreary place. The dull green and grey paint immediately created a sense of an old and faded schoolroom. The blackboards, covered in layers of ancient chalk dust ground into grey patterns by filthy erasers, spoke of neglect and apathy. Even the bulletin boards, which had no tacks, no notices, and no pictures, offered nothing to please the eye. <u>The student desks were awful.</u> The teacher's desk was really a chipped wooden table accompanied by a chipped metal folding chair.

revisions: _____

_____

Transitions

As you revise your descriptive paragraph, you may notice places that seem choppy or abrupt. That is, one sentence may end, and another may start, but the two sentences don't seem to be connected. Reading your paragraph aloud, you might sense that it is not very smooth.

You can make the writing smoother and make the content clearer by using *transitions*. Transitions are words or phrases that link one idea to another. They tell the reader what he or she has just read and what is coming next. Every kind of writing has its own transitions. Here are some transitions you may want to use in writing a description:

ALONG THESE LINES/Pearson Education Canada

INFOBOX   **TRANSITIONS FOR A DESCRIPTIVE PARAGRAPH**

To show ideas brought together: and, also, in addition, as well as

To show a contrast: although, but, however, in contrast, on the contrary, on the other hand, unlike, yet

To show a similarity: all, both, each, like, similarly

To show a time sequence: after, always, before, first (second, third, and so forth), meanwhile, next, often, soon, then, when, while

To show a position in space: above, ahead of, alongside, among, around, away, below, beside, between, beneath, beyond, by, close, down, far, here, in front of, inside, near, nearby, next to, on, on top of, outside, over, there, toward, under, up, underneath

There are many other transitions you can use, depending on how you need to link your ideas. Take a look at the draft of the description paragraph of a bedroom. Compare it to the outline. You will notice that more sense details have been added. Transitions have been added, too. Pay particular attention to the transitions in this draft.

> A Draft of a Descriptive Paragraph (*transitions are underlined*)

My brother's bedroom reflected his fascination with fantasy and science fiction. Stars were pasted on the ceiling where, at night, they glowed in the dark. <u>Then</u> the room appeared to be covered by a starry sky. Movie posters covered the walls. A poster of Steven Spielberg's film *AI: Artificial Intelligence* hung <u>next to</u> a poster of *The Matrix* in a shiny chrome frame. <u>Below</u> the posters, two steel bookcases were full of books about science fiction. I remember *Fahrenheit 451* and *The War of the Worlds*. DVDs of old movies like *Raiders of the Lost Ark* were also stacked on the bookshelves. The bed was piled high with *Star Trek* pillows.

EXERCISE
15

RECOGNIZING TRANSITIONS

Underline the transitions in the following paragraph.

Waiting for my bus, I felt like a stranger on the scene. Under the roof of the small bus shelter, I was all alone. In front of me was a strip of dead grass littered with soft drink cans and cigarette butts. A six-lane highway was beyond the grass patch. Cars and trucks sped by me, focused on passing each other, making the green light, and getting somewhere fast. The drivers did not have time to notice me. A few cars in the outside lane swerved toward me as they temporarily lost control. Far ahead of me, on the other side of the highway, tall buildings with blank glass fronts stared. Maybe they were staring at me, the only human being who was not enclosed in metal or glass.

EXERCISE 16

COMBINING SENTENCES AND USING TRANSITIONS

The following description has some choppy sentences that could be combined to create a smoother paragraph. Combine each pair of underlined sentences by revising them in the space above each pair and using appropriate transitions.

The street fair was filled with tempting objects to buy and food to eat. First, there was a booth selling bright straw hats. <u>People strolled by. The vendor popped a hat on each person's head.</u> He said the hat looked stunning and tried to make a deal. <u>A stall offering shiny silver bracelets was in the same area. So was a stall selling discount CDs.</u> Food was a tremendous attraction. <u>Dozens of people crowded around an ice-cream truck. A group of people pushed to buy hot pretzels at a pushcart.</u> Food smells filled the air wherever people went. <u>Bakery smells were nearby. So was the odour of pizza.</u> They were irresistible. <u>The spicy aroma of Indian curry came. It was not so close.</u> When people reached the end of the fair, they turned around to walk through it one more time. <u>They had seen, tasted, and bought many things. They wanted to do it all again.</u>

Proofreading and Polishing: Description

In preparing the final version of a descriptive paragraph, you add the finishing touches to your paragraph, making changes in words, changing or adding transitions, and sharpening details. In the final version of the description paragraph, you will notice these changes:

- The phrase "had lots of books" has been changed to "were crammed with books." (The phrases "lots of" and "a lot" are not specific, and some writers use them repetitively. Try not to use them.)
- "My brother" has been identified by name, Michael.
- A few more sense details have been added.
- Another specific name of a movie has been added.
- In the draft paragraph, the ending of the paragraph is a little sudden. The paragraph needs a sentence that pulls all the details together and reminds the reader of the topic sentence. A sentence has been added to the final version that ties the paragraph together.

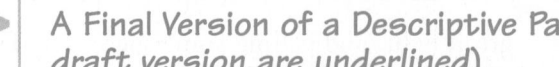

A Final Version of a Descriptive Paragraph (*changes from the draft version are underlined*)

My brother <u>Michael's</u> bedroom reflected his fascination with fantasy and science fiction. Stars were pasted on the ceiling where, at night, they glowed in the dark. Then the room appeared to be covered by a starry sky. Movie posters covered the walls. A poster of Steven Spielberg's film *AI: Artificial Intelligence*

ALONG THESE LINES/Pearson Education Canada

hung next to a poster of *The Matrix* in a shiny chrome frame. Below the posters, two <u>black</u> steel bookcases were crammed with books about science fiction. I remember *Fahrenheit 451* and *The War of the Worlds*. DVDs of old movies like *Raiders of the Lost Ark* and *Alien* were also stacked on the bookshelves. The bed was piled high with <u>huge, soft</u> *Star Trek* pillows. <u>Anyone entering the room would know at once that Michael liked to escape to fantastic and futuristic places.</u>

Before you prepare the final copy of your descriptive paragraph, check your latest draft for errors in spelling and punctuation, and for any errors made in typing or recopying.

EXERCISE 17	PROOFREADING TO PREPARE THE FINAL VERSION

Below are two descriptive paragraphs with the kinds of errors that are easy to overlook when you write the final version of an assignment. Correct the errors, writing above the lines. There are twelve errors in the first paragraph and eight errors in the second paragraph.

1. I have an old dilapidated sweatshirt that I'll allways cherish for the memmories it holds. It is a ratty-looking, grey shirt that belongs in the rag pile but I wore that shirt on many happy occassions. The greasy stain on one sleeve is a memory of how I got covered in oil when i was working on my first motorcycle the tear at the neck reminds me of a crazy game of football. At the game where I tore the shirt, I also met my current girlfreind. The pale white blotches acrost the front of the shirt are from bleech. But to me they are a memory of the time my girlfriend and I was fooling around at the laundry room and put to much bleach in the washer. Every mark or stain on my shirt means something to me and I'll never through that old shirt away.

2. When I finally got around to cleaning my refrigerator, I was horrified at the items I had been storing. First, I surveyed the boxes and jar's on the door shelves. Among them was a jar of gourmet salsa that some one had given me for Christmas four years ago. I also found a handful of brown rice in a bag and an empty box of vanila puding mix. I did not stop to wonder why I had kep a empty box of pudding mix, or enough brown rice to feed a small mouse. Instead, I moved on to the back of the refrigerator, where I found jars full of a mysterous green and orange fuzz. Behind the jars were shrivelled lemons and rock-hard pieces of cheese. Underneath it all was a slice of slimy pizza wrapped in ancient aluminum foil. I had no idea my refrigerator had become such health hazard.

Lines of Detail: A Walk-Through Assignment

Your assignment is to write a paragraph describing a popular place for socializing. Follow these steps:

Step 1: To begin, freewrite about a place where people socialize. For example, you could write about a place where people go to eat, or dance, or shop, or just "hang out."

Step 2: Read your freewriting. Underline all the words, phrases, and sentences of description.

Step 3: List everything you underlined, grouping the ideas in some order. Maybe the details can be listed from inside to outside, or can be put into categories, like walls, floor, and furniture, or scenery and people.

Step 4: After you've surveyed the list, write a sentence about the dominant impression of the details.

Step 5: Using the dominant impression as your topic sentence, write an outline. Add specific details where you need them. Concentrate on details that appeal to the senses.

Step 6: Write a first draft of your paragraph. Be sure to check the order of your details. Combine short sentences and add transitions.

Step 7: Revise your first draft version, paying particular attention to order, specific details, and transitions.

Step 8: After a final check for punctuation, spelling, and word choice, prepare the final version of the paragraph.

Writing Your Own Descriptive Paragraph

When you write on any of the following topics, work through the stages of the writing process in preparing your descriptive paragraph. Be sure that your paragraph is based on a dominant impression, and put the dominant impression into your topic sentence.

1. Write a paragraph that describes one of the following items:

> the contents of your purse or wallet
> the contents of your refrigerator
> what you ate for breakfast
> children riding the school bus
> a hospital waiting room
> people riding the subway or bus
> the best meal you ever had
> a toddler in a car seat or stroller
> a dentist's waiting room
> an exciting sports event
> your favourite teacher
> an irritating customer
> your first impression of a school
> a person who was a positive influence in your life

ALONG THESE LINES/Pearson Education Canada

2. Describe a place that creates one of these impressions:

peace	tension	depression
excitement	cheerfulness	hurry
friendliness	danger	fun

3. Describe a person who conveys one of these impressions:

confidence	warmth	pride
hostility	fear	style
shyness	rebellion	intelligence
conformity	strength	beauty

4. Online dating services such as Lavalife.com and Match.com are experiencing a steady increase in subscribers. You (or a friend) would like to post a profile. Write a paragraph in which you describe yourself or your friend.

5. Select a photograph of a person or place. You can use a photograph from a magazine or newspaper, or one of your own photographs. Write a paragraph describing that photograph. Attach the photograph to the completed paragraph.

6. Interview a partner to gather details for a descriptive paragraph with the title, "My Perfect Room."

First, prepare a list of at least six questions to ask your partner. Write down the answers your partner gives and use these answers to form more questions. For example, if your partner says her dream room would be a game room, ask her what games she'd like to have in it. If your partner says his perfect room would be a workshop, ask him what kind of workshop.

When you've finished the interview, switch roles. Let your partner interview you. Feel free to add more questions or to follow up on previous ones.

Finally, give your partner his or her interview responses, then take your own responses and use them as the basis for gathering as many details as you can on your perfect room. Finally, build the thought lines of your paragraph. Then go on to the outline, draft, and final versions. Be prepared to read your completed paragraph to your partner.

WRITING FROM READING: DESCRIPTION

A Present for Popo
Elizabeth Wong

The child of Chinese immigrants, Elizabeth Wong was born in Los Angeles, California. She has a master's degree in fine arts and has worked as a writer for newspapers and television. She has also written several plays. In "A Present for Popo," Wong describes a beloved grandmother.

Before you read this essay, consider these questions:

Are you afraid of growing old?

Do you think most old people in North America are treated well?

Are they respected? Ignored?

Are you close to anyone over sixty-five?
Did you grow up in close contact with a grandparent?
Is there one person who holds your family together?

When my Popo opened a Christmas gift, she would shake it, smell it, listen to it. She would size it up. She would open it **nimbly,** with all enthusiasm and delight, and even though the mittens were ugly or the blouse too small or the card obviously homemade, she would coo over it as if it were the baby Jesus.

nimbly: quickly, gracefully

Despite that, buying a gift for my grandmother was always problematic. Being in her late 80s, Popo didn't seem to need any more sweaters or handbags. No books certainly, as she only knew six words of English. Cosmetics might be a good idea, for she was just a wee bit **vain.**

vain: excessively proud of one's appearance

But ultimately, nothing worked. "No place to put anything anyway," she used to tell me in Chinese. For in the last few years of her life, Popo had a bed in a room in a house in San Gabriel owned by one of her sons. All her belongings, her money, her very life was now **co-opted** and controlled by her sons and their wives. Popo's daughters had little power in this matter. This was a traditional Chinese family.

co-opted: taken over

For you see, Popo had begun to forget things. Ask her about something that happened 20 years ago, and she could recount the details in the heartbeat of a New York minute. But it was those **niggling** little everyday matters that became so troubling. She would forget to take her heart medicine. She would forget where she put her handbag. She would forget she talked to you just moments before. She would count the few dollars in her billfold, over and over again. She would ask me for the millionth time, "So when are you going to get married?" For her own good, the family decided she should give up her beloved one-room Chinatown flat. Popo herself recognized she might be a danger to herself, "I think your grandmother is going crazy," she would say.

niggling: unimportant

That little flat was a bothersome place, but Popo loved it. Her window had a view of several import-export shops below, not to mention the **grotesque** plastic hanging lanterns and that nasty loudspeaker serenading tourists with 18 hours of top-40 popular hits.

grotesque: incongruous; comically or repulsively distorted

My brother Will and I used to stand under her balcony on Mei Ling Way, shouting up, "Grandmother on the Third Floor! Grandmother on the Third Floor!" Simultaneously, the wrinkled faces of a half-dozen grannies would peek cautiously out their windows. Popo would come to the balcony and proudly claim us: "These are my grandchildren coming to take me to *dim sum.*" Her neighbours would cluck and sigh, "You have such good grandchildren. Not like mine."

dim sum: an assortment of dumplings with savoury fillings

In that cramped room of Popo's, I could see past Christmas presents. A full-wall **collage** of family photos that my mother and I made together and presented one year with lots of fanfare. Popo had attached additional snapshots by way of paper clips and Scotch tape. And there, on the window sill, a little **terrarium** to which Popo had tied a small red ribbon. "For good luck," as she gleefully pointed out the sprouting buds. "See, it's having babies."

collage: abstract collection of photos, pieces of paper, and so on, glued to a pictorial surface

terrarium: a small container where plants and small creatures are kept alive under conditions imitating their natural environment

Also, there were the utility shelves on the wall, groaning from a wide assortment of junk, stuff, and whatnot. Popo was fond of salvaging discarded things. After my

ALONG THESE LINES/Pearson Education Canada

brother had installed the shelving, she did a little jig, then took a whisk broom and lightly swept away any naughty spirits that might be lurking on the walls. "Shoo, shoo, shoo, away with you, Mischievous Ones!" That apartment was her independence, and her pioneer spirit was everywhere in it.

Popo was my mother's mother, but she was also a second mother to me. Her death was a great blow. The last time I saw her was Christmas 1990, when she looked hale and hearty. I thought she would live forever. Last October, at 91, she had her final heart attack. The next time I saw her, it was at her funeral.

An open casket, and there she was, with a shiny new penny poised between her lips, a silenced warrior woman. Her sons and daughters placed colourful pieces of cloth in her casket. They burned incense and paper money. A small marching band led a New Orleans–like procession through the streets of Chinatown. Popo's picture, larger than life, in a flatbed truck to survey the world of her adopted country.

This little 4-foot, 9-inch woman had been the glue of our family. She wasn't perfect, she wasn't always even nice, but she learned from her mistakes, and, ultimately, she forgave herself for being human. It is a lesson of forgiveness that seems to have **eluded** her own sons and daughters.

eluded: escaped

And now she is gone. And with her—the **tenuous, cohesive** ties of blood and duty that bound us to family. My mother predicted that once the distribution of what was left of Popo's estate took place, no further words would be exchanged between Popo's children. She was right.

tenuous: slight, insubstantial

cohesive: holding together

But this year, six of the 27 grandchildren and two of the 18 great-grandchildren came together for a holiday feast of honey-baked ham and mashed potatoes. Not a gigantic family reunion. But I think, for now, it's the one yuletide present my grandmother might have truly enjoyed.

Merry Christmas, Popo!

UNDERSTANDING "A PRESENT FOR POPO"

1. Why was Popo's life co-opted and controlled by her sons and their wives?

2. Although it was noisy and cramped, why did Popo love her little flat (apartment)?

3. The author writes of many presents that Popo had received over the years. List two gifts that she treasured.

4. What was the most important present, the one mentioned in the title "A Present for Popo"?

WRITING FROM READING "A PRESENT FOR POPO"

1. Elizabeth Wong uses many details about her grandmother's apartment to describe the woman. Write a paragraph in which you use many details about a person's environment (for example, her office, his apartment) to describe that person.

2. Wong's essay includes a description of a funeral in a Chinese-American family. Write a description of some custom or ritual in your family. You could write, for instance, about a wedding, a funeral, the celebration of a holiday, or a religious occasion.

3. "A Present for Popo" is a tribute to a beloved person. Write a description of someone who holds a special place in your life.

4. The grandmother in Wong's essay is an immigrant, a Chinese woman who moved to America. Describe an immigrant that you know. Focus on how the person is a combination of two countries or cultures.

5. Describe an older person you know well. In your description, you can use details of appearance and behaviour. Focus on how these details reveal personality.

6. Describe yourself at age ninety. Use your imagination to give details of appearance, behaviour, and family relationships.

CHAPTER 5
Narration

After you have read this chapter and completed its exercises
and assignments, you should be able to

- write a narrative with a point
- make your narrative interesting and engaging
- use dialogue effectively in your narrative
- add effective detail to your narrative
- draft and edit your narrative

*"If you would understand your own age,
read the works of fiction produced in it.
People in disguise speak freely."*

~ SIR ARTHUR HELPS

▼

SIR ARTHUR HELPS WAS
A NINETEENTH-CENTURY
ENGLISHMAN KNOWN
FOR HIS PARTICIPATION
IN A GROUP CALLED THE
APOSTLES, WHOSE
PURPOSE WAS TO
DISCUSS LITERATURE
AND SOCIETY.

WHAT IS NARRATION?

Narration means telling a story. Everybody tells stories; some people are better
storytellers than others. When you write a *narrative paragraph*, you can tell a story
about something that happened to you or to someone else, or about something that
you saw or read.

Because it relies on specific details, a narrative is like a description. But it is
also different from a description, because it covers events in a time sequence.
While a description can be about a person, a place, or an object, a narrative is
always about happenings: events, actions, incidents.

Interesting narratives do more than tell what happened. They help the reader
become involved in the story by providing vivid detail. You can get that detail
from your memory or observation or reading. Using good details, you don't just
tell the story, you *show* it.

Giving the Narrative a Point

We all know people who tell long stories that seem to lead nowhere. These people
talk on and on; they recite an endless list of activities and soon become boring.
Their narratives have no point.

The difficult part of writing a narrative is making sure that it has a *point*. That point will be included in the topic sentence. The point of a narrative is the *meaning* of the incident or incidents you are writing about. To get to the point of your narrative, ask yourself questions like these:

What did I learn?
What's the meaning of this story?
What's my attitude toward what happened?
Did it change me?
What emotion did it make me feel?
Was the experience a good example of something (like unfairness, or kindness, or generosity)?

The answers to such questions can lead you to the topic sentence.

An effective topic sentence for a narrative is

not this: I'm going to tell you about the time I flunked my driving test. (This is an announcement; it does not make a point.)
but this: When I failed my driving test, I learned not to be over-confident.

not this: Yesterday my car stalled in rush-hour traffic. (This identifies the incident but does not make a point. It is also too narrow to be a good topic sentence.)
but this: When my car stalled in rush-hour traffic, I was annoyed and embarrassed.

The topic sentence, stating the point of your narrative paragraph, can be placed in the beginning or middle or end of the paragraph. You may want to start your story with the point, so that the reader knows exactly where your story is headed, or you may want to conclude your story by leaving the point until last. Sometimes the point can even fit smoothly into the middle of your paragraph.

Consider the following narrative paragraphs. The topic sentences are in various places.

Topic Sentence at the Beginning

<u>When I was five, I learned how serious it is to tell a lie.</u> One afternoon, my seven-year-old friend Tina asked me if I wanted to walk down the block to play ball in an empty lot. When I asked my mother, she said I couldn't go because it was too close to dinner time. I don't know why I lied, but when Tina asked me if my mother had said yes, I nodded my head in a lie. I wanted to go play, and I did. Yet as I played in the dusty lot, a dull buzz of guilt or fear distracted me. As soon as I got home, my mother confronted me. She asked me whether I had gone to the sandlot and whether I had lied to Tina about getting permission. This time, I told the truth. Something about my mother's tone of voice made me feel very dirty and ashamed. I had let her down.

Topic Sentence in the Middle

When I was little, I was afraid of diving into water. I thought I would go down and never come back up. Then one day, my father took me to a pool where we swam and fooled around, but he never forced me to try a dive. After about an hour of playing, I walked around and around the edge of the pool, trying to get the courage to dive in. Finally, I did it. <u>When I made that first dive, I felt blissful because I did something I had been afraid to do.</u> As I came to the surface, I wiped the water from my eyes and looked around. The sun seemed more dazzling, and the water sparkled. Best of all, I saw my father looking at me with a smile. "You did it," he said. "Good for you! I'm proud of you."

Topic Sentence at the End

It seemed as if I'd been in love with Reeza for years. Unfortunately, Reeza was always in love with someone else. Finally, she broke up with her boyfriend Nelson. I saw my chance. I asked Reeza out. After dinner, we talked and talked. Reeza told me all about her hopes and dreams. She told me about her family and her job, and I felt very close to her. We talked late into the night. When she left, Reeza kissed me. "Thanks for listening," she said. "You're like a brother to me." <u>Reeza meant to be kind, but she shattered my hopes and dreams.</u>

EXERCISE 1

FINDING THE TOPIC SENTENCE IN A NARRATIVE PARAGRAPH

Underline the topic sentence in each of the following narrative paragraphs.

Paragraph 1

I was eager to get a place of my own. I figured that having my own apartment meant I was free at last because there would be no rules, no curfew, no living by someone else's schedule. My first day in the apartment started well. I arranged the furniture, put up all my pictures, and phoned each of my friends to say hi. Then I called out for pizza. When it came, I tried to start a conversation with the delivery man, but he was in a hurry. I ate my pizza alone while I watched the late movie. It was too late to call any of my friends to come over, and I definitely wasn't going to call my mother and let her know I wanted some company. In truth, my first day in my apartment showed me the lonely side of living on my own.

Paragraph 2

Last Saturday I took a bus downtown to have lunch with a friend. After lunch, my friend and I split the bill, and I reached for my wallet to pay my share. I was horrified to discover I had lost my wallet. My friend drove me home, and the first thing I saw was the blinking message light on my answering machine. The message said someone had found my wallet and wanted to return it. I couldn't believe anyone in the city would be so kind and honest, but losing something changed my mind. When I met the man in a nearby coffee shop, he gave me the wallet with all my money and credit cards still in it. He said he had found it on a seat on the bus and had been calling my apartment for hours. He was such a good person he wouldn't even take a small reward. He even paid the cheque at the coffee shop because he said I'd had a bad day and deserved a break!

Paragraph 3

Yesterday, one person showed me what it means to be a good parent. I was walking in the mall, and just ahead of me a toddler was holding his father's hand and struggling to keep up. Pretty soon, the child got tired and started to cry. Within minutes, his crying had become a full-fledged tantrum. The little boy squatted on the ground, refusing to go any farther, his face purple. Some parents would have shouted at the child, threatened him, or scooped him up and carried him away. This father, however, just sat down on the ground by his son and talked to him, very calmly and quietly. I couldn't hear his words, but I got the feeling he was sympathizing with the tired little boy. Pretty soon, the child's screams became little sniffles, and father and son walked quietly away.

EXERCISE 2	WRITING THE MISSING TOPIC SENTENCES IN NARRATIVE PARAGRAPHS

Below are three paragraphs. If the paragraph already has a topic sentence, write it in the lines provided. If it doesn't have a topic sentence, create one. (Two of the paragraphs have no topic sentence.)

Paragraph 1

When I got up, I realized I must have turned off my alarm clock and gone back to sleep because I was already an hour behind schedule. I raced into the shower, only to find I had used up the last of the shampoo the day before. I barely had time to make a cup of coffee to take with me in the car. I grabbed the cup of coffee, rushed to the car, and turned the ignition. The car wouldn't start. Two hours later, the emergency service finally came to jump-start the car. I arrived at work three hours late, and the supervisor was not happy with me.

_____

_____

_____

Paragraph 2

Since I gave my first speech in my Public Speaking class, I'm not as shy as I used to be. On the day I was supposed to give my speech, I seriously considered cutting class, taking an F on the speech, or even dropping the course. All I could think of was what could go wrong. I could freeze up and go blank, or I could say something really stupid. In spite of my terror, I managed to walk up to the front of the class. When I started talking, I could hear my voice shaking. I wondered if everyone in the room could see the cold sweat on my forehead. By the middle of the speech, I was concentrating so intensely on *what* to say that I forgot about my nerves. When I finished, I couldn't believe people were clapping! I never believed I could stand up and speak to the entire class. Once I did that, it seemed so easy to talk in a class discussion. Best of all, the idea of making another speech doesn't seem as frightening anymore.

Paragraph 3

Last weekend I was driving home alone, at about 10:00 p.m., when a carload of young men pulled their car up beside mine. They began shouting and making strange motions with their hands. At first I ignored them, hoping they'd go away. But then I got scared because they wouldn't pass me. They kept driving right alongside my car. I rolled up my car windows and locked the doors. I couldn't hear their shouts, but I was still afraid. I was more afraid when I stopped at a red light and they pulled up next to me. Suddenly, one of the men screamed at me, at the top of his lungs, "Hey! You have a broken tail light!"

HINTS FOR WRITING A NARRATIVE PARAGRAPH

Everyone tells stories, but some people tell stories better than others. When you write a story, be sure to

- be clear
- be interesting
- stay in order
- pick a topic that is not too big

1. **Be clear.** Put in all the information the reader will need to follow your story. Sometimes you need to explain the time, or place, or the relationships of the people in your story to make the story clear. Sometimes you

need to explain how much time has elapsed between one action and another. This paragraph is not clear:

> I've never felt so stupid as I did on my first day of work. I was stocking the shelves when Mr. Cimino came up to me and said, "You're doing it wrong." Then he showed me how to do it. An hour later, he told me to call the produce supplier and check on the order for grapefruit. Well, I didn't know how to tell Mr. Cimino that I didn't know what phone to use or how to get an outside line. I also didn't know how to get the phone number of the produce supplier, or what the order for the grapefruit was supposed to be and when it was supposed to arrive. I felt really stupid asking these questions.

What's wrong with the paragraph? It lacks all kinds of information. Who is Mr. Cimino? Is he the boss? Is he a produce supervisor? And, more importantly, what kind of place is the writer's workplace? The reader knows the place has something to do with food, but is it a supermarket, or a fruit market, or a warehouse?

2. **Be interesting.** A boring narrative can make the greatest adventure sound dull. Here is a dull narrative:

> I had a wonderful time on prom night. First, we went out to dinner. The meal was excellent. Then we went to the dance and saw all our friends. Everyone was dressed up great. We stayed until late. Then we went out to breakfast. After breakfast we watched the sun come up.

Good specific detail is the difference between an interesting story and a dull one.

3. **Stay in order.** Put the details in a clear order, so that the reader can follow your story. Usually, time order is the order you follow in narration. This narrative has a confusing order:

> My impatience cost me twenty dollars last week. There was a pair of shoes I really wanted. I had wanted them for weeks. So, when payday came around, I went to the mall and checked the price on the shoes. I had been checking the price for weeks before. The shoes were expensive, but I really wanted them. On payday, my friend, who works at the shoe store, told me the shoes were about to go on sale. But I was impatient. I bought them at full price, and three days later, the shoes were marked down twenty dollars.

There's something wrong with the order of events here. Tell the story in the order it happened: first, I saw the shoes and wanted them; second, the shoes were expensive; third, I checked the price for several weeks; fourth, I got paid; fifth, I checked the price again; sixth, my friend told me the shoes were about to go on sale; seventh, I paid full price right away; eighth, the shoes went on sale. A clear time sequence helps the reader follow your narrative.

4. **Pick a topic that is not too big.** If you try to write about too many events in one paragraph, you run the risk of being superficial. You can't describe anything well if you cover too much. This paragraph covers too much:

ALONG THESE LINES/Pearson Education Canada

Starting Grade 10 at a new high school was a difficult experience. Because my family had just moved to town, I didn't know anybody at school. On the first day of school, I sat by myself at lunch. Finally, two students at another table started a conversation with me. I thought they were just feeling sorry for me. At the end of the first week, it seemed like the whole school was talking about exciting plans for the weekend. I spent Friday and Saturday night at home, doing all kinds of things to keep my mind off my loneliness. On Monday, people casually asked, "Have a good weekend?" I lied and said, "Of course."

This paragraph would be better if it discussed one shorter time period in greater depth and detail. It could cover the first day at school, or the first lunch at school, or the first Saturday night at home alone, when the writer was doing "all kinds of things" to keep from feeling lonely.

communication at work

In a job interview, you may expect to be asked a question that begins with the phrase, "Tell me about a time when you. . . ." These kinds of questions are called *behavioural* questions, and give the interviewer some insight into how you would behave in certain situations. Your response will be told in the form of a *narrative*, with a main point, in chronological order, and with as much detail as you can possibly include. Common behavioural questions include: "Tell me about a time when you went 'above and beyond' at work," and "Tell me about a time when you had to deal with a difficult co-worker or client." Your instructor may ask you to write a paragraph in which you respond to one of these questions.

Using a Speaker's Exact Words in Narrative

Some of the examples of narrative that you have already seen have included the exact words someone said. You may want to include part of a conversation in your narrative. To do so, you need to know how to punctuate speech.

A person's exact words need quotation marks around them. If you change the words, you do not use quotation marks.

exact words: "You're being silly," he told me.
not exact words: He told me that I was being silly.

exact words: My sister said, "I'd love to go to the party."
not exact words: My sister said that she would love to go to the party.

There are a few other points to remember about punctuating a person's exact words. Once you've started quoting a person's exact words, periods and commas generally go inside the quotation marks. Here are two examples:

Richard said, "Nothing can be done."
"Be careful," my mother warned us.

When you introduce a person's exact words with phrases like "She said," or "The teacher told us," put a comma before the quotation marks. Here are two examples:

She said, "You'd better watch out."
The teacher told us, "This will be a challenging class."

If you are using a person's exact words and have other questions about punctuation, check the section on punctuation in this book.

WRITING THE NARRATIVE PARAGRAPH IN STEPS

THOUGHT LINES   ### GATHERING IDEAS: NARRATION

Finding something to write about can be the hardest part of writing a narrative paragraph because you may find it difficult to think of anything interesting or significant that you've experienced. By answering the following questions, you can gather topics for your paragraph.

EXERCISE 3

QUESTIONNAIRE FOR GATHERING NARRATIVE TOPICS

Answer the following questions as best you can. Then read your answers to a group. The members of the group should then ask you follow-up questions. Write your answers on the lines provided; the answers will add detail to your list.

Finally, ask each member of your group to circle one topic or detail on your questionnaire that could be developed into a narrative paragraph. Discuss the suggestions. Repeat this process for each member of the group.

Narrative Questionnaire

1. Did you ever have a close call? When? _____ Write four details you remember about it:

   a. _____

   b. _____

   c. _____

   d. _____

   Additional details to add after working with the group:

   _____

   _____

2. Have you ever tried out for a team? Write four details about what happened before, during, and after:

   a. _____

   b. _____

   c. _____

   d. _____

   Additional details to add after working with the group:

   _____

   _____

3. Have you ever had a day when everything went wrong? Write four details about that day:

   a. _____

   b. _____

c. _____

d. _____

Additional details to add after working with the group:

_____

_____

4. Have you ever applied for a job? Write four details about what happened when you applied for a job:

   a. _____

   b. _____

   c. _____

   d. _____

   Additional details to add after working with the group:

   _____

   _____

Freewriting for a Narrative Topic

One good way to discover something to write about is to freewrite. For example, if your instructor asks you to write a narrative paragraph about something that changed you, you might begin by freewriting.

> ### Freewriting for a Narrative Paragraph
>
> **Topic: Something That Changed Me**
>
> Something that changed me. I don't know. What changed me? Lots of things happened to me, but I can't find one that changed me. Graduating from high school? Everybody will write about that, how boring, and anyway, what was the big deal? I haven't gotten married. No big change there. Divorce. My parents' divorce really changed the whole family. A big shock to me. I couldn't believe it was happening. I was really scared. Who would I live with? They were real calm when they told me. I've never been so scared. I was too young to understand. Kept thinking they'd just get back together. They didn't. Then I got a step-mother. The year of the divorce a hard time for me. Kids suffer in divorce.

Narrowing and Selecting a Suitable Narrative Topic

After you freewrite, you can assess your writing, looking for words, phrases, or sentences that you could expand into a paragraph. The sample writing has several ideas for a narrative:

high-school graduation

learning about my parents' divorce

adjusting to a stepmother

the year of my parents' divorce

Looking for a topic that is not too big, you could use

high-school graduation

learning about my parents' divorce

Since the freewriting has already labelled graduation as a boring topic, the divorce seems to be a more attractive subject. In the freewriting, you already have some details related to the divorce; add to these by **brainstorming**. Follow-up questions and answers might include the following:

How old were you when your parents got divorced?

I was seven years old when my mom and dad divorced.

Are you an only child?

My sister was ten.

Where did you parents tell you? Did they both tell you at the same time?

They told us at breakfast, in the kitchen. Both my folks were there. I was eating toast. I remember I couldn't eat it when they both started talking. I remember a piece of toast with one bite out of it.

What reasons did they give?

They said they loved us, but they couldn't get along. They said they would always love us kids.

If you didn't understand, what did you *think* was happening?

At first I just thought they were having another fight.

Did you cry? Did they cry?

I didn't cry. My sister cried. Then I knew it was serious. I kept thinking I would have to choose which parent to live with. Then I knew I'd really hurt the one I didn't choose. I felt so much guilt about hurting one of them.

What were you thinking?

I felt ripped apart.

Questions can help you form the *point of your narrative*. After brainstorming, you can go back and survey all the details. Do they lead you to a point? Try asking yourself the questions listed at the beginning of this chapter: What did I learn? What's the meaning of this story? What's my attitude toward what happened? Did it change me? What emotion did it make me feel? Was the experience a good example of something (like unfairness, or kindness, or generosity)?

For the topic of the divorce, the details refer to a number of emotions: confusion, pain, shock, disbelief, fear, guilt. The *point* of the paragraph can't list all these emotions, but it could say

When my parents announced they were divorcing, I felt confused by all my emotions.

Now that you have a point and a good-sized list of details, you can move to the outlines stage of writing a narrative paragraph.

ALONG THESE LINES/Pearson Education Canada

EXERCISE
4

DISTINGUISHING GOOD TOPIC SENTENCES FROM BAD ONES IN NARRATION

Below are sentences. Some would make good topic sentences for a narrative paragraph. Others would not; they are too big to develop in a single paragraph, or they are so narrow they can't be developed, or they make no point about an incident or incidents. Put an *X* by the sentences that would *not* make good topic sentences.

1. _____ I bought a flat-screen television yesterday.
2. _____ I learned a lot during my co-op work placement.
3. _____ The motorist who stopped to help me on the highway taught me a valuable lesson about trust.
4. _____ My two-year battle for child custody was a nightmare.
5. _____ This is the story of the birth of my son.
6. _____ I saw true compassion when I visited the home for babies with AIDS.
7. _____ Our team's victory over the Rangers demonstrated the power of endurance.
8. _____ I've seen drugs ruin the lives of four of my friends in four years.
9. _____ The robbery took place at the deli near my house.
10. _____ I never knew what it was like to be afraid until our house was burglarized.

EXERCISE
5

DEVELOPING A TOPIC SENTENCE FROM A LIST OF DETAILS

Below are two lists of details. Each has an incomplete topic sentence. Read the details carefully; then complete each topic sentence.

1. **topic sentence:** When he _____, my brother made me feel _____.

   details: My brother always borrows my clothes.
   Sometimes I wish he wouldn't.
   Last week he took my new leather jacket.
   I went to my closet, and the jacket wasn't there.
   I wanted to wear it that night.
   Later, he came home wearing it.
   I could have punched him.
   He gave it back.
   He swore he didn't know it had a big slash in the back.
   He acted innocent.
   I told him he'd have to pay to fix the jacket.
   He still hasn't paid me.

2. **topic sentence:** An incident at a traffic light showed me_____
   _____.

   details: I was stopped at a traffic light one afternoon.
   Cars were stopped on all sides of me.
   Suddenly, a driver from the car beside me leaped out of his car.

He ran to the car in front of me.
He started screaming at the driver of the car.
The driver inside that car wouldn't open his window.
The man who was screaming began to pound on the window.
Then he started kicking the car, hard.
I watched, in terror.
I couldn't drive out of this situation.
I was stuck and afraid of being the next victim.
The crazy, shouting driver stopped.
He got back in his car.
When the light changed, he raced into the intersection.
I felt safer, but still shaken.

 DEVISING A PLAN: NARRATION

The topic of how an experience changed you has led you to a point and a list of details. You can now write a rough outline, with the *point* as the *topic sentence*. Once you have the rough outline, check it for these qualities:

Relevance: Does all the detail connect to the topic sentence?
Order: Is the detail in a clear order?
Development: Does the outline need more detail? Is the detail specific enough?

Your revised outline might look like the following:

> ### An Outline for a Narrative Paragraph
>
> **topic sentence:** When my parents announced that they were divorcing, I felt confused by all my emotions.
>
> **details:**
>
> background of the narrative
>
> I was seven when my mom and dad divorced.
>
> My sister was ten.
>
> Both my folks were there.
>
> They told us at breakfast, in the kitchen.
>
> I was eating toast.
>
> I remember I couldn't eat anything when they started talking.
>
> I remember a piece of toast with one bite out of it.
>
> story of the divorce announcement
>
> My parents were very calm when they told us.
>
> They said they loved us but couldn't get along.
>
> They said they would always love us kids.
>
> my reactions at each stage
>
> It was a big shock to me.
>
> I couldn't believe it was happening.
>
> At first I just thought they were having another fight.

ALONG THESE LINES/Pearson Education Canada

> I was too young to understand.
>
> I didn't cry.
>
> My sister cried.
>
> Then I knew it was serious.
>
> I kept thinking I would have to choose which parent to live with.
>
> I knew I'd really hurt the one I didn't choose.
>
> I felt so much guilt about hurting one of them.
>
> I was ripped apart.

Once you have a revised outline, you're ready to move on to the rough lines stage of the narrative paragraph.

EXERCISE
6

FINDING DETAILS THAT ARE OUT OF ORDER IN A NARRATIVE OUTLINE

The following outlines have details that are out of order. Put them in the correct order by numbering the first event with a 1, and so on.

1. **topic sentence:** Renewing my driver's licence was a frustrating experience.

   details: _____ I got in the shortest line.
   _____ The office was packed with people.
   _____ When I got through the crowd, I went straight to the information desk.
   _____ The clerk at the information desk just gave me a form and said, "Get in line."
   _____ After an hour, I got to the head of the line.
   _____ I gave my form to the man behind the counter.
   _____ I waited in line for an hour.
   _____ The man behind the counter said, "You're in the wrong line."

2. **topic sentence:** Yesterday I saw something that showed me the good side of people.

   details: _____ My traffic lane was at a standstill, so I had time to look around.
   _____ I was driving down the highway.
   _____ As I waited for the traffic to move, I saw a ragged man by the side of the road, holding a sign.
   _____ The sign said, "Will Work for Food."
   _____ I saw a car pull off the road, right next to the man.
   _____ The ragged man shrank back, as if he were afraid the car would hit him.
   _____ The driver motioned to the homeless man through the open window.
   _____ The driver of the car rolled down his window on the passenger side.
   _____ The homeless man crept over.
   _____ The driver handed him a big bag of food from Burger King.

EXERCISE 7

RECOGNIZING IRRELEVANT DETAILS IN A NARRATIVE OUTLINE

Below are two outlines. One of them has details that aren't relevant to the topic sentence. Cross out the details that don't fit.

1. **topic sentence:** I saw another side of my sister when her husband was in a car accident.

   details: My sister Julia is usually very helpless.
   She lets her husband Leo make all the decisions.
   She doesn't like to go anywhere without him.
   Then one day she got a call from the hospital.
   Leo had been in a car accident.
   He was in critical condition.
   Julia suddenly became very strong.
   She calmly told us she was going to the hospital to wait.
   She went right up to the desk at the emergency room and asked to see Leo.
   When the nurses tried to make her wait, she demanded to see him.
   She stayed by Leo's side for twenty-four hours.
   The only time she left was to talk to his doctors.
   She was very firm and businesslike with the doctors.
   She questioned them about the right treatment for Leo.
   She got the name of a famous surgeon.
   She called the surgeon and got him to come to the hospital.
   Today, Leo says she saved his life.

2. **topic sentence:** The most embarrassing thing I've ever experienced happened to me in the supermarket checkout line.

   details: I always shop with a list of what I need to buy.
   The cashier was running the items through the scanner.
   Our store uses scanners now instead of cash registers.
   When he was finished, he said, "That'll be $23.50."
   I reached into my wallet for the money.
   All I found was a ten-dollar bill.
   I searched frantically through all the folds of my wallet.
   There was nothing but the ten-dollar bill.
   I was *sure* I had put a twenty in my wallet when I left for the store.
   Then I remembered—I had spent the twenty at the gas station.
   I whispered to the cashier, "Oops! I didn't bring enough money."
   He just looked at me.
   The groceries were already bagged.
   I had to take them out of the bags and get rid of items that added up to $13.50.
   Meanwhile, the people in line behind me wanted to kill me.
   At that moment, I wished they had.

ROUGH LINES **DRAFTING AND REVISING: NARRATION**

After you have a revised outline for your narration paragraph, you can begin working on a rough draft of the paragraph. As you write your first draft, you can combine some of the short sentences of the outline. Once you have a draft, you can check it for places you'd like to improve. The list below may help you check your draft.

CHECKLIST FOR REVISING THE DRAFT OF A NARRATIVE PARAGRAPH

✓ Is my narrative vivid?
✓ Are the details clear and specific?
✓ Does the topic sentence fit all the details?
✓ Are the details written in a clear order?
✓ Do the transitions make the narrative easy to follow?
✓ Have I made my point?

Revising for Sharper Details

A good idea for a narrative can be made better if you revise for sharper detail. In the following paragraph, the underlined words and phrases could be revised to create better details. In the next example, see how the second draft has more vivid details than the first draft.

First Draft: Details Are Dull

A woman at the movies showed me just how rude and selfish people can be. It all started when I was in line with <u>a lot</u> of other people. We had been waiting <u>a long time</u> to buy our tickets. We were outside, and it <u>wasn't pleasant</u>. We were impatient because time was running out and the movie was about to start. Some people were <u>making remarks</u>, and <u>others were pushing</u>. Then <u>a woman cut</u> to the front of the line. The cashier at the ticket window <u>told</u> the woman there was a line and she would have to go to the end of it. The woman <u>said she didn't want to wait because her son didn't want to miss the beginning of the movie.</u>

Second Draft: Better Details

A woman at the movies showed me just how rude and selfish people can be. It all started when I was in line with <u>forty or fifty other people.</u> We had been waiting to buy our tickets for <u>twenty minutes.</u> We were outside, <u>where the temperature was about 30 degrees, and it looked like rain.</u> We were all getting impatient because time was running out and the movie was about to start. <u>I heard two people mutter about how ridiculous the wait was, and someone else kept saying, "Let's go!" The man directly behind me kept pushing me, and each new person at the end of the line pushed the whole line forward, against the ticket window. Then a woman with a loud voice and a large purse thrust her purse and her body in front of the ticket window.</u> The cashier <u>politely</u> told the woman there was a line and she had to go to the end of it. But the woman answered <u>indignantly. "Oh no," she said. "I'm with my son Mickey. And Mickey really wants to see *The Phantom Menace*. And he hates to miss the first part of any movie. So I can't wait. I have got to have those tickets now."</u>

Checking the Topic Sentence

Sometimes you think you have a good idea and a good topic sentence and details, but when you write the draft of the paragraph, you realize the topic sentence doesn't quite fit all the details. When that happens, you can either revise the details or rewrite the topic sentence.

In the following paragraph, the topic sentence (underlined) doesn't quite fit all the details, so it needs to be rewritten.

> <u>I didn't know what to do when a crime occurred in front of my house.</u> At 9:00 p.m. I was sitting in my living room, watching television, when I heard what sounded like a crash outside. At first I thought it was a garbage can that had fallen over. Then I heard another crash and a shout. I ran to the window, and I looked out into the dark. I couldn't see anything because the street light in front of my house was broken. But I heard at least two voices, and they sounded angry and threatening. I heard another voice, and it sounded like someone moaning. I was afraid. I ran to the telephone. I was going to call 911, but then I froze in fear. What if the police came and people got arrested? Would the suspects find out I was the one who had called the police? Would they come after me? Would I be a witness at a trial? I didn't want to get involved. So I just stood behind the curtain, peeking out and listening. Pretty soon the shouting stopped, but I still heard sounds like hitting. I couldn't stand it anymore. I called the police. When they came, they found a young teenager, badly beaten, in the street. They said my call may have saved his life.

The paragraph above has good details, but the story has more of a point than "I didn't know what to do." The person telling the story did, finally, do something. A better topic sentence would cover the whole story. Here is the topic sentence rewritten:

> I finally found the courage to do the right thing when a crime occurred in front of my house.

| EXERCISE 8 | COMBINING SENTENCES IN A DRAFT OF A NARRATIVE |

The following paragraph contains some short, choppy sentences, which are underlined. Wherever you see two or more underlined sentences clustered next to each other, combine them into one clear, smooth sentence. Write your revised version of the paragraph in the spaces above the lines.

Getting lost in the city gave me my first taste of panic. When I was fourteen, I convinced my mother I was old enough to travel to my aunt's apartment in the city. My mother gave me clear directions. She wrote the address on a slip of paper. She also drew a map of the streets I had to cross once I got off the bus. I had been to my aunt's place many times with my family. I was sure I would have no problems. When I got off the bus, I began walking confidently toward my aunt's street. However, after I had walked a few blocks, nothing looked familiar. I convinced myself I had to keep walking until I found a store or restaurant I knew. I walked farther. Everything seemed strange. The streets began to look unfriendly, even dangerous. I felt the people were staring at me. They were staring with hostility. Desperate, I approached a stranger. I asked him for directions. He looked at me for a moment. He laughed. He told me I had gotten off at the wrong bus stop. My aunt's street was fifteen blocks away. I felt relieved. I felt foolish. I felt both emotions about my mistakes and my panic.

| EXERCISE 9 | ADDING BETTER DETAILS TO THE DRAFT OF A NARRATIVE |

The following paragraph has some details that could be more vivid. Rewrite the paragraph in the lines below, replacing the underlined details with more vivid words, phrases, or sentences.

Roberto showed he is a great athlete when he lost the wrestling match. The match had been very close, but someone had to lose, and that someone turned out to be Roberto. After the match, the winner, Tom, was getting all the attention. He was acting very full of himself. Roberto was just keeping to himself. Roberto looked hurt. His eyes were sad. Nevertheless, he went to Tom and shook hands. Tom looked mean and didn't say much. Roberto, on the other hand, said the right thing. Then Roberto walked away, his head held high.

rewrite:

_____

_____

_____

_____

_____

_____

_____

_____

_____

EXERCISE **10**	**WRITING A BETTER TOPIC SENTENCE FOR A NARRATIVE**

The following paragraphs could use better topic sentences. (In each paragraph, the current topic sentence is underlined.) Read each paragraph carefully, then write a new topic sentence for it in the lines provided.

   1. <u>My visit to my old school was interesting.</u> I hadn't been back to Miller Road Public School since Grade 5, so I expected it to be changed. I just didn't expect it to be so drastically changed. When I entered the schoolyard, I saw that the playground that had once been full of trees and bright green grass was now a muddy, empty lot. All the trees were gone. The school, once a new, golden brick building, was sooty and decrepit. Several of the windows were broken. I walked into the entrance hall and saw graffiti all over the walls. The school was silent. Wandering the halls, I peeped into the classrooms. I saw rickety desks and blackboards so faded you could hardly see the words chalked on them. Then I found Room 110, my old Grade 1 classroom. I went in and sat down at one of the desks, and the room that had once seemed so big and so exciting suddenly seemed small and sad.

new topic sentence:_____

_____

   2. <u>I had dinner with my family last week.</u> My two younger brothers, Simon and David, started it by fighting over who was going to sit in the seat next to my father. When we all sat down to eat, my sister provoked my mother by complaining, "Chicken again? All we eat is chicken." Of course, my mother jumped right in and said if my sister wanted to take the responsibility for planning menus and cooking

ALONG THESE LINES/Pearson Education Canada

meals, she could go right ahead. Meanwhile, my father was telling David not to kick Simon under the table, and Simon was spitting mashed potatoes at David. I got irritated and said I wished that once, just once, we could eat dinner like a normal family. So then my father and I had an argument about what I meant by a normal family. By that time, Simon had spilled his milk on the floor, and my mother had caught my sister feeding chicken to the dog. We all left the dinner table in a bad mood.

new topic sentence:_____

_____

Using Transitions Effectively in Narration

When you tell a story, you have to be sure that your reader can follow you as you move through the steps of your story. One way to make your story easier to follow is to use *transitions*, words that connect one event to another. Most of the transitions in narration have to do with time. Following is a list of transitions that writers often use in writing narration.

INFOBOX **TRANSITIONS FOR A NARRATIVE PARAGRAPH**

after, again, always, at first, at last, at once, at the same time, before, during, finally, first (second, etc.), frequently, immediately, in the meantime, later, later on, meanwhile, next, now, soon, soon after, still, suddenly, then, until, when, while

The Draft

Below is a revised draft of the paragraph on divorce. It has been revised several ways, using the checklist. Some ideas from the outline have been combined. The details have been put in order and transitions (underlined) have been added. Exact words of dialogue have been used to add vivid details.

A Draft of a Narrative Paragraph (*transitions are underlined*)

When my parents announced that they were divorcing, I felt confused by all my emotions. At the time of their announcement, I was seven and my sister was ten. Both my folks were there to tell us. They told us at breakfast, in the kitchen. I was eating toast, but I remember I couldn't eat anything when they started talking. I remember a piece of toast with one bite taken out of it. My parents were very calm when they told us. "We love both you kids very much," my father said, "but your mother and I aren't getting along." They said they would always love us. The announcement was such a shock to me that I couldn't believe it was happening. At first, I just

(continued)

ALONG THESE LINES/Pearson Education Canada

thought they were having another fight. Because I was too young to understand, I didn't cry. <u>Suddenly</u>, my sister started to cry, <u>and then</u> I knew it
was serious. I kept thinking I would have to choose which parent to live with.
I knew I'd really hurt the one I didn't choose, so I felt so much guilt about
hurting one of them. I felt torn apart.

EXERCISE 11

RECOGNIZING TRANSITIONS IN A NARRATIVE PARAGRAPH

Underline the transitions in the following paragraph.

The salesman who called last night was a master of manipulation.
He first asked for me by name. He didn't ask for the head of the house,
which is always a sure sign that the call is a sales pitch. After confirming
I was Mr. Johnson, he told me he was checking on my newspaper
delivery. Then he asked if I had been getting my paper regularly and on
time. When I said yes, he quickly added that I could get a better deal by
extending my subscription, right away, at a discounted rate for long-term
customers. By that time, I was getting tired of what I now knew was a
sales call. Just before I tried to end the conversation, the salesman offered
me a chance to win a trip to the Bahamas. Suddenly, he had my interest
again. While I listened to him explain the contest, I seriously thought about
extending my newspaper subscription. Finally, I even thanked him for the
information about the vacation contest. Maybe the next time a salesman
calls, I'll first ask him about any contests and my real chances of winning.

EXERCISE 12

ADDING THE RIGHT TRANSITIONS TO A NARRATIVE PARAGRAPH

In the following paragraph, circle the correct transition in each of the pairs.

I ran into trouble when I was taking my art history test yesterday;
(later/at once) I solved my problem. I was doing fine (after/at first),
completing the matching questions about the painters and their paintings.
(Then/Still), I ran into five short-answer questions about the Impressionists, and my mind went blank. I knew I had studied the material, but
I couldn't remember a thing. Who or what were the Impressionists?
I froze, and the harder I tried to remember, the less confident I felt. I
decided to go on to the other questions on the test (before/while) I lost my
confidence. I took a deep breath and completed the rest of the test, ignor-
ing the five questions about the Impressionists and focusing on what I
knew about the remaining questions. (Soon after/Finally) I had done that,

> I felt much calmer, for I had found the rest of the test fairly easy. I began to feel confident (frequently/again). (Before/Suddenly), all that I had studied about the Impressionists came back to me.

PROOFREADING AND POLISHING: NARRATION

As you prepare the final copy of the narrative paragraph, make any minor changes in word choice or transitions that will refine your writing. Below is the final copy of the narrative paragraph on divorce. Notice these changes in the final version:

- The draft version used both formal and informal words such as "folks," "parents," "dad," and "father."
- The final version uses only "parents" and "father."
- A few details have been added.
- A few details have been changed.
- A transition has been added.

> ### A Final Version of a Narrative Paragraph (*changes from the draft are underlined*)
>
> When my parents announced that they were divorcing, I felt confused by all my emotions. At the time of the announcement, I was seven, and my sister was ten. Both <u>my parents</u> were there to tell us. They told us at breakfast, in the kitchen. I was eating toast, but I remember I couldn't eat anything when they started talking. <u>In fact,</u> I remember <u>staring at</u> a piece of toast with one bite taken out of it. My parents were very calm when they told us. "We both love you very much," my father said. "But your mother and I aren't getting along." They said they would always love us. The announcement was such a shock to me that I couldn't believe it was happening. At first, I just thought they were having another fight. Because I was too young to understand, I didn't cry. Suddenly, my sister started to cry, and then I knew it was serious. I kept thinking I would have to choose which parent to live with. I knew I'd really hurt the one I didn't choose, so I felt <u>terrible</u> guilt about hurting one of them. I felt torn apart.

Before you prepare the final copy of your narrative paragraph, check your latest draft for errors in spelling and punctuation, and for any errors made in typing or recopying.

EXERCISE 13 — PROOFREADING TO PREPARE THE FINAL VERSION

Following are two narrative paragraphs with the kind of errors that are easy to overlook when you prepare the final version of an assignment. Correct the errors, writing above the lines. There are ten errors in the first paragraph and seven errors in the second paragraph.

1.   When my girl friend tossed my ring out the window, I knew she was

not ready to forgive me one more time. It all started on Saturday, at MacDonald's, when I ran into my girlfriend Lakisha. I could see she was'nt in a good mood. As soon as we sat down, she asked me about Yvonne. A girl I've been seeing behind Lakisha's back. Well, of course I lied and said "Yvonne means nothing to me." However, Lakisha said she seen me and Yvonne at the mall the night before, and we looked like was rommanticly involved. I asked, "How could you tell?" Well, naturally that was the wrong thing to say since I was admitting Yvonne and I had been together. After I asked that stupid question, Lakisha took my ring off her finger and tossed that ring right threw the window at McDonald's.

2.   My son Scott's first day at preschool was an emotional one for me. i was up early on that day, planning his cloths and worrying about his fears and tears when I dropped him off at his first school. However, when I woke Scott up, I tried to be cheerful. I smiled and acted as if he were about to begin an exciting adventure. "Today is the day you get to make friends and have some fun," I said. Scott didn't seem to unhappy or reluctant as he ate breakfast. He was pleased when I let him wear him faverite baseball cap and shorts. In the car on the way to school, Scott sat quietly, but I could hardly hold back my tears. I was picturing my little boy along, afraid, crieing in a corner of the classroom. Yet when I handed him over to the friendly teacher, Scott did not protest. He took the teacher's hand and walked, wide-eyed, to a new world.

Lines of Detail: A Walk-Through Assignment

Write a paragraph about an incident in your life that embarrassed (or amused, or frightened, or saddened, or angered) you. In writing the paragraph, follow these steps:

Step 1: Begin by freewriting. Then read your freewriting, looking for both the details and the focus of your paragraph.

Step 2: Brainstorm for more details. Then write all the freewriting and the brainstorming as a list.

Step 3: Survey your list. Write a topic sentence that makes a point about the details.

Step 4: Write an outline. As you write the outline, check that your details fit the topic sentence and are in a clear order. As you revise your outline, add details where they are needed.

Step 5: In the rough lines stage, write and revise a draft of your paragraph. Revise until your details are specific and in a clear order, and your transitions are smooth. Combine any sentences that are short and choppy. Add a speaker's exact words if they will make the details more specific.

Step 6: In preparing the final copy, check for punctuation, spelling, and word choice.

Writing Your Own Narrative Paragraph

When you write on any of the following topics, be sure to work through the stages of the writing process in preparing your narrative paragraph.

1. Write about some event you saw that you'll never forget. Begin by freewriting. Then read your freewriting, looking for both the details and the focus of your paragraph.

   If your instructor agrees, ask a writing partner or a group to (a) listen to you read your freewriting, (b) help you focus it, (c) help you add details by asking questions.

2. Write a narrative paragraph about how you met your boyfriend or girlfriend, your husband or wife, or your best friend. Start by listing as many details as you can, and, if your instructor agrees, ask a writing partner or a group to (a) survey your list of details, (b) ask questions that will lead you to more details.

3. Write about a time when you got what you wanted. Start by listing as many details as you can, and, if your instructor agrees, ask a writing partner or a group to (a) survey your list of details, and (b) ask questions that will lead you to more details.

4. Interview an older family member or friend. Ask him or her to tell you an interesting story about the past. Ask questions as the person speaks. Take notes. If you have a tape recorder, you can tape the interview, but take notes as well.

   When you've finished the interview, review the information with the person you've interviewed. Would he or she like to add anything? If you wish, ask follow-up questions.

   Next, on your own, find a point to the story. Work through the stages of the writing process to turn the interview into a narrative paragraph.

WRITING FROM READING: NARRATION

One Caring Teacher Set Things Right
Richard Wagamese

Richard Wagamese is a member of the Ojibway Nation in northwestern Ontario. A successful journalist, he began writing novels in 1993. His latest novel, Ragged Company, *was published in the Summer of 2008.*

Before you read this selection, consider these questions:

What are your most vivid childhood memories?

Who has been your most memorable teacher, and why?

Have you ever experienced an 'act of kindness' that has changed your life?

I write in the dimness of morning. Outside, the world is a shape shifter. Light eases things back into definition, their boundaries called from shadow, hardening, forming, beginning to hold again and the land shrugs itself into wakefulness. Purple moving upward into pearl grey.

It's good to be up and working at this time. I can feel the power of life and light around me and as the letters form upon the screen, race each other to the sudden halt of punctuation, I understand where this need to write comes from.

palpable: tangible, obvious

communion: a feeling of connectedness

It comes from this **palpable** mystery. This first light breaking over everything, altering things, arranging them, setting them down into patterns again and tucking shadow back into folds behind the trees. It comes from the need of **communion,** of joining with that Great Mystery, that force, that energy.

I always wanted to write. There isn't a time I can recall when I didn't carry the desire to frame things, order things upon a page, sort them out, make sense of them. But in the beginning, learning to write was a test, a challenge, an ordeal.

I was the only Indian kid in a mill town school in northern Ontario in the early 1960s. It was a different world then, harder maybe, colder and the idea of Indians was set like concrete, particularly in the **parochial,** working class confines of a saw mill town 200 miles from nowhere.

parochial: narrowly restricted perspective

The school was set between the railroad tracks and the pipeline in a hollow between hills above the mill. We sat with the thick **sulphur** smell coming through the windows and the **spume** of the stacks on the horizon above the trees. In the classroom, I was ignored, set down near the back and never called upon for anything.

sulphur: a chemical smelling of rotten eggs

spume: column of smoke

lethargic: listless, tired

They said I was slow, a difficult learner, far too quiet for a kid and **lethargic.**

They said I hadn't much hope for a future and after they held me back a year, they just let me be. But I wanted to learn. I was hungry for it and I went to school every day eager and excited about the things we were given to learn.

But I couldn't see. No one had spent enough time with me to learn that.

The reason I was slow to pick things up was that I could never see the board. Even at the front of the room where they put me so they could keep a better eye on me, I could never **discern** the writing on the blackboard. Everything I learned I learned by memory, by listening hard to what the teacher said and memorizing it.

discern: to recognize

When I was adopted in 1965, I was sent to my first big school in a southern Ontario town called Bradford, just north of Toronto.

There were hundreds of kids in that school and it seemed like I walked in waves of them on my way to school that first day. Walking through those big glass doors was terrifying for me.

I was in Grade 3 and my teacher wanted to introduce me and she asked me to write my name on the blackboard for the other kids to read. I went to the board, leaned close to it, squinted and began to write. I heard snickers at the first letter and open laughter when I'd finished.

I'd written my name upside down and backwards. To the rest of my classmates it was odd, strange and hilarious but it was how I'd learned and I felt the weight of their laughter like stones. Walking back to my seat that day I felt ashamed, stupid and terribly alone.

But I had a teacher who cared. She walked me down to the nurse's station herself and waited while I got my eyes tested.

astigmatism: a condition that results in blurred vision

Astigmatism, the nurse told her. Terrible astigmatism. Then she listened closely to me when I explained why my writing was wrongly shaped.

I taught myself to write by squinting back over my shoulder. When we were taught to write in script, I wasn't given any teacher attention, wasn't offered any help in forming the letters.

ALONG THESE LINES/Pearson Education Canada

mimicked: to have copied

skewed: crooked, off-centre

penmanship: handwriting

So I watched the kid behind me and I **mimicked** what I saw on my own page. Unfortunately, what I saw was upside down and backwards and that was how I taught myself to write. I could spell everything correctly but it was all **skewed**.

Well, I got glasses very shortly after that and my world changed. Once I could see what was written on the board, my ability to learn accelerated and I graduated Grade 3 with straight As. Especially in **penmanship**.

See, for that teacher I wasn't an Indian. I was a kid in need. So she took the time to show me how to write properly. Every day, before and after school, she and I sat at a desk and we worked through the primary writing books. I shaped letters time after time after time until I gradually unlearned the awkward process I'd taught myself.

Like life, unlearning something was a lot harder than learning it. I struggled with breaking down my method and at times it seemed I would never get it right. But I persisted with the help and encouragement of that teacher and I learned how to write in the right direction. But I still shape my Gs and Ds wrong today. I still write them back to front after all this time.

I write on a keyboard these days. But there isn't a time when I set a pen to paper that I don't remember learning how to write and what it took to get me there.

See, there's a story behind every difference. There's a reason we become the people we become and it's having the courage and consideration to hear those stories that allows us to help each other. Sometimes, life turns us upside down and backwards. It's caring that gets us back on our feet again and pointed in the right direction.

UNDERSTANDING "ONE CARING TEACHER SET THINGS RIGHT"

1. The first few paragraphs of "One Caring Teacher Set Things Right" describe the pre-dawn contrast between light and dark. Why do you think Wagamese prefers to write at this time?

2. According to Wagamese, why does he feel the need to write?

3. What two meanings do "upside down and backwards" have for the narrative?

WRITING FROM READING "ONE CARING TEACHER SET THINGS RIGHT"

When you write on any of the following topics, be sure to work through the stages of the writing process.

1. Write a narrative paragraph about a time when you helped someone who was in trouble.

2. Write a story that describes your most vivid school-related memory.

3. Many people have had a teacher who has helped shape their lives, either positively or negatively. Write a narrative paragraph that describes what that teacher did to impact your life.

CHAPTER 6
Process

"Logic takes care of itself; all we have to do is to look and see how it does it."

~ LUDWIG WITTGENSTEIN

▼ LUDWIG WITTGENSTEIN WAS A TWENTIETH-CENTURY AUSTRIAN PHILOSOPHER.

WHAT IS PROCESS?

A **process** paragraph explains how to do something or describes how something happens or is done. When you tell the reader how to do something (a *directional process*), you speak directly to the reader and give him or her clear, specific instructions about performing some activity. Your purpose is to explain an activity so that a reader can do it. For example, you may have to leave instructions telling a new employee how to close the cash register or use the copy machine.

When you describe how something happens (an *informational process*), your purpose is to explain an activity, but not to tell a reader how to do it. For example, you may have to explain how a boxer trains for a fight or how the special effects for a film were created. Instead of speaking directly to the reader, an informational process speaks about *I*, *he*, *she*, *we*, *they*, or about a person by his or her name. A directional process uses *you* or, in the way it gives directions, the word *you* is understood.

A Process Involves Steps in Time Order

Whether a process is directional or informational, it describes something that is done in steps, and these steps are in a specific order: a **time order**. The process can involve steps that are followed in minutes, hours, days, weeks, months, or

ALONG THESE LINES/Pearson Education Canada

even years. For example, the steps in changing a tire may take minutes, whereas the steps taken to lose ten pounds may take months.

The important thing to remember is that a process involves steps that *must follow a certain order*, not just a range of activities that can be placed in any order. This sentence *signals a process*:

> Learning to search the internet is easy if you follow a few simple directions. (*Using the internet involves following steps in order; that is, you cannot search before you turn the machine on.*)

The following sentence *does not signal a process*:

> There are several ways to get a person to like you. (*Each way is separate; there is no time sequence here.*)

Telling a person, in a conversation, how to do something or how something is done gives you the opportunity to add important points that you may have forgotten or to throw in details that you may have left out. Your listener can ask questions if he or she doesn't understand you. Writing a process, however, is more difficult. Your reader isn't there to stop you, to ask you to explain further, to question you. In writing a process, you must be organized and clear.

Hints for Writing a Process Paragraph

1. **In choosing a topic, find an activity you know well.** If you write about something familiar to you, you'll have a clearer paragraph.

2. **Choose a topic that includes steps that must be done in a specific time sequence.**

not this:	I find lots of things to do on a rainy day.
but this:	I have a plan for cleaning out my closet.

3. **Choose a topic that is fairly small.** A complicated process cannot be covered well in one paragraph. If your topic is too big, the paragraph can become vague, incomplete, or boring.

too big:	There are many stages in the parliamentary process of a bill before it becomes a law.
smaller and manageable:	Willpower and support were the most important elements in my struggle to quit smoking.

4. **Write a topic sentence that makes a point.** Your topic sentence should do more than announce. Like the topic sentence for any paragraph, it should have a point. As you plan the steps of your process and gather details, ask yourself some questions: What point do I want to make about this process? Is the process hard? Is it easy? Does the process require certain tools? Does the process require certain skills, like organization, patience, endurance?

an announcement:	This paragraph is about how to change the oil in your car.
a topic sentence:	You don't have to be a mechanic to change the oil in your car, but you do have to take a few simple precautions.

5. **Include all the steps.** If you are explaining a process, you are writing for someone who does not know the process as well as you do. So keep in mind that what seems clear or simple to you may not be clear or simple to the reader. Be sure to tell what is needed before the process starts, too. For instance, what ingredients are needed to cook the dish? Or what tools are needed to assemble the toy?

6. **Put the steps in the right order.** Nothing is more irritating to a reader than trying to follow directions that skip back and forth. Careful planning, drafting, and revision can help you get the time sequence right.

7. **Be specific in the details and steps.** To be sure you have sufficient detail and clear steps, keep your reader in mind. Put yourself in the reader's place. Could you follow your own directions or understand your steps?

If you remember that a process explains, you will focus on being clear. Now that you know the purpose and strategies of writing a process, you can begin the thought lines step of writing one.

communication at work

Process is everywhere! Be sure to make yourself aware of your school's fire evacuation procedures; here is the procedure used at Simon Fraser University (2007) in Vancouver:

If You Discover a Fire in the Building

1. Immediately sound the fire alarm by activating the nearest fire alarm pull station.
2. Alert people in the immediate area.
3. Dial (9) 911 (Vancouver Fire Department):
   a.   state your name
   b.   state that a fire is in progress and give address
   c.   provide information about the fire (i.e., what floor, how fast the fire is spreading, people trapped, etc.)
4. Leave the building using the nearest exit. DO NOT USE THE ELEVATOR.

| EXERCISE **1** | **RECOGNIZING GOOD TOPIC SENTENCES FOR PROCESS PARAGRAPHS** |

If a sentence is a good topic sentence for a process paragraph, put *OK* on the line provided. If a sentence has a problem, label that sentence with one of these letters:

A This is an **announcement**; it makes no point.

B This sentence covers a topic that is **too big** for one paragraph.

NS This sentence describes a topic that does **not require steps**.

ALONG THESE LINES/Pearson Education Canada

1. _____ There is a simple plan for finding the best deals on car insurance.
2. _____ How I learned to clean fish is the subject of this paragraph.
3. _____ There are several reasons for updating your home computer.
4. _____ The process of building a house is challenging.
5. _____ Selling your car for the best price means knowing how to clean it to look its best.
6. _____ This paper shows the method of refinishing an antique chair.
7. _____ Civil rights in Canada evolved in several stages.
8. _____ There are many things to remember when you enter college.
9. _____ If you learn just a few trade secrets, you can install your own hardwood floors.
10. _____ Fred learned the right way to apply for a car loan.

EXERCISE
2

INCLUDING NECESSARY MATERIALS IN A PROCESS

Below are three possible topics for a process paragraph. For each topic, work with a partner or a group and list the items (materials, ingredients, tools, utensils, supplies) that the reader will have to gather before he or she begins the process. When you've finished the exercise, check your lists with another group to see if you've missed any items.

1. **topic:** making and packing a school lunch for a six-year-old

   needed items: _____

   _____

   _____

2. **topic:** cooking a hamburger on a barbecue

   needed items: _____

   _____

   _____

3. **topic:** preparing a package for mailing (the package contains a breakable item)

   needed items: _____

   _____

   _____

WRITING THE PROCESS PARAGRAPH IN STEPS

 ### GATHERING IDEAS: PROCESS

The easiest way to start writing a process paragraph is to pick a small topic, one that you can cover well in one paragraph. Then you can gather ideas by listing or freewriting or both.

If you decided to write about how to find the right apartment, you might begin by freewriting.

Then you might check your freewriting, looking for details that have to do with the process of finding an apartment. You can underline those details, as in the example that follows.

> ### Freewriting for a Process Paragraph
>
> #### Topic: Finding the Right Apartment
>
> You have to <u>look around. Don't pick the first apartment you see.</u> Sean did that, and he wound up with a dump. <u>Look at a bunch.</u> But <u>not too many,</u> or you'll get confused. <u>The lease,</u> too. <u>Check it carefully.</u> <u>Do you pay the hydro?</u> <u>Do you want a one-bedroom?</u> <u>Friends can help</u> if they know of any nice apartments. I found my place that way. Maybe somebody you know lives in <u>a good neighbourhood.</u> <u>A convenient location can be more expensive.</u> But <u>can save you money on transportation.</u>

Next, you can put what you've underlined into a list, in correct time sequence:

before the search
>
> do you want a one-bedroom?
>
> friends can help

a good neighbourhood
>
> convenient location can be more expensive
>
> can save you money on transportation

during the search
>
> look around
>
> don't pick the first apartment you see
>
> look at a bunch
>
> but not too many

after the search
>
> check the lease carefully
>
> do you pay the hydro?

Check the list. Are some details missing? Yes. A reader might ask, "What other ways (besides asking friends) can help you find apartments? What else should you do before you search? When you're looking at apartments, what should you be looking for? What questions should you ask? After the search, how do you decide which apartment is best? And what, besides the hydro, should you check on the lease?" Answers to questions like these can give you the details needed to write a clear and interesting directional process.

Writing a Topic Sentence for a Process Paragraph

Freewriting and a list can now help you focus your paragraph by identifying the point of your process. You already know what the subject of your paragraph is: finding the right apartment. But what's the point? Is it easy to find the right apartment? Is it difficult? What does it take to find the right apartment?

Maybe a topic sentence could be

> Finding the right apartment takes planning and careful investigation.

Once you have a topic sentence, you can think about adding details that explain your topic sentence and can begin the outlines stage of writing.

EXERCISE **3**	**FINDING THE STEPS OF A PROCESS IN FREEWRITING**

Read the following freewriting, then reread it, looking for all the words, phrases, or sentences that have to do with steps. Underline all those items. Once you've underlined the freewriting, put what you've underlined into a list, in a correct time sequence.

How I Found a Great Gift for My Father: Freewriting

Birthdays are tough. How do you find the right gift? Especially for a parent. Usually I give my dad a tie or a sweater, something very ordinary which he stashes in the back of his closet. This year he was really surprised when he saw his present draped across the couch. It was a small blanket, called a "throw," with a pattern of hockey jerseys and team names. It began when I decided to get my father something he would really use. I started to observe his habits and interests. He gardened; he played cards with some friends. Hockey was his favourite sport on television. He always fell asleep watching it. He would curl up as if he were cold. Now I had some gift ideas. I went to the stores to see if there were any new gardening gadgets, accessories for card tables, or books on hockey. Nothing appealed to me. Finally I found the perfect gift. I bought what I knew he would use and like.

_____

_____

_____

_____

_____

_____

_____

_____

 **DEVISING A PLAN: PROCESS**

Using the freewriting and topic sentence on finding the right apartment, you could make an outline. Then you could revise it, checking the topic sentence and list of details, improving them where you think they could be better. A revised outline of finding an apartment follows.

An Outline for a Process Paragraph

topic sentence: Finding the apartment you want takes planning and careful investigation.

details:

before the search

Decide what you want.

Ask yourself, "Do I want a one-bedroom?" and "What can I afford?"

A convenient location can be more expensive.

It can also save you money on transportation.

Friends can help you with names of nice apartments.

Maybe somebody you know lives in a good neighbourhood.

Check the classified advertisements in the newspapers.

Look around.

during the search

Don't pick the first apartment you see.

Look at several.

But don't look at too many.

Check the cleanness, safety, plumbing, and appliances of each one.

Ask the manager about the laundry room, additional storage, parking facilities, and maintenance policies.

after the search

Compare the two best places you saw.

Consider the price, location, and condition of the apartments.

Check the leases carefully.

Check the cost of monthly hydro.

Check the requirements for first and last month's rent deposits.

The following checklist may help you to revise an outline for your own process paragraph.

CHECKLIST   FOR REVISING A PROCESS OUTLINE

✓ Is my topic sentence focused on some point about the process?

✓ Does it cover the whole process?

✓ Do I have all the steps?

✓ Are they in the right order?

✓ Have I explained clearly?

✓ Do I need better details?

EXERCISE **4**	**REVISING THE TOPIC SENTENCE IN A PROCESS OUTLINE**

The following topic sentence doesn't cover all the steps of the process. Read the outline several times; then write a topic sentence that covers all the steps of the process and has a point.

topic sentence: If you want to save money at the supermarket, write a list at home.

details: First, leave a pencil and a piece of paper near your refrigerator.
Each time you use the last of some item, like milk, write that item on the paper.
Before you go to the store, read what's written on the paper and add to the list.
Then rewrite the list, organizing it according to the layout of your store.
Put all the dairy products together on the list, for instance.
Put all the fresh fruits and vegetables together.
At the store, begin with the first items on your list.
Move purposefully through the aisles.
Keep your eyes on your list so you don't see all kinds of goodies that you don't need.
Pass by the gourmet items.
Keep going through each aisle, buying only what is on your list.
At the end of the last aisle, check what's in your cart against your list.
Get any item you forgot.
When you stand in the checkout line, avoid looking at the overpriced and tempting snacks that fill the area.

revised topic sentence:

_____

_____

EXERCISE **5**	**REVISING THE ORDER OF STEPS IN A PROCESS OUTLINE**

The steps in each of these outlines are out of order. Put numbers in the spaces provided, indicating what step should be first, second, and so on.

1. **topic sentence:** The empty lot near our house evolves into a dog park every afternoon.

   details: _____ A German shepherd mix is the first arrival.
   _____ The shepherd comes with a blonde woman who throws sticks for him.

_____ A teenager with two feisty little terriers releases them to play with the other two dogs.

_____ The terriers' owner throws them a bright green ball.

_____ The shepherd is very excited to see a beagle puppy run into the lot, straining at her leash.

_____ Free of her leash, the beagle begins to dance and leap around the shepherd mix.

_____ Soon all four dogs are racing for the green ball.

_____ After about half an hour, the first exhausted dog, the beagle, is carried home.

_____ The other three continue to play until it begins to get dark.

2. **topic sentence:** Cody knows exactly how to persuade me to go to the movies.

   details: _____ He says, "The paper says there's a new movie opening today. We could go to that."

   _____ "It's supposed to be a really good movie," he adds.

   _____ Then he says, "If you go to the movies with me, I'll pay."

   _____ He starts by looking in the *TV Guide* and sighing.

   _____ "There's nothing on television," he says, "so what will we do tonight?"

   _____ He looks through the newspaper and asks if I know about any new movies.

   _____ I say I don't know about any new movies.

   _____ Suddenly, going to the movies seems very attractive to me.

3. **topic sentence:** Ken has a perfect system for getting out of work early.

   details: _____ Ken's excuse always gets him out of work early because our boss thinks Ken has done so much extra work all day.

   _____ By the time our boss arrives, Ken looks as if he is hard at work.

   _____ He makes sure she notices him as soon as she arrives because he immediately asks her a question or strolls by her work area.

   _____ Then, about an hour before his shift is over, he comes up with an excuse.

   _____ He starts by getting to work earlier than our boss does.

   _____ As he acts busy, he calls attention to himself by sighing or racing around.

   _____ Ken acts busy all morning and most of the afternoon.

   _____ His excuse can be a headache, or a dentist's appointment, or a sudden need to buy more fax paper or other office supplies.

| EXERCISE **6** | **LISTING ALL THE STEPS IN AN OUTLINE** |

Below are three topic sentences for process paragraphs. Write all the steps needed to complete an outline for each sentence. After you've listed all the steps, number them in the correct time order.

1. **topic sentence:** Anyone can create his or her own exercise plan.

   steps: _____

   _____

   _____

   _____

   _____

   _____

   _____

   _____

2. **topic sentence:** You can devise a plan for saving money on your credit card bills.

   steps: _____

   _____

   _____

   _____

   _____

   _____

   _____

   _____

3. **topic sentence:** There is a simple method for getting to work on time.

   steps: _____

   _____

   _____

   _____

   _____

   _____

   _____

   _____

 **DRAFTING AND REVISING: PROCESS**

If you take the outline and write it in paragraph form, you'll have a first draft of the process paragraph. As you write the first draft, you can combine some of the short sentences from the outline. Then you can review your draft and revise it for organization, detail, clarity, grammar, style, and word choice.

Using the Same Grammatical Person

Remember that the *directional* process speaks directly to the reader, calling him or her *you*. Sentences in a directional process use the word *you*, or they imply *you*.

> directional: *You* need a good paint brush to get started. Begin
>   by making a plan. (*You* is implied in the second
>   sentence.)

Remember that the *informational* process involves somebody doing the process. Sentences in an informational process use words like *I* or *we* or *he* or *she* or *they* or a person's name.

> informational: *Sandra* needs a good paint brush to get started.
>   First, *I* can make a list.

One problem in writing a process paragraph is shifting from describing how somebody did something to telling the reader how to do an activity. When that shift happens, the two kinds of processes get mixed. That shift is called a **shift in person**. In grammar, the words *I* and *we* are considered to be in the first person; *you* is in the second person; and *he*, *she*, *it*, and *they* are in the third person.

If these words refer to one, they are called *singular*; if they refer to more than one, they are called *plural*. The following list may help.

INFOBOX	A LIST OF PERSONS

1st person singular: I
2nd person singular: you
3rd person singular: he, she, it, or a person's name

1st person plural: we
2nd person plural: you
3rd person plural: they, or the names of more than one person

In writing your process paragraph, decide whether your process will be directional or informational, and stay with one kind. Below are two examples of a shift in person. Look at them carefully and study how the shift is corrected.

Shift in person:

> After **I** preheat the oven to 350 degrees, **I** mix the egg whites and sugar
> with an electric mixer set at high speed. **Mix** until stiff peaks form.
> Then **I** put the mixture in small mounds on an ungreased cookie sheet.

("Mix until stiff peaks form" is a shift to the *you* person.)

ALONG THESE LINES/Pearson Education Canada

Shift corrected:

> After **I** preheat the oven to 350 degrees, **I** mix the egg whites and sugar with an electric mixer set at high speed. **I** mix until stiff peaks form. Then **I** put the mixture in small mounds on an ungreased cookie sheet.

Shift in person:

> **A salesperson** has to be very tactful when customers try on clothes. **The salesperson** can't hint that a suit may be a size too small. **You** can insult a customer with a hint like that.

(The sentences shifted from *salesperson* to *you*.)

Shift corrected:

> **A salesperson** has to be very careful when customers try on clothes. **The salesperson** can't hint that a suit may be a size too small. **He** (or **she**) can insult a customer with a hint like that.

Using Transitions Effectively

As you revise your draft, you can add transitions. Transitions are particularly important in a process paragraph because you are trying to show the steps in a *specific sequence*, and you are trying to show the *connections* between steps. Good transitions will also keep your paragraph from sounding like a choppy, boring list.

Below is a list of some of the transitions you can use in writing a process paragraph. Be sure that you use transitional words and phrases only when it's logical to do so, and try not to overuse the same transitions in a paragraph.

INFOBOX | **TRANSITIONS FOR A PROCESS PARAGRAPH**

after, afterward, as, as he is . . . , as soon as . . . , as you are . . . , at last, at the same time, before, begin by, during, eventually, finally, first, second, third, etc., first of all, gradually, in the beginning, immediately, initially, last, later, meanwhile, next, now, quickly, sometimes, soon, suddenly, the first step, the second step, etc., then, to begin, to start, until, when, whenever, while, while I am . . .

When you write a process paragraph, you must pay particular attention to clarity. As you revise, keep thinking about your audience to be sure your steps are easy to follow. The following checklist can help you revise your draft.

✓ **CHECKLIST** | **FOR REVISING A PROCESS PARAGRAPH**

✓ Does the topic sentence cover the whole paragraph?
✓ Does the topic sentence make a point about the process?
✓ Is any important step left out?
✓ Should any step be explained further?
✓ Are the steps in the right order?
✓ Should any sentences be combined?
✓ Have I used the same person throughout the paragraph to describe the process?
✓ Have I used transitions effectively?

EXERCISE

7

CORRECTING SHIFTS IN PERSON IN A PROCESS PARAGRAPH

Below is a paragraph that shifts from an informational to a directional process in several places. Those places are underlined. Rewrite the underlined parts, directly above the underlining, so that the whole paragraph is an informational process.

Kathleen has an efficient system for paying her bills. As soon as a bill arrives in the mail, she stacks it in a tray marked "To Pay." Every week-end, she takes the bills out of the tray and pays them. She could wait and pay them all at the end of each month, as some people do, but she feels that by waiting <u>you</u> might miss a bill that is due sooner and have to pay a late penalty. Once she has paid all the bills, she writes "Paid" and the date on her bill stub. <u>File</u> that customer's stub in a file divided into sections like Hydro Bills, Rent, Telephone Bills, and Car Payments. Once a year, Kathleen surveys that file and discards stubs more than six months old. With her system, <u>your</u> unpaid bills are all in one place, and <u>you have</u> clear records of paid bills.

EXERCISE 8	REVISING TRANSITIONS IN A PROCESS PARAGRAPH

The transitions in this paragraph could be better. Rewrite the underlined transitions, directly above each one, so that the transitions are smoother.

In a few simple steps, you can make a delicious ice cream sundae. <u>First,</u> gather a deep bowl or sundae glass, one large and one small spoon, ice cream, chocolate syrup, nuts, and a spray can of whipped cream. <u>Second,</u> use the large spoon to put mounds of ice cream into the glass or bowl. <u>Third,</u> cover the ice cream with the chocolate syrup. <u>Fourth,</u> sprinkle the ice cream with nuts. <u>Fifth,</u> spray the whipped cream to form a peak at the top of the ice cream. <u>Sixth,</u> dip the small spoon into the sundae and enjoy the treat.

EXERCISE 9	COMBINING SENTENCES IN A PROCESS PARAGRAPH

The paragraph below has many short, choppy sentences, which are underlined. Wherever you see two or more underlined sentences clustered next to each other, combine them into one clear, smooth sentence. Write your revised version of the paragraph in the spaces above the lines.

The servers at The Barbecue House have a routine that encourages customers to relax and eat large meals. <u>First, each server greets a table of patrons. The server hands out menus. He or she takes a drink order.</u> While the customers wait for their drinks, they have plenty of time to study the extensive menu. <u>In addition, they do not become impatient because they have already seen a server. They know drinks are on the way.</u> As soon as the server returns, he or she recites a list of the day's specials. <u>They always sound delicious. They are always described as juicy, crispy, spicy, or mouth-watering.</u> Later, when the server brings the food, he or she is sure to check that everyone at the table is satisfied, asking, "Is everything all right?" After the table has finished dinner, the server has one more duty. <u>He or she offers three flavours of coffee.</u> <u>He or she describes seven luscious desserts.</u> Few people can resist this smooth and friendly process of offering and serving a meal.

The Draft

Below is a draft of the process paragraph on finding an apartment. The draft has more details than the outline. Some short sentences have been combined, and transitions have been added.

A Draft of a Process Paragraph

Finding the apartment you want takes planning and careful investigation. First of all, you must decide what you want. Ask yourself, "Do I want a one-bed-room?" and "Do I want a studio apartment?" Most important, ask yourself, "What can I afford?" A convenient location can be expensive; on the other hand, that location can save you money on transportation. Before you start looking for a place, do some research. Friends can help you with names of nice apart-ments. Be sure to check the classified advertisements in the newspapers. Once you begin your search, don't pick the first apartment you see. You should look at several places, but looking at too many can make your search confusing. Just be sure to check each apartment's cleanness, safety, plumbing, and appli-ances. Then ask the manager about the laundry room, additional storage, park-ing facilities, and maintenance policies. After you've completed your search, compare the two best places you saw. Consider each one's price, location, and condition. Carefully check the leases, studying the cost of monthly hydro and the deposits for first and last month's rent.

 **PROOFREADING AND POLISHING: PROCESS**

Below is the final version of the process paragraph on finding the apartment you want. You'll notice that it contains several changes from the previous draft.

- The word "nice" has been changed to "suitable" to make the description more specific.
- The sentence that began "You should look" has been rewritten so that it follows the pattern of the preceding sentences. Three sentences in a row now include the parallel pattern of "Be sure," "don't pick," and "Look at."
- The second use of "be sure" has been changed to "remember" to avoid repetition.
- New details about what to check for in the leases have been added.
- A final sentence that relates to the topic of the paragraph has been added.

> ### A Final Version of a Process Paragraph (*changes from the draft are underlined*)

Finding the apartment you want takes planning and careful investigation. First of all, you must decide what you want. Ask yourself, "Do I want a one-bedroom?" and "Do I want a studio apartment?" Most important, ask yourself, "What can I afford?" A convenient location can be expensive; on the other hand, that location can save you money on transportation. Before you start looking for a place, do some research. Friends can help you with names of <u>suitable</u> apartments. Be sure to check the classified advertisements in the newspapers. Once you begin your search, don't pick the first apartment you see. <u>Look</u> at several places, but <u>be aware that</u> looking at too many can make your search confusing. Just <u>remember</u> to check each apartment's cleanness, safety, plumbing, and appliances. Then ask the manager about the laundry room, additional storage, parking facilities, and maintenance policies. After you've completed your search, compare the two best places you saw. Consider each one's price, location, and condition. Carefully check the leases, studying the cost of monthly hydro, the deposits for first and last month's rent, <u>and the rules for tenants. When you've completed your comparison, you're ready to choose the apartment you want</u>.

Before you prepare the final copy of your process paragraph, check your latest draft for errors in spelling and punctuation, and for any errors made in typing or recopying.

EXERCISE 10 — PROOFREADING TO PREPARE THE FINAL PARAGRAPH

Below are two process paragraphs with the kinds of errors that are easy to overlook when you prepare the final version of an assignment. Correct the errors, writing above the lines. There are eleven errors in the first paragraph and nine in the second paragraph.

1.   The best way to deal with cockroaches is to never give up. Let's say you get up in the nite for a glass of water. Suddenly, when you turn on the light, an enormous roach skitters across you're bear feet. Of course, the first thing you do is scream, as if a Peeping Tom were at the window. Next, you begin to plan an extermination You grab a newspaper and swat at the insect just as the ugly bug slips between the sink and the kitchen counter. You've missed it. Immediately, you being a search for the can of insect spray that You keep for emergencies. Eventually you find it, and spray the entire kitchen. You spray so much that every roach within twenny mile should be dead. Unfortunately, you don't know if youv'e killed the roach that crossed your toes in the kitchen. Now is the time to persevere.

Never go back to bed in defeat. Instead, stand guard in the kitchen until one big roach staggers out in to the open.

2.   Pretending to enjoy a dinner you hate can be accomplished if you follow several sneaky steps. First, don't shudder when your father announces he have spent allday making his famous turkey stew. Do not remind him that you have allways despised that recipe. Instead, say something like, "Oh, I remember that stew." It would be a little too phony to say how much you use to love it. When the stew is placed in front of you, begin by moving it around on the plate, meanwhile chewing on a role or salad so that you give the illusion of eating the main coarse. As you pretend to eat, look around you. Is there a hungry dog under the table. Help him out by providing him with a secret meal. If there is no dog, try concealing the stew under some other food on your plate. Put the meat under a potato skin or a lettuce leaf. If you have a paper napkin, consider wrapping it around some stew and concealing the package in your pocket. At the end of the meal, be sure to comment that you're fathers stew is as good as it ever was.

Lines of Detail: A Walk-Through Assignment

Your assignment is to write a paragraph on how to plan a special day. Follow these steps:

Step 1: Focus on one special day. If you want to, you can begin by using your own experience. Ask yourself such questions as these: "Have I ever planned a birthday party? A baby or wedding shower? A surprise party? A picnic? A reunion? A barbecue? A celebration of a religious holiday? Have I ever seen anyone else plan such a day? If so, how would I teach a reader about planning for such a day?"

Step 2: Once you have picked the day, freewrite. Write anything you can remember about the day and how you or someone else planned it.

Step 3: When you've completed the freewriting, read it. Underline all the details that refer to steps in planning that event. List the underlined details, in time order.

Step 4: Add to the list by brainstorming. Ask yourself questions that can lead to more details. For example, if an item on your list is, "Send out invitations early," ask questions like, "How early?" and "How do you decide whom to invite?"

Step 5: Survey your expanded list. Write a topic sentence that makes some point about your planning for this special day. To reach a point, think of questions like, "What makes a plan successful?" or "If you are planning for a special day (birthday, barbecue, surprise party, etc.), what must you remember?"

ALONG THESE LINES/Pearson Education Canada

Step 6: Use the topic sentence to prepare an outline. Be sure that the steps in the outline are in the correct time order.

Step 7: Write a first draft of the paragraph. In this first draft, add more details and combine short sentences.

Step 8: Revise your draft. Be careful to use smooth transitions, and check that you have included all the necessary steps.

Step 9: Prepare and proofread the final version of your paragraph.

Writing Your Own Process Paragraph

When you write on one of these topics, be sure to work through the stages of the writing process on preparing your paragraph.

1. Write a **directional or informational process** about one of these topics:

   packing a suitcase

   preparing for a garage sale

   painting a room

   preparing for a test

   losing weight

   choosing a roommate

   doing holiday shopping early

   breaking up with a boyfriend or girlfriend

   getting good tips while working as a waiter or waitress

   finding the right mate

   avoiding morning traffic jams

   getting up in the morning

   getting children to eat vegetables

   sizing up a new acquaintance

   quitting a job gracefully

   changing the oil in a car

   changing a tire

   breaking a specific habit

   buying the cheapest airline tickets online

   installing speakers in a car

2. Write about the wrong way to do something, or the wrong way you (or someone else) did it. You can use any of the topics in the list in question 1, or you can choose your own topic.

3. Imagine that a friend is about to register for classes at your college. This will be your friend's first semester at the college. Write a paragraph giving your friend clear directions for registering. Be sure to have an appropriate topic sentence.

4. Interview one of the counsellors at your college. Ask the counsellor to tell you the steps for applying for financial aid. Take notes or tape the interview. Get copies of any forms that are included in the application process. Ask questions about these forms.

   After the interview, write a paragraph explaining the process of applying for financial aid. Your explanation is directed at a high-school senior who has never applied for aid.

5. Interview someone whose cooking you admire. Ask that person to tell you the steps involved in making a certain dish. Take notes or tape the interview.

   After the interview, write a paragraph (*not* a recipe) explaining how to prepare the dish. Your paragraph will explain the process to someone who is a beginner at cooking.

WRITING FROM READING: PROCESS

How to Get a Reference Letter
Andrew Potter

Andrew Potter is a columnist for Maclean's *magazine. This article originally appeared in the magazine's University issue, 2007.*

Before you read this selection, consider these questions:

   Have you ever asked for a reference letter? Why?

   How do you decide whom to ask for a reference letter?

   What do you think is the best way to get the best possible reference letter?

distressing: upsetting

With **distressing** regularity, anyone who has taught in a university for any length of time receives an email that goes something like this:

Dear Professor Smith,

You probably don't remember me, but I was a student in your Intro 101 class back in 200X. After working for a few years, I've decided I would like to go to graduate school, and was wondering if I could possibly trouble you for a reference letter. I got a 74 per cent in your class, and I have appended my résumé showing what I have been up to since I graduated. I know this is a shot in the dark, but you are almost the only professor I could even ask, and I could really use your help.

Sincerely yours,
"A" student

Reference letters are a necessary part of any application to graduate or professional school, along with a writing sample, statement of research interest, standardized test scores, and a transcript. The relative importance of each of these varies depending on the discipline and department, with grades and test scores mattering a great deal for admission to law and medicine, whereas humanities departments tend

ubiquitous: everywhere

to pay more attention to the writing sample. Yet backing it all up are the **ubiquitous**

ALONG THESE LINES/Pearson Education Canada

reference letters, testimonials written on the student's behalf speaking to his or her ability, character and personality.

Unfortunately, many students shoot themselves in the foot when it comes to getting reference letters, and those who write **meek** pleas like the one above are making two fundamental errors. The first is pretty simple to fix: don't be **sheepish** or apologetic. Writing reference letters for students is not a favour that professors grant to their students, it is one of their professional obligations. Crazy as it seems, professors want to get their best students into grad schools, and writing strong letters on their behalf is part of the job.

The second mistake is a bit harder to fix after the fact. The time to start making your case for a reference letter is not when you decide to go to graduate school. Rather, you need to start setting the stage for possible letters when you are still an undergrad, with your academic future still dimly imagined. This stage is built on three pillars: your course selection, your choice of professors, and your behaviour in class.

Start with course selection. It is hard for profs to get to know you in a class of 200 or 300 students, which is why you have to find at least a couple of courses, preferably in the upper years, that have a maximum enrolment of 30 students or so. Take these courses even if you aren't particularly interested in the topic, since the attention and recognition you will get from the professor will more than make up for dull content.

Second of all, pay attention to who is teaching the class. At almost every university in Canada a great deal of instruction is being **off-loaded** to grad students, **adjunct** faculty and contract workers. They tend to be young and desperate, and consequently put a lot of effort into their teaching. But they are also **itinerant** workers, with very little status within the profession. When you go looking for reference letters a few years down the road it might be hard just finding them, since they could be literally anywhere in the world. And even when you do track them down, chances are that they will be either still working on contracts, or even out of the academic business altogether. In either case, any reference they give you will carry relatively little weight within the profession. So when selecting your courses, do a quick check in the department calendar and find out which instructors are permanent members of the faculty, and take as many of their classes as you can.

Finally, it is useful to keep one thing in mind: professors can only write you a good letter if they know who you are, what you are like, and how your mind works. It is very hard to write a strong letter for a student when all you can really say is that "so-and-so took my class and got a B+." So do all the readings and go to class. And when you are in class, ask a lot of questions. Then make a point of dropping by during the prof's office hours, and pepper him or her with comments about the lecture or the readings or the assignment. In short, be the annoying keener that everyone hates.

References aren't the most important part of your application, and it would take a truly outstanding letter to make up for miserable grades or an incompetent writing sample. But reference letters are a necessary part of your application, and they

meek: submissive

sheepish: embarrassed

off-loaded: given

adjunct: someone or something of lesser rank

itinerant: traveling

mercenary: acting just
for money or other
reward

signal your acceptance into a community of scholars. If you are an undergraduate student with even the slightest thought that you might someday want to go on to graduate school, it is never too early to start working on getting those letters. Be as strategic and **mercenary** about it as possible—you have nothing to apologize for.

UNDERSTANDING "HOW TO GET A REFERENCE LETTER"

1. What are the two mistakes Potter claims students make when requesting reference letters?

2. Why does Potter suggest that it is important to consider who is teaching the course?

3. Why do you think it might be difficult for students to be "strategic and mercenary" about securing reference letters, as Potter suggests?

WRITING FROM READING "HOW TO GET A REFERENCE LETTER"

When you write on any of these topics, be sure to work through the stages of the writing process in preparing your process paragraph.

1. Andrew Potter encourages being an "annoying keener." However, there is a fine line between being memorable and being annoying. Write a humorous process paragraph that describes how to ensure you get a *negative* reference letter.

2. Reverse the roles: pretend *you* are the professor, and one of your students has asked you to write him or her a reference letter. Write a process paragraph describing how to write (a) a positive reference letter or (b) a negative reference letter.

3. Has anyone ever asked you for a favour? What if you didn't feel comfortable doing this favour? Write a paragraph outlining the steps you would take to decline without hurting the other person's feelings.

4. Many schools have very specific processes that candidates must follow when applying to their programs. Do some research and write a process paragraph detailing the steps a prospective student must follow to apply.

ALONG THESE LINES/Pearson Education Canada

CHAPTER 7
Comparison and Contrast

LEARNING OBJECTIVES

After you have read this chapter and completed its exercises and assignments, you should be able to

- choose appropriate topics for your comparison or contrast paragraph
- write a comparison or contrast paragraph in either subject-by-subject or point-by-point format
- use appropriate transitions in your comparison or contrast paragraph
- draft and edit your paragraph

"Shadow owes its birth to light."

~ JOHN GAY

▼
JOHN GAY WAS AN
EIGHTEENTH-CENTURY
POET AND DRAMATIST.

WHAT IS COMPARISON? WHAT IS CONTRAST?

To **compare** means to point out *similarities*. To **contrast** means to point out *differences*. When you compare or contrast, you need to come to some conclusion. It's not enough to say, "These two things are similar," or "They are different." Your reader will be asking, "So what? What's your point?" You may be showing the differences between two restaurants to explain which is the better place to eat:

> If you like Mexican food, you can go to either Café Mexicana or Juanita's, but Juanita's has better spicing.

Or you may be explaining the similarities between two family members to show how people with similar personalities can clash:

> My cousin Bill and my brother Karram are both so stubborn they can't get along.

Hints for Writing a Comparison or Contrast Paragraph

1. **Limit your topic.** When you write a comparison or contrast paragraph, you might think that the easiest topics to write about are broad ones with many similarities or differences. However, if you make your topic too large, you will not be able to cover it well, and your paragraph will be full of very general, boring statements.

   Here are some topics that are too large for a comparison or contrast paragraph: two countries, two periods in history, two kinds of addiction, two wars, two economic or political systems, two prime ministers.

2. **Avoid the obvious topic.** Some students may think it is easier to write about two things if the similarities or differences between them are obvious, but with an obvious topic you'll have nothing new to say, and you'll risk writing a boring paragraph.

   Here are some obvious topics: the differences between high school and college, the similarities between *Men in Black* and *Men in Black II*. If you are drawn to an obvious topic, *try a new angle* on the topic. Write about the unexpected, using the same topic. Write about the similarities between high school and college, or the differences between *Men in Black* and *Men in Black II*. You may have to do more thinking before you come up with ideas, but your ideas may be more interesting to write about and to read.

3. **Make your point in the topic sentence of your comparison or contrast paragraph.** Indicate whether the paragraph is about similarities or differences in the topic sentence like this:

   Because he is so reliable and loyal, Michael is a much better friend to me than Stefan is.

   (The phrase "much better" indicates differences.)

   My two botany teachers share a love of the environment and a passion for protecting it.

   (The word "share" indicates similarities.)

4. **Do not announce in the topic sentence.** The sentences below are announcements, not topic sentences.

   Let me tell you about why Michael is a different kind of friend than Stefan is.

   This paper will explain the similarities between my two botany teachers.

5. **Make sure your topic sentence has a focus.** It should indicate similarities or differences; it should focus on the specific kind of comparison or contrast you will make.

   not focused: My old house is different from my new house.
   focused: My new home is bigger, brighter, and more comfortable than my old one.

6. **The topic sentence should cover both subjects to be compared or contrasted.**

only one subject:	The beach at Santa Lucia was dirty and crowded.
both subjects:	The beach at Santa Lucia was dirty and crowded, but the beach at Fisher Bay was clean and private.

Be careful. It's easy to get so carried away by the details of your paragraph that you forget to put both subjects into one sentence.

EXERCISE 1

IDENTIFYING SUITABLE TOPIC SENTENCES FOR A COMPARISON OR CONTRAST PARAGRAPH

Below is a list of possible topic sentences for a comparison or contrast paragraph. Some would make good topic sentences. The ones that wouldn't make good topic sentences have one or more of these problems: They are announcements, they don't indicate whether the paragraph will be about similarities or differences, they don't focus on the specific kind of comparison or contrast to be made, they cover subjects that are too big to write about in one paragraph, or they don't cover both subjects.

Mark the problem sentences with an *X*. If a sentence would make a good topic sentence for a comparison or contrast paragraph, mark it *OK*.

1. _____ I have two friends, Rick and Luke.
2. _____ My two close friends, Rick and Luke, are very similar.
3. _____ My two close friends, Rick and Luke, are alike in their athletic ability and obsession with sports.
4. _____ Canada and the United States are similar in their economic system, history, and culture.
5. _____ The Palm Club has better music and a friendlier atmosphere.
6. _____ This paragraph will discuss the similarities between tea and Red Bull energy drink.
7. _____ Men and women are different in their physical, intellectual, and emotional makeup.
8. _____ On the one hand, there is Jack's Pizza Parlour, and then there is the Italian Palace.
9. _____ Mr. Sheridan is a more energetic and enthusiastic teacher than Mr. Smith.
10. _____ My second semester in college was a big improvement over my first.

Organizing Your Comparison or Contrast Paragraph

Whether you decide to write about similarities (to compare) or differences (to contrast), you will have to decide how to organize your paragraph. You can choose between two patterns of organization: *subject-by-subject* or *point-by-point*.

Subject-by-Subject Organization In the subject-by-subject pattern, you support and explain your topic sentence by first writing all your details on one subject and then writing all your details on the other subject. If you choose a subject-by-subject pattern, be sure to discuss the points for your second subject *in the* *same order* as you did for the first subject. For example, if your first subject is an amusement park, you might cover (1) the price of admission, (2) the length of lines at rides, and (3) the quality of the rides. When you discuss the second subject, another amusement park, you should write about its prices, length of lines, and quality of rides in the same order.

Look carefully at the outline and comparison paragraph for a subject-by-subject pattern.

A Comparison Outline: Subject-by-Subject Pattern

topic sentence: Once I realized that my brother and my mother are very much alike in temperament, I realized why they don't get along.

details:

first subject, James—temper, unkind words, stubbornness

My brother James is a hot-tempered person.

It is easy for him to lose control of his temper.

When he does, he often says things he later regrets.

James is also very stubborn.

In an argument, he will never admit he is wrong.

Once we were arguing about baseball scores.

Even when I showed him the right score, printed in the paper, he wouldn't admit he was wrong.

He said that the newspaper had made a mistake.

James' stubbornness overtakes his common sense.

second subject, mother—temper, unkind words, stubbornness

James has inherited many of his character traits from our mother.

She has a quick temper, and anything can provoke it.

Once, she got angry because she had to wait too long at a traffic light.

She also has a tendency to use unkind words when she's angry.

She never backs down from a disagreement or concedes that she was wrong.

My mother even quit a job because she refused to admit she'd made a mistake in taking inventory.

Her pride can lead her into foolish acts.

After I realized how similar my brother and mother are, I understood how such inflexible people are likely to clash.

A Comparison Paragraph: Subject-by-Subject Pattern

first subject, James

Once I realized that my brother and my mother are very much alike in temperament, I realized why they don't get along. My brother James is a hot-tempered person. It's easy for him to lose control of his temper, and when he does, he often says things he regrets. James is also very stubborn. In an argument, he will never admit he is wrong. I remember one time when we

(continued)

ALONG THESE LINES/Pearson Education Canada

were arguing about baseball scores. Even when I showed him the right score, printed in the newspaper, he wouldn't admit he was wrong. James insisted that the newspaper must have made a mistake in printing the score. As this example shows, sometimes James' stubbornness overtakes James' common sense.

second subject, mother It took me a while to realize that my stubborn brother James has inherited many of his traits from our mother. Like James, she has a quick temper, and almost anything can provoke it. She once got angry because she had to wait too long at a traffic light. She also shares James' habit of saying unkind things when she's angry. And just as James refuses to back down when he's wrong, my mother will never back down from a disagreement or concede she's wrong. In fact, my mother once quit a job because she refused to admit she'd made a mistake in taking inventory. Her pride is as powerful as James' pride, and it can be just as foolish. After I realized how similar my mother and brother are, I understood how such inflexible people are likely to clash.

Look carefully at the paragraph in the *subject-by-subject* pattern, and you'll note that it

- begins with a topic sentence about both subjects—James and his mother,
- gives all the details about one subject—James,
- then gives all the details about the second subject—his mother—in the same order.

Point-by-Point Organization In the point-by-point pattern, you support and explain your topic sentence by discussing each point of comparison or contrast, switching back and forth between your subjects. You explain one point for each subject, then explain another point for each subject, and so on.

Look carefully at the outline and the following comparison paragraph below for the point-by-point pattern.

> ## A Comparison Outline: Point-by-Point Pattern
>
> **topic sentence:** *Once I realized that my brother and my mother are very much alike in temperament, I realized why they don't get along.*
>
> **details:**
>
> 1st point, temper
>
> My brother James is a hot-tempered person.
>
> It is easy for him to lose control of his temper.
>
> My mother has a quick temper, and anything can provoke it.
>
> Once she got angry because she had to wait too long at a traffic light.
>
> *(continued)*

2nd point, unkind words

When my brother gets angry, he often says things he regrets.

My mother has a tendency to use unkind words when she's angry.

3rd point, stubbornness

James is very stubborn.

In an argument, he will never admit he is wrong.

Once we were arguing about baseball scores.

Even when I showed him the right score, printed in the paper, he wouldn't admit he was wrong.

He said the newspaper had made a mistake.

James' stubbornness overtakes his common sense.

My mother will never back down from a disagreement or admit that she is wrong.

She even quit a job because she refused to admit she'd made a mistake in taking inventory.

She was foolish in her stubbornness.

After I realized how similar my mother and brother are, I understood how such inflexible people are likely to clash.

> ## A Comparison Paragraph: Point-by-Point Pattern

Once I realized that my brother and my mother are very much alike in temperament, I realized why they don't get along.

1st point My brother is a hot-tempered person, and it is easy for him to lose control of his temper. My mother shares James' quick temper, and anything can provoke her anger. Once, she got angry because she had to wait too long at a traffic light. When my

2nd point brother gets angry, he often says things he regrets. Similarly, my mother is known for the unkind things she's said in anger. James

3rd point is a very stubborn person. In an argument, he will never admit he's wrong. I can remember one argument we were having over baseball scores. Even when I showed him the right score, printed in the newspaper, he wouldn't admit he had been wrong. He simply insisted the paper had made a mistake. At times like this, James' stubbornness overtakes his common sense. Like her son, my mother will never back down from an argument or admit she was wrong. She even quit a job because she refused to admit she'd made a mistake in taking inventory. In that case, her stubbornness was as foolish as James'. It took me a while to see the similarities between my brother and mother. Yet after I realized how similar these two people are, I understood how two inflexible people are likely to clash.

Look carefully at the paragraph in the point-by-point pattern, and you'll note that it

- begins with a topic sentence about both subjects—James and his mother,
- discusses how both James and his mother are alike in these points: their quick tempers, the unkind things they say in a temper, their often foolish stubbornness, and
- switches back and forth between the two subjects.

Subject-by-subject and point-by-point patterns can be used for either a comparison or a contrast paragraph. But whatever pattern you choose, remember these hints:

1. **Be sure to use the same points to compare or contrast two subjects.** If you are contrasting two cars, you can't discuss the price and safety features of one, and the styling and speed of the other. You must discuss the price of both, or the safety features, or styling, or speed of both.

   You don't have to list the points in your topic sentence, but you can include them, like this: "My old Celica turned out to be a cheaper, safer, and faster car than my boyfriend's new Taurus."

2. **Be sure to give roughly equal space to both subjects.** This rule doesn't mean you must write the same number of words—or even sentences—on both subjects. It does mean you should be giving fairly equal attention to the details of both subjects.

   Since you will be writing about two subjects, this type of paragraph can involve more details than other paragraph formats. Thus, a comparison or contrast paragraph may be longer than twelve sentences.

3. **Consider using two paragraphs, one for each subject.** If your comparison or contrast becomes too lengthy, use one paragraph for all your details on one subject and then a second paragraph for all your details on the other subject.

Using Transitions Effectively for Comparison or Contrast

The transitions you use in a comparison or a contrast paragraph, as well as when to use them, all depend on the answers to two questions:

1. Are you writing a comparison or a contrast paragraph?

   - When you choose to write a *comparison* paragraph, you use transition words, phrases, or sentences that point out *similarities*.
   - When you choose to write a *contrast* paragraph, you use transition words, phrases, or sentences that point out *differences*.

2. Are you organizing your paragraph in the point-by-point or subject-by-subject pattern?

   - When you choose to organize your paragraph in the *point-by-point pattern*, you need transitions *within each point* and *between points*.
   - When you choose to organize your paragraph in the *subject-by-subject pattern*, you need to place *most of your transitions* in the *second half* of the paragraph, to remind the reader of the points you made in the first half.

The Infobox shows some transitions you can use in writing comparison or contrast. There are many others that may be appropriate for your ideas.

INFOBOX	**TRANSITIONS FOR A COMPARISON OR A CONTRAST PARAGRAPH**

To show similarities: additionally, again, also, and, as well as, both, each of, equally, furthermore, in addition, in the same way, just like, like, likewise, similarly, similar to, too, so

To show differences: although, but, conversely, different from, despite, even though, except, however, in contrast to, instead of, in spite of, nevertheless, on the other hand, otherwise, still, though, unlike, whereas, while, yet

Writing a comparison or contrast paragraph challenges you to make decisions: Will I compare or contrast? Will I use a point-by-point or a subject-by-subject pattern? These decisions will determine what kind of transitions you will use and where you will use them.

EXERCISE 2	**WRITING APPROPRIATE TRANSITIONS FOR A COMPARISON OR CONTRAST PARAGRAPH**

Below are pairs of sentences. First, decide whether each pair shows a comparison or a contrast. Then combine the two sentences into one, using an appropriate transition (either a word or phrase).

You may have to rewrite parts of the original sentences to create one smooth sentence. The first pair is done for you.

1. Dr. Cheung is a professor of art.

    Dr. Mbala is a professor of history.

    combined: <u>Dr. Cheung is a professor of art while Dr. Mbala is a professor</u>
    <u>of history.</u>

2. *Dr. Doolittle* featured animals that talked.

    In *Babe*, farm animals spoke.

    combined: _____

    _____

3. Small children are often afraid to leave their parents.

    Teenagers can't wait to get away from their parents.

    combined: _____

    _____

4. Sandra Jessop is a singer with a popular band.

    Her brother Nick can't sing a note.

    combined: _____

    _____

5. Exercise can help you lower cholesterol levels, fight heart disease, and relieve stress.

    A doctor can give you medicine for heart disease, high cholesterol, or stress.

    combined: _____

    _____

6. Mrs. Colletti volunteers at the animal shelter.

    Mr. Colletti donates his free time to the soup kitchen.

    combined: _____

    _____

7. Introduction to Philosophy was a challenging course that developed my skills in reasoning.

    College Writing, a tough course, taught me how to think and reason.

    combined: _____

    _____

8. Camping out takes work and can be uncomfortable.

    Staying in a motel is easy and pleasant.

    combined: _____

    _____

9. Staying in a motel costs money.

    Camping out requires expensive supplies.

    combined: _____

    _____

10. My co-workers at The Sports Store were friendly and supportive.

    The people I worked with at Bruno's Subs created a warm and helpful working environment.

    combined: _____

    _____

WRITING THE COMPARISON OR CONTRAST PARAGRAPH IN STEPS

THOUGHT LINES **GATHERING IDEAS: COMPARISON OR CONTRAST**

One way to get started on a comparison or a contrast paragraph is to list as many differences or similarities as you can on one topic. Then you can see whether you have more similarities (comparisons) or more differences (contrasts), and decide which approach to use. For example, if you are asked to compare or contrast two restaurants, you could begin with a list like this:

> List for Two Restaurants: Victor's and The Garden

similarities
> both offer lunch and dinner
> very popular
> nearby

differences

Victor's	The Garden
formal dress	informal dress
tablecloths	placemats
food is bland	spicy food
expensive	moderate
statues, fountains, fresh flowers	dark wood, hanging plants

Getting Points of Comparison or Contrast

Whether you compare or contrast, you are looking for points of comparison or contrast, items you can discuss about both subjects.

If you surveyed the list on the two restaurants and decided you wanted to contrast the two restaurants, you'd see that you already have these points of contrast:

dress   food   decor   prices

To write your paragraph, start with several points of comparison or contrast. As you work through the stages of writing, you may decide you don't need all the points you've jotted down, but it is better to start with too many points than with too few.

EXERCISE

3

DEVELOPING POINTS OF COMPARISON OR CONTRAST

Do this exercise with a partner or a group. Below are some topics that could be used for a comparison or a contrast paragraph. Underneath each topic, write three points of comparison or contrast. Be prepared to share your answers. The first topic is done for you.

1. **topic:** Compare or contrast two television reality shows.

   points of comparison or contrast:

   a. the host _____

   b. the kinds of "challenges" participants face _____

   c. the prizes _____

2. **topic:** Compare or contrast a movie and its sequel.

   points of comparison or contrast:

   a. _____

   b. _____

   c. _____

3. **topic:** Compare or contrast two holidays.

   points of comparison or contrast:

   a. _____

   b. _____

   c. _____

4. **topic:** Compare or contrast two college courses.

   points of comparison or contrast:

   a. _____

   b. _____

   c. _____

5. **topic:** Compare or contrast two professional hockey players.

   points of comparison or contrast:

   a. _____

   b. _____

   c. _____

EXERCISE
4

FINDING DIFFERENCES IN SUBJECTS THAT LOOK SIMILAR

Below are pairs of subjects that are very similar but that do have some differences. List three differences for each pair.

1. **subject:** Burger King and McDonald's

   differences:

   a. _____

   b. _____

   c. _____

2. **subject:** Facebook and MySpace

   differences:

   a. _____

   b. _____

   c. _____

3. **subject:** CD-ROMs and thumb drives

   differences:

   a. _____

   b. _____

   c. _____

4. **subject:** SUVs and minivans
    differences:

    a. _____

    b. _____

    c. _____

5. **subject:** motorcycles and motor scooters
    differences:

    a. _____

    b. _____

    c. _____

EXERCISE	FINDING SIMILARITIES IN SUBJECTS
5	**THAT LOOK DIFFERENT**

Below are pairs of subjects that are different but have some similarities. List three similarities for each pair.

1. **subject:** attending college part-time and attending college full-time
    similarities:

    a. _____

    b. _____

    c. _____

2. **subject:** renting a movie and going to a movie
    similarities:

    a. _____

    b. _____

    c. _____

3. **subject:** working the night shift and working daytime hours
    similarities:

    a. _____

    b. _____

    c. _____

4. **subject:** love and hate
    similarities:

    a. _____

    b. _____

    c. _____

ALONG THESE LINES/Pearson Education Canada

5. **subject:** starting a new business and starting a new relationship
   similarities:

   a. _____

   b. _____

   c. _____

Adding Details to Your Points

Once you have some points, you can begin adding details. The details may lead you to more points. Even if they don't, the process will help you to develop the ideas of your paragraph.

If you were to write about the differences in restaurants, for example, your new list with added details might look like this:

> ### List for a Contrast of Restaurants

<u>Victor's</u>	<u>The Garden</u>
dress—formal	informal dress
men in jackets, women in dresses	all in jeans
decor—pretty, elegant statues, fountains	lots of dark wood, brass, green hanging plants
fresh flowers on tables, tablecloths	place mats, on table is a card listing specials
food—bland-tasting, traditional, broiled fish or chicken, steaks, traditional appetizers like shrimp cocktail, onion soup	spicy and adventurous, noodles in sambal or lemon grass, peppers in everything, curry, appetizers like tiny tortillas, ribs in smoked pepper sauce
price—expensive	moderate
everything costs extra, like appetizer, salad	price of dinner includes appetizer and salad

---

Reading the list about restaurants, you might conclude that some people may prefer The Garden to Victor's. Why? There are several hints within your list: The Garden has cheaper food, better food, and a more casual atmosphere.

Now that you have a point, you can put it into a topic sentence. A topic sentence contrasting the restaurants could be

> Some people would rather eat at The Garden than at Victor's because The Garden gives them better, cheaper food in a more casual environment.

Once you have a possible topic sentence, you can begin working on the outlines stage of your paragraph.

ALONG THESE LINES/Pearson Education Canada

EXERCISE

6

WRITING TOPIC SENTENCES FOR COMPARISON OR CONTRAST

Below are lists of details. Some are for comparison paragraphs; some are for contrast paragraphs. Read each list carefully; then write a topic sentence for each list.

1. topic sentence: _____

_____

List of Details

living alone	**having a roommate**
advantages—privacy; no need to share; quiet; no conflicts	lots of space; cheaper; never lonely; always have support
disadvantages—more costly; emotional support	conflicts may arise; different lifestyles

2. topic sentence: _____

_____

List of Details

traditional books	**digital books**
availability—to the general public	to those with access to the appropriate technology
cost—anywhere from free at the public library to $45 for a hardcover new release; value may rise with age	approximately $15 for a newly released downloaded book; value of a digital book is not yet determined
longevity: can last indefinitely with proper care	likely deleted after reading to free up space for other books

3. topic sentence: _____

_____

List of Details

pick-up truck	**sport utility vehicle (like Bronco, Explorer)**
seating—for two	seats four or five
room to carry things—large truck, large bed, can be open space, covered by a canvas cover, or permanently closed	large covered space behind seats, but not as big as pick-up's space
uses—good for rough terrain, hunting and fishing, hauling and moving, construction work	good for country driving but also for suburban families with space for toys, baby strollers, car seats

4. topic sentence: _____

_____

List of Details

pick-up truck	sport utility vehicle
buyers—popular with young people, outdoors enthusiasts, farmers	people in their twenties, people who camp or fish
image—a rugged, solid, practical vehicle	fashionable, rugged, useful
accessories available—CD players, fancy speakers, air conditioning	luxurious interiors, CD players and speakers, air conditioning

communication at work

On the job, many employers turn to their experienced and specialized staff to help them make sound business decisions. For instance, your boss may tell you that your company is thinking of outsourcing its network security. Knowing that you are an expert in the field, she may ask you to prepare a report comparing and/or contrasting two competing vendors. What aspects do you think you would compare or contrast?

 ## DEVISING A PLAN: COMPARISON OR CONTRAST

Once you have a topic sentence, you can begin to draft an outline. Before you can write an outline, however, you have to make a decision: What pattern do you want to use in organizing your paragraph? Do you want to use the subject-by-subject or the point-by-point pattern?

The following is an outline of a contrast paragraph in point-by-point form.

> ### An Outline of a Contrast Paragraph: Point-by-Point Pattern
>
> **topic sentence:** Some people would rather eat at The Garden than at Victor's because The Garden gives them better, cheaper food in a more casual environment.
>
> **details:**
>
> **1st point: food**
>
> Food at Victor's is bland-tasting and traditional.
>
> The menu has broiled fish, chicken, traditional steaks.
>
> The spices used are mostly parsley and salt.
>
> The food is the usual 1950s food, with a little French food on the list.
>
> Appetizers are the usual things like shrimp cocktail or onion soup.
>
> Food at The Garden is more spicy and adventurous.
>
> There are noodle dishes in sauces such as sambal or lemon grass.
>
> There are peppers in just about everything.
>
> *(continued)*

The Garden serves four different curry dishes.

It has all kinds of international food.

Appetizers include items like tiny tortillas and hot, smoked-pepper ribs.

2nd point: prices

The prices of the two restaurants differ.

Victor's is expensive.

Everything you order costs extra.

An appetizer and a salad cost extra.

Food at The Garden is more moderately priced.

The price of a dinner includes an appetizer and a salad.

3rd point: environment

Certain diners may feel uncomfortable in Victor's, which has a formal environment.

Everyone is dressed up, the men in jackets and ties and the women in dresses. Less formal diners would rather eat in a more casual environment.

People don't dress up to go to The Garden; they wear jeans.

conclusion

Many people prefer a place where they can relax, with reasonable prices and unusual food, to a place that's a little stuffy, with a traditional and expensive menu.

Once you've drafted an outline, check it. Use the checklist below to help you review and revise your outline.

✓ **CHECKLIST** **FOR AN OUTLINE OF A COMPARISON OR A CONTRAST PARAGRAPH**

✓ Do I have enough details?

✓ Are all my details relevant?

✓ Have I covered all the points on both sides?

✓ If I'm using a subject-by-subject pattern, have I covered the points in the same order on both sides?

✓ Have I tried to cover too many points?

✓ Have I made my main idea clear?

Using this checklist as your guide, compare the outline with the thought lines list. You may notice some changes:

- Some details on decor in the list have been omitted because there were too many points.
- A concluding sentence has been added to reinforce the main idea.

ALONG THESE LINES/Pearson Education Canada

EXERCISE **7**	ADDING A POINT AND DETAILS TO A COMPARISON OR A CONTRAST OUTLINE

The following outline is too short. Develop it by adding a point of contrast and details to both subjects, to develop the contrast.

topic sentence: Carson College is a friendlier place than Wellington College.

details: When a person enters Carson College, he or she sees groups of students who seem happy.
They are sprawled on the steps and on the lawns, looking as if they are having a good time.
They are laughing and talking to each other.
At Wellington College, everyone seems to be a stranger.
Students are isolated.
They lean against the wall or sit alone, reading intently or staring into space.
The buildings at Carson seem open and inviting.
There are many large glass windows in each classroom.
There are wide, large corridors.
Many signs help newcomers find their way around.
Wellington College seems closed and forbidding.
It has dark, windowless classrooms.
The halls are narrow and dirty.
There are no signs or directions posted on the buildings.

Add a new point of contrast, and details, about each college: _____

_____

_____

_____

_____

_____

_____

EXERCISE **8**	FINDING IRRELEVANT DETAILS IN A COMPARISON OR CONTRAST OUTLINE

The following outline contains some irrelevant details. Cross out the details that don't fit.

topic sentence: My daughter's fourth birthday party and my high-school graduation ceremony showed that people of all ages celebrate in similar ways.

details: Last week, my daughter Nina's friends dressed in their best for her birthday party.
The girls wore frilly or flowered dresses.
The boys sported new shirts and clean shoes.

I always loved to go barefoot when I was a child.
Years ago, my classmates and I were also elaborately dressed.
We were self-conscious in our graduation caps and gowns.
Some of us wore special hoods or coloured tassels.
The children at the party were eager for the fun to get started.
They wanted to play, but their parents had told them to behave.
Some children are too good to be true.
They misbehave at home but are angels in public.
The graduates were eager to get their diplomas.
They fidgeted in their chairs as the guest speaker droned on.
He was the president of a large corporation.
They looked behind them at their families and friends.
But they tried to behave because the vice-principal had warned them that she would be watching.
When Nina's four-year-old friends heard some music playing, they began to loosen up.
They started to jump around, dance, and giggle.
Soon they were wild with happiness.
When the graduates had all received their diplomas, they let themselves go.
They jumped up, tossed their caps in the air, and hugged each other.
Their parents started taking photographs.
Soon the graduates filled the air with laughter and shouts of victory.

EXERCISE 9

REVISING THE ORDER IN A COMPARISON OR A CONTRAST OUTLINE

Below is an outline written in the subject-by-subject pattern. Rewrite the second half of the outline so that the points in the second half follow the order of the first half. You do not have to change any sentences; just rearrange them.

topic sentence: Young people and old people are both victims of society's prejudices.

details: Some people think young people are not capable of mature thinking.
They think the young are on drugs.
They think the young are alcoholics.
The young are considered parasites because they do not earn a great deal of money.
Many young people are in college and not working full-time.
Many young people rely on help from their parents.
The young are outcasts because their appearance is different.
The young wear trendy fashions.
They have strange haircuts.
People may think the young are punks.
The way young people look makes other people afraid.
Old people are also judged by their appearance.

They are wrinkled or scarred or frail-looking.
People are afraid of growing old and looking like that.
So they are afraid of the old.
Some people think elderly people are not capable of mature thinking.
They think the old are on too much medication to think straight.
They think the old are senile.
Some people consider the old to be parasites because elderly people do not earn a great deal of money.
Some of the elderly have small pensions.
Some have only old age pensions.
The young and the old are often stereotyped.

Rewritten order: _____

_____

_____

_____

_____

_____

_____

_____

_____

_____

ROUGH LINES   ## DRAFTING AND REVISING: COMPARISON OR CONTRAST

When you've revised your outline, you can write the first draft of the restaurant paragraph. After making a first draft, you may want to combine more sentences, rearrange your points, fix your topic sentence, or add vivid detail. You may also need to add transitions.

The Draft

Here is a draft version of the paragraph on contrasting two restaurants. As you read it, notice the changes from the outline: the order of some details in the outline has been changed, sentences have been combined, and transitions have been added.

> ### A Draft of a Contrast Paragraph, Point-by-Point Pattern (transitions are underlined)
>
> Some people would rather eat at The Garden than at Victor's because The Garden gives them better and cheaper food in a more casual environment. The food at Victor's is bland-tasting and traditional. The menu has broiled fish, chicken, and traditional steaks. The food is the usual 1950s food with a little

(continued)

French food on the list. Appetizers are the usual things like shrimp cocktail and onion soup. The spices used are mainly parsley and salt. Food at The Garden, <u>however,</u> is more spicy and adventurous. The restaurant has all kinds of international food. There are many noodle dishes with sauces such as sambal or lemon grass. The menu has four kinds of curry on it. The appetizers include items like tiny tortillas and hot, smoked-pepper ribs. <u>And if parsley is the spice of choice at Victor's,</u> jalapeño pepper is the favourite spice at The Garden. The prices at the restaurants differ, <u>too.</u> Victor's is expensive because everything you order costs extra. An appetizer or a salad costs extra. Food at The Garden, in contrast, is more moderately priced because the price of a dinner includes an appetizer and a salad. <u>Price and menu are important, but the most important difference between the restaurants has to do with environment.</u> Certain diners may feel uncomfortable at Victor's, which has a formal kind of atmosphere. Everyone is dressed up, the men in jackets and ties and the women in dresses. Less formal diners would rather eat in a more casual place like The Garden, where everyone wears jeans. Many people prefer a place where they can relax, with reasonable prices and unusual food, to a place that's a little stuffy, with a traditional and expensive menu.

The following checklist may help you revise your own draft:

CHECKLIST   **FOR REVISING THE DRAFT OF A COMPARISON OR A CONTRAST PARAGRAPH**

✓   Did I include a topic sentence that covers both subjects?
✓   Is the paragraph in a clear order?
✓   Does it stick to one pattern, either subject-by-subject or point-by-point?
✓   Are both subjects given roughly the same amount of space?
✓   Do all the details fit?
✓   Are the details specific and vivid?
✓   Do I need to combine any sentences?
✓   Are transitions used effectively?
✓   Have I made my point?

EXERCISE 10

REVISING THE DRAFT OF A COMPARISON OR A CONTRAST PARAGRAPH BY ADDING VIVID DETAILS

You can do this exercise alone, with a writing partner, or with a group. The following contrast paragraph lacks the vivid details that could make it interesting. Read it, then rewrite the underlined parts in the space above the underlining. Replace the original words with more vivid details.

My new car is giving me the same problems that I had in my old car. My old car, a Honda Civic, cost at least a hundred dollars a month to keep on the road. I was constantly paying for some minor but expensive repairs. One month, the car needed <u>three things</u> repaired. In addition, my Honda was uncomfortable. The seats were <u>not good,</u> and I always had to <u>sit funny.</u> Another irritation in the Honda was its little quirks. For example, the radio <u>never worked right.</u> I had hoped to put all those problems behind me when I bought my new Nissan Pathfinder, but my hopes were not fulfilled. Just like my old car, my new one costs me <u>a lot</u> to keep on the road. This time the money doesn't go to repairs; it goes to filling the gas tank. I had not realized such a big car would use so much gas. And while the Pathfinder has <u>nice</u> seats, I'm still uncomfortable. I'm not used to sitting so high off the ground. Also, I'm not used to stepping so far down when I get out of the vehicle. Finally, the car shares a radio problem with my old one. The Nissan's radio worked right—for a while. Then someone broke off my antenna, and now the radio doesn't work at all. Thinking of all the similar flaws in my two cars, I have concluded that I must accept them and pray that they will not show up in my next car.

EXERCISE **11**	**REVISING A DRAFT BY COMBINING SENTENCES**

The paragraph below has many short, choppy sentences, which are underlined. Whenever you see two or more underlined sentences clustered next to each other, combine them into one smooth, clear sentence. Write the new sentence above the underlined portions.

Both my mother and my older sister, Andrea, treat me like a little boy. First of all, they both criticize my eating habits. <u>My mother is disturbed when she sees me eating chocolate-chip cookies for breakfast. She is upset if I drink Sprite for breakfast.</u> She doesn't believe I am getting the proper nutrition. <u>Andrea eats only health food. She gets concerned about my diet.</u>

<u>She is upset when she sees me eating junk food like Whoppers or fried chicken nuggets.</u> My mother and Andrea also monitor my comings and goings. <u>If I am late getting home from work, my mother asks questions. She wants to know if the traffic was bad. She wonders if I had an accident.</u> Similarly, Andrea is always asking why I am leaving late for school or whether I am skipping classes. Worst of all, these two women investigate and evaluate my friends, particularly my girlfriends. My mother will ask, "Whatever happened to that sweet girl you were seeing? I really liked her." My sister is blunter. She is likely to say, "You'll never find a finer girl than your last girlfriend. You should apologize to her." If she doesn't like a girl I'm seeing, Andrea says, "You can do better than that." Although these comments irritate me, I love my mother and Andrea. <u>I know my mother and sister care about me. I wish they would treat me like an adult.</u>

FINAL LINES   ## PROOFREADING AND POLISHING: COMPARISON OR CONTRAST

Contrast Paragraph: Point-by-Point Pattern

Below is the revised version of the paragraph contrasting restaurants, using a point-by-point pattern. When you read it, you'll notice several changes:

- "Usual" or "usually" had been used too often, so synonyms were substituted.
- "Onion soup" became "*French* onion soup," to emphasize the detail.
- "Everything *you* order" was changed to "everything *a person* orders," to avoid sounding as if the reader is ordering food at Victor's.
- "A formal *kind of atmosphere*" became "a formal environment" to eliminate extra words.

> ### A Final Version of a Contrast Paragraph, Point-by-Point Pattern (changes from the draft are underlined)
>
> Some people would rather eat at The Garden than at Victor's because The Garden gives them better and cheaper food in a more casual environment. The food at Victor's is bland-tasting and traditional. The menu has broiled fish, chicken, and traditional steaks. The food is <u>typical</u> 1950s food with a little French food on the list. Appetizers are <u>standard items</u> like shrimp cocktail and <u>French</u> onion soup. The spices are mostly parsley and salt. Food at The Garden, however, is more spicy and adventurous. The restaurant has all kinds of international food. There are many noodle dishes with sauces such as sambal or lemon grass. The menu has four kinds
>
> *(continued)*

ALONG THESE LINES/Pearson Education Canada

of curry on it. The appetizers include items like tiny tortillas and hot, smoked-pepper ribs. And if parsley is the spice of choice at Victor's, jalapeño pepper is the favourite spice at The Garden. The prices at the restaurants differ, too. Victor's is expensive because everything <u>a person</u> orders costs extra. An appetizer or a salad costs extra. Food at The Garden, in contrast, is more moderately priced because the price of a dinner includes an appetizer and a salad. Price and menu are important, but the most important difference between the two restaurants has to do with <u>environment</u>. Certain diners may feel uncomfortable at Victor's, which has a formal environment. Everyone is dressed up, the men in jackets and ties and the women in dresses. Less formal diners would rather eat in a more casual place like The Garden, where everyone wears jeans. Many people prefer a place where they can relax, with reasonable prices and unusual food, to a place that's a little stuffy, with a traditional and expensive menu.

Before you prepare the final copy of your comparison or contrast paragraph, check your latest draft for errors in spelling and punctuation, and for any errors made in typing or recopying.

The Same Contrast Paragraph: Subject-by-Subject

To show you what the same paragraph contrasting restaurants would look like in a subject-by-subject pattern, the outline, draft, and final versions follow.

An Outline: Subject-by-Subject Pattern

topic sentence: Some people would rather eat at The Garden than at Victor's because The Garden gives them better, cheaper food in a more casual environment.

details:

    1st subject: Victor's

        Food at Victor's is bland-tasting and traditional.

        The menu has broiled fish, chicken, and traditional steaks.

        The spices used are mostly parsley and salt.

        The food is the usual 1950s food, with a little French food on the list.

        Appetizers are the usual things like shrimp cocktail and onion soup.

        Victor's is expensive.

        Everything you order costs extra.

        An appetizer or salad costs extra.

        Certain diners may feel uncomfortable at Victor's, which has a formal environment.

        Everyone is dressed up, the men in jackets and ties and the women in dresses.

(continued)

2nd subject: The Garden

> Food at The Garden is more spicy and adventurous.
>
> There are many noodle dishes in sauces such as sambal or lemon grass.
>
> There is jalapeño pepper in just about everything.
>
> The Garden serves four different curry dishes.
>
> It has all kinds of international food.
>
> Appetizers include items like tiny tortillas and hot, smoked-pepper ribs.
>
> Food at The Garden is moderately priced.
>
> The price of a dinner includes an appetizer and a salad.
>
> The Garden is casual.
>
> People don't dress up to go there; they wear jeans.
>
> Many people prefer a place where they can relax, with reasonable prices and unusual food, to a place that's a little stuffy, with a traditional and expensive menu.

A Draft: Subject-by-Subject Pattern (transitions are underlined)

Some people would rather eat at The Garden than at Victor's because The Garden gives them better, cheaper food in a more casual environment. The food at Victor's is bland-tasting and traditional. The menu has broiled fish, chicken, and traditional steaks on it. The food is the usual 1950s food, with a little French food on the list. Appetizers are the usual things like shrimp cocktail and onion soup. At Victor's, the spices are mostly parsley and salt. Eating traditional food at Victor's is expensive because everything you order costs extra. An appetizer or a salad, for instance, costs extra. Victor's prices make some people nervous, and the restaurant's formal environment makes them uncomfortable. At Victor's, everyone is dressed up, the men in jackets and ties and the women in dresses. <u>The formal atmosphere, the food, and the prices attract some people, but many diners would rather go to The Garden for a meal.</u> The food at The Garden is more spicy and adventurous <u>than the offerings at Victor's.</u> The place has all kinds of international food. There are many noodle dishes in sauces such as sambal or lemon grass, and The Garden serves four different curry dishes. Appetizers include items like tiny tortillas and hot, smoked-pepper ribs. <u>If Victor's relies on parsley and salt to flavour its food,</u> The Garden sticks to jalapeño pepper, which is in just about everything. Prices are lower at The Garden <u>than they are at Victor's.</u> The Garden's meals are more moderately priced because, <u>unlike Victor's,</u> The Garden includes an appetizer and a salad in the price of a dinner. <u>And in contrast to Victor's,</u> The Garden is a casual restaurant. People don't dress up to go to The Garden; everyone wears jeans. Many people prefer a place where they can relax, with unusual food at reasonable prices, to a place that's a little stuffy, with a traditional and expensive menu.

> A Final Version: Subject-by-Subject Pattern (changes from the draft are underlined)

Some people would rather eat at The Garden than at Victor's because The Garden gives them better, cheaper food in a more casual environment. The food at Victor's is bland-tasting and traditional. The menu has broiled fish, chicken, and traditional steaks on it. The food is typical 1950s food, with a little French food on the list. Appetizers are the <u>standard</u> things like shrimp cocktail and <u>French</u> onion soup. At Victor's, the spices are mostly parsley and salt. Eating traditional food at Victor's is expensive because everything <u>a person</u> orders costs extra. An appetizer or a salad, for instance, costs extra. Victor's prices make some people nervous, and the restaurant's formal environment makes them uncomfortable. At Victor's, everyone is dressed up, the men in jackets and ties and the women in dresses. The formal atmosphere and the prices attract some people, but many diners would rather go to The Garden for a meal. The food at The Garden is more spicy and adventurous than the offerings at Victor's. The place has all kinds of international food. There are many noodle dishes in sauces such as sambal or lemon grass, and The Garden serves four different curry dishes. Appetizers include items like tiny tortillas and hot, smoked-pepper ribs. If Victor's relies on parsley and salt to flavour its food, The Garden sticks to jalapeño pepper, which is in just about everything. Prices are lower at The Garden than they are at Victor's. The Garden's meals are moderately priced because, unlike Victor's, The Garden includes an appetizer and a salad in the price of a dinner. And in contrast to Victor's, The Garden is a casual restaurant. People don't dress up to go to The Garden; everyone wears jeans. Many people prefer <u>The Garden because</u> they prefer a place where they can relax, with unusual food at reasonable prices, to a place that's a little stuffy, with a traditional and expensive menu.

EXERCISE 12 — PROOFREADING TO PREPARE THE FINAL VERSION

Below are two comparison paragraphs with the kinds of errors that are easy to overlook in a final copy of an assignment. Correct the errors, writing your corrections above the lines. There are thirteen errors in the first paragraph and nine errors in the second paragraph.

1. My nephew's stuffed dog and my portable MP3 player meet the same needs in both of us. Brendan, who is four, won't go anywhere without the ragged stufed dog he loves. To him, that dog represents security I have seen him cry so long and so hard that his parents had to turn the car around and drive fifty kilometres to pick up the dog they forgot. My MP3 player is my security, and

I take it everywere. I even take it to the library when I study; I just plug in the earphones. When Brendan feels tense, he runs to grab his dog. One day Brendans mother was yelling at him, an his face got puckered up and red. Brendan ran out of the room and hid in the corner of the hallway. He was clutching his dog. While I dont clutch my MP3 player, I do turn to my mussic to relax whenever I felt anxious. Brendan uses his toy to excape the world. I seen him sit silent for half an hour, holding his dog and starring into space. He is involved in some fantasy with his puppy. Whenever I feel tense, I turn on my music. It soothes me and puts me in a world of my own. I guess adults and children have there own ways of coping with conflict, and they have their own toys, too!

2.   The last two Thanksgivings I celebrated were as different as the people who invited me to them. Two years ago, my sister Teresa asked me to come to her house for Thanksgiving dinner. When I arrive, the first think I noticed was an elaborately set table with white linen napkins, china plates, and a centrepiece of fresh flowers and autumn leaves. When we sat down at the table, Teresa set the tone for the formal diner. She made sure that her two sons pulled out chairs for their two great ants, and she slowly passed around the platters of food while her husband carved the turkey. After dinner, Teresa, who likes to be organized. got everyone to sit queitly in the living room, where we chatted politely about past holidays. My sister Camille had a completely diffrent kind of Thanksgiving last year. Camille is a casual person, so I was not surprised to see that when I got to her house, the table was not even sit. Instead, three or four people were coming from the kitchen, loading the table with bowls and platters of food. A pile of plastic utensils and paper plates sat on top of some large paper napkins. In the middle of all this food was a centrepiece of a paper turkey. At dinner time, everyone piled food on a paper plate and sat somewhere in the living room, or den. People kept coming and going, grabbing or offering more food. After dinner, Camile sat back and watched the football game while others played cards or napped. From one holiday to the next, I had witnessed how personalities reveal themselves in family holidays.

Lines of Detail: A Walk-Through Assignment

Write a paragraph that compares or contrasts any experience you've heard about with your own experience living it. For example, you could compare or contrast what you heard about starting college with your actual experience of starting college. You could compare or contrast what you heard about falling in love with your experience of falling in love, or what you heard about playing a sport with your own experience playing that sport. To write your paragraph, follow these steps:

Step 1: Choose the experience you will write about, then list all the similarities and differences between the experience as you heard about it and the experience as you lived it.

Step 2: To decide whether to write a comparison or a contrast paragraph, survey your list to see which has more details, the similarities or the differences.

Step 3: Add details to your comparison or contrast list. Survey your list again, and group the details into points of comparison or contrast.

Step 4: Write a topic sentence that includes both subjects, focuses on comparison or contrast, and makes a point.

Step 5: Decide whether your paragraph will be in the subject-by-subject or point-by-point pattern. Write your outline in the pattern you choose.

Step 6: Write a draft of your paragraph. Revise your draft, checking the transitions, the order of the points, and the space given to each point. For each subject, check the relevance and vividness of the details. Combine any short, choppy sentences.

Step 7: Before you prepare the final copy of your paragraph, edit for word choice, spelling, punctuation, and transitions.

Writing Your Own Comparison or Contrast Paragraph

When you write on one of these topics, be sure to follow the stages of the writing process.

1. Contrast what your appearance (or your behaviour) makes others think of you and what you are like below the surface of your appearance (or behaviour). If your instructor agrees, you can ask a writing partner or a group to give you ideas on what your appearance or behaviour says about you.

2. Contrast something you did in the past with the way you do the same thing today. For example, you could contrast the two ways (past and present) of studying, shopping, treating your friends, spending your free time, driving a car, or getting along with a parent or child.

3. Compare or contrast any of the following:

two fashion designers	two newspapers	two movies
two cars	two websites	two TV shows
two stores	two family traditions	two jobs
two athletic teams	two birthdays	two classes

If your instructor agrees, you may want to brainstorm points of comparison or contrast with a writing partner or with a group.

4. Imagine that you are a reporter who specializes in helping consumers get the best for their money. Imagine that you are asked to rate two brands of the same supermarket item. Write a paragraph advising your readers which is the better buy. You can rate two brands of cola,

yogurt, potato chips, toothpaste, ice cream, chocolate-chip cookies, or paper towels—any item you can get in a supermarket.

Be sure to come up with *enough* points of contrast. You can't, for example, do a well-developed paragraph on just the taste of two cookies. But you can also discuss texture, colour, smell, price, fat content, calories, number of chocolate chips, and so on. If your instructor agrees, you may want to brainstorm topics or points of contrast with a group, as a way of beginning the writing process. Then work on your own on the outlines, draft, and final version.

5. Contrast your taste in music, or dress, or ways of spending leisure time with that of another generation.

6. If you have ever shopped online for sales or bargains offered by your favourite store, or store without outlets in your area, contrast this experience with shopping inside the store itself. Select one specific store for this assignment, but be sure to contrast the specific differences between the two shopping choices. You should include three points of contrast in your paragraph.

7. Interview a person of your age group who comes from a different part of the country. (Note: There may be quite a few people from different parts of the country in your class.) Ask him or her about similarities or differences between his or her former home and this part of the country. You could ask about similarities or differences in dress, music, dating, nightlife, ways to spend leisure time, favourite entertainers, or anything else that you like.

After the interview, write a paragraph that either shows how people of the same age group from different parts of the country have different tastes in music, dress, and so on, or share the same tastes in music, dress, and so on. Whichever approach you choose, use details you collected in the interview.

WRITING FROM READING: COMPARISON AND CONTRAST

Hey, Canada's One Cool Country
Samantha Bennett

Samantha Bennett is a columnist at the Pittsburgh Post-Gazette *and vice-president of the National Society of Newspaper Columnists. This article was later published in the* Toronto Star.

Before you read this selection, consider these questions:

Compare Canada to its closest neighbour and largest trading partner, the United States. Consider each country's politics, social programs, and culture. How are they similar? How are they different?

Do you think the United States is becoming more or less progressive?

Would you ever leave a country if you disagreed with its social or international policies?

You live next door to a clean-cut, quiet guy. He never plays loud music or throws **raucous** parties. He doesn't gossip over the fence, just smiles politely and offers you

raucous: loud

ALONG THESE LINES/Pearson Education Canada

neat as a pin:
extremely tidy

Coalition of the Willing: term used by President George W. Bush to refer to countries that would assist the United States in the war in Iraq

freedom bacon: Canadian bacon. This is a reference to the reaction some American restaurateurs had to France's refusal to join the "Coalition of the Willing": "French Fries" were changed to "freedom fries" on their menus.

bong: device used to smoke marijuana or other drugs

pinkos: slang; a term once used to describe a person with leftist political views

Ho-Hos: American snack, something like a small cake

Dudley Do-Right: a Canadian Mountie featured in a television cartoon

some tomatoes. His lawn is cared-for, his house is **neat as a pin** and you get the feeling he doesn't always lock his front door. He wears Dockers. You hardly know he's there.

And then one day you discover that he has pot in his basement, spends his weekends at peace marches and that guy you've seen mowing the yard is his spouse.

Allow me to introduce Canada.

The Canadians are so quiet that you may have forgotten they're up there, but they've been busy doing some surprising things. It's like discovering that the mice you are dimly aware of in your attic have been building an espresso machine.

Did you realize, for example, that our reliable little tag-along brother never joined the **Coalition of the Willing?** Canada wasn't willing, as it turns out, to join the fun in Iraq. I can only assume American diner menus weren't angrily changed to include **"freedom bacon,"** because nobody here eats the stuff anyway.

And then there's the wild drug situation: Canadian doctors are authorized to dispense medical marijuana. Parliament is considering legislation that would not exactly legalize marijuana possession, as you may have heard, but would reduce the penalty for possession of under 15 grams to a fine, like a speeding ticket. This is to allow law enforcement to concentrate resources on traffickers. If your garden is full of wasps, it's smarter to go for the nest rather than trying to swat every individual bug. Or, in the United States, **bong.**

Now, here's the part that I, as an American, can't understand. These poor benighted **pinkos** are doing everything wrong. They have a drug problem. Marijuana offences have doubled since 1991. And Canada has strict gun control laws, which mean that the criminals must all be heavily armed, the law-abiding civilians helpless and the government on the verge of a massive confiscation campaign. (The laws have been in place since the '70s, but I'm sure the government will get around to the confiscation eventually.) They don't even have a death penalty!

And yet, nationally, overall crime in Canada has been declining since 1991. Violent crimes fell 13 per cent in 2002. Of course, there are still crimes committed with guns—brought in from the United States, which has become the major illegal weapons supplier for all of North America—but my theory is that the surge in pot-smoking has rendered most criminals too relaxed to commit violent crimes. They're probably more focused on shoplifting boxes of **Ho-Hos** from convenience stores.

And then there's the most reckless move of all. Just last month, Canada decided to allow and recognize same-sex marriages. Merciful moose, what can they be thinking? Will there be married Mounties (they always get their man!)? **Dudley Do-Right** was sweet on Nell, not Mel! We must be the only ones who really care about families. Not enough to make sure they all have health insurance, of course, but more than those libertines up north.

This sort of behaviour is a clear and present danger to all our stereotypes about Canada. It's supposed to be a cold, wholesome country of polite, beer-drinking hockey players, not founded by freedom fighters in a bloody revolution, but quietly assembled by loyalists and royalists more interested in order and good government than liberty and independence.

lockstep: a rigid process, often mindlessly followed

But if we are the rugged individualists, why do we spend so much of our time trying to get everyone to march in **lockstep**? And if Canadians are so reserved and moderate, why are they so progressive about letting people do what they want to?

Canadians are, as a nation, less religious than we are, according to polls. As a result, Canada's government isn't influenced by large, well-organized religious groups and thus has more in common with those of Scandinavia than those of the United States, or, say, Iran.

Canada signed the Kyoto global warming treaty, lets 19-year-olds drink, has more of its population living in urban areas and accepts more immigrants per capita than the United States.

These are all things we've been told will wreck our society. But I guess Canadians are different, because theirs seems oddly sound.

Like teenagers, we fiercely idolize individual freedom but really demand that everyone be the same. But the Canadians seem more adult—more secure. They aren't afraid of foreigners. They aren't afraid of homosexuality. Most of all, they're not afraid of each other.

I wonder if America will ever be that cool.

UNDERSTANDING "HEY, CANADA'S ONE COOL COUNTRY"

1. Does Bennett use the subject-by-subject or point-by-point form of contrast? Do you think this form is more or less effective than the other for this topic?

2. Bennett uses humour throughout the article. Do you think this makes her article more or less effective?

3. Canada has been described as being more "moderate" than the United States. Why do you think this might be?

WRITING FROM READING "HEY, CANADA'S ONE COOL COUNTRY"

When you write on any of the following topics, be sure to work through the stages of the writing process in preparing your paragraph.

1. Have you noticed any similarities between Canada and your home country? Write a paragraph comparing or contrasting one element (i.e. importance of family, or approach to health care, child care, welfare, etc.) of the two countries.

2. What are some of the most common misperceptions that Americans have of Canada and Canadians? That Canadians have of Americans? Write a paragraph in which you compare or contrast these misperceptions.

3. It has long been thought that weather can impact behaviour; Shakespeare alluded to this in *Romeo and Juliet* when a character suggests that, because of the hot weather, a fight would break out. Do you think Canadians are often considered "polite" because of our cool weather? Write a paragraph in which you compare or contrast "weather behaviours."

CHAPTER 8
Classification

LEARNING OBJECTIVES

After you have read this chapter and completed its exercises
and assignments, you should be able to

- choose an appropriate topic for classification
- choose a basis for classification
- organize your classification paragraph effectively
- draft and edit your classification paragraph

*"Order is repetition of units. Chaos is
multiplicity without rhythm."*

~ M. C. ESCHER

▼

M. C. ESCHER, BORN IN
THE LATE NINETEENTH
CENTURY, WAS A DUTCH
GRAPHIC DESIGNER
BEST KNOWN FOR HIS
INTRICATE ARTWORK.

WHAT IS CLASSIFICATION?

When you **classify,** you divide something into different categories, and you do
it according to some basis. For example, you may classify the people in
your neighbourhood into three categories: those you know well, those you
know slightly, and those you don't know at all. Although you may not be
aware of it, you have chosen a basis for this classification; that is, you are
classifying the people in your neighbourhood according to *how well you
know them.*

Hints for Writing a Classification Paragraph

1. **Divide your subject into three or more categories.** If you are thinking
   about classifying DVD players, for instance, you might think about
   dividing them into cheap DVD players and expensive DVD players.
   Your basis for classification would be the price of DVD players. But you
   would need at least one more price category—moderately priced DVD
   players. Using at least three categories helps you to be reasonably
   complete in your classification.

2. **Pick one basis for classification and stick with it.** If you're classifying DVD players on the basis of price, you can't divide them into cheap, expensive, and Japanese. Two of the categories relate to price, but "Japanese" does not.

In the following examples, notice how one item doesn't fit its classification and has been crossed out:

anglers
anglers who fish every day
weekend anglers
~~anglers who own their own boat~~
anglers who fish once a year
(If you are classifying anglers on the basis of how often they fish, "anglers who own their own boat" doesn't fit.)

tests
essay tests
objective tests
~~math tests~~
combination essay and objective tests
(If you are classifying tests on the basis of the type of questions they ask, "math tests" doesn't fit because it describes the subject being tested.)

3. **Be creative in your classification.** While it is easy to classify drivers according to their age, your paragraph will be more interesting if you choose another basis of comparison, such as how drivers react to a very slow driver in front of them.

4. **Have a reason for your classification.** You may be classifying to help a reader understand a topic or to help a reader choose something. You may be trying to prove a point, to criticize, or to attack.

A classification paragraph must have a unifying reason behind it, and the details for each category should be as descriptive and specific as possible. Determining your audience and deciding why you are classifying can help you stay focused and make your paragraph more interesting.

| EXERCISE 1 | FINDING A BASIS FOR CLASSIFYING |

Write three bases for classifying each of the following topics. The first topic is done for you.

1. **topic to classify:** jobs
You can classify jobs on the basis of

   a. what kind of education is required

   b. which industry they're in

   c. how much they pay

2. **topic to classify:** cars
    You can classify cars on the basis of

    a. _____

    b. _____

    c. _____

3. **topic to classify:** children
    You can classify children on the basis of

    a. _____

    b. _____

    c. _____

4. **topic to classify:** books
    You can classify books on the basis of

    a. _____

    b. _____

    c. _____

EXERCISE
2

IDENTIFYING WHAT DOESN'T FIT THE CLASSIFICATION

In each list below, one item doesn't fit because it is not classified on the same basis as the others in the list. First, determine the basis for the classification. Then, cross out the one item on each list that doesn't fit.

1. **topic:** parties

    basis for classification: _____

    list: anniversary parties
              birthday parties
              small parties
              retirement parties

2. **topic:** liars

    basis for classification: _____

    list: constant liars
              frequent liars
              occasional liars
              vicious liars

3. **topic:** jewellery

basis for classification: _____

list: earring
        diamond
        necklace
        bracelet

4. **topic:** sleepers

basis for classification: _____

list: late sleepers
        people who snore
        people who toss and turn
        people who talk in their sleep

5. **topic:** police

basis for classification: _____

list: captain
        detective
        officer of the year
        constable

EXERCISE 3

FINDING CATEGORIES THAT FIT ONE BASIS FOR CLASSIFICATION

In the lines under each topic, write three categories that fit the basis of classification that is given. The first one is done for you.

1. **topic:** cartoons on television
   basis for classification: when they are shown
   categories:

   a. Saturday morning cartoons _____

   b. weekly cartoon series shown in the evening _____

   c. cartoons that are holiday specials _____

2. **topic:** doctors
   basis for classification: their specialty
   categories:

   a. _____

   b. _____

   c. _____

3. topic: computers
   basis for classification: price
   categories:
   a. _____
   b. _____
   c. _____

4. topic: music
   basis for classification: genre
   categories:
   a. _____
   b. _____
   c. _____

5. topic: vacations
   basis for classification: how long they are
   categories:
   a. _____
   b. _____
   c. _____

communication at work

In today's competitive marketplace, companies are constantly striving to keep their employees' skills current and up-to-date. To this end, most corporations have invested some-times large portions of their budgets in—and entire departments to—training and develop-ment. Many corporations have classified their training initiatives on the basis of how the learning is delivered: through e-learning, in a classroom, in a virtual classroom, or through blended learning, a combination of methods. In what other ways is classification used in the workplace?

WRITING THE CLASSIFICATION PARAGRAPH IN STEPS

THOUGHT LINES   ### GATHERING IDEAS: CLASSIFICATION

First, pick a topic for your classification. The next step is to choose some basis for your classification.

Brainstorming a Basis for Classification

Sometimes the easiest way to choose one basis is to brainstorm about different types related to your topic and to see where your brainstorming leads you. For example, if you were to write a paragraph classifying phone calls, you could begin by listing anything about phone calls that occurs to you:

Phone Calls

sales calls at dinner time	people talk too long
short calls	calls I hate getting
calls in middle of night	wrong number
long distance calls	waiting for a call

The next step is to survey your list. See where it is leading you. The list of phone calls includes a few *unpleasant phone calls*:

sales calls at dinner time

wrong number

calls in middle of night

Maybe you can label these "Calls I Do Not Want," and that will lead you toward a basis for classification. You might think about calls you *do not* want and calls you *do* want. You think further and realize that you want or do not want certain calls because of their effect on you. You decide to use the effect of the calls on you as the basis for classification. Remember, however, that you need at least three categories. If you stick with this basis for classification, you can come up with three categories:

Calls that please me

Calls that irritate me

Calls that frighten me

You can then gather details about your three categories by brainstorming:

> **Added Details for Three Categories**
>
> **Calls that please me**
>
> from boyfriend
>
> good friends
>
> catch-up calls—someone I haven't talked to for a while
>
> make me feel close
>
> **Calls that irritate me**
>
> sales calls at dinner time
>
> wrong numbers
>
> calls that irritate or interrupt
>
> invade privacy
>
> **Calls that frighten me**
>
> emergency call in middle of night
>
> "let's break up" call from boyfriend
>
> change my life, indicate some bad change

Matching the Points within the Categories

As you begin thinking about details for each of your categories, try to write about the same points in each category. For instance, in the list of phone calls, each category includes some details about who made the call.

> Calls that please me—from good friends, my boyfriend
>
> Calls that irritate me—from salespeople, unknown callers
>
> Calls that frighten me—from the emergency room, my boyfriend

Each category also includes some details about why you react to them in a specific way:

> Calls that please me—make me feel close
>
> Calls that irritate me—invade privacy
>
> Calls that frighten me—indicate some bad change

You achieve unity by covering the same points for each category.

Writing a Topic Sentence for a Classification Paragraph

The topic sentence for a classification paragraph should do two things:

1. It should mention what you are classifying.
2. It should indicate the basis for your classification by stating the basis or listing your categories, or both.

Consider the details on phone calls. To write a topic sentence about the details, you

1. mention what you are classifying: phone calls, and
2. indicate the basis for classifying by (a) stating the basis (whether I want to get the calls), or (b) listing the categories (calls that please me, calls that irritate me, and calls that frighten me). You may also state both the basis and the categories in the topic sentence.

Following these guidelines, you can write a topic sentence like this:

> I can classify phone calls according to their effect on me.

or

> Phone calls can be grouped into the ones that please me, the ones that irritate me, and the ones that frighten me.

Both of these topic sentences state what you're classifying and give some indication of the basis for the classification. Once you have a topic sentence, you are ready to begin the outlines stage of writing the classification paragraph.

EXERCISE **4** 	CREATING QUESTIONS TO GET DETAILS FOR A CLASSIFICATION PARAGRAPH

Do this exercise with a partner or group. Each of the following lists includes a topic, the basis for classifying that topic, and three categories. For each list, think of three questions that you could ask to get more details about the types. The first list is done for you.

1. **topic:** moviegoers

    basis for classification: how they behave during the movie

    categories: the quiet moviegoers, the irritating moviegoers, the
    obnoxious moviegoers

    questions you can ask:

    a. Does each type use a cellphone?

    b. Does each type talk during the movie?

    c. Does each type come and go during the movie?

2. **topic:** sports fans at a game

    basis for classification: how much they like the sport

    categories: fanatics, ordinary fans, and bored observers

    questions you can ask:

    a. _____

    b. _____

    c. _____

3. **topic:** people in line at the supermarket

    basis for classification: their reason for shopping

    categories: the convenience food singles, the responsible parents,
    the healthy dieters

    questions you can ask:

    a. _____

    b. _____

    c. _____

4. **topic:** cellphone users

    basis for classification: the features of their phones

    categories: those who use cellphones with internet access, those who use
    cellphones with cameras and camcorders, those who use
    basic cellphones

    questions you can ask:

    a. _____

    b. _____

    c. _____

5. **topic:** college students

    basis for classification: what they carry in their backpacks

    categories: those who carry the bare essentials, those who carry a few
    extras, those who carry more than they need

    questions you can ask:

    a. _____

    b. _____

    c. _____

EXERCISE	WRITING TOPIC SENTENCES FOR
5	**A CLASSIFICATION PARAGRAPH**

Review the topics, bases for classification, and categories in Exercise 4. Then, using that material, write a good topic sentence for each topic.

Topic Sentences

for topic 1: _____

_____

_____

for topic 2: _____

_____

_____

for topic 3: _____

_____

_____

for topic 4: _____

_____

_____

for topic 5: _____

_____

_____

OUT LINES   DEVISING A PLAN: CLASSIFICATION

Effective Order in Classifying

After you have a topic sentence and a list of details, you can create an outline. Think about which category you want to write about first, second, and so forth. The order of your categories will depend on what you're writing about. If you're classifying ways to meet people, you can save the best one for last. If you're classifying three habits that are bad for your health, you can save the worst one for last.

If you list your categories in the topic sentence, list them in the same order that you will explain them in the paragraph.

Below is an outline for a paragraph classifying phone calls. The thought lines have been put into categories. The underlined sentences have been added to clearly define each category before the detail is given.

> An Outline for a Classification Paragraph

topic sentence: Phone calls can be grouped into the ones that please me, the ones that irritate me, and the ones that frighten me.

category 1 details

There are some calls that please me.

They make me feel close to someone.

I like calls from my boyfriend, especially when he calls just to say he is thinking of me.

I like to hear from good friends.

I like catch-up calls.

These are calls from people I haven't talked to in a while.

category 2 details

There are some calls that irritate me.

These calls invade my privacy.

Sales calls always come at dinner time.

They offer me newspaper subscriptions or "free" vacations.

I get at least four wrong number calls each week.

All these calls irritate me, and I have to interrupt what I'm doing to answer them.

category 3 details

There are some calls that frighten me.

They are the calls that tell me about some bad change in my life.

I once got a call in the middle of the night.

It was from a hospital emergency room.

The nurse said my brother had been in an accident.

I once got a call from a boyfriend.

He said he wanted to break up.

You can use the following checklist to help you revise your own classification outline.

CHECKLIST   **FOR REVISING THE CLASSIFICATION OUTLINE**

✓ Do I have a consistent basis for classifying?

✓ Does my topic sentence mention what I'm classifying and indicate the basis for classification?

✓ Do I have enough to say about each category in my classification?

✓ Are the categories presented in the most effective order?

✓ Am I using clear and specific detail?

With a revised outline, you can begin writing your draft.

EXERCISE
6

RECOGNIZING THE BASIS FOR CLASSIFICATION WITHIN THE TOPIC SENTENCE

The topic sentences below do not state a basis for classification, but you can recognize the basis nevertheless. After you've read each topic sentence, write the basis for classification on the lines provided. The first one is done for you.

1. **topic sentence:** Neighbours can be classified into complete strangers, acquaintances, and buddies.
   basis for classification: how well you know them

2. **topic sentence:** At the Thai restaurant, you can order three kinds of hot sauce: hot sauce for beginners, hot sauce for the adventurous, and hot sauce for fire eaters.

   basis for classification: _____

3. **topic sentence:** When it comes to photographs of yourself, there are three types: the ones that make you look good, the ones that make you look fat, and the ones that make you look ridiculous.

   basis for classification: _____

4. **topic sentence:** On any airplane, there are some passengers who bring one small piece of luggage, others who bring a couple of large pieces, and some who bring enough luggage to fill the trunk of a car.

   basis for classification: _____

5. **topic sentence:** nternet users can be grouped into those who rely on it for news, those who use it for research, and those who use it for entertainment.

   basis for classification: _____

EXERCISE
7

ADDING DETAILS TO A CLASSIFICATION OUTLINE

Do this exercise with a partner or group. In this outline, add details where the blank lines indicate. Match the points covered in the other categories.

topic sentence: My jobs can be categorized into pleasant jobs, acceptable jobs, and unbearable jobs.

details: My first job was a pleasant job.
I worked at a small coffee shop.
I worked behind the take-out counter.
Business was steady but never hectic.
The staff was friendly and helpful to new employees.
The customers were regulars who enjoyed visiting the café.
Another job was an acceptable job.
I worked in the library at college.

I worked at the book check-out and return counter.
Sometimes there was no one in the library, and the job
was boring.

_____.

My last job was an unbearable job.
I worked at a movie theatre.
I sold tickets.

_____

_____

There were very few staff members, so it was lonely.

ROUGH LINES **DRAFTING AND REVISING: CLASSIFICATION**

You can transform your outline into a first draft of a paragraph by writing the topic sentence and the detail in paragraph form. As you write, you can begin combining some of the short sentences, adding details, and inserting transitions.

Transitions in Classification

Various transitions can be used in a classification paragraph. The transitions you select will depend on what you are classifying and the basis you choose for classifying. For example, if you are classifying roses according to how pretty they are, you can use transitions like, "One lovely kind of rose," and "Another, more beautiful kind," and "The most beautiful kind." In other classifications you can use transitions like "The first type," "Another type," or "The final type." In revising your classification paragraph, use the transitions that most clearly connect your ideas.

As you write your own paragraph, you may want to refer to a "kind" or a "type." For variety, try other words like "class," "category," "group," "species," "form," or "version," if it is logical to do so.

After you have a draft of your paragraph, you can revise and review it. The checklist below may help you with your revisions.

CHECKLIST FOR REVISING THE DRAFT OF A CLASSIFICATION PARAGRAPH

✓ Does my topic sentence include what I'm classifying?
✓ Does it indicate the basis of my classification?
✓ Should any of my sentences be combined?
✓ Do my transitions clearly connect my ideas?
✓ Should I add more details to any of the categories?
✓ Are the categories presented in the most effective order?

Below is a revised draft of the classification paragraph on phone calls with these changes from the outline:

- An introduction has been added, in front of the topic sentence, to make the paragraph smoother.
- Some sentences have been combined.
- Some details have been added.
- Transitions have been added.
- A final sentence has been added, so that the paragraph makes a stronger point.

> ## A Draft of a Classification Paragraph
>
> I get many phone calls, but they fit into three types. Phone calls can be grouped into the ones that please me, the ones that irritate me, and the ones that frighten me. There are some calls that please me because they make me feel close to someone. I like calls from my boyfriend, especially when he calls just to say he is thinking of me. I like to hear from my good friends. I like catch-up calls, the calls from people I haven't talked to in a while that fill me in on what friends have been doing. There are also calls that irritate me because they invade my privacy. Sales calls, offering me newspaper subscriptions and "free" vacations, always come at dinner time. In addition, I get at least four wrong-number calls each week. All these calls irritate me, and I have to interrupt what I'm doing to answer them. The more serious calls are the ones that frighten me. They are the calls that tell me about some bad change in my life. Once, in the middle of the night, a call from a hospital emergency room told me my brother had been in an accident. Another time, a boyfriend called to tell me he wanted to break up. When I get bad news by phone, I realize that the telephone can bring frightening calls as well as friendly or irritating ones.

EXERCISE 8

COMBINING SENTENCES FOR A BETTER CLASSIFICATION PARAGRAPH

The following paragraph has some short sentences that would be more effective if they were combined. Combine each pair of underlined sentences into one sentence. Write the new sentence in the space above the old ones.

In the dog world, there are yipper-yappers, authoritative barkers, and boom-box barkers. <u>Yipper-yappers have a short, high-pitched bark. Their bark sounds like hysterical nagging.</u> Yipping dogs are usually small dogs like miniature poodles or terriers. <u>The fiercely emotional quality of their bark is frightening. I am not too afraid of these dogs.</u> I know they can only get to my ankles if they attack. There is a moderate kind of dog. It is the authoritative barker. This type of dog has a deep bark; it signifies that the dog means business. Boxers, collies, and other medium-size dogs possess this commanding voice. <u>They demand my respect. I am afraid of them. Their low, growling bark and their size make me afraid.</u> The third kind of dog has a boom-box bark. <u>Its bark is very loud. It can be heard from blocks away.</u> Dogs that sound like this are usually the enormous ones like Great Danes or German shepherds. These dogs strike fear in my heart. They sound intimidating, and they have large bodies and giant teeth. <u>People say you can't judge a book by its cover. You can tell quite a bit about a dog by its bark.</u>

EXERCISE 9 — IDENTIFYING TRANSITIONS IN A CLASSIFICATION PARAGRAPH

Underline all the transitions in the following paragraph. The transitions may be words or groups of words.

At the supermarket where I work as a cashier, I classify my customers according to how they relate to me. First, there are those who are polite and kind to me. After I say, "Hello, how are you today?" they usually say, "Fine." Some make a funny comment about the weather or the traffic. This type of customer often makes pleasant conversation while I ring up the groceries. Another class of customer doesn't talk at all. As far as this kind is concerned, I do not exist. This kind simply stares right through me or, even worse, talks on a cellphone as I ring up and bag the groceries. Recently, I have seen customers glued to their phones throughout their time at the checkout counter, not even acknowledging me when I announce the total or hand them their change. The final and most dreaded type of customer is the angry customer. This kind is angry at me, at the other customers, and possibly at the whole world. Members of this group argue about the price of every item, complain about how long it takes to ring them up, and criticize the way I pack their groceries. They always leave shaking their heads in disgust. Dealing with these varieties of customers each day, I am grateful that most people fit into the first category, the good-natured, pleasant group.

 **PROOFREADING AND POLISHING: CLASSIFICATION**

Below is the final version of the classification paragraph on phone calls. If you compare the draft and final versions, you'll notice these changes:

- The first sentence has been rewritten so that it is less choppy and a word of transition, "My," links the second sentence to the first.
- Some words have been eliminated and sentences rewritten so that they are not too wordy.
- The word choice has been refined: "bad change" has been replaced by "crisis," "someone" has been changed to "a person I care about," to make the details more precise, and "irritate" has been changed to "annoy" to avoid repetition.

> ### A Final Version of a Classification Paragraph
>
> I get many phone calls, but most of them fall into one of three types. My phone calls can be grouped into the ones that please me, the ones that irritate me, and the ones that frighten me. There are some calls I want to receive because they make me feel close to <u>a person I care about.</u> I like calls from my boyfriend, especially when he calls just to say he is thinking of me. I like to hear from my good friends. I like catch-up calls from friends I haven't talked to in a while. There are also calls I don't want because they invade my privacy. Sales calls, offering me newspaper subscriptions and "free" vacations, always come at dinner time. In addition, I get at least four wrong-number calls each week. All these calls <u>annoy</u> me, and I have to interrupt what I'm doing to answer them. The more serious calls are the ones <u>I really don't want to receive.</u> They are the calls that tell me about some <u>crisis</u> in my life. <u>I once got a midnight call from a hospital emergency room, informing me my brother had been in an accident.</u> Another time, a boyfriend called to tell me he wanted to break up. When I get bad news by phone, I realize that the telephone can bring frightening calls as well as friendly or irritating ones.

Before you prepare the final version of your own classification paragraph, check your latest draft for errors in spelling and punctuation, and for any errors made in typing or recopying.

EXERCISE 10

PROOFREADING TO PREPARE THE FINAL VERSION

Below are two classification paragraphs with the kinds of errors that are easy to overlook when you prepare the final version of an assignment. Correct the errors, writing above the lines. The first paragraph has thirteen errors; the second has eleven errors.

   1.   My experince in school has shown me their are three kinds of

pencils, and they are the pencils that work great, the pencils that barely work,

and the pencils that dont work at all. The pencil's that work are the ones that are perfectly sharpened to a razor-fine point and have huge, clean erasers at the end. These pencils produce a dark, clear line when I write with them unfortunatly, I never do write with them. Great pencils are the ones I always come accross, all over the house, when i'm looking for something else. The pencils I usually rite with are the damaged pencils. They work, but not well. They need sharpening, or their erasers are worn so far down that using them leaves rips across the page. Sometimes these pencils leave a faded, weak line on the paper. Sometimes the line is so thick it look like a crayon. The third kind of pencl is the worst of all. Pencils in this group just don't work. They have no point. Or if they have a point, it brakes off as soon as I write. They have no eraser. The pencils are so chewed and mutilated they might have been previously owned by woodpeckers. Non-working pencils are the ones I bring to class on test days. I just do'nt seem to have much luck with pencils.

2.   Sleepers fall into three categories and they are the light sleeper, the average sleepers, and the heavy sleepers. Light sleepers have a hard time falling asleep and staying asleep. My mother is a light sleeper, and she cant fall asleep unless the room is totaly quite and completely dark. She have a sleep mask and earplugs to help her get to sleep. Even after she falls asleep, she does not sleep soundly. She swears she can hear me tiptoe acrost the living room when she is wearing her earplugs in bed. She wakes up and reads, raids the refridgerator, or turns on the television at least twice each night. Unlike my mother, I am a average sleeper. I fall asleep fairly easily, unless I have a problem on my mind. Even if I toss and turn until I get to sleep, I tend to sleep through the night. Loud noises like car alarms or sirens can wake me, but I am usually deep in sleep until my clock radio blasts me awake. My roommate is a much deeper sleeper then I am. He falls into the class of sleeper who can fall asleep in an instant. He can climb into bed and be unconscience in a minute. I may come in late, slam the door, and bump into a chair, but my roommate won't wake up. A car wreck outside the window doesn't disturb him. He sleeps trough the alarm clock, every morning until I shake him into awareness. He has a gift for sleeping that I wish he could share with my mother.

Lines of Detail: A Walk-Through Assignment

Write a paragraph that classifies bosses on the basis of how they treat their employees. To write the paragraph, follow these steps.

Step 1: List all the details you can remember about bosses you have worked for or known.

Step 2: Survey your list. Then list three categories of bosses, based on how they treat their employees.

Step 3: Now that you have three categories, study your list again, looking for matching points for all three categories. For example, all three categories could be described by this matching point: where the boss works.

Step 4: Write a topic sentence that (a) names what you are classifying, and (b) states the basis for classification or names all three categories.

Step 5: Write an outline. Check that your outline defines each category, uses matching points for each category, and puts the categories in an effective order.

Step 6: Write a draft of the classification paragraph. Check the draft, revising it until it has specific detail, smooth transitions, and effective word choice.

Step 7: Before you prepare the final copy of your paragraph, check your last draft for any errors in punctuation, spelling, word choice, or mechanics.

Writing Your Own Classification Paragraph

When you write on any of these topics, be sure to work through the stages of the writing process in preparing your classification paragraph.

1. Write a classification paragraph on any of the following topics. If your instructor agrees, brainstorm with a partner or with a group to come up with (1) a basis for your classification, (2) categories related to the basis, and (3) points you can make to give details about each of the categories.

horror movies	cars	MP3 players
romantic movies	hockey players	scams
children	fans at a concert	excuses
parents	fans at a sports event	cellphone options
students	neighbours	dogs
teachers	restaurants	fears
drivers	dates	weddings
salespeople		

2. Adapt one of the topics in question 1 by making your topic smaller. You can classify Chinese restaurants, for example, instead of restaurants, or sports cars, instead of cars. Then write a classification paragraph that helps your reader make a choice about your topic.

3. Below are some topics. Each one already has a basis for classification. Write a classification paragraph on one of these choices. If your instructor

agrees, work with a partner or with a group to brainstorm categories, matching points and details for the categories.

Classify

1. exams on the basis of how difficult they are.

2. weekends on the basis of how busy they are.

3. Valentines on the basis of how romantic they are.

4. breakfasts on the basis of how healthy they are.

5. snowboarders (or people who engage in some other sport) on the basis of how experienced they are.

6. singers on the basis of the kind of audience they appeal to.

7. parties on the basis of how much fun they are.

8. television commercials on the basis of what time of day or night they are broadcast.

9. radio stations on the basis of what kind of music they play.

10. urban legends on the basis of how illogical they are.

WRITING FROM READING: CLASSIFICATION

I'm a Banana and Proud of It

Wayson Choy

Wayson Choy is the author of The Jade Peony *and* All That Matters, *the latter having won the Trillium Book Award for writing in English in 2005. Born in Vancouver, he currently teaches creative writing at Humber College.*

Before you read this essay, consider these questions:

Why do you think people use stereotypes?

How can we fight stereotypes?

What challenges do first-generation children of immigrants face?

Because both my parents came from China, I took Chinese. But I cannot read or write Chinese and barely speak it. I love my North American citizenship. I don't mind being called a "banana," yellow on the outside and white inside. I'm proud I'm a banana.

After all, in Canada and the United States, native Indians are "apples" (red outside, white inside); blacks are "Oreo cookies" (black and white); and Chinese are "bananas." These metaphors assume, both rightly and wrongly, that the culture here has been primarily anglo-white. Cultural history made me a banana.

History: My father and mother arrived separately to the B.C. coast in the early part of the century. They came as unwanted "aliens." Better to be an alien here than to be dead of starvation in China. But after the Chinese Exclusion laws were passed in North America (late 1800s, early 1900s), no Chinese immigrants were granted citizenship in either Canada or the United States.

concibine: mistress

Like those Old China village men from Toi San who, in the 1850s, laid down cliff-edge train tracks through the Rockies and the Sierras, or like those first women who came as mail-order wives or **concubines** and who as bond-slaves were turned into cheaper labourers or even prostitutes—like many of those men and women, my father and mother survived ugly, unjust times. In 1917, two hours after he got off the boat from Hong Kong, my father was called "chink" and told to go back to China. "Chink" is a hateful racist term, stereotyping the shape of Asian eyes: "a chink in the armour," an undesirable slit. For the Elders, the past was humiliating. Eventually, the Second World War changed hostile attitudes toward the Chinese.

During the war, Chinese men volunteered and lost their lives as members of the American and Canadian military. When hostilities ended, many more were proudly in uniform waiting to go overseas. Record Chinatown dollars were raised to buy **War Bonds**. After 1945, challenged by such money and ultimate sacrifices, the Exclusion laws in both Canada and the U.S. were revoked. Chinatown residents claimed their citizenship and sent for their families.

War Bonds: certificates sold by the government to raise money to fight the War

By 1949, after the Communists took over China, those of us who arrived here as young children, or were born here, stayed. No longer "aliens," we became legal citizens of North America. Many of us also became "bananas."

Historically, "banana" is not a racist term. Although it clumsily stereotypes many of the children and grandchildren of the Old Chinatowns, the term actually follows the old Chinese tendency to assign **endearing** nicknames to replace formal names, semicomic names to keep one humble. Thus, "banana" describes the generations who assimilated so well into North American life.

endearing: to make beloved

In fact, our families encouraged members of my generation in the 1950s and sixties to "get ahead," to get an English education, to get a job with good pay and prestige. "Don't work like me," Chinatown parents said. "Work in an office!" The lao wah-kiu (the Chinatown old-timers) also warned, "Never forget—you still be Chinese!"

None of us ever forgot. The mirror never lied.

Many Chinatown teenagers felt we didn't quite belong in any one world. We looked Chinese, but thought and behaved North American. Impatient Chinatown parents wanted the best of both worlds for us, but they bluntly labelled their children and grandchildren "juk-sing" or even "mo no." Not that we were totally "shallow bamboo butt-ends" or entirely "no brain," but we had less and less understanding of Old China traditions, and less and less interest in their village histories. Father used to say we lacked Taoist ritual, Taoist manners. We were, he said, "mo li."

This was true. Chinatown's younger brains, like everyone else's of whatever race, were being colonized by "whitebread" U.S. family television programs. We began to feel Chinese home life was inferior. We co-operated with English-language magazines that showed us how to act and what to buy. Seductive Hollywood movies made some of us secretly weep that we did not have movie-star faces. American music made Chinese music sound like noise.

By the 1970s and eighties, many of us had consciously or unconsciously distanced ourselves from our Chinatown histories. We became bananas.

Finally, for me, in my 40s and 50s, with the death first of my mother, then my father, I realized I did not belong anywhere unless I could understand the past. I needed to find the foundation of my Chinese-ness. I needed roots.

I spent my college holidays researching the past. I read Chinatown oral histories, located documents, searched out early articles. Those early citizens came back to life for me. Their long toil and blood sacrifices, the proud record of their patient, legal challenges, gave us all our present rights as citizens. Canadian and American Chinatowns set aside their family tongue differences and encouraged each other to fight injustice. There were no borders. "After all," they affirmed, "Daaih ga tohng yahn...We are all Chinese!"

In my book, *The Jade Peony*, I tried to re-create this past, to explore the beginnings of the conflicts trapped within myself, the struggle between being Chinese and being North American. I discovered a truth: these "between world" struggles are universal.

In every human being, there is "the Other"—something that makes each of us feel how different we are to everyone else, even to family members. Yet, ironically, we are all the same, wanting the same security and happiness. I know this now.

I think the early Chinese pioneers actually started "going bananas" from the moment they first settled upon the West Coast. They had no choice. They adapted. They initiated assimilation. If they had not, they and their family would have starved to death. I might even suggest that all surviving Chinatown citizens eventually became bananas. Only some, of course, were more ripe than others.

paradox: a seemingly self-contradictory expression

That's why I'm proudly a banana: I accept the **paradox** of being both Chinese and not Chinese.

Now at last, whenever I look in the mirror or hear ghost voices shouting, "You still Chinese!" I smile.

I know another truth: In immigrant North America, we are all Chinese.

UNDERSTANDING "I'M A BANANA AND PROUD OF IT"

1. According to Choy, what does the term "banana" mean?

2. Many of the classifications Choy mentions ("apple," "Oreo cookie") could be considered offensive. Why is Choy not offended by the term "banana"?

3. Choy's father was called a "chink," a "hateful racist term." What is the difference between this term and "banana," what Choy calls a nickname?

4. According to Choy, why did Chinese parents encourage their children to assimilate into Canadian culture?

5. What do you think Choy means by "We are all Chinese"? Do you agree or disagree?

WRITING FROM READING "I'M A BANANA AND PROUD OF IT"

When you write on any of the following topics, be sure to work through the stages of the writing process.

1. Wayson Choy progresses from mentioning the derogatory classifications of "apple" and "Oreo cookie" to stating that "We are all Chinese." Does the immigrant experience give us all a common ground? Do we really have the same experiences? Do some informal research and write a humorous paragraph in which you classify some common immigrant experiences.

2. Think about your childhood experiences. Which are strongest in your memory? Write a paragraph in which you clearly categorize these experiences.

3. Choy distinguishes between hateful, racist terms and nicknames. Write a paragraph in which you classify some of the terms in common use today, and their effects.

ALONG THESE LINES/Pearson Education Canada

CHAPTER 9
Cause and Effect

LEARNING OBJECTIVES

After you have read this chapter and completed its exercises and assignments, you should be able to

- choose an appropriate topic for a cause or effect paragraph
- write an appropriate topic sentence for a cause or effect paragraph
- provide clear and specific causes or effects in a paragraph
- use appropriate transitions in a cause or effect paragraph
- draft and edit your cause or effect paragraph

"Life is a perpetual instruction in cause and effect."

~ RALPH WALDO EMERSON

▼

RALPH WALDO EMERSON WAS A NINETEENTH-CENTURY POET AND ESSAYIST. HE WAS ALSO CONSIDERED ONE OF THE GREATEST ORATORS (SPEECHMAKERS) OF HIS TIME.

WHAT IS CAUSE AND EFFECT?

Almost every day, you consider the causes or effects of events so that you can make choices and take action. In writing a paragraph, when you explain the *reasons* for something, you are writing about **causes**. When you write about the *results* of something, you are writing about **effects**. Often in writing, you consider both the causes and effects of a decision, an event, a change in your life, or a change in society, but in this chapter you will be asked to concentrate on *either* causes (reasons) *or* effects (results).

Hints for Writing a Cause or Effect Paragraph

1. **Pick a topic you can handle in one paragraph.** A topic you can handle in one paragraph is one that (a) is not too large, and (b) doesn't require research.

    Some topics are so large that you probably can't cover them in one paragraph. Topics that are too large include ones like

    Why People Get Angry

    Effects of Unemployment on My Family

Other topics require you to research the facts and to include the opinions of experts. They would be good topics for a research paper, but not for a one-paragraph assignment. Topics that require research include ones like

The Causes of Divorce

The Effects of Television Viewing on Children

When you write a cause or effect paragraph, choose a topic you can write about by using what you already know. That is, make your topic smaller and more personal. Topics that use what you already know are ones like

Why Children Love Video Games

The Causes of My Divorce

What Enlistment in the Armed Forces Did for My Sister

How Alcoholics Anonymous Changed My Life

2. **Try to have at least three causes or effects in your paragraph.** Be sure you consider immediate and remote causes or immediate and remote effects. Think about your topic and gather as many causes or effects as you can *before* you start drafting your paragraph.

An event usually has more than one cause. Think beyond the obvious, the *immediate cause*, to more *remote causes*. For example, the immediate cause of your car accident might be the other driver who hit the rear end of your car. But more remote causes might include the weather conditions or the condition of the road.

Situations can have more than one result, too. If you take Algebra I for the second time and you pass the course with a "C," an *immediate result* is that you fulfill the requirements for graduation. But there may be other, more *remote results*. Your success in algebra may help to change your attitude toward mathematics courses. Or your success may build your confidence in your ability to handle college work. Or your success may lead you to sign up for another course taught by the same teacher.

3. **Make your causes and effects clear and specific.** If you are writing about why Facebook is popular, don't write, "Facebook is popular because everybody is on it," or "Facebook is popular because it's a trend." If you write either of these statements, you're really saying, "Facebook is popular because it's popular."

Think further. Don't people get back in touch with friends they haven't seen in years? What about the applications and groups? By giving specific details that explain, illustrate, or describe a cause or effect, you help the reader understand your point.

4. **Write a topic sentence that indicates whether your paragraph is about causes or effects.** You shouldn't announce, but you can *indicate*.

not this: The effects of my winning the scholarship are going to be discussed. (an announcement)

but this: Winning the scholarship changed my plans for college. (indicates effects will be discussed)

You can *list* a short version of all your causes or effects in your topic sentence, like this:

ALONG THESE LINES/Pearson Education Canada

The popularity of "foreign" cars has forced North American car makers to change their products, close manufacturing plants, and create a whole new line of hybrid cars.

You can *hint* at your points by summarizing them, like this:

The popularity of "foreign" cars has challenged and even threatened its competition, but it has also created new business opportunities.

Or you can use words that *signal* causes or effects.

words that signal causes: reasons, why, because, motives, intentions
words that signal effects: results, impact, consequences, changed, threatened, improved

---

EXERCISE 1

SELECTING A SUITABLE TOPIC FOR A CAUSE OR EFFECT PARAGRAPH

Below is a list of topics. Some topics are suitable for a cause or effect paragraph. Some are too large to handle in one paragraph, some would require research, and some are both too large and would require research. Put *OK* next to any topic that is suitable, and an *X* next to any topic that is not.

Topics—Suitable and Not Suitable

1. _____ Why Dinosaurs Appeal to Children
2. _____ Effects of Smoking Cigarettes
3. _____ Reasons I Attend College Part-Time
4. _____ Why Kids Love Soccer
5. _____ The Impact of Technology on Education
6. _____ The Causes of Drug Abuse
7. _____ The Effects of AIDS on Our Society
8. _____ How Magic Johnson Changed My Perceptions of AIDS
9. _____ Why Marriages Fail
10. _____ The Causes of Anorexia

EXERCISE 2

RECOGNIZING CAUSE AND EFFECT IN TOPIC SENTENCES

In the following list, if the topic sentence is for a "cause" paragraph, put a *C* next to it. If the topic sentence is for an "effect" paragraph, put an *E* next to it.

Topic Sentences for Cause or Effect Paragraphs

1. _____ Taking on shift work at the shop had interesting consequences on my part-time studies.
2. _____ I decided to pierce my eyebrow out of a desire to look different, to do something exciting, and to shock my parents.
3. _____ Jack has several motives for proposing marriage.
4. _____ Until I actually owned one, I never knew how a laptop could change a person's work habits.
5. _____ The television's remote control device has created conflicts in my marriage.

6. _____ Children enjoy horror movies because the movies allow them to deal with their fears in a nonthreatening way.

7. _____ People buy clothes with designer labels to impress others, to feel successful, and to feel accepted into a high social class.

8. _____ The birth of my little sister had an unexpected impact on my life.

9. _____ I am beginning to understand why my mother was a strict disciplinarian.

10. _____ Illegal downloading has changed the music industry.

WRITING THE CAUSE OR EFFECT PARAGRAPH IN STEPS

 GATHERING IDEAS: CAUSE OR EFFECT

Once you've picked a topic, the next—and very important—step is getting ideas. Because this paragraph will contain only causes or effects and details about them, you must have enough causes or effects to write a developed paragraph.

Freewriting on a Topic

One way to get ideas is to freewrite on your topic. Because causes and effects are clearly connected, you can begin by freewriting about both and then choose one— causes or effects—later.

If you were thinking about writing a cause or effect paragraph on owning a car, you could begin by freewriting something like this:

> **Freewriting on Owning a Car**
>
> A car of my own. Why? I needed it. Couldn't get a part-time job without one. Because I couldn't get to work. Needed it to get to school. Of course I could have taken the bus to school. But I didn't want to. Feel like an adult when you have a car of your own. Freedom to come and go. I was the last of my friends to have a car. Couldn't wait. An old Camaro. But I fixed it up nicely. Costs a lot to maintain. Car payments, car loan. Car insurance.

Now you can review the freewriting and make separate lists of causes and effects you wrote down:

Causes (Reasons)
needed to get a part-time job
needed to get to school
my friends had cars

Effects (Results)
feel like an adult
freedom to come and go
costs a lot to maintain
car payments
car loan
car insurance

Because you have more details on the effects of owning a car, you decide to write an effects paragraph.

Your list of effects can be used several ways. You can add to it if you think of ideas as you are reviewing your list. You can begin to group ideas in your list and then add to it. Below is a grouping of the list of effects. Grouping helps you see how many effects and details you have.

Effects of Getting My Own Car

one effect:	I had to pay for the car and related expenses.
details:	costs a lot to maintain
	car payments
	car loan
	car insurance
second effect:	I had the freedom to come and go.
details:	none
third effect:	I felt like an adult.
details:	none

Will these effects work in a paragraph? One way to decide is to try to add details to the effects that have no details. Now ask questions to get the details.

second effect: I had the freedom to come and go.

What do you mean?

Well, I didn't have to beg my father for his truck anymore. I didn't have to get rides from friends. I could go to the city when I wanted. I could ride around just for fun.

third effect: I felt like an adult.

What do you mean, "like an adult"?

Adults can go where they want, when they want. They drive themselves.

If you look carefully at the answers to the questions above, you'll find that the two effects are really *the same*. By adding details to both effects, you'll find that both are saying that owning a car gives you the adult freedom to come and go.

So the list needs another effect of owning a car. What else happened? How else did things change when you got your car? You might answer:

I worried about someone hitting my car.

I worried about bad drivers.

I wanted to avoid the scratches you get in parking lots.

With answers like these, your third effect could be

I became a more careful driver.

Now that you have three effects and some details, you can rewrite your list. You can add details as you rewrite.

List of Effects of Getting My Own Car

one effect:	I had to pay for the car and related expenses.
details:	costs a lot to maintain
	car payments
	car loans
	car insurance

(continued)

ALONG THESE LINES/Pearson Education Canada

> **second effect:** I had the adult freedom to come and go.
>
> **details:** didn't have to beg my father for his truck
> didn't have to get rides from friends
> could go to the city when I wanted
> could ride around for fun
>
> **third effect:** I became a more careful driver.
>
> **details:** worried about someone hitting the car
> worried about bad drivers
> wanted to avoid the scratches cars get in parking lots

Designing a Topic Sentence

With at least three effects and some details for each effect, you can create a topic sentence. The topic sentence for this paragraph should indicate that the subject is the *effects* of getting a car. You can summarize all three effects in your topic sentence, or you can just hint at them. A possible topic sentence for the paragraph can be

> Owning my own car cost me money, gave me freedom, and made me more
> careful about how I drive.

or

> Once I got a car of my own, I realized the good and bad sides of ownership.

With a topic sentence and a fairly extensive list of details, you are ready to begin the outlines step in preparing your paragraph.

EXERCISE 3

DESIGNING QUESTIONS FOR A CAUSE OR EFFECT PARAGRAPH

Below are four topics for cause or effect paragraphs. For each topic, write five questions that could lead you to ideas on the topic. (The first one is completed for you.) After you've written five questions for each topic, give your list to a member of your writing group. Ask him or her to add one question to each topic and then to pass the exercise on to the next member of the group. Repeat the process so that each group member adds to the lists of all the other members.

Later, if your instructor agrees, you can answer the questions (and add more questions and answers) as a way to begin writing a cause or effect paragraph.

1. **topic:** the effects of camera phones on crime

   questions that can lead to ideas and details:

   a. Are unsuspecting people photographed and blackmailed?

   b. Can the cameras be used to photograph confidential documents?

   c. Are the cameras used by Peeping Toms?

   d. Can criminals use the camera phones to photograph banks?

   e. Can citizens photograph a crime in progress?

   additional questions: Can citizens photograph a suspect or perpetrator? Can police use the cameras in surveillance?

2. **topic:** why college students work part- or full-time
    questions that can lead to ideas and details:

    a. _____

    b. _____

    c. _____

    d. _____

    e. _____

    additional questions: _____

    _____

    _____

    _____

    _____

3. **topic:** the effects of portable technology (e.g. PDAs, laptops, wireless Internet access, cellphones) on family life
    questions that can lead to ideas and details:

    a. _____

    b. _____

    c. _____

    d. _____

    e. _____

    additional questions: _____

    _____

    _____

    _____

    _____

4. **topic:** why Canadians are eating more meals away from home
    questions that could lead to ideas and details:

    a. _____

    b. _____

    c. _____

    d. _____

    e. _____

    additional questions: _____

    _____

    _____

    _____

    _____

ALONG THESE LINES/Pearson Education Canada

5. **topic:** the effects of high gas prices on drivers
   questions that could lead to ideas and details:

   a. _____

   b. _____

   c. _____

   d. _____

   e. _____

   additional questions: _____

   _____

   _____

   _____

   _____

EXERCISE 4 | **CREATING CAUSES OR EFFECTS FOR TOPIC SENTENCES**

For each of the following topic sentences, create three causes or effects, depending on what the topic sentence requires. The first one is completed for you.

1. **topic sentence:** Voicemail has both improved and complicated my life.

   a. I don't miss important calls anymore.

   b. Now I have to deal with all the messages left on my answering machine.

   c. I also have to decide whether to answer my phone or to "screen" calls when I am at home and the phone rings.

2. **topic sentence:** Small children may fear the dark for a number of reasons.

   a. _____

   _____

   b. _____

   _____

   c. _____

   _____

3. **topic sentence:** There are several reasons why students are afraid to speak in class.

   a. _____

   _____

   b. _____

   _____

   c. _____

   _____

4. **topic sentence:** Credit cards can have negative effects on those who use them.

   a. _____
   _____

   b. _____
   _____

   c. _____
   _____

5. **topic sentence:** Taking too many college courses at one time can have serious consequences.

   a. _____
   _____

   b. _____
   _____

   c. _____
   _____

communication at work

Academic institutions are very clear about the consequences of what they call "academic dishonesty," which includes cheating and plagiarism. Consider these passages, taken from the Kwantlen University College website:

> **Cheating**, which includes plagiarism, occurs where a student or group of students uses or attempts to use unauthorized aids, assistance, materials or methods.
> **Plagiarism** occurs where a student represents the work or ideas of another person as his or her own.*

What happens if a student plagiarizes? At Kwantlen University College,

- for most first offences, a grade of zero will be awarded for the affected assignment, test, paper, analysis, etc.;
- for most second offences, a failing grade will be assigned in the affected course;
- depending upon the circumstances surrounding a first or second offence, a more severe level of discipline may be imposed by the university college;
- where deemed appropriate in the circumstances, for any third offence, the matter will be referred to the vice president, academic, for the assignment of discipline which may include, but is not limited to, suspension or expulsion from the university college.

Can you think of other examples of cause and effect at your college? At work?

Source: Kwantlen University College, http://www.kwantlen.ca/registrar/honesty.pdf
Review Chapter 2 of this text to learn how to avoid plagiarism, or ask your instructor for assistance.

 **DEVISING A PLAN: CAUSE OR EFFECT**

With a topic sentence and a list of causes (or effects) and details, you can draft an outline of your paragraph. Once you have a rough outline, you can work on revising it. You may want to add to it, take out certain ideas, rewrite the topic sentence, or change the order of the ideas. The checklist below may help you revise your outline.

ALONG THESE LINES/Pearson Education Canada

CHECKLIST　**FOR REVISING THE OUTLINE OF A CAUSE OR EFFECT PARAGRAPH**

✓ Does my topic sentence make my point?

✓ Does it indicate whether my paragraph is about causes or effects?

✓ Does the topic sentence fit the rest of the outline?

✓ Have I included enough causes or effects to make my point?

✓ Have I included enough details?

✓ Should I eliminate any ideas?

✓ Is the order of my causes or effects clear and logical?

The Order of Causes or Effects

Looking at a draft outline can help you decide on the best order for your reasons (causes) or results (effects). There is no single rule for organizing reasons or results. Instead, you should think about the ideas you are presenting and decide on the most logical and effective order.

For example, if you are writing about some immediate and some long-range effects, you might want to discuss the effects in a **time order**. You might begin with the immediate effect, then discuss what happens later, and end with what happens last of all. If you are discussing three or four effects that are not in any particular time order, you might save the most important effect for last, for an **emphatic order**. If one cause leads to another, then use the **logical order** of discussing the causes.

Compare the following outline on owning a car to the previous list of effects. Notice that the carefree side of owning a car comes first, and the cares of owning a car, the expense and the worry, come later. The topic sentence follows the same order.

An Outline for an Effects Paragraph

topic sentence: Owning my own car gave me freedom, cost me money, and made me careful about how I drive.

effect 1: I had the adult freedom to come and go.

details: I didn't have to beg my father for his truck.

I didn't have to get rides from my friends.

I could go to the city when I wanted.

I could ride around for fun.

effect 2: I had to pay for the car and related expenses.

details: A car costs a lot to maintain.

I had car payments.

I had a car loan to pay.

I had car insurance.

effect 3: I became a more careful driver.

details: I worried about someone hitting the car.

I worried about bad drivers.

I wanted to avoid the scratches cars can get in a parking lot.

Once you have a revised outline of your cause or effect paragraph, you are ready to begin your draft.

EXERCISE **5**	**WRITING TOPIC SENTENCES FOR CAUSE** **OR EFFECT OUTLINES**

Below are two outlines. They have no topic sentences. Read the outlines carefully, several times. Then write a topic sentence for each.

1. topic sentence: _____

    _____

    _____

    _____

    details: When I don't get enough sleep, I get irritable.
               Little things, like my friend's wise remarks, make me angry.
               At work, I am not as patient as I usually am when a customer
               complains.
               Lack of sleep also slows me down.
               When I'm tired, I can't think as fast.
               For instance, it takes me ten minutes to find a number in the
               phone book when I can usually find one in a minute.
               When I'm tired, I am slower in restocking the shelves at the
               store where I work.
               Worst of all, I make more mistakes when I'm tired.
               Last Monday, I was so tired I locked myself out of my car.
               And a sleepless night can cause me to ring up a sale the
               wrong way.
               Then I have to spend hours trying to fix my mistake before
               my boss catches it.

2. topic sentence: _____

    _____

    _____

    _____

    details: Denise wasn't really interested in the things I like to do.
               She hated sports.
               She always complained when we went to football games together.
               Denise was not much fun to be with.
               Whenever we were together, we wound up fighting over some
               trivial thing.
               For example, we once spent a whole evening fighting about
               what movie we should see.
               My main reason for breaking up was Denise's lack of trust
               in me.
               Denise couldn't believe I cared about her unless I showed her,
               every minute.
               She made me call her at least three times a day.
               She needed to know where I was at all times.
               She was jealous of the time I spent away from her.

EXERCISE 6	**REVISING THE ORDER OF CAUSES OR EFFECTS**

Below are topic sentences and lists of causes or effects. Reorder each list according to the directions given at the end of the list. Put 1 by the item that would come first, 2 by the next one, and so forth.

1. **topic sentence:** My brother went on a diet for several reasons.

   _____ He couldn't exercise for as long as he was used to.

   _____ His clothes were too tight.

   _____ A doctor told him his weight was raising his cholesterol to a dangerous level.

   Use this order: From least important to most important (emphatic order).

2. **topic sentence:** Cellphones have had a serious impact on driving.

   _____ Some areas are banning the use of cellphones by drivers.

   _____ Many accidents involved distracted drivers talking on their cellphones.

   _____ People began to use cellphones while they drove because the phones were so convenient.

   Use this order: Time order.

3. **topic sentence:** Losing my job had negative and positive effects on me.

   _____ I was in a state of shock because I had no idea I'd be laid off.

   _____ I eventually realized the job had been a dead-end job and I could do better.

   _____ I went from shock to a feeling of failure.

   Use this order: The order indicated by the topic sentence, from bad to good.

EXERCISE 7	**DEVELOPING AN OUTLINE**

The outlines below need one more cause or effect and details related to that cause or effect. Fill in the missing parts.

1. **topic sentence:** A promotion at work can be both rewarding and frightening.

   effect 1: Moving up is a sign that others respect a person's work.

   details: My father was thrilled to be promoted to assistant manager.
   His boss had told him the promotion was a reward for good work.
   It also signalled his boss' faith in him.

effect 2: In addition, a promotion is a chance to use more of one's talents and skills.

details: I was delighted to move up in the shipping company I worked for.
I knew I would no longer be locked into the same dull, daily routine.
Instead, I could make some of my own decisions.

effect 3: _____

_____

_____

details (at least two sentences): _____

_____

_____

2. **topic sentence:** People give many reasons for running red lights.

cause 1: Some claim it was safe to do so.

details: They say they were all alone on a deserted road.
They say there was no traffic coming or going.
Therefore, they say, they didn't need to stop.

cause 2: Many drivers swear they didn't see the light.

details: Some swear they were distracted by their children misbehaving in the car.
Others blame the dog; they say it jumped on them.
A few say they were changing the radio station and didn't look up in time.

cause 3: _____

_____

_____

details (at least three sentences): _____

_____

_____

_____

_____

_____

ROUGH LINES **DRAFTING AND REVISING: CAUSE OR EFFECT**

Once you have an outline in good order, with a sufficient number of causes or effects and a fair number of details, you can write a first draft of the paragraph. When the first draft is complete, you can read and reread it, deciding how you'd like to improve it. The checklist that follows may help you revise.

ALONG THESE LINES/Pearson Education Canada

✓

CHECKLIST   **FOR REVISING THE DRAFT OF A CAUSE OR EFFECT PARAGRAPH**

    ✓   Does my topic sentence indicate cause or effect?

    ✓   Does it fit the rest of the paragraph?

    ✓   Do I have enough causes or effects to make my point?

    ✓   Do I have enough details for each cause or effect?

    ✓   Are my causes or effects explained clearly?

    ✓   Is there a clear connection between my points?

    ✓   Do I need to combine sentences?

    ✓   Do I need an opening or closing sentence?

Linking Ideas in Cause or Effect

When you write about how one event or situation causes another, or about how one result leads to another, you have to be clear in showing the connections between events, situations, or effects.

One way to be clear is to rely on transitions. Some transitions are particularly helpful in writing cause and effect paragraphs.

INFOBOX   **TRANSITIONS FOR A CAUSE OR EFFECT PARAGRAPH**

For cause paragraphs: because, due to, for, for this reason, since

For effect paragraphs: as a result, consequently, hence, in consequence, then, therefore, thus, so

Making the Links Clear

Using the right transition word is not always enough to make your point. Sometimes you have to write the missing link in your line of thinking so that the reader can understand your point. To write the missing link means writing phrases, clauses, or sentences that help the reader follow your point.

> **not this:** Many parents are working outside the home. Consequently, take-out and convenience foods are popular.

> **but this:** Many parents are working outside the home and have less time to cook. Consequently, take-out and convenience foods, which are located near the entrance of most grocery stores, are popular.

The hard part of making clear links between ideas is that you have to put yourself in your reader's place. Remember that your reader cannot read your mind, only your paper. Connections between ideas may be clear in your mind, but you must spell them out on paper.

ALONG THESE LINES/Pearson Education Canada

Revising the Draft

Below is a draft of the paragraph on owning a car. When you read it, you'll notice many changes from the outlines stage:

- The details on "car payments" and "a car loan" said the same thing, so the repetition has been cut out.
- Some details about the costs of maintaining a car and about parking have been added.
- The order of the details about the costs of a car has been changed. Now, paying for a car comes first, maintaining it comes after.
- Sentences have been combined.
- Transitions have been added.

A Draft of an Effects Paragraph (*transitions are underlined*)

Owning my own car gave me freedom, cost me money, and made me more careful about how I drive. <u>First of all,</u> my car gave me the adult freedom to come and go. I didn't have to beg my father for his truck or get rides from my friends anymore. I could go to the city or even ride around for fun when I wanted. <u>On the negative side,</u> I had to pay for the car and related expenses. I had to pay for the car loan. I also paid for car insurance. <u>A car costs a lot to maintain, too.</u> I paid for oil changes, tune-ups, tires, belts, and filters. <u>With so much of my money put into my car,</u> I became a more careful driver. I worried about someone hitting the car and watched out for bad drivers. <u>In addition,</u> I wanted to avoid the scratches a car can get in a parking lot, so I always parked far away from other cars.

EXERCISE 8

MAKING THE CONNECTIONS CLEAR

Below are ideas that are connected, but the connection is not clearly explained. Rewrite each pair of ideas, making the connection clear.

1. I never wrote a research paper in high school. Therefore, I did poorly in Canadian Economic History in college.

   rewritten: _____

   _____

   _____

   (Hint: Did your Canadian Economic History class require a research paper? Did you know how to write one?)

2. Young teens see musicians and actors with elaborate tattoos. These celebrities seem cool, so the young teens want to get tattoos.

   rewritten: _____

   _____

   _____

   (Hint: Do the young teens want to look cool?)

3. I drank three cups of coffee last night. Consequently, I couldn't sleep.

   rewritten: _____

   _____

   _____

   (Hint: Do you usually or rarely drink coffee at night? What substance in the coffee kept you awake?)

4. Some cities are facing massive traffic jams on the highways. As a result, the cities have created carpool-only lanes.

   rewritten: _____

   _____

   _____

   (Hint: Are the carpool-only lanes designed to attract drivers to share rides? What makes the lanes attractive?)

5. Pine Tree College was nearer to home than Lake College. As a result, I went to Pine Tree College.

   rewritten: _____

   _____

   _____

   (Hint: Did you want a college close to home? Did you want to save money by attending college and living at home? Did you want a shorter trip to school?)

EXERCISE 9　　**REVISING A PARAGRAPH BY ADDING DETAILS**

Each of the following paragraphs is missing details. Add details—at least two sentences—to each paragraph using the blank lines.

　　1.　Becoming a parent has made me a happier, more cautious, and more ambitious person. I had never believed the friends who told me that parenthood would change my life, but they were right. First of all, parenthood has brought the joy of watching my child grow and change every day. I am constantly amazed when I realize that I am a part of this little person. My happiness is mixed with caution because I am protective of my child. I now listen to the weather report every day because I don't want my child to catch cold in the snow or sniffle in the rain. I scan every room in my apartment to clear it of the stray pencil or china coffee mug that my baby might pick up. Being a parent has made me more careful than I have ever been, and also more ambitious.

_____

_____

_____

Now that I have a child, I feel that I have been reborn as a more fulfilled, careful, and motivated person.

2.   The school board had good reasons for closing Maple Heights Secondary School. First, the school was extremely overcrowded. Maple Heights Secondary was designed to hold 2,000 students; last year, it held 4,500. Expanding it to accommodate a population that continues to grow would be more expensive than building a new school. The school was not only too small; it was also in the wrong place. When it opened thirty-five years ago, Maple Heights was surrounded by neighbourhoods with families, but shortly after, the neighbourhood changed. Today the school is surrounded by empty lots and decaying warehouses. Maple Heights has not kept up with the changing times in another respect. It lacks the modern technology a good school needs.

_____

_____

_____

Although it is always difficult to see a secondary school close, Maple Heights is too crowded, poorly located, and outdated to save.

EXERCISE **10**	**REVISING A DRAFT BY COMBINING SENTENCES**

Combine the underlined sentences in the following paragraph. Write your combinations in the space above the original sentences.

The latest television commercial is designed to make viewers think that freedom, excitement, and nature come with the car. First of all, the ad starts with a tired executive. The executive rips off his tie and leaps into his convertible. As he speeds out of the city, the viewers get a sense of freedom. The freedom is connected to a sense of excitement. <u>The car zips past slower cars. Loud rock 'n' roll plays on the soundtrack.</u> The car races around curves and conquers dangerous corners. Soon, viewers see the ultimate effect of owning the convertible. <u>The car brings the executive to the middle of a green area. There is a gorgeous lake. Everything is unspoiled.</u> The rock 'n' roll music fades away, and the only sounds heard are bird calls and gentle breezes. Truly, this commercial says, a new car can change viewers' lives. This ad is not really for a car; instead, it sells a dream of excitement and escape.

FINAL LINES   PROOFREADING AND POLISHING: CAUSE OR EFFECT

Below is the final version of the paragraph on owning a car. When you contrast the final version with the draft, you'll notice several changes:

- An introductory sentence has been added.
- Some sentences have been combined.
- Transitions have been revised.
- Some words have been changed so that the language is more precise.

Changes in style, word choice, sentence variety, and transitions can all be made before you decide on the final version of your paragraph. You may also want to add an opening or closing to your paragraph.

A Final Version of an Effects Paragraph (*changes from the draft are underlined*)

<u>When I bought my first car, I wasn't prepared for all the changes it made in my life.</u> Owning my own car gave me freedom, cost me money, and made me careful about how I drive. First of all, my car gave me the adult freedom to come and go. I didn't have to beg my father for his truck or get rides from my friends anymore. I could go to the city or even ride around for fun when I wanted. On the negative side, I had to pay for the car and related expenses. <u>I had to pay for both the car loan and car insurance.</u> A car costs <u>money</u> to maintain, too. I paid for oil changes, tune-ups, tires, belts, and filters. With so much of my money put into my car, I became a more careful driver. I worried about someone hitting the car and watched out for bad drivers. <u>To avoid dangers in the parking lot as well as on the road,</u> I always parked <u>my car far</u> away from other cars, <u>keeping my car safe from scratches.</u>

Before you prepare the final copy of your paragraph, check your latest draft for errors in spelling and punctuation, and for any errors made in typing or recopying.

| EXERCISE **11** | PROOFREADING TO PREPARE THE FINAL VERSION |

Below are one cause paragraph and one effects paragraph with the kinds of errors that are easy to overlook when you prepare the final version of an assignment. Correct the errors, writing above the lines. There are nine errors in the first paragraph and ten errors in the second paragraph.

1.   I signed up for an Introduction to Computers class this semster so that I could get some useful skills. One reason I took the Course is that, I want to be able to use my son's computer. He is ten years old and knows all about email and the Internet, but I don't know anything. At thirty, I should be able to keep up with my son. I also want to know some thing my son doesn't know, and that is how to do word processing. Now that I am in college, I have many written assinments that would be much easier if I knew word processing. A basic knowledge of computers would also be a important asset in my future. Right now I am in a low-paying job, but I think I get a better job if I had some computer skills. I know that banks, stores, schools, buisnesses, and hospitals all want to hire people who know how to use technolgy. I believe learning computer skills will help me at home, at school, and at work.

2.   A major traffic jam can have a number of affects. Of coarse, the tie-up directly affects those caught in it and the drivers forced to find alternite routes. These people experience frustration and even rage as they realize they will be late for work, school, or other responsibility. When they finally excape the traffic snarl they take their nasty moods with them. They should consider themselves lucky to get out with no damage but lost time. Others has more to complain about. They get caught in the overheating cars or minor accidents that occur when traffic cannot move. these poor drivers have to deal with tow trucks, repair services, and even insurance agents. While most people think of a traffic jam's effects on drivers, not many think of it's effect on law enforcement. The local or provincial police must not only find the cause of the gridlock but also deal with impatient drivers. While some search for the source of the traffic snarl. Other officers direct the masses of cars to merge or take a detour. A traffic jam calls for patience in every direction.

ALONG THESE LINES/Pearson Education Canada

Lines of Detail: A Walk-Through Assignment

Write a paragraph on this topic: "Why Canadians Are Eating More Meals away from Home." To write your paragraph, follow these steps:

Step 1: Go back to Exercise 3, topic 4 of this chapter. Topic 4 is the same topic as this assignment. If you have done that exercise, you have already written five or more questions that can lead you to ideas and details. If you haven't done the exercise, do topic 4 now.

Step 2: Use the answers to your questions to prepare a list of ideas and details. Put the items on your list into groups of reasons and related details. Add to the groups until you have at least three reasons (and related details) why Canadians are eating more meals away from home.

Step 3: Write a topic sentence that fits your reasons.

Step 4: Write an outline. Check that your outline has sufficient details and that you have put the reasons in the best order.

Step 5: Write a rough draft of your paragraph. Revise it until you have enough specific details to explain each reason, and the links between your ideas are smooth and clear. Check whether any sentences should be combined and whether your paragraph could use an opening sentence or a concluding one.

Step 6: Before you prepare the final copy of your paragraph, check your latest draft for word choice, punctuation, transitions, and spelling.

Writing Your Own Cause or Effect Paragraph

When you write on any of the topics below, be sure to work through the stages of the writing process.

1. Write a cause paragraph on one of the following topics. Create the topic by filling in the blanks.

   Why I Chose _____

   Why I Stopped _____

   Why I Enjoy _____

   Why I Started _____

   Why I Hate _____

   Why I Bought _____

   Why I Decided _____

2. Write a one-paragraph letter of complaint to the manufacturers of a product you bought or to the company that owns a hotel, restaurant, airline, or some other service you used. In your letter, write at least three reasons why you (1) want your money refunded or (2) want the product replaced. Be clear and specific about your reasons. Be sure your letter has a topic sentence.

   If your instructor agrees, read a draft of your letter to a writing partner, and ask your partner to pretend to be the manufacturer or the head of the company. Ask your partner to point out where your ideas are not clear or convincing and where you make your point effectively.

3. Think of a current fad or trend. The fad can be a popular style of clothing, a kind of movie, a kind of music, a sport, a pastime, an actor, an athlete, a gadget, an invention, or an appliance. Write a paragraph on the causes of this fad or trend or the effects of it.

If your instructor agrees, begin by brainstorming with a group. Create a list of three or four fads or trends. Then create a list of questions to ask (and answer) about each fad or trend. If you are going to write about causes, for example, you might ask questions like

What changes in society have encouraged this trend?
Have changes in the economy helped to make it popular?
Does it appeal to a specific age group? Why?
Does it meet any hidden emotional needs? For instance, is it a way to gain status, or to feel safe, or powerful?

If you are going to write about effects, you might ask questions like

Will this trend last?
Has it affected competitors?
Is it spreading?
Is the fad changing business, or education, or the family?
Has it improved daily life?

WRITING FROM READING: CAUSE AND EFFECT

Saving the Planet One Swamp at a Time
David Suzuki

David Suzuki is arguably Canada's most famous and well-respected environmental educator. He has worked in the media as a journalist and broadcaster, and in 1990 founded the David Suzuki Foundation, a nonprofit organization dedicated to examining public policy and educating the public about environmental issues.

Before you read this selection, consider these questions:

Do you have a special memory of nature?

Aside from the obvious environmental impacts, what other impacts might global warming have?

Currently, what efforts do you and your family take to reduce your impact on the environment?

Do you have a swamp? I don't mean literally. I mean a special place where, at **indelible:** unforgettable some point, you really connected with nature—a place that made an **indelible** imprint on your mind, the smell, the sound, the feel of which has stayed with you forever.

Maybe yours was a family cabin at the lake. Or a special river where you canoed with your grandfather. Or a tree you climbed in your backyard. Mine actually was a swamp near my home in London, Ont. I spent hours there, looking for frogs and **brackish:** slightly salty birds, and wading through the **brackish** water, searching for new life. Afterward, I would lie on my back in the tall grass, drying off, breathing the humid air, staring **puny:** very small up at the sky, and wondering about it all. How vast it all seemed and how **puny** I felt in comparison.

Back then, I would never have imagined human beings could significantly alter something as huge as the planet's atmosphere. It was beyond comprehension. Sure, when I was very young, I remember smoke fogs from wood and coal burning in Vancouver, where I was born, that settled in on the city and made it difficult to see across the street. But a good wind would eventually clear the smoke. That's the way it always was. Nature took care of our waste, cleansing our air and water and making them pure again.

What I didn't know as a boy was that my swamp and the sky above me were not actually separate things at all. Our atmosphere, our oceans, our lakes, soils and all living things are intricately connected. Making a major change to any one thing in this zone of life, our biosphere, will have profound repercussions throughout the entire system. It can actually affect how our natural services function. That's why global warming is such a big deal.

In Canada, it's tempting to shrug off global warming as something that will make life in our cold country more pleasant. Vineyards in Winnipeg, farms in the Arctic. But the reality is not so simple. And decidedly less fun.

By burning vast quantities of fossil fuels like coal, oil and gas, and by cutting down massive forested areas, humans have released enough greenhouse gases and reduced the absorptive capacity of nature enough to fundamentally alter our atmosphere. There is now 32 per cent more carbon dioxide, the main greenhouse gas, in our atmosphere today than there was before the industrial revolution.

The trouble with greenhouse gases like carbon dioxide is that they trap heat, much like a blanket, and hold it near the planet's surface. If we didn't have any of these gases, heat from the sun would shine onto the planet and then radiate back into space, and our planet would be either too hot or too cold. Over millions of years, our Earth has created the perfect conditions for life, with just the right amount of greenhouse gases to ensure that it is never too hot or too cold. Without this stable climate, human civilization would likely never have developed to where we are today. We depend on it.

But all the extra carbon dioxide and other gases we keep adding to the air are disrupting the stable climate that has been so very important to us. I say "disrupting" because it is really a more accurate description of what happens. Adding heat to the atmosphere also means adding energy that can **manifest** itself in unusual ways—more frequent or extreme storms, for example.

manifest: show, display

In other words, global warming does not equate to a modest, pleasant warming. Rather, it means higher global temperatures overall, which translates to a host of other, often unforeseen, problems. This year, the headlines have been full of these issues: falling water tables, retreating lakeshores, acidification of oceans, shrinking ice caps and glaciers, expanded ranges for invasive species, and more. Even noxious weeds like poison ivy are expected to blossom in a carbon-dioxide enriched atmosphere.

Air quality in urban areas will also be affected. Smog is created from a chemical interaction in the atmosphere between automobile and smokestack pollution, and heat and sunlight. More heat and more sunlight will mean more smog. Resulting new

ALONG THESE LINES/Pearson Education Canada

infrastructure: the basic
foundation of a system
or organization

infrastructure needs and increasing health care costs add up quickly. Already, the Ontario Medical Association says air pollution costs the province more than $1 billion in hospital charges and lost workdays. That will only get worse as our climate warms.

But enough about the risks—most people are aware of them by now. Scary stories have been all over the news for the past six months. In fact, it seems like results of yet another study are published practically every day confirming something bad about global warming. It's getting to the point where I worry people will be tempted to just throw up their hands and say "I give up!" Yet that would be a huge mistake, because it's not too late to avoid what scientists call "dangerous warming." Yes, some warming has already occurred and more will come, but we can still avoid the

brunt: the main burden

brunt of a disrupted climate by taking action now.

Sir Nicholas Stern, former chief economist with the World Bank, has estimated that to pay for all the changes necessary to avoid dangerous warming, it will cost the global economy about 1 per cent of the world's annual GDP. That's not insignificant. But what's astounding is what it will cost us if we carry on with business as usual: up to 20 per cent of the global economy per year, which could lead to a worldwide depression.

prudent: commonsense,
practical

So taking action now is far and away the most **prudent** financial course. We simply cannot afford to wait. A recent statement by the scientific academies of 13 countries put it this way: "The problem is not yet insoluble, but becomes more difficult with each passing day."

Tackling the problem sufficiently will involve all sectors of society, from governments to businesses and individuals. It means having firm national targets and timelines that will spur innovation and provide certainty and a level playing field for industry.

It means giving individuals options so they can more easily pick the most sustainable choice. And it means leadership at all levels to break us away from the status quo and put us on a new path.

Individuals can learn about reducing their own footprint at dozens of environmental websites or they can take the initiative and:

Leave the car at home and sometimes walk, bike, or take transit.
Switch all their light bulbs to modern energy-efficient CFLs.
Buy fuel-efficient vehicles.
Choose more local foods.
Use a programmable thermostat.
Buy Energy Star appliances.
Weather-strip their homes.
Encourage friends or political leaders to take action.
I could go on and on.

Many people are already doing these things, but to really solve global warming we need our leaders to take it seriously, too. Because right now, Canada is still falling behind. And our world, which once seemed so vast and limitless, is actually far smaller and more interconnected than we could ever have imagined.

ALONG THESE LINES/Pearson Education Canada

UNDERSTANDING "SAVING THE PLANET ONE SWAMP AT A TIME"

1. According to the article, what are two causes of global warming?

2. List at least three effects of global warming, according to Suzuki's article. Are any of these surprising or new to you?

3. Suzuki has listed some ways in which individuals can help the environment. What do you, your family, and your friends do to minimize your impact on the environment? What else might you consider doing? What would it take for you to consider doing more?

WRITING FROM READING "SAVING THE PLANET ONE SWAMP AT A TIME"

When you write on any of the following topics, be sure to work through the stages of the writing process.

1. Environmentalists have often encouraged the public to "think globally, act locally." What do you think this means? Write a paragraph in which you discuss some of the effects of doing this.

2. Suzuki mentions fond memories of a swamp he visited in childhood as one of the reasons he is so environmentally aware today. Think of some of the issues you feel strongly about; what are your reasons for feeling that way? Write a paragraph in which you discuss the causes of your passion.

3. It has been said that the effects of global warming affect the poor more than the well-off. Do you agree or disagree? Write a paragraph on the effects of global warming on the poor.

4. Do you think global warming affects countries differently? Write a paragraph in which you explore how global warming uniquely affects Canada or another country.

CHAPTER 10
Argument

LEARNING OBJECTIVES

After you have read this chapter and completed its exercises and assignments, you should be able to

- choose an appropriate topic for an argument paragraph
- take a stand on a topic of your choice
- use clear, specific, and logical details in support of your stand
- address objections to your argument
- draft and edit your argument paragraph

"When I'm getting ready to reason with a man, I spend one-third of my time thinking about myself and what I am going to say—and two-thirds thinking about him and what he is going to say."

~ ABRAHAM LINCOLN

▼

KNOWN FOR HIS POWERFUL SPEECHES, ABRAHAM LINCOLN WAS THE SIXTEENTH PRESIDENT OF THE UNITED STATES AND BROUGHT AN END TO SLAVERY IN HIS COUNTRY.

WHAT IS ARGUMENT?

A written **argument** is an attempt to *persuade* a reader to think or act in a certain way. When you write an argument paragraph, your goal is to get people to see your point, to agree with it, and perhaps to act on it.

In an argument paragraph, you take a stand. Then you support your stand with reasons. In addition, you give details for each reason. Your goal is to persuade your reader by making a point that has convincing reasons and details.

Hints for Writing an Argument Paragraph

1. **Pick a topic you can handle.** Your topic should be small enough to be covered in one paragraph. For instance, you can't argue effectively for world peace in just one paragraph.
2. **Pick a topic you can handle based on your own experience and observation.** Such topics as drug legalization, gun control, capital punishment, or air pollution require extensive research into facts, figures, and expert opinions to make a complete argument. They are topics you can write

ALONG THESE LINES/Pearson Education Canada

about convincingly in a longer research paper, but for a one-paragraph argument, pick a topic based on what you've experienced yourself.

> **not this topic:** Organized Crime
> **but this topic:** Starting a Crime Watch Program in My Neighbourhood

3. **Do two things in your topic sentence: Name the subject of your argument, and take a stand.** The following topic sentences do both:

   subject   takes a stand

   The college cafeteria should serve more healthy snacks.

   subject   takes a stand

   High school athletes who fail a course should not be allowed to play on a school team.

   You should take a stand, but *don't announce it*:

   > **not this:**   This paragraph will explain why Springfield needs a teen centre.
   > **but this:**   Springfield should open a teen centre. (A topic sentence with a subject and a stand.)

4. **Consider your audience.** Consider why these people should support your points. How will they be likely to object? How will you get around these objections? For instance, you might want to argue, to the residents of your community, that the intersection of Hawthorne Road and Sheridan Street needs a traffic light. Would anyone object?

   At first, you might think, "No. Why would anyone object? The intersection is dangerous. There's too much traffic there. People risk major accidents while getting across the intersection." But if you think further about your audience, which is the people in your community, you might identify these objections: Some town residents may not want to pay for a traffic signal. Some drivers may not want to spend extra time waiting for a light to change.

   There are several ways to handle objections. First, you can *refute* an objection. To refute it means to prove it isn't valid. For instance, if someone says that a light wouldn't do any good, you might say that a new light has already worked in a nearby neighbourhood.

   Sometimes it's best to admit that the other side has a point. You have to *concede* that point. For instance, traffic lights do cost money. And waiting for a light to change does take time.

   Sometimes you can *turn an objection into an advantage*. When you acknowledge the objection and yet use it to make your own point, you show that you've intelligently considered both sides of the argument. This is what Lincoln meant in the quotation at the beginning of this chapter. For instance, you might say that the cost of a traffic signal at the intersection is well worth it because that light will buy safety for all the drivers who try to cross Hawthorne Road and Sheridan Street. Or you might say that waiting a few moments for the light to change is better than waiting many minutes for an opening in the heavy traffic of the intersection.

5. **Be specific, clear, and logical in your reasons.** As always, think before you write. Think about your point and your audience. Try to come up with at least three reasons for your position.

Be careful that your reasons do not overlap. For instance, you might write the following:

topic sentence: College students should get discounts on transit passes.

audience: chair of the Transit Commission.

reasons: 1. Given their limited budgets, many college students can't afford to pay as much as adults who work full-time.
2. The cost of passes is high for most students.
3. More people taking public transit reduces emissions.

Notice that reasons 1 and 2 overlap; they are really part of the same reason.

Be careful not to argue in a circle. For instance, if you say, "One reason for having an afterschool program at Riverside Elementary School is that we need one there," you've just said, "We need an afterschool program because we need an afterschool program."

Finally, be specific in stating your reasons.

not this: One reason to start a bus service to and from the college is to help people.

but this: A bus service to and from the college would encourage students to leave their cars at home and use travel time to study.

| **EXERCISE**
1 | **RECOGNIZING GOOD TOPIC SENTENCES**
IN AN ARGUMENT PARAGRAPH |

Some of the following topic sentences are appropriate for an argument paragraph. Some are for topics that are too large for one paragraph or require research. Others are announcements or do not take a stand. Put *OK* next to the sentences that would work well in an argument paragraph.

1. _____ People should try to cure their own addictions.
2. _____ Graffiti is a much-maligned art form.
3. _____ We must ban offshore oil drilling in Canadian waters.
4. _____ Junk food should be banned at all elementary schools.
5. _____ We need stricter penalties for young offenders.
6. _____ Something should be done about victims' rights.
7. _____ The city should incorporate bicycle lanes on all major streets.
8. _____ Local bank branches should be open on Saturday so that working people can do their banking.
9. _____ The reasons to ban bottled water will be the subject of this essay.
10. _____ College students deserve more financial aid.

EXERCISE

2

RECOGNIZING AND HANDLING OBJECTIONS

Below are topic sentences of arguments. Working with a group, list two possible objections to each argument that might come from the specific audience identified. Then think of ways to handle each objection, either by refuting it, or conceding it, or trying to turn it to your advantage. On the lines provided, write the actual sentence(s) you would use in a paragraph.

1. **topic sentence:** The college library, which is currently open until 10:00 p.m., should be open until midnight every night.

   audience: the deans, the vice-president, and the president of the college

   possible objections from this audience:

   a. _____

   b. _____

   answering objections:

   a. _____

   b. _____

2. **topic sentence:** During the summer, the municipal government should keep public schools open for community programs.

   audience: the schools' local communities

   possible objections from this audience:

   a. _____

   b. _____

   answering objections:

   a. _____

   b. _____

3. **topic sentence:** Broadleaf Public School should ban junk food vending machines in their hallways.

   audience: principal of Broadleaf Public School, trustees, and superintendents

   possible objections from this audience:

   a. _____

   b. _____

   answering objections:

   a. _____

   b. _____

4. **topic sentence:** The Downtown Donut Shop should stop serving coffee in Styrofoam cups.

   audience: the owners of the Downtown Donut Shop

   possible objections from this audience:

   a. _____

   b. _____

   answering objections:

   a. _____

   b. _____

5. **topic sentence:** Local day-care centres should be required, by law, to provide one adult supervisor for every two children under the age of one year.

   audience: the owners of the Happy Child Day-Care Centre, which currently has one adult supervisor for every three children under the age of one year

   possible objections from this audience:

   a. _____

   b. _____

   answering objections:

   a. _____

   b. _____

WRITING THE ARGUMENT PARAGRAPH IN STEPS

GATHERING IDEAS: ARGUMENT

Imagine that your instructor has given you this assignment:

> Write a one-paragraph letter to the editor of your local newspaper.
> Argue for something in your town that needs to be changed.

One way to begin is to brainstorm for some specific point that you can write about.

> Is there a part of town that needs to be cleaned up?
>
> Should something be changed at a school?
>
> What do I notice on my way to work, or school, that needs improvement?
>
> What could be improved in my neighbourhood?

By answering these questions, you may come up with one topic, and then you can list ideas about it.

> **topic:**   Cleaning Up Roberts Park
>
> **ideas:**   dirty and overgrown
>
> benches are all cracked and broken

full of garbage

could be fixed up

I work nearby

I'd use it

You can consider your audience and possible objections:

audience: Local people of all ages who read the local paper.

possible objections   Would cost money.
from this audience: More important things to spend money on.

answering objections: Money would be well spent to beautify the downtown. City children could play there in the fresh air and in nature; workers could eat lunch there.

Grouping Your Ideas

Once you have a list, you can start grouping the ideas in your list. Some of the objections you wrote down may actually lead you to reasons that support your argument. That is, by answering objections, you may come up with reasons that support your point. Below is a list with a point to argue, three supporting reasons, and some details about cleaning up Roberts Park.

> ### A List for an Argument Paragraph
>
> **point:**   We should clean up Roberts Park.
>
> **reason:**   Improving the park would make the downtown area more attractive to shoppers.
>
> **details:**   Shoppers could stroll in the park or rest from their shopping.
> Friends could meet in the park for a day of shopping and lunch.
>
> **reason:**   City children could play in the park.
>
> **details:**   They could get fresh air.
> They could play in a natural setting.
>
> **reason:**   Workers could eat lunch outdoors.
>
> **details:**   Several office buildings are nearby.
> Workers would take a break outdoors.

With three reasons and some details for each, you can draft a topic sentence. Remember that your topic sentence for an argument should (1) name your subject and (2) take a stand. Below is a topic sentence about Roberts Park that does both.

subject   takes a stand

Roberts Park   should be cleaned up and improved.

With a topic sentence, you are ready to move on to the outlines stage of preparing an argument paragraph.

EXERCISE 3

DISTINGUISHING BETWEEN REASONS AND DETAILS

Each list below has three reasons and details for each reason. Write *reason 1*, *reason 2*, or *reason 3* next to the reasons on each list. Then write *detail for 1*, *detail for 2*, or *detail for 3* next to the items that give details about each reason. There may be more than one sentence of details connected to one reason.

1. **topic sentence:** The city needs to pick up garbage at my apartment complex three times, not twice, a week.

_____ Garbage spills out past the dumpster.

_____ People throw their garbage on top of already loaded dumpsters; the bags fall and split open.

_____ Garbage that piles up, uncovered, is a health hazard.

_____ Too much garbage accumulates when the schedule allows for only two pickups.

_____ Flies buzz over the garbage, a sign of dangerous contamination that can spread.

_____ The roaches from the garbage area move into the apartments, carrying disease.

_____ Garbage piles make people lose pride in their neighbourhood.

_____ Apartment residents are starting to litter the parking lot because they've lost respect for their homes.

_____ One long-time resident is thinking of moving to a better neighbourhood.

2. **topic sentence:** Children under ten years of age should not be permitted in the Mountain Mall unless they are accompanied by an adult.

_____ It is not safe for children to be alone in the mall.

_____ Unsupervised children cause trouble for mall merchants.

_____ Children left alone in the mall are not always happy with their freedom.

_____ I saw one nine-year-old boy roam the mall for hours, looking forlorn.

_____ Sometimes pairs of sad young girls wait by the food court for an hour, until Mom, who is late, remembers to pick them up.

_____ Once I saw two seven-year-old boys walk back and forth in front of my store for half an hour, with nothing to do.

_____ Children have been kidnapped in malls.

_____ If a child gets sick at the mall, will he or she know what to do?

_____ Bored children run through stores, chasing each other.

_____ I saw one child shoplifting.

EXERCISE 4

FINDING REASONS TO SUPPORT AN ARGUMENT

Give three reasons that support each point. In each case, the readers of your local newspaper will be the audience for an argument paragraph.

1. **point:** The province should ban all telephone sales calls between the hours of 5:00 p.m. and 8:00 p.m.

    reasons:

    a. _____

    b. _____

    c. _____

2. **point:** Our city must ban the use of office lighting after work hours.

    reasons:

    a. _____

    b. _____

    c. _____

3. **point:** Cellphones should be banned in classrooms.

    reasons:

    a. _____

    b. _____

    c. _____

4. **point:** Public education should start with preschool, at age three.

    reasons:

    a. _____

    b. _____

    c. _____

OUT LINES   ## DEVISING A PLAN: ARGUMENT

With a topic sentence and a list of reasons and details, you can draft an outline. Then you can review it, making whatever changes you think it needs. The following checklist may help you to review and revise your outline.

✓

CHECKLIST	FOR REVISING AN ARGUMENT OUTLINE

> ✓ Does my topic sentence make my point? Does it state a subject and take a stand?
>
> ✓ Have I considered the objections to my argument so that I am arguing intelligently?
>
> ✓ Do I have all the reasons I need to make my point?
>
> ✓ Do any reasons overlap?
>
> ✓ Are my reasons specific?
>
> ✓ Do I have enough details for each reason?
>
> ✓ Are my reasons in the best order?

communication at work

Argument and conflict are inevitable whenever you have to work with other people; different personalities, work experiences, and styles, combined with the stress of our daily lives, can make for an explosive environment. In recognition of this, most corporations today have devoted numerous programs and workshops to help train their employees to deal with conflict. Though there are many theories on how to deal with conflict, many have the same premise as your argument paragraph: clearly, objectively stated details in support of your argument, along with an acknowledgment of the other person's point of view, will often give you a "win-win" situation.

The Order of Reasons in an Argument

When you are giving several reasons, it is a good idea to keep the most convincing or most important reason for last. Saving the best for last is called using **emphatic order**. For example, you might have these three reasons to tear down an abandoned building in your neighbourhood: (1) The building is ugly, (2) Drug dealers are using the building, and (3) The building is infested with rats. The most important reason, the drug dealing, should be used last, for an emphatic order.

Below is an outline on improving Roberts Park. When you look at the outline, you'll notice several changes from the previous list:

- Since the safety of children at play is important, it is put as the last detail.
- Some details have been added.
- A sentence has been added to the end of the outline. It explains why improving the park is a good idea even to people who will never use the park themselves. It is a way of answering these people's objections.

ALONG THESE LINES/Pearson Education Canada

> ### An Outline for an Argument Paragraph

topic sentence: Roberts Park should be cleaned up and improved.

reason: Improving the park would make the downtown area more attractive to shoppers.

details: Shoppers could stroll through the park or rest there after shopping.
Friends could meet at the park for a day of shopping and lunch.

reason: Workers from nearby offices and stores could eat lunch outdoors.

details: Several office buildings are nearby.
An hour outdoors is a pleasant break from work.

reason: City children could play there.

details: They would get fresh air.
They would play on grass, not on asphalt.
They would not have to play near traffic.

final idea: An attractive park improves the city, and all residents benefit when the community is beautified.

EXERCISE 5

WORKING WITH THE ORDER OF REASONS IN AN ARGUMENT OUTLINE

Below are topic sentences and lists of reasons. For each list, put a star or asterisk in the blank beside the reason that is the most significant—the reason you would save for last in an argument paragraph.

1. **topic sentence:** Manufacturers of vitamins should stop the double packaging of their products.

   reason 1: _____   Putting a small jar into a big box is deceptive, making buyers think they are getting more for their money.

   reason 2: _____   Consumers with arthritis find it difficult to open two packages.

   reason 3: _____   Double packaging wastes valuable natural resources.

2. **topic sentence:** Our city should not sell public space, such as benches and garbage cans, to advertisers.

   reason 1: _____   Advertising is ugly.

   reason 2: _____   The city should not be able to decide on the use of public space without asking the opinion of the public.

   reason 3: _____   There is already too much advertising in the city.

3. **topic sentence:** The province's highway speed limit should not be raised.

    reason 1: _____ A slower speed limit has been shown to save lives.

    reason 2: _____ One hundred kilometres an hour is the ideal speed limit to maximize fuel efficiency.

    reason 3: _____ The current speed limit maintains the ideal traffic flow.

4. **topic sentence:** Seven-year-olds should be given a small allowance, to spend as they wish.

    reason 1: _____ Seven-year-olds see other children their age with spending money.

    reason 2: _____ Children need to learn to handle money responsibly.

    reason 3: _____ Learning to make change develops math skills.

EXERCISE 6

RECOGNIZING REASONS THAT OVERLAP

Below are topic sentences and lists of reasons. In each list, two reasons overlap. Put an X beside the two reasons that overlap.

1. **topic sentence:** The college cafeteria should lower its prices.

    a. _____ Prices are too high for most students.

    b. _____ Lower prices would actually mean a profit for the cafeteria because more students would use it.

    c. _____ Many students can't afford to eat in the cafeteria.

    d. _____ The cafeteria has to compete with nearby, cheaper restaurants.

2. **topic sentence:** Advertising should be banned from all Saturday morning children's TV programs.

    a. _____ Young children are too innocent to know the way advertising works.

    b. _____ Much advertising is for unhealthy food, like sugary cereals and junk food.

    c. _____ Advertising manipulates unsuspecting children.

    d. _____ Toy commercials push expensive toys that many parents cannot afford.

3. **topic sentence:** Our college needs a larger, lighted sign at the entrance.

    a. _____ Some residents of our town have never heard of our college, so a large sign would be good publicity.

    b. _____ Visitors to the college have a hard time finding it.

    c. _____ Students who are preoccupied sometimes drive right past the entrance to their college at night.

    d. _____ A better sign would make people more aware of the college.

EXERCISE **7**	**IDENTIFYING A REASON THAT IS NOT SPECIFIC**

In each of the following lists, put an *X* by the reason that is not specific.

1. **topic sentence:** The college library should ban access to social networking sites on its computers.

   a. _____ Students who need to use the library's computers for research often cannot find an available computer.

   b. _____ Students who access social networking sites often use the computer for hours.

   c. _____ Computers are frequently infected by viruses from the sites.

   d. _____ There aren't enough computers in the library.

2. **topic sentence:** Canadian college students should learn a foreign language.

   a. _____ Countries that compete with us economically, like Japan and Germany, have a competitive edge because their children routinely learn English.

   b. _____ It is often easier for a person to get a good job when he or she speaks two or more languages.

   c. _____ Learning a new language broadens a person's horizons.

   d. _____ Most Canadians, at home or at work, have to interact with immigrants or visitors who do not speak English or French.

3. **topic sentence:** Our college should open a fitness centre in the gym.

   a. _____ Health clubs are too expensive for many students.

   b. _____ A fitness centre would be good for students.

   c. _____ Students who have an hour or two between classes could work out in the gym.

   d. _____ Students new to the college could make friends by using the fitness centre.

EXERCISE **8**	**ADDING DETAILS TO AN OUTLINE**

Below is part of an outline. It includes a topic sentence and three reasons. Add at least two sentences of detail to each reason. Your details may be examples or descriptions.

topic sentence: The staff at Bargain Supermarket should enforce the "9 Items or Fewer" rule at the Express Checkout lane.

reason: Customers who follow the rule suffer because of people who don't obey the rule.

detail: _____

_____

detail: _____

_____

reason: Not enforcing the rule can create unpleasant confrontations among customers.

detail: _____

_____

detail: _____

reason: If it doesn't enforce the rule, Bargain Supermarket may lose customers.

detail: _____

_____

detail: _____

_____

ROUGH LINES   ## DRAFTING AND REVISING: ARGUMENT

Once you are satisfied with your outline, you can write the first draft of your paragraph. When you have completed it, you can begin revising the draft so that your argument is as clear, smooth, and convincing as it can be. The checklist below may help you with your revisions.

✓

CHECKLIST   **FOR REVISING THE DRAFT OF AN ARGUMENT PARAGRAPH**

✓ Do any of my sentences need combining?

✓ Have I left out a serious or obvious reason?

✓ Should I change the order of my reasons?

✓ Do I have enough details?

✓ Are my details specific?

✓ Do I need to explain the problem or issue I am writing about?

✓ Do I need to link my ideas more clearly?

✓ Do I need a final sentence to stress my point?

Checking Your Reasons

Be sure that your argument has covered all the serious or obvious reasons. Sometimes writers get so caught up in drafting their ideas that they forget to mention something very basic to the argument. For instance, if you were arguing for a leash law for your community, you might give the reason that dogs that run free can hurt people, scare children, and damage property. But don't forget to mention another serious reason to keep dogs on leashes: Dogs that are not restrained can get hurt or killed by cars.

One way to see if you have left out a serious or obvious reason is to ask a friend or classmate to read your draft and to react to your argument. Another technique is to put your draft aside for an hour or two and then read it as if you were a reader, not the writer.

Explaining the Problem or the Issue

Sometimes your argument discusses a problem so obvious to your audience that you don't need to explain it. On the other hand, sometimes you need to explain a problem or issue so your audience can understand your point. If you tell readers of your local paper about teenage vandalism at Central High School, you probably need to explain what kind of vandalism has occurred there and how often. Sometimes it's smart to convince readers of the seriousness of a situation by explaining it a little, so they'll be more persuaded by your argument.

Transitions That Emphasize

In writing an argument paragraph, you can use different transitions, depending on how you present your point. But no matter how you present your reasons, you will probably want to *emphasize* one of them. The Infobox below shows some transitions that can be used for emphasis.

INFOBOX	TRANSITIONS TO USE FOR EMPHASIS

above all, especially, finally, mainly, most important, most of all, most significant, primarily

For example, by saying, "*Most important,* broken windows at Central High School are a safety problem," you put the emphasis for your audience on this one idea.

A Draft

Below is a draft of the argument paragraph on Roberts Park. When you read it, you'll notice these changes from the outline:

- A description of the problem has been added.
- Details have been added.
- Short sentences have been combined.
- Transitions, including two sentences of transition, have been added. "Most important" and "best of all"—transitions that show emphasis—have been included.

 ### A Draft of an Argument Paragraph (*transitions are underlined*)

Roberts Park was once a pretty little park, but today it is overgrown with weeds, cluttered with garbage and rusty benches. Roberts Park should be cleaned up and improved. Improving the park would make the downtown area more attractive to shoppers. Shoppers could stroll through a renovated park or rest there after shopping. Friends could also meet there for a day of shopping and lunch. <u>Shoppers are not the only ones who could enjoy the park.</u> Workers from nearby offices and stores could eat lunch outdoors. Several office buildings are near the park, and workers from these offices could bring their lunch to work and eat outside in good weather. I think many people would agree that an hour spent outdoors is a pleasant break from work. <u>Most important,</u> city

(continued)

children could play in an improved Roberts Park. They would get fresh air while they played on grass, not asphalt. <u>Best of all,</u> they would not have to play near traffic. <u>Children, shoppers, and workers would benefit from a clean-up of Roberts Park, but so would others.</u> An attractive park improves the city, and all residents benefit when a community is beautified.

EXERCISE 9

ADDING AN EXPLANATION OF THE PROBLEM TO AN ARGUMENT PARAGRAPH

This paragraph could use an explanation of the problem before the argument is stated. Write a short explanation of the problem in the lines provided.

_____

_____

_____

Directional and exit signs on Lake Highway must be designed with larger lettering. Larger lettering would help a significant number of our residents. Lake Valley has many older residents whose vision is not perfect. Signs in large letters would make driving easier for those who are currently straining to see the right exit, only to find it as they pass it. Another group that would appreciate bigger lettering is the visitors to the area. Many of them are struggling to find their way to a motel, restaurant, or store they've never seen, and they are not sure where to turn. Better signs would reduce their confusion and make their visit more pleasant. Most of all, larger lettering would result in safer driving. If signs were larger, drivers would see them sooner. Thus they could change lanes sooner and more safely as they merged into the correct lane or got to an exit ramp. Many of the accidents caused by drivers suddenly switching lanes would be avoided. Better signs would then lead to safer, smoother driving.

EXERCISE 10

RECOGNIZING TRANSITIONS IN AN ARGUMENT PARAGRAPH

Underline all the transitions—words, phrases, or sentences—in the following paragraph. Put a double line under any transitions that emphasize.

At the start of each workday, millions head to their jobs with good intentions. However, many start the day already tired and stressed and therefore unable to make their best efforts. They are living proof that

ALONG THESE LINES/Pearson Education Canada

workers in Canada need four weeks' annual paid vacation. Employees need more time off because they are facing more stress in the workplace. Many are working longer hours; some hold a second job to supplement their income. Bosses demand more productivity and new skills. Employees face further stress at home, too. When both parents work outside the home, they strain to find time for their children and their household duties. When one parent works, the family may face economic hardship due to the loss of income of the stay-at-home parent. Single parents struggle to cope alone. Those without partners or children may seem lucky, but they, too, fight to pay the bills and find time for a personal life. More vacation time would de-stress these workers, but most of all, it would also benefit employers. Exhausted, burned-out workers cannot give their best when they are struggling just to get through the day. On the other hand, people who have sufficient time to rest return to work with renewed energy. Thus, everybody—employees and employers—profits from more vacation for workers.

EXERCISE 11

REVISING A DRAFT BY COMBINING SENTENCES

In the following paragraph, combine each cluster of underlined sentences into one clear, smooth sentence. Write your combinations in the space above the original sentences.

<u>At Ashley Apartments, there are large clusters of residents' mailboxes.</u> <u>They appear in front of each building.</u> Each cluster houses a couple of dozen individual mailboxes, each opened by a resident's key. <u>The system works well. The mailboxes have one problem.</u> These mailboxes need to be repaired immediately. <u>They create a bad image for the apartments. They have crumbling plaster. They have rotten wood.</u> Few people looking for an apartment and seeing the mailboxes would decide to rent at Ashley Apartments. The current renters are also affected by the sagging, chipped boxes. <u>These residents lose respect for the apartment complex. This disrespect can be seen in the increase of litter. It can also</u>

be seen in the garbage bags. <u>They are casually tossed beside the dumpsters, not inside them.</u> The most significant reason to repair the mailboxes is a safety issue. The boxes are made of wood, plaster, and metal. As they begin to fall apart, they expose rough wooden boards and sharp metal edges. <u>Children play in the parking lots. The parking lots are next to the mailboxes.</u> One day soon, a child may run right into one of these wooden boards or sharp edges. Clearly, it is time to fix the situation.

EXERCISE 12

ADDING A FINAL SENTENCE TO AN ARGUMENT PARAGRAPH

The following paragraph would benefit from a final sentence to sum up the reasons or to reinforce the topic sentence. Add that final sentence in the space provided.

I am twenty years old, and I live with my parents while I work and attend college. Living at home, I am comfortable and save money, but I am in constant conflict with my parents. Parents of grown children who live at home should remember that these children are adults. Attempting to monitor grown children as if they were still in high school does not work. My parents continually ask me, "Where are you going? When will you be back?" They want to know when I plan to study or how I am spending my money. The more questions they fire at me, the less I tell them. Questioning doesn't achieve its goal, and trying to control an adult child doesn't work, either. I have heard the warning, "You are still living under our roof, and as long as you do, you must follow our rules." This is a logical point, but most of the time, I am not under their roof. I am at my job, at school, or with friends, so my folks must learn to trust me, not control me. The most significant reason why parents should respect their children's adult status is that respect leads to co-operation. I am always happy when my parents praise one of my decisions—a decision made without their nagging. When they don't push me, I am more likely to make choices they would approve of.

_____

_____

_____

ALONG THESE LINES/Pearson Education Canada

 **PROOFREADING AND POLISHING: ARGUMENT**

Below is the final version of the argument paragraph on Roberts Park. When you read the final version, you'll notice some changes from the draft:

- Some words have been changed to improve the details.
- The first sentence has been changed so that it is more descriptive and uses a parallel pattern for emphasis.

> **A Final Version of an Argument Paragraph (*changes from the draft are underlined*)**
>
> Roberts Park was once a pretty little park, but today it is overgrown with weeds, <u>littered with garbage, and cluttered with rusty benches.</u> Roberts Park should be cleaned up and improved. Improving the park would make the downtown area more attractive to shoppers. Shoppers could stroll through a <u>restored</u> park or rest there after shopping. Friends could also meet at the park for a day of shopping and lunch. Shoppers are not the only ones who could enjoy the park. Workers from nearby offices and stores could eat lunch outdoors. Several office buildings are near the park, and workers from these offices could bring <u>a bag</u> lunch to work and eat outside in good weather. I think many people would agree that an hour spent outdoors is a pleasant break from work. Most important, city children could play in an improved Roberts Park. They would get fresh air while they played on grass, not asphalt. Best of all, they would not have to play near traffic. Children, shoppers, and workers would benefit from a clean-up of Roberts Park, but so would others. An attractive park improves the city, and all residents benefit when a community is beautified.

Before you prepare the final copy of your argument paragraph, check your latest draft for errors in spelling and punctuation, and look for any errors made in typing or recopying.

EXERCISE 13

PROOFREADING TO PREPARE THE FINAL VERSION

Below are two paragraphs with the kinds of errors that are easy to overlook when you prepare the final version of an assignment. Correct the errors, writing above the lines. There are twelve errors in the first paragraph and ten errors in the second paragraph.

1.   Our college should put a pencil sharpener in every classroom. First of all putting a sharpener in each class would help many students. Most student take notes and tests in pencil. Often, a pencil point breaks or gets worn down while a student is writing. A pencil sharpener in the room takes care of the problem. Secondly, a pencil sharpner would eliminate distractions in class. For instance, I was in my math class yesterday when my pencil point broke. I didn't

have another pencil, and there was no sharpener in the room. I had to interrupt the lesson to ask to borow a pencil. last of all, a pencil sharpner in each room would solve the problem of wandering students. At least once a day, a student comes into one of my classes, politely asking, "Does this room have a pencil sharpener? Its embarrassing to have to do this. And its worse to wander desperately threw the halls, trying to find one of the few rooms with a sharpener. Pencil sharpeners wouldn't cost the college much, but they would sure make a diference.

    2.   My local Cable Television Service, Friendly Cable Company, needs to live up to the terms of its contract with subscribers. For one thing, Friendly Cable Company promises fast service, but their response is slow. When I call the company I have to go through an entire menu of sales offers, before I get to press number five for cable service. Than I am placed on hold for as long as twenty minutes. When I finally reach a service representative, I am given a service appointment that is three days later. Friendly Cable isn't very fast, and it isn't too friendly, either. Once I asked to speak to the Manager. The representative said I couldn't speak to the manager, but I could leave my number, and the manager would get back to me. The manager never cal me. Most importantly, the Friendly Cable Company contract provides cable television in return for money. The contract says that if I don't pay my cable bill, I don't get to watch cable television. I always pay my bill, but I do'nt get functioning cable television. Twice in this month alone, my cable has been out. I think Friendly Cable owes me some money for the times when I didn't get my money's worth. I like watching cable television, but I wish my cable service did it's job.

Lines of Detail: A Walk-Through Assignment

    Write a one-paragraph letter to the editor of your local newspaper. Argue for some change you want for your community. You could argue for a traffic light, turn signal, or stop sign at a specific intersection. Or you could argue for bike paths in certain places, a recycling program, more bus service, or for any other specific change you feel is needed. To write your paragraph, follow these steps:

Step 1: Begin by listing all the reasons and details you can about your topic. Survey your list and consider any possible objections. Answer the objections as well as you can, and see if the objections can lead you to more reasons.

Step 2: Group your reasons, listing the details that fit under each reason. Add details where they are needed and check to see if any reasons overlap.

ALONG THESE LINES/Pearson Education Canada

Step 3: Survey the reasons and details, and draft a topic sentence. Be sure that your topic sentence states the subject and takes a stand.

Step 4: Write an outline. Then revise it, checking that you have enough reasons to make your point. Also check that your reasons are specific and in an effective order. Be sure that you have sufficient details for each reason. Check that your outline includes answers to any significant objections.

Step 5: Write a draft of your argument. Revise the draft until it includes any necessary explanations of the problem being argued, all serious or obvious reasons, and sufficient specific details. Also check that the most important reason is stated last. Add all the transitions that are needed to link your reasons and details.

Step 6: Before you prepare the final copy of your paragraph, decide whether you need a final sentence to stress your point and whether your transitions are smooth and logical. Refine your word choice. Then check for errors in spelling, punctuation, and grammar.

Writing Your Own Argument Paragraph

When you write on any of the following topics, be sure to work through the stages of the writing process in preparing your argument paragraph.

1. Write a paragraph for readers of your local newspaper, arguing for one of the following:

   a. a ban on all advertising of alcohol
   b. mandatory jail terms for those convicted of impaired driving
   c. the inclusion of more locally grown, organic food in grocery stores
   d. secondary school guidance counsellors to encourage students to enter the trades, as an alternative to university

2. In a paragraph, argue one of the following topics to the audience specified. If your instructor agrees, brainstorm your topic with a group before you start writing. Ask the group to "play audience," reacting to your reasons, raising objections, and asking questions.

   topic a: Early-morning classes should be abolished at your college.
   audience: the Dean of Academic Affairs

   topic b: Attendance in college classes should be optional.
   audience: the instructors at your college

   topic c: College students should be forgiven a portion of their student loans.
   audience: your MP (Member of Parliament)

   topic d: Your college should provide a free day-care facility for students with children.
   audience: the president of your college

   topic e: Businesses should hire more student interns.
   audience: the president of a company (name it) that you'd like to work for

3. Write a paragraph for or against any of the following topics. Your audience for the argument is your classmates and your instructor.

For or Against
a. privatized health care
b. "do-it-yourself" projects
c. inviting doctors trained in other countries to practise in Canada
d. passing a law that requires all businesses to disclose what they pollute the environment with and by how much
e. having a public, online rating system for health care professionals
f. funding for religion-based schooling
g. banning cellphones in the classroom
h. increasing the maximum speed limit on Canada's highways
i. "big box" stores
j. imported produce
k. reality TV
l. a minimum percentage of Canadian content on all Canadian radio and television stations
m. online dating services
n. lowering the young offenders' age limit

WRITING FROM READING: ARGUMENT

Have We Forgotten the Trojan Horse?
Charles Gordon

Charles Gordon is a columnist for the Ottawa Citizen *and* Maclean's *magazine.*

Before you read this selection, consider these questions:

Have you noticed an increase in advertising in public spaces?

Does advertising affect your purchase decisions?

How important are brand name products to you?

Do you shop exclusively at specific stores? Do you buy only certain brands?

The commercialization of just about everything began the day the Berlin Wall came down. That event represented the triumph of capitalism over communism, which no one will dispute, and the right of corporations to do anything they please, which hardly anyone seems to dispute either.

At least not yet. The free market is in. Regulation is out. Taxation is discredited. Government spending is passé. And what corporations do, provided it is within the letter of the law, is OK, even putting advertising on boxes of Girl Guide cookies.

Is nothing **sacred**? *The Globe and Mail* felt **constrained** to comment. Here is its editorial: "The Girl Guides of Canada are going to solicit advertising sponsors for their cookies. Sigh." Although the Guides founder "would probably have harrumphed herself into a coronary over it, advertising isn't immoral," the *Globe* continues, "we are a culture as much defined by what we buy as what we believe. And thinking

sacred: made holy by religious association

constrained: forced

creatively, it is just possible that, in addition to badges in pet-keeping, fishing and canoe safety, future Girl Guides could receive awards for demonstrating mastery in the fine art of product placement. Still. Sigh."

dilemma: choice between two equally undesirable alternatives

Could there be a better illustration of our modern **dilemma**? The *Globe,* as demonstrated by all the sighing, clearly knows that something is not quite right. But it cannot bring itself to say so, because "advertising isn't immoral" and because the Girl Guides are responding to market forces that are, by definition, good. Still. Sigh. This is not the only example of cherished institutions entering into partnerships with the corporate world. There is the well-publicized relationship between the Royal Canadian Mounted Police and Walt Disney. There is the Walt Disney Co.'s involvement with Canada Post, which issued a series of stamps featuring a Disney character.

More recently, there is a peculiar relationship between a doughnut company, the Canadian armed forces and the minister of national defence, as illustrated by a Tim Hortons commercial aired during the Super Bowl game. It shows the minister's limousine pulling up beside a Canadian Forces ship and several cases of Tim Hortons coffee being unloaded from the trunk for the coffee-hungry crew. This is likely to become a trend. Explained a Forces public affairs officer: "Next time I want to put out a brochure on a navy ship, I'm going to track down some company that's willing to put its logo on the back and cover the costs."

No money seems to have changed hands here, but are we, the Canadian public, ready for the idea of our armed forces being sponsored? Well, we know how strapped the armed forces are, and how much demands are already being placed on the taxpayer. If a corporation wants to help out, where's the harm? That's the conventional logic. Still, sigh.

Further examples are all around. Some are almost too familiar, particularly in the world of sports, where corporations are able to attach their names to anything that moves, not to mention skis, skates or drives. We take for granted the advertising on the boards in hockey arenas, or on the uniforms worn by tennis players and race car drivers. Rare now is the tournament, stadium or big game that does not have some corporation's name on it. And now Girl Guide cookies. Next: the northern lights.

Can we do anything but sigh at this corporate invasion of our public and private spaces? Well, sigh. To legislate bans would be in violation of many fundamental human rights. And that's assuming that the political will to take such action existed, which it doesn't.

The answer lies, as it usually does, with us as individuals. If we protest and make a noise, things can happen. The Nike corporation came to Ottawa last year to offer a free gymnasium floor, then withdrew its offer when city councillors asked questions about the corporation's record in the **Third World.**

Third World: developing nations of Africa, Asia, and Latin America

Continuing attempts by corporations to get their names into schools have also met with resistance. The most recent example involves a school being offered a satellite dish and television monitors in classrooms, on which students are shown 12-minute news broadcasts that include two to $2^1/_2$ minutes of commercials.

ALONG THESE LINES/Pearson Education Canada

It is funding cuts, of course, that increase the appeal of such proposals. The school (or the city, or the hospital, or the team) gets some equipment it would not otherwise be able to afford, virtually free. Only on rare occasions does someone dare to suggest that virtually free is too high a price. But, in the case of the schools, that has happened in the past, with groups of parents and educators being able to convince departments of education to look gift horses in the mouth. That could work again, and it wouldn't hurt either to do some serious **lobbying** against funding cuts.

lobbying: influencing members of legislature

More direct approaches can work, too. Corporations are sensitive about their public image (otherwise, why spend vast sums to be just above the elbow on the left sleeve of a race car driver's jacket?), and will respond to letters of protest. A smart corporation president is like a smart politician—able to recognize when the mail, be it snail or e-, represents a segment of public opinion that it would be risky to offend. The president of a company thinking of putting the company logo on either the vanilla crème or the chocolate mint, would certainly think again after receiving some personal letters urging him or her to take another advertising approach.

If we want to stop the commercialization of everything, if we want corporations to keep their names to themselves, then we have to let them know. A sigh is just a sigh.

UNDERSTANDING "HAVE WE FORGOTTEN THE TROJAN HORSE?"

1. Charles Gordon cites several examples of public or private organizations teaming up with corporations. List three examples here:

   _____ and _____

   _____ and _____

   _____ and _____

2. Why does "conventional logic" see no harm in this trend toward free corporate advertising for public and private organizations?

   _____

   _____

   _____

3. What does a school or a team gain from allowing corporate advertising in its classrooms or on its uniforms?

   _____

   _____

   _____

4. The title of Charles Gordon's article refers to the Trojan horse. In classical Greek mythology, the Greek army hid soldiers inside a large, hollow horse made of wood. They presented the horse to their enemies, the Trojans (residents of Troy). Thinking the horse was a gift for their goddess, the Trojans brought it inside their city walls. The soldiers inside the wooden horse then broke out and opened the city gates for the Greek army. The Greeks burned the city of Troy and defeated the Trojans.

According to Gordon, how is the "commercialization of just about everything" like a Trojan horse?

_____

_____

_____

_____

_____

WRITING FROM READING "HAVE WE FORGOTTEN THE TROJAN HORSE?"

1. Write a one-paragraph summary of Gordon's article. Focus on the point of his argument and the details he uses to support his point.

2. Write an argument that agrees or disagrees with any of the statements below. You can support your argument with reasons or specific examples. Your audience is your classmates and your instructor.

> Advertising is misleading and makes people buy what they don't need.

> Schools should form partnerships with corporations to ensure up-to-date technology for today's students.

> Governments should increase funding to education, health, and sports.

WRITING FROM READING: ARGUMENT

Assimilation, Pluralism, and "Cultural Navigation": Multiculturalism in Canadian Schools

Hiren Mistry

Hiren Mistry is a Toronto educator and author whose activist and research interests focus on pluralism in education.

Before you read this selection, consider these questions:

> *In your everyday life, how many different people do you meet? what ages? what races? what cultural backgrounds?*

> *How many times have you heard someone say in reference to newcomers to Canada, "Why don't they just go back to where they came from?"*

> *What makes Canada different from the United States? from the United Kingdom? from European countries? from other former Commonwealth countries?*

pedagogical gurus: influential teachers

proverbial: customary, usual

camp: group of supporters

advocates: promotes, recommends

Arguably, Canadian public high-schools are giant cultural-laboratories: Canada's multicultural future is tested, experimented with, and reproduced here. Teachers, administrators and **pedagogical gurus** are the **proverbial** lab-technicians of this cultural experiment. The "test subjects" are the students who fill Canadian classrooms from all over the globe. The formula? This is where opinions differ in the lab. A larger, more historically established **camp advocates** a policy of assimilation, while

paradigms: examples or patterns of thought

a smaller, growing camp asserts a policy of pluralism. A world of difference separates these two **paradigms**. I would equally argue that the failure or success of our nation is also caught up in the differences between these two approaches to dealing with multiculturalism in our schools. After all, what is tested and reproduced in our schools will leave a mark on the future of Canada. We would, therefore, do well to examine our choices carefully before we experiment any further.

assimilation: absorbing into a system, making all alike

Assimilation is the paradigm of choice amongst a significant number of established and therefore powerful educators in this country. They argue that participation in Canadian public life should foster a sense of common national heritage, regardless of where one emigrates from. For these educators, this nationalist ethic is first fostered in the classroom; hence their belief that the celebration of "traditional" Canadian values should be given priority in the curricular, as well as extracurricular, life of our schools. Flag Day, Remembrance Day, and Thanksgiving, for instance, should be given precedence over school-wide celebrations of Ramadan or the establishment of multicultural councils. Assemblies and curriculum in support of Black History or Asian Heritage Month would be seen as equally distracting. While advocates of assimilation would agree that cultural diversity is a fact of Canadian life, they would be quick to point out that Canadian students, and their families, have all the freedom to celebrate and practice their cultural ancestry in the privacy of their *own homes*. However, they believe it is the moral duty of all Canadians to separate their *public* and *private* cultural obligations.

implicit: hinted at, indirect

For assimilationists, their argument for the promotion of common Canadian values and identity underlies a not-so-**implicit** fear of difference. For one, they believe a focus on cultural diversity in schools will weaken Canada's already fragile identity. Secondly, they claim that, by encouraging students to explore the cultural ancestry of their peers, or even themselves, schools will culturally *ghettoize*. Rather than learning how to get along, they believe students would end up becoming more self-interested, racist, and prone to establishing gangs and **instigating** violence. As an extension to this argument, they claim that, in a world of increasing international tension between competing cultural and religious groups, nationalist conflicts and historical **vendettas** would be played out in the halls of Canadian high-schools.

instigating: causing, encouraging

vendettas: bitter quarrels, blood feuds

While I do not doubt that the above concerns are very real in the minds of those educators advocating a multicultural policy of assimilation, I hesitate to take their alarm too seriously. Their arguments for assimilation—and against pluralism—are founded equally on their fear of change (and the loss of cultural **hegemony**), as well as on a **naive** understanding of culture. The consequences of their blind-spots are too critical to ignore, for all Canadians.

hegemony: leadership

naive: innocent, child-like

pluralist: belief in a society where minority groups maintain independent traditions

Advocates of a **pluralist** approach to multiculturalism envision an environment where the global connections of our Canadian students are actively engaged and thoroughly integrated into all facets of curricular and extracurricular school life. Their argument is, quite simply, that the cultural composition of Canada has irreversibly changed. If a casual look at a typical urban classroom won't silence

ALONG THESE LINES/Pearson Education Canada

doubters, then the 2001 Canadian census statistics for Toronto, Montreal, and Vancouver would quickly put any doubts to rest. In the 1990s, 73 percent of all new immigrants settled in these three cities, of which nearly 77 percent were of South Asian, African, South American and Chinese descent.[1] More significantly, Canada wide, immigrants from these regions grew by over 24 percent from 1991 to 2001, and there is no sign that this is a receding trend. Pluralists, therefore, see it as the obligation of the education system to *prepare* students for the future, rather than enchant them with romantic notions of cultural **homogeneity**. Assimilation might have been a *possible* response (though, still morally questionable) to multiculturalism, when ethnic minorities in fact lived up (or rather down) to this **demographic** classification. However, in urban communities, such as in Brampton, Ontario, where more than 40 percent of the population is of non-European and American descent, assimilation is no longer a viable option. New immigrants do not leave their ancestral customs and beliefs at the border when they enter Canada or Canadian schools. Indeed, they take their culture with them and import it into their Canadian lives: publicly and privately. Unless Canadian students, therefore, know how to interact with their multicultural peers in public space, we need to be concerned about the outcome of their ignorance once their lives move beyond the classroom.

Pluralists, however, do not advocate an "either-or" scenario of cultural loyalties. Why can't nationalist heritage of Canadian identity be fostered at the same time as the multicultural heritages of our students? Our brains are **cognitively** equipped to deal with such cultural diversity, for our brains are no more necessarily mono-cultural than they are mono-lingual. Just as one with the **requisite** exposure to a second language gains enough competence to become bilingual, it also follows that those who gain exposure to and competence in more than one culture will become moderately, if not successfully, bi-cultural. "Having such a capacity is no more a threat to one's personal integrity than bi-lingualism is a cause for brain damage."[2] There is no need for Canada's national heritage to be at odds with the ancestral cultures of Canadian students. They needn't cancel each other out. All that is required is exposure to and engagement with culture.

The consequences for not engaging in this bold, yet practical, experiment are **manifold**. If Canadian schools continue to respond to the presence of diversity through assimilation, they will see their worst fears come true. Students who do not see their world views recognized in their school environment will seek other ways, outside of the school environment, to reinforce their personal and cultural integrity. This is doubly reinforced when ESL students, in particular, find little academic success after receiving minimal language training before mainstreaming to regular academic courses. The polarization between cultural groups and the mainstream of Canadian schools—and the fallout of ignorance, fear, and prejudice—has a source closer to home than most Canadian educators would like to think.

homogeneity: sameness, uniformity

demographic: analyzing populations by statistics of birth, death, disease, and so on

cognitively: knowingly, perceptually

requisite: necessary, essential

manifold: many and various

However, all is not "doom and gloom." The choice is clear. If Canadian educators take seriously the challenge to foster the "cultural intelligence" of their students and adopt a pluralist pedagogy to prepare them to engage the multicultural world beyond their classroom walls, Canada can proudly live up to its reputation for being a global model of multiculturalism. If not, the seeds of ignorance, fear, and bigotry—which **purveyors** of multiculturalism most wish to avoid—will most certainly be sown. And, unfortunately, Canadian educators will have only themselves to blame.

purveyors: suppliers

1. Cf. "Canada 2nd to Australia in foreign-born residents: census," Tue., 21 Jan. 2003 (http://cbc.ca/stories/2003/01/21/census_immigrants030121).

2. Roger Ballard, "Race, Culture and Ethnicity," CASAS Occasional Papers, University of Manchester, 2002, p. 25.

UNDERSTANDING "ASSIMILATION, PLURALISM, AND 'CULTURAL NAVIGATION': MULTICULTURALISM IN CANADIAN SCHOOLS"

1. According to the author, Hiren Mistry, what are the two paradigms used to study the multicultural future of Canada?

    _____

    _____

    _____

2. Assimilationists argue that promotion of cultural diversity may "ghettoize" Canada's high-schools. What consequences do they fear?

    _____

    _____

    _____

3. Why does the author believe that "assimilation is no longer a viable option" for modern-day Canada?

    _____

    _____

    _____

4. The article "Assimilation, Pluralism, and 'Cultural Navigation': Multiculturalism in Canadian Schools" includes two endnotes, marked with numbers [1] and [2]. What purposes do these endnotes serve?

    _____

    _____

    _____

5. In your opinion, does multiculturalism mean "your culture *or* my culture" or "your culture *and* my culture"? Give three reasons for your view.

    _____

    _____

    _____

WRITING FROM READING "ASSIMILATION, PLURALISM, AND 'CULTURAL NAVIGATION': MULTICULTURALISM IN CANADIAN SCHOOLS"

1. The author, Hiren Mistry, asserts that Canadian students of all backgrounds need to "know how to interact with their multicultural peers in public space." Interview your classmates to find out what their experiences have been. Do they consider themselves part of the dominant Canadian culture? part of their traditional culture? part of both cultures? Do they get along with some cultural groups more easily than others? Why or why not? Then write a paragraph arguing *one* of the following views:

   a. Most young people in Canada today accept and understand other cultures on a day-to-day basis.

   b. Many young people in Canada today feel that they do not belong and that they are misunderstood due to their cultural backgrounds.

2. Based on 2001 Canadian census statistics, the author states that almost one-quarter of all newcomers to Canada from 1991 to 2001 were of non-European and American backgrounds. What do you think are the Canadian values that appealed to these immigrants and influenced their choice to settle here?

3. Each pair of topic sentences below offers opposing views on multiculturalism in Canada. Choose one position *only* and provide reasons and details to support it. (To expand your ability to debate effectively, try arguing the point of view that you do not personally agree with.) Your audience is your classmates and your instructor.

   a. Learning more about other cultures in school results in better relations in society.

      or

      Learning more about other cultures in school will do little to change the attitudes that children learn at home.

   b. People from all over the world immigrate to Canada to take advantage of economic opportunities, not to become part of Canadian society.

      or

      People from all over the world choose Canada as their home to build a new life that blends both traditional and Canadian values.

   c. Public schools should remain nondenominational and provide a secular education only.

      or

      Celebrating cultural and religious differences in public schools excludes no one and acknowledges recent changes in Canadian society.

4. In the late 1960s, Canada promoted a policy of bilingualism and biculturalism that reflected the history of English and French Canada. This federal policy ensured that English-speaking and French-speaking Canadians had separate but equal rights and privileges. Has this separation of cultures helped or hurt Canada? Should this policy be extended now to other language groups and cultures? Support your argument with reasons or predictions. Your audience again is your instructor and your classmates.

CHAPTER 11
Writing an Essay

"Nobody trips over mountains. It is the small pebble that causes you to stumble. Pass all the pebbles in your path and you will find you have crossed the mountain."

~ AUTHOR UNKNOWN

WHAT IS AN ESSAY?

You write an essay when you have more to say than can be covered in one paragraph. An essay can be one paragraph, but in this book we take it to mean a writing of more than one paragraph. An essay has a main point, called a **thesis**, which is supported by subpoints. The subpoints are the **topic sentences**. Each paragraph in the **body**, or main part, of the essay has a topic sentence. In fact, every paragraph in the body of an essay is like the paragraphs you've already written, because each one makes a point and then supports it.

COMPARING THE SINGLE PARAGRAPH AND THE ESSAY

Read the paragraph and the essay that follow, both about Bob, the writer's brother. You'll notice many similarities.

ALONG THESE LINES/Pearson Education Canada

A Single Paragraph

I think I'm lucky to have a brother who is two years older than I am. For one thing, my brother Bob fought all the typical child–parent battles, and I was the real winner. Bob was the one who made my parents understand that seventeen-year-olds shouldn't have an 11:00 p.m. curfew on weekends. He fought for his rights. By the time I turned seventeen, my parents had accepted the later curfew, and I didn't have to fight for it. Bob also paved the way for me at school. He was such a great athlete that I benefited from his reputation. When I tried out for the basketball team, I had an advantage before I hit the court. I was Bob Cruz's younger brother, so the coach thought I had to be pretty good. At home and at school, my big brother was a big help to me.

An Essay

Some people complain about being the youngest child or the middle child in the family. These people believe older children get all the attention and grab all the power. I'm the younger brother in my family, and I disagree with the complainers. I think I'm lucky to have a brother who is two years older than I am.

For one thing, my brother Bob fought all the typical child–parent battles, and I was the real winner. Bob was the one who made my parents understand that seventeen-year-olds shouldn't have an 11:00 p.m. curfew on weekends. He fought for his rights, and the fighting wasn't easy. I remember months of arguments between Bob and my parents as Bob tried to explain that not all teens on the street at 11:30 are punks or criminals. Bob was the one who suffered from being grounded or who lost the use of my father's car. By the time I turned seventeen, my parents had accepted the later curfew, and I didn't have to fight for it.

Bob also paved the way for me at school. Because he was so popular with the other students and the teachers, he created a positive image of what the boys in our family were like. When I started school, I walked into a place where people were ready to like me, just as they liked Bob. I remember the first day of class when the teachers read the new class rolls. When they got to my name, they asked, "Are you Bob Cruz's brother?" When I said yes, they smiled. Bob's success opened doors for me in school sports, too. He was such a great athlete that I benefited from his reputation. When I tried out for the basketball team, I had an advantage before I hit the court. I was Bob Cruz's younger brother, so the coach thought I had to be pretty good.

I had many battles to fight as I grew up. Like all children, I had to struggle to gain independence and respect. In my struggles at home and at school, my big brother was a big help to me.

If you read the two sample selections carefully, you noticed that they make the same main point, and they support that point with two subpoints.

> **main point:**   I think I'm lucky to have a brother who is two years older than I am.
>
> **subpoints:**   1.   My brother Bob fought all the typical child–parent battles, and I was the real winner.
>   2.   Bob also paved the way at school.

You'll notice that the essay is longer because it has more details and examples to support the points.

ORGANIZING AN ESSAY

When you write an essay of more than one paragraph, the thesis is the *focus* of your entire essay; it is the major point of your essay. The other important points that are part of the thesis are in topic sentences.

> **Thesis:** Working as a salesperson has changed my character.
> **Topic sentence:** I have had to learn patience.
> **Topic sentence:** I have developed the ability to listen.
> **Topic sentence:** I have become more tactful.

Notice that the thesis expresses a bigger idea than the topic sentences following it, and that it is supported by the topic sentences. The essay has an introduction, a body, and a conclusion.

1. **Introduction:** The first paragraph is usually the introduction. The thesis most often goes here.
2. **Body:** This central part of the essay is the part in which you support your main point (the thesis). Each paragraph in the body of the essay has its own topic sentence.
3. **Conclusion:** Usually one paragraph long, the conclusion reminds the reader of the thesis.

WRITING THE THESIS

There are several characteristics of a thesis:
1. It is expressed in a sentence. A thesis is *not* the same as the topic of the essay, or as the title of the essay:

> **topic:**   quitting smoking
> **title:**   Why I Quit Smoking
> **thesis:**   I quit smoking because I was concerned for my health, and I wanted to prove to myself that I could break the habit.

2. A thesis *does not announce*; it makes a point about the subject:

> **announcement:** This essay will explain the reasons why young adults should watch what they eat.
>
> **thesis:**   Young adults should watch what they eat so they can live healthy lives today and prevent future health problems.

ALONG THESE LINES/Pearson Education Canada

3. A thesis *is not too broad*. Some ideas are just too big to cover well in an essay. A thesis that tries to cover too much can lead to a superficial or boring essay.

thesis too broad:	People should work on solving their interpersonal communication problems.
an acceptable thesis:	As an immigrant, I had a hard time understanding that many Canadians thought my imperfect English meant I was uneducated.

4. A thesis *is not too narrow*. Sometimes, students start with a thesis that looks good because it seems specific and precise. Later, when they try to support such a thesis, they can't find anything to say.

thesis too narrow:	My sister pays forty dollars a week for a special formula for her baby.
an acceptable thesis:	My sister had no idea what it would cost to care for a baby.

Hints for Writing a Thesis

1. Your thesis can *mention the specific subpoints* of your essay. For example, your thesis might be

I hated *No Country for Old Men* because the film is extremely violent and it glorifies criminals.

With this thesis, you have indicated the two subpoints of your essay: *No Country for Old Men* is extremely violent; *No Country for Old Men* glorifies criminals.

2. Or your thesis can make a point without mentioning the specific subpoints of your essay. For example, you can write a thesis like the following:

I hated *No Country for Old Men* because of the way it makes the unspeakable into entertainment.

With this thesis, you can still use the subpoints stating that the movie was extremely violent and glorified criminals. You just don't have to mention all your subpoints in the thesis. Be sure to check with your instructor about the type of thesis you should use.

EXERCISE	**RECOGNIZING GOOD THESIS SENTENCES**
1	Below is a list of thesis statements. Some are acceptable, but others are too broad or too narrow. Some are announcements; others are topics, not sentences. Put a *G* next to the good thesis sentences.

1. _____ Why oat bran is an important part of a healthy diet will be discussed in the following essay.
2. _____ My family was a small family unit.
3. _____ The environment is a major concern of people in today's society.
4. _____ How to install speakers in a car.

5. _____ Computers are changing the world.

6. _____ Being an only child has its advantages.

7. _____ The government should stop making pennies because they have outlived their usefulness.

8. _____ A crisis in the banking industry.

9. _____ Newfoundland and Labrador is Canada's youngest province.

10. _____ The advantages of buying a North American car.

EXERCISE 2

SELECTING A GOOD THESIS SENTENCE

In each pair of thesis statements below, put a *G* next to the good thesis sentence.

1. a. _____ Road rage incidents and people under stress.

   b. _____ People under stress are more likely to be involved in incidents of road rage.

2. a. _____ Drinking bottled water is a popular but expensive habit.

   b. _____ Pollution of the oceans, rivers, and lakes of the world is threatening to change life as we know it.

3. a. _____ The challenges of being a foreign student will be discussed in this essay.

   b. _____ Foreign students face academic, social, and financial challenges.

4. a. _____ The need for a better highway system in Northwestern Ontario.

   b. _____ The province needs to expand and restructure its highway system in Northwestern Ontario.

5. a. _____ I failed my third sociology test last Friday.

   b. _____ Sociology has too many strange terms, boring statistics, and complicated studies for me to remember.

6. a. _____ The old house needs basic repairs in several areas.

   b. _____ Where the old house needs basic repair work is the subject of this paper.

7. a. _____ The differences between a foster child and an adopted child in the provincial legal system.

   b. _____ In the provincial legal system, there are three significant differences between a foster child and an adopted child.

8. a. _____ Becoming a vegan benefits one's health, one's community, and the environment.

   b. _____ Why everyone should be vegan.

9. a. _____ Gold jewellery and its quality.

   b. _____ There are three signs that a piece of jewellery is real gold.

10. a. _____ Child abuse is a problem in families of every social class.

   b. _____ The local child abuse hotline is helping to save lives.

EXERCISE 3

WRITING A THESIS THAT RELATES TO THE SUBPOINTS

Below are lists of subpoints that could be explained in an essay. Write a thesis for each list. Remember that there are two ways to write a thesis: you can write a thesis that includes the subpoints, or you can write one that makes a point without listing the subpoints. As an example, the first one is done for you, using both kinds of topic sentences.

1. **one kind of thesis:** Cities that demonstrate a commitment to urban planning see less urban sprawl within their boundaries.

   another kind of thesis: Cities that are committed to mixed-use practices, to green space, and to defensible space see less urban sprawl within their boundaries.

   subpoints:

   a. Paris, for instance, has increased densification by including a mixture of residential, commercial, and work space in parts of the city.

   b. Central Park, designed in 1858, was envisioned as an oasis for New York's citizens.

   c. The use of cobblestone streets, leafy trees, and the like is termed defensible space, meaning the use of strategies to decrease crime in an area.

2. **thesis:** _____

   _____

   subpoints:

   a. Employers look for workers who are prepared to work hard.

   b. Employers will hire people with the right training.

   c. Employers want workers who have a positive attitude.

3. **thesis:** _____

   _____

   subpoints:

   a. Neighbours will often collect your mail when you're out of town.

   b. In an emergency, neighbours can lend you the tools you need.

4. thesis: _____

   _____

   subpoints:

   a. Neighbours will often collect your mail when you're out of town.

   b. In an emergency, neighbours can lend you the tools you need.

   c. Neighbours can be nosy and critical.

   d. Neighbours can invade your living space.

5. thesis: _____

   _____

   subpoints:

   a. The local news website gives me the weather forecast.

   b. It tells me about crimes in my neighbourhood.

   c. It informs me of major car accidents.

WRITING THE ESSAY IN STEPS

In an essay, you follow the same steps you learned in writing a paragraph—thought lines, outlines, rough drafts, final version—but you adapt them to the longer essay form.

THOUGHT LINES

GATHERING IDEAS: AN ESSAY

Often the thought lines part begins with *narrowing a topic*. Your instructor may give you a large topic so that you can find something smaller, within the broad one, that you'd like to write about.

Some students think that, because they have several paragraphs to write, they'd better pick a large topic, one that will give them enough to say. But large topics can lead to boring, shallow, general essays. A smaller topic can challenge you to find the specific, concrete examples and details that make an essay interesting and effective.

If your instructor asked you to write about college, for instance, you might *freewrite* some ideas as you narrow the topic:

> ### Narrowing the Topic of College
>
> What college means to me—too big, and it could be boring
>
> College vs. high school—everyone might choose this topic
>
> College students—too big
>
> College students who have jobs—better!
>
> Problems of working and going to college—okay!

In your freewriting, you can consider your *purpose*—to write an essay about some aspect of college—and *audience*—your instructor and your classmates. Your narrowed topic will appeal to this audience because many students hold jobs and instructors are familiar with the problems of working students.

Listing Ideas

Once you have a narrow topic, you can use whatever process works for you. You can brainstorm by writing a series of questions and answers about your topic, you can freewrite on the topic, you can list ideas on the topic, or you can do any combination of these processes.

Below is a sample listing of ideas on the topic of the problems of working and going to college.

Problems of Working and Going to College

early classes

too tired to pay attention

tried to study at work

got caught

got reprimanded

slept in class

constantly racing around

no sleep

little time to do homework

weekends only time to study

no social life

apartment a mess

missed work for make-up test

get behind in school

need salary for tuition

rude to customers

girlfriend ready to kill me

Clustering the Ideas

By clustering the items on the list, you'll find it easier to see the connections between ideas. The following items have been clustered (grouped), and they have been listed under a subtitle.

Problems of Working and Going to College: Ideas in Clusters

Problems at School	**Problems at Work**
early classes	tried to study at work
too tired to pay attention	got caught
slept in class	got reprimanded

(continued)

little time to do homework	missed work for make-up test
get behind in school	rude to customers

Problems Outside of Work and School

weekends only time to study

no social life

apartment a mess

girlfriend ready to kill me

When you surveyed the clusters, you probably noticed that some of the ideas from the original list were left out. These ideas, on racing around, not getting enough sleep, and needing tuition money, could fit into more than one place and might not fit anywhere. You might come back to them later.

When you name each cluster by giving it a subtitle, you move toward a focus for each body paragraph of your essay. By beginning to focus the body paragraphs, you start thinking about the main point, the thesis of your essay. Concentrating on the thesis and on focused paragraphs helps you *unify* your essay.

Reread the clustered ideas. When you do so, you'll notice that each cluster is about problems at a different place. You can incorporate that concept into a thesis with a sentence like this:

> Students who work while they attend college face problems at school, at work, and at home.

Once you have a thesis and a list of details, you can begin working on the outlines part of your essay.

EXERCISE

4

NARROWING TOPICS

Working with a partner or with a group, narrow these topics so the new topics are related, but smaller, and suitable for short essays that are between four and six paragraphs. The first topic is narrowed for you.

1. topic: summer vacation
   smaller, related topics:

   a. a car trip with children

   b. Disney World: not a vacation paradise

   c. my vacation job

2. topic: driving
   smaller, related topics:

   a. _____

   b. _____

   c. _____

3. **topic:** sports

smaller, related topics:

a. _____

b. _____

c. _____

4. **topic:** the environment

smaller, related topics:

a. _____

b. _____

c. _____

5. **topic:** money

smaller, related topics:

a. _____

b. _____

c. _____

6. **topic:** urban living

smaller, related topics:

a. _____

b. _____

c. _____

EXERCISE

5

CLUSTERING RELATED IDEAS

Below are two topics, each with a list of ideas. Mark all the related items on the list with the same number (*1, 2,* or *3*). Some items might not get a number. When you've finished marking the list, write a title for each number that explains the cluster of ideas.

1. **topic:** giving a speech

_____ audience may be large

_____ begin by thinking of a good topic

_____ right before you speak, take a deep breath

_____ make eye contact with your audience as you speak

_____ make a list of what you want to say

_____ organize your list onto note cards

_____ relax as you get up to speak

_____ speak slowly

_____ as you wait to speak, remember all speakers are nervous

_____ stand confidently

The ideas marked 1 can be titled _____

The ideas marked 2 can be titled _____

The ideas marked 3 can be titled _____

2. **topic:** why a new job is stressful

_____ boss may be bad tempered

_____ you may feel all your co-workers are watching you

_____ you don't know anyone who works there

_____ you think you can't learn the new routines

_____ a different computer program is challenging

_____ you may be given very little autonomy

_____ the salary may be low

_____ you may think all the co-workers are gossiping about you

_____ you may be afraid you won't get the work done quickly enough

_____ the boss may have strong dislikes

The ideas marked 1 can be titled _____

The ideas marked 2 can be titled _____

The ideas marked 3 can be titled _____

OUT LINES   DEVISING A PLAN: AN ESSAY

In the next stage of writing your essay, draft an outline. Use the thesis to focus your ideas. There are many kinds of outlines, but all are used to help a writer organize ideas. When you use a **formal outline,** you show the difference between a main idea and its supporting details by *indenting* the supporting details. In a formal outline, Roman numerals (I, II, III, and so on) and capital letters are used. Each Roman numeral represents a paragraph, and the letters beneath the numeral represent supporting details.

> The Structure of a Formal Outline

first paragraph	I. Thesis
second paragraph	II. Topic sentence
	⎡ A.
	⎢ B.
details	⎨ C.
	⎢ D.
	⎣ E.

(continued)

ALONG THESE LINES/Pearson Education Canada

third paragraph	III. Topic sentence
details	A. B. C. D. E.
fourth paragraph	IV. Topic sentence
details	A. B. C. D. E.
fifth paragraph	V. Conclusion

Hints for Outlining

Developing a good, clear outline now can save you hours of confused, disorganized writing later. The extra time you spend to make sure your outline has sufficient details and that *each paragraph stays on one point* will pay off in the long run.

1. **Check the topic sentences:** Keep in mind that each topic sentence in each body paragraph should support the thesis sentence. If a topic sentence is not carefully connected to the thesis, the structure of the essay will be confusing. Here is a thesis with a list of topic sentences; the topic sentence that doesn't fit is crossed out.

thesis:	I A home-cooked dinner can be a rewarding experience for both the cook and the guests.
topic sentences:	II Preparing a meal is a satisfying activity. III It is a pleasure for the cook to see guests enjoy the meal. IV ~~Many recipes are handed down through generations.~~ V Dinner guests are flattered when someone cooks for them.
conclusion:	VI Dining at home is a treat for everyone at the table or in the kitchen.

Since the thesis of this outline is about the pleasure of dining at home, for the cook and the guests, topic sentence IV doesn't fit: it isn't about the joy of cooking *or* about being a dinner guest. It takes the essay off track. A careful check of the links between the thesis and the topic sentences will help keep your essay focused.

2. **Include some details:** Some writers believe that they don't need many details in the outline. They feel they can fill in the details later, when

they actually write the essay. Even though some writers do manage to add details later, others who are in a hurry or who run out of ideas can have problems.

Imagine, for example, that a writer has included very few details in an outline, like this:

II A burglary makes the victim feel unsafe.
    A. The person has lost property.
    B. The person's home territory has been invaded.

The paragraph created from this outline might be too short and lack specific details, like this:

A burglary makes the victim feel unsafe. First of all, the victim has lost property. Second, a person's home territory has been invaded.

If you have difficulty thinking of ideas when you write, try to tackle the problem in the outline. The more details you put into your outline, the more detailed and effective your draft essay will be. For example, suppose the same outline on the burglary topic had more details, like this:

II A burglary makes the victim feel unsafe.

more detail about burglary itself:

    A. The person has lost property.
    B. The property could be worth hundreds of dollars.
    C. The victim can lose a television or camera or laptop.
    D. The burglars may take cash.
    E. Worse, items with personal value, like family jewellery or heirlooms, can be stolen.

more detail about safety concerns:

    F. Even worse, a person's territory has been invaded.
    G. People who thought they were safe know they are not safe.
    H. The fear is that the invasion can happen again.

You will probably agree that the paragraph will be more detailed, too.

3. **Stay on one point:** It's a good idea to check the outline of each body paragraph to see if each paragraph stays on one point. Compare each topic sentence, which is at the top of the list for the paragraph, against the details indented under it. Staying on one point gives each paragraph unity.

Below is the outline for a paragraph that has problems staying on one point. See if you can spot the problem areas.

III Sonya is a generous person.

    A. I remember how freely she gave her time when our club had a car wash.
    B. She is always willing to share her lecture notes with me.
    C. Sonya gives ten percent of her salary to her church.
    D. She is a member of Big Sisters and spends every Saturday with a disadvantaged child.
    E. She can read people's minds when they are in trouble.
    F. She knows what they are feeling.

The topic sentence of this paragraph is about generosity. But sentences E and F talk about Sonya's insight, not her generosity.

When you have a problem staying on one point, you can solve the problem in one of two ways:

   a. Eliminate details that don't fit your main point.

or

   b. Change the topic sentence so that it relates to all the ideas in the paragraph.

For example, you could cut out sentences E and F about Sonja's insight, getting rid of the details that don't fit. Or you could change the topic sentence in the paragraph so that it relates to all the ideas in the paragraph: "Sonya is a generous and an insightful person."

Revisiting the Thought Lines Stage

Writing an outline can help you identify underdeveloped places in your plan— places where your paragraphs need more details. You can develop these details in two ways:

   1. Go back to the writing you did in the thought lines stage. Check whether items on a list or ideas from freewriting can lead you to more details for your outline.
   2. Brainstorm for more details by a question-and-answer approach. For example, if the outline includes "My apartment is a mess," you might ask, "Why? How messy?" Or if the outline includes "I have no social life," you might ask, "What do you mean? Parties? Clubs?"

The time you spend writing and revising your outline will make it easier for you to write an essay that is well developed, unified, and coherently structured. The following checklist may help you revise.

CHECKLIST   **FOR REVISING THE OUTLINE OF AN ESSAY**

   ✓ **Unity:** Do the thesis and topic sentences all lead to the same point? Does each paragraph make one, and only one, point? Do the details in each paragraph support the topic sentence? Does the conclusion unify the essay?
   ✓ **Support:** Do the body paragraphs have enough supporting details?
   ✓ **Coherence:** Are the paragraphs in the most effective order? Are the details in each paragraph arranged in the most effective order?

A sentence outline on the problems of working and going to college follows. It includes the thesis in the first paragraph. The topic sentences have been created from the titles of the ideas clustered earlier. The details have been drawn from ideas in the clusters and from further brainstorming. The conclusion has just one sentence that unifies the essay.

An Outline for an Essay

paragraph 1

 introduction

 I   Thesis: Students who work while going to college face problems
              at school, at work, and at home.

paragraph 2

 topic sentence

 II   Trying to juggle job and school responsibilities creates problems at school.

 details

   A. Early classes are difficult.

   B. I am too tired to pay attention.

   C. Once I slept in class.

   D. I have little time to do homework.

   E. I get behind in school assignments.

paragraph 3

 topic sentence

 III   Work can suffer when workers attend college.

 details

   A. I tried to study at work.

   B. I got caught by my boss.

   C. I was reprimanded.

   D. Sometimes I come to work very tired.

   E. When I don't have enough sleep, I can be rude
        to customers.

   F. Rudeness gets me in trouble.

   G. Another time, I had to cut work to take a make-up test.

paragraph 4

 topic sentence

 IV   Working students suffer outside of classes and the workplace.

 details

   A. I work nights during the week.

   B. The weekends are the only time I can study.

   C. My apartment is a mess since I have no time to clean it.

   D. Worse, my girlfriend is ready to kill me because I have no
        social life.

   E. We never even go to the movies anymore.

   F. When she comes over, I am busy studying.

paragraph 5 conclusion

 V   I have learned that working students have to be very organized
      to cope with their responsibilities at college, work, and home.

ALONG THESE LINES/Pearson Education Canada

EXERCISE 6

COMPLETING AN OUTLINE FOR AN ESSAY

Below is part of an outline that has a thesis and topic sentences, but no details. Add the details and write in complete sentences. Write one sentence for each capital letter. Be sure that the details are connected to the topic sentence.

I **thesis:** Video cameras have several beneficial uses in today's society.

II People use their video cameras to record memorable family events.

A. _____

B. _____

C. _____

D. _____

E. _____

III Video cameras are being used to prevent or detect crimes.

A. _____

B. _____

C. _____

D. _____

E. _____

IV Video cameras have given ordinary people an opportunity to feel what it's like to be a TV director or an actor.

A. _____

B. _____

C. _____

D. _____

E. _____

V The video camera has changed the way people celebrate family rituals, has contributed to the prevention and detection of crime, and has made ordinary people into TV directors and performers.

EXERCISE **7**	FOCUSING AN OUTLINE FOR AN ESSAY

The following outline has a thesis and details, but it has no topic sentences for the body paragraphs. Write the topic sentences.

I thesis: After my last meal at Don's Diner, I swore I'd never eat there again.

II _____

_____

     A. My friend and I were kept waiting for a table for half an hour.

     B. During that time, several tables were empty, but no one bothered to clear the dirty dishes.

     C. We just stood in the entrance, waiting.

     D. Then, when we were seated, the waitress was surly.

     E. It took fifteen minutes to get a menu.

     F. The plates of food were slammed down on the table.

     G. The orders were mixed up.

III _____

_____

     A. The hamburger was full of gristle.

     B. Toasting the hamburger bun couldn't hide the fact that it was stale.

     C. The french fries were as hard as cardboard.

     D. The iced-tea powder was floating on top of the glass.

     E. The lettuce had brown edges.

     F. Ketchup was caked all over the outside of the ketchup bottle.

IV I never want to repeat the experience I had at Don's Diner.

ROUGH LINES   **DRAFTING AND REVISING: AN ESSAY**

When you are satisfied with your outline, you can begin drafting and revising the essay. Start by writing a first draft of the essay, which includes these parts: introduction, body paragraphs, and conclusion.

WRITING THE INTRODUCTION

Where Does the Thesis Go?

The thesis should appear in the **introduction** of the essay, in the first paragraph. But most of the time it should not be the first sentence. In front of the thesis, write three or more sentences of introduction. Generally, the thesis is the *last sentence* in the introductory paragraph.

ALONG THESE LINES/Pearson Education Canada

Why put the thesis at the end of the first paragraph? First of all, writing several sentences in front of your main idea gives you a chance to lead into it gradually and smoothly without immediately confronting the reader with it. This method will help you build interest and gain the reader's attention.

Finally, if your thesis is at the end of the introduction, it states the main point of the essay just before that point is supported in the body paragraphs. Putting the thesis at the end of the introduction is like inserting an arrow that points to the supporting ideas in the essay.

Hints for Writing the Introduction

There are a number of ways to write an introduction.

1. **You can begin with some general statements** that gradually lead to your thesis:

   general statements
   : Students face all kinds of problems when they start college. Some students struggle with a lack of basic math skills; others have never learned to write a term paper. Students who were stars in high school have to cope with being just another student number at a large institution. Students with small children have to find a way to be good parents and good students, too. Although all these problems are common,

   thesis at end
   : I found an even more typical conflict. <u>My biggest problem in college was learning to organize my time.</u>

2. **You can begin with a quote** that smoothly leads to your thesis. The quote can be from someone famous, or it can be an old saying. It can be something your mother always told you, a slogan from an advertisement, or the words of a song.

   quote
   : Everybody has heard the old saying, "Time flies," but I never really thought about that statement until I started college. I expected college to challenge me with demanding course work. I expected it to excite me with the range of people I would meet. I even thought it might amuse me with the fun and intrigue of dating and romance. But I never expected college to exhaust me. I was surprised to discover

   thesis at end
   : that <u>my biggest problem in college was learning to organize my time.</u>

   (Note: You can add transitional words or phrases to your thesis, as in the sample above.)

3. **You can tell a story** as a way of leading into your thesis. You can open with the story of something that happened to you or to someone you know, or a story that you read about or heard on the news.

   story
   : My friend Phyllis is two years older than I am, and so she started college before I did. When Phyllis came home from college for the Thanksgiving weekend, I called her with a huge list of activities she and I could enjoy. I was really surprised when Phyllis told me she planned to spend most of the weekend sleeping. I didn't understand

thesis at end

her when she told me she was worn out. When I started college myself, I understood her perfectly. Phyllis was a victim of that old college ailment: not knowing how to handle time. I developed the same disease. <u>My biggest problem in college was learning to organize my time.</u>

4. You can explain why this topic is worth writing about. Explaining could mean giving some background on the topic, or it could mean discussing why the topic is an important one.

explain

I don't remember a word of what was said during my freshman orientation, and I wish I did. I'm sure somebody somewhere warned me about the problems I'd face in college. I'm sure somebody talked about getting organized. Unfortunately, I didn't listen, and I had to learn the hard way. I hope other students will listen and learn and be spared my hard lesson and my big problem. <u>My biggest problem in college was learning to organize my time.</u>

thesis at end

5. You can use one or more questions to lead into your thesis. You can open with a question or questions that will be answered by your thesis. Or you can open with a question or questions that catch the reader's attention and move toward your thesis.

question

Have you ever stayed up all night to study for an exam, then fallen asleep at dawn and slept right through the time of the exam? If you have, then you were probably the same kind of college student I was. I was the student who always ran into class three minutes late, the one who begged for an extension on the term paper, the one who pleaded with the teacher to postpone the test. I just could not get things done on schedule. <u>My biggest problem in college was learning to organize my time.</u>

thesis at end

6. You can open with a contradiction of your main point as a way of attracting the reader's interest and leading to your thesis. The contrast between your opening and your thesis creates interest.

contradiction

People who knew me in my freshman year probably felt really sorry for me. They saw a girl with dark circles under her bloodshot eyes, a girl who was always racing from one place to another. Those people probably thought I was exhausted from overwork. But they were wrong. My problem in college was definitely not too much work; it was the way I handled my work. <u>My biggest problem in college was learning to organize my time.</u>

thesis at end

| EXERCISE **8** | WRITING AN INTRODUCTION |

Below are five thesis sentences. Pick one. Then write an introductory paragraph on the lines provided. Your last sentence should be the thesis sentence. If your instructor agrees, read your introduction to others in the class who wrote an introduction for the same thesis, or read your introduction to the entire class.

Thesis Sentences

1. Young girls are becoming dangerously preoccupied with their weight.
2. Our city should invest more in public transit.
3. People are often surprised at the occupational hazards of my job.
4. One family member has been my greatest role model.
5. People should be more careful in protecting their homes from thieves.

Write an introduction: _____

_____

_____

_____

_____

_____

_____

_____

_____

_____

WRITING THE BODY OF THE ESSAY

In the body of the essay, the paragraphs *explain*, *support*, and *develop* your thesis. In this part of the essay, each paragraph has its own topic sentence, which does two things:

1. It focuses the sentences in the paragraph.
2. It makes a point connected to the thesis.

The thesis and the topic sentences are ideas that need to be supported by details, explanations, and examples. You can visualize the connections among the parts of an essay like this:

Introduction with Thesis

Body {
    Topic Sentence
      Details
    Topic Sentence
      Details
    Topic Sentence
      Details
}

Conclusion

When you write topic sentences, you can help to organize your essay by referring to the following checklist.

CHECKLIST   **FOR TOPIC SENTENCES OF AN ESSAY**

✓ Does the topic sentence give the point of the paragraph?
✓ Does the topic sentence connect to the thesis of the essay?

How Long Are the Body Paragraphs?

Remember that the body paragraphs of an essay are the place where you explain and develop your thesis. These paragraphs should be long enough to explain, not just list, your points. To do this well, try to make your body paragraphs *at least seven sentences* long. As you develop your writing skills, you may find that you can support your ideas in fewer than seven sentences.

Developing the Body Paragraphs

You can write well-developed body paragraphs by following the same steps you used in writing single paragraphs for the earlier assignments in this text. By working through the stages of gathering ideas, outlining, drafting, revising, editing, and proofreading, you can create clear, effective paragraphs.

To focus and develop the body paragraphs, ask the questions in the checklist as you revise.

CHECKLIST   **FOR DEVELOPING BODY PARAGRAPHS FOR AN ESSAY**

✓ Does the topic sentence cover everything in the paragraph?
✓ Do I have enough details to explain the topic sentence?
✓ Do all the details in the paragraph support, develop, or illustrate the topic sentence?

EXERCISE

9

CREATING TOPIC SENTENCES

Below are thesis sentences. For each thesis, write topic sentences (as many as are indicated by the numbered blanks). The first one is done for you.

1. **thesis:** These days, parents are over-programming their children.

   topic sentence   1: *Often, children have activities planned for every day of the week.*

   topic sentence   2: *Unstructured time is important to children's emotional well-being.*

   topic sentence   3: *Doctors have said that some children are as stressed as adults.*

2. **thesis:** Professor Thompson is willing to help his students both in class and during his office hours.

   topic sentence 1: _____

   _____

   topic sentence 2: _____

   _____

3. **thesis:** It's easy to recognize the student who is at college just to have a good time.

   topic sentence 1: _____

   _____

   topic sentence 2: _____

   _____

   topic sentence 3: _____

   _____

4. **thesis:** The ideal roommate has several characteristics.

   topic sentence 1: _____

   _____

   topic sentence 2: _____

   _____

   topic sentence 3: _____

   _____

5. **thesis:** Moving to a new town has its good and bad points.

   topic sentence 1: _____

   _____

   topic sentence 2: _____

   _____

   topic sentence 3: _____

   _____

   topic sentence 4: _____

   _____

WRITING THE CONCLUSION

The last paragraph in the essay is the **conclusion**. It does not have to be as long as a body paragraph, but it should be long enough to tie the essay together and remind the reader of the thesis. You can use any of these strategies in writing the conclusion:

1. **You can restate the thesis, in new words.** Go back to the first paragraph of your essay and reread it. For example, this could be the first paragraph of an essay:

   introduction   Even when I was a child, I did not like being told what to do. I wanted to be my own boss. When I grew up, I figured that the best way to be my own boss was to own my own business. I thought that being in charge would be easy. I now know how difficult being an independent businessperson can

   thesis at end   be. <u>Independent business owners have to be smart, highly motivated, and hard-working.</u>

   The thesis, underlined above, is the sentence that you can restate in your conclusion. Your task is to *make the point again but to use different words*. Then work that restatement into a short paragraph, like this:

          People who own their own business have to be harder on themselves than any employer would ever be. Their success is their own responsibility; they cannot blame company policy or rules because they set the policy and make the rules. <u>If the

   restating the thesis   business is to succeed, their intelligence, drive, and effort are essential.</u>

2. **You can make a judgment, evaluation, or recommendation.** Instead of simply restating your point, you can end by making some comment on the issue you've described or the problem you've illustrated. If you were looking for another way to end the essay on owning one's own business, for example, you could end with a recommendation.

          People often dream of owning their own business. Dream-

   ending with a recommendation   ing is easy, but the reality is tough. <u>Those who want to succeed in their own venture should find a role model.</u> Studying a role model would teach them that know-how, ambition, and constant effort lead to success.

3. **You can conclude your essay by framing it.** You can tie your essay together neatly by using something from your introduction as a way of concluding. When you take an example, a question, or even a quote from your first paragraph and refer to it in your last paragraph, you are "framing" the essay.

   frame   Children <u>who do not like to take directions</u> may think

   frame   that <u>being their own boss will be easy.</u> Adults who try to start a business soon discover that they must be totally self-directed; that is, they must be strong enough

   frame   to <u>keep learning</u>, to <u>keep pushing forward</u>, and to <u>keep working.</u>

EXERCISE **10**	CHOOSING A BETTER WAY TO RESTATE THE THESIS

Below are five clusters. Each cluster consists of a thesis sentence and two sentences that try to restate the thesis. Each restated sentence could be used as part of the conclusion to an essay. Put *B* next to the sentence in each pair that is a better restatement. Remember that the better choice repeats the same idea as the thesis but does not rely on too many of the same words.

1. **thesis:** Students choosing a college major should consider their abilities, their interests, and their financial goals.

    restatement 1: _____ Before they choose a major, students should think about what they do well, what they like to do, and what they want to earn.

    restatement 2: _____ Abilities, interests, and financial goals are things students choosing a major should consider.

2. **thesis:** One of the best ways to meet people is to take a college class.

    restatement 1: _____ Taking a class in college is one of the best ways to meet people.

    restatement 2: _____ College classes can make strangers into friends.

3. **thesis:** The three frosh week activities I enjoyed the most were the scavenger hunt, the club night, and the boat cruise.

    restatement 1: _____ Frosh week organizers obviously know what activities will help students make new friends.

    restatement 2: _____ The scavenger hunt, club night and boat cruise were my favourite frosh week activities.

4. **thesis:** My first job taught me the importance of being on time.

    restatement 1: _____ On my first job, I learned how important it is to be on time.

    restatement 2: _____ Punctuality was the key lesson of my first job.

5. **thesis:** Saving even a small amount of money each month is better than not saving at all.

    restatement 1: _____ Saving a little money every month can be better than not saving at all.

    restatement 2: _____ No matter how small it is, making a monthly deposit in a bank account is better than living from paycheque to paycheque.

Revising the Draft

Once you have a rough draft of your essay, you can begin revising it. The following checklist may help you to make the necessary changes in your draft.

✓ CHECKLIST   FOR REVISING THE DRAFT OF AN ESSAY

✓ Does the essay have a clear, unifying thesis?
✓ Does the thesis make a point?
✓ Does each body paragraph have a topic sentence?
✓ Is each body paragraph focused on its topic sentence?
✓ Are the body paragraphs roughly the same size?
✓ Do any of the sentences need to be combined?
✓ Do any of the words need to be changed?
✓ Do the ideas seem to be smoothly linked?
✓ Does the introduction catch the reader's interest?
✓ Is there a definite conclusion?
✓ Does the conclusion remind the reader of the thesis?

Transitions within Paragraphs

In an essay, you can use two kinds of transitions: those within a paragraph and those between paragraphs.

Transitions that link ideas *within a paragraph* are the same kinds you've used previously. Your choice of words, phrases, or even sentences depends on the type of connection you want to make. Here is a list of some common transitions and the kind of connection they express.

INFOBOX   COMMON TRANSITIONS WITHIN A PARAGRAPH

To join two ideas: again, also, and, another, besides, furthermore, in addition, likewise, moreover, similarly

To show a contrast or a different opinion: but, however, in contrast, instead, nevertheless, on the contrary, on the other hand, otherwise, or, still, yet

To show a cause-and-effect connection: accordingly, as a result, because, consequently, for, so, therefore, thus

To give an example: for example, for instance, in the case of, like, such as, to illustrate

To show time: after, at the same time, before, finally, first, meanwhile, next, recently, shortly, soon, subsequently, then, until

Transitions between Paragraphs

When you write something that is more than one paragraph long, you need transitions that link each paragraph to the others. There are several effective ways to link paragraphs and to remind the reader of your main idea and of how the smaller points connect to it. Restatement and repetition are two ways:

1. **Restate an idea** from the preceding paragraph at the start of a new paragraph. Look closely at the following two paragraphs and notice how the second paragraph repeats an idea from the first paragraph and provides a link.

If people were more patient, driving would be less of an ordeal. If, for instance, the driver behind me didn't honk his horn as soon as the traffic light turned green, both he and I would probably have lower blood pressure. He wouldn't be irritating himself by pushing so hard. And I wouldn't be reacting by slowing down, trying to irritate him even more, and getting angry at him. When I get impatient in heavy traffic, I just make a bad situation worse. Hurrying doesn't get me to my destination any faster; it just stresses me out.

transition restating an idea

The impatient driver doesn't get anywhere; neither does the impatient customer at a restaurant. Impatience at restaurants doesn't pay. I work as a hostess at a restaurant, and I know that the customer who moans and complains about waiting for a table won't get one any faster than the person who makes the best of the wait. In fact, if a customer is too aggressive or obnoxious, the restaurant staff may actually slow down the process of getting that customer a table.

2. **Use synonyms and repetition** as a way of reminding the reader of an important point. For example, in the following two paragraphs, notice how certain repeated words, phrases, and synonyms all remind the reader of a point about facing fear. The repeated words and synonyms are underlined.

Some people just avoid whatever they fear. I have an uncle who is afraid to fly. Whenever he has to go on a trip, he does anything he can to avoid getting on an airplane. He will drive for days, travel by train, take a bus trip. Because he is so terrified of flying, he lives with constant anxiety that some day he may have to fly. He is always thinking of the one emergency that could force him to confront what he most dreads. Instead of dealing directly with his fear, he lets it haunt him.

Other people are even worse than my uncle. He won't attack his fear of something external. But there are people who won't deal with their fear of themselves. My friend Sam is a good example of this kind of person. Sam has a serious drinking problem. All Sam's friends know he is an alcoholic. But Sam will not admit his addiction. I think he is afraid to face that part of himself. So he denies his problem, saying he can stop drinking any time he wants to. Of course, until Sam has the courage to admit what he is most afraid of—his alcoholism—he won't be able to change.

A Draft Essay

Below is a draft of the essay on working and going to college. As you read it, you'll notice many changes from the outline:

- An introduction has been added, phrased in the first person, "I," to unify the essay.
- Transitions have been added within and between paragraphs.
- General statements have been replaced by more specific ones.
- Word choice has been improved.

- A conclusion has been added. Some of the ideas added to the conclusion came from the original list about the topic of work and school. They are ideas that didn't fit in the body paragraphs but are useful in the conclusion.

A Draft of an Essay (*thesis and topic sentences are underlined*)

I work thirty hours a week at the front desk of a motel in Riverside. When I first signed up for college classes, I figured college would be fairly easy to fit into my schedule. After all, college students are not in class all day, as high-school students are. So I thought the twelve hours a week I'd spend in class wouldn't be too much of a load. But I was in for a big surprise. <u>My first semester at college showed me that students who work while going to school face problems at school, at work, and at home.</u>

<u>First of all, trying to juggle job and school responsibilities creates problems at school.</u> Early-morning classes, for example, are particularly difficult for me. Because I work every weeknight from six to midnight, I don't get home until 1:00 a.m., and I can't fall asleep until 2:00 a.m. or later. I am too tired to pay attention in my 8:00 a.m. class. Once, I even fell asleep in that class. My work hours create other conflicts. They cut into my study time, so I have little time to do all the assigned reading and papers. I get behind in these assignments, and I never seem to have enough time to catch up. Consequently, my grades are not as good as they could be.

Because I both work and go to school, I have problems doing well at school. But <u>work can also suffer when workers attend college.</u> Students can't bring school into the workplace. One night I tried to study at work, but my boss caught me reading my biology textbook at the front desk. I was reprimanded, and now my boss doesn't trust me. Sometimes I come to work very tired. When I don't get enough sleep, I can be rude to hotel guests who give me a hard time. Then the rudeness can get me into trouble. I remember one particular guest who reported me because I was sarcastic to her. She had spent half an hour complaining about her bill, and I had been too tired to be patient. Once again, my boss reprimanded me. Another time, school interfered with my job when I had to cut work to take a make-up test at school. I know my boss was unhappy with me then, too.

As a working student, I run into trouble on the job and at college. <u>Working students also suffer outside of college and the workplace.</u> Since I work nights during the week, the weekends are the only time I can study. Because I have to use my weekends to do schoolwork, I can't do other things. My apartment is a mess since I have no time to clean it. Worse, my girlfriend is ready to kill me because I have no social life. We never even go to the movies anymore. When she comes over, I am busy studying.

(continued)

> With responsibilities at home, at work, and at college, I face a cycle of stress. I am constantly racing around, and I can't break the cycle. I want a college education, and I must have a job to pay my tuition. The only way I can manage is to learn to manage my time. <u>I have learned that working students have to be very organized to cope with their responsibilities at college, at work, and at home.</u>

EXERCISE **11**	IDENTIFYING THE MAIN POINTS IN THE DRAFT OF AN ESSAY

Below is the draft of a five-paragraph essay. Read it, then reread it and underline the thesis and the topic sentences in each body paragraph and in the conclusion.

Until this year, I had never considered spending my free time helping others in my community. Volunteer work, I thought, was something retired folks and rich people did to fill their days. Just by chance, I became a volunteer for the public library's Classic Connection, a group that arranges read-a-thons and special programs for elementary school children. Although I don't receive a salary, working with some perceptive and entertaining third graders has been very rewarding in other ways.

Currently, I meet with my small group of four girls and three boys each Saturday morning from ten to eleven o'clock, and they have actually taught me more than I ever thought possible. I usually assign the children various passages in an illustrated children's classic like *The Little Prince*, and I help them with the difficult words as they read aloud. When I occasionally read to them, they follow right along, but when it's their turn, they happily go off track. I've learned that each child has a mind of his or her own, and I now have much more respect for day-care workers and elementary school teachers who must teach, entertain, and discipline thirty rowdy children all day long. I'm tired after just one hour with only seven children.

I have also learned the value of careful planning. I arrive at each session with a tape recorder and have them record a sound effect related to the story we'll be reading. At certain points during the session, we stop to hear the sound effects. They love to hear themselves and seem more focused on reading when I use this method. When I am well prepared, I feel more relaxed, and the sessions go smoothly.

I've enjoyed making several new friends and contacts through the Classic Connection. I've become friendly with the parents of the kids in my reading group, and one of the fathers has offered me a good-paying job at his printing business. He even mentioned he could be flexible about my schedule. I asked him if he could help me put a collection together of the group's most outrageous original stories, and he said he'd be glad to do it in *his* free time. I've thus learned that the spirit of volunteerism is indeed contagious.

I plan to keep volunteering for the Classic Connection's programs and look forward to a new group that should be starting soon. I don't know if I'm ready to graduate to an older group. After all, third graders still have much to teach me.

EXERCISE 12

ADDING TRANSITIONS TO AN ESSAY

The following essay needs transitions. Add the transitions where indicated, and add the type of transition—word, phrase, or sentence—that is needed.

When I finished high school, I was determined to go to college. What I hadn't decided was *where* I would go to college. Most of my friends were planning to go away from home to attend college. They wanted to be responsible for themselves and to be free of their parents' supervision. Like my friends, I thought of going away to college. But I finally decided to go to a college near my home. I chose a college near home for several reasons.

_____ (add a phrase), I can save money by attending a community college near home. _____ (add a word) I am still living at home, I do not have to pay for room and board at a college residence or pay rent for an apartment off-campus. I do not have to pay for the transportation costs of visits home. My friends who are away at school tell me about all the money they are spending on the things I get at home, for free. These friends are paying for things like doing their laundry or hooking up their cable TV. _____ (add a phrase), my college expenses are basically just tuition, fees, and books. I think I have a better deal than my friends who went away to college.

_____

_____ (add a sentence). By attending college near home, I have kept a secure home base. I think it would be very hard for me to handle a new school, a new town, a new set of classmates, and a new place to live all at the same time. I have narrowed my challenges to a new school and new classmates. _____ (add a word) I come home after a stressful day at college, I still have Mom's home cooking and Dad's sympathy to console me. I still sleep in my own comfortable—and comforting—room. Students who go away to school may have more freedom, _____ (add a word) I have more security.

_____

_____ (add a sentence). My decision to stay home for college gave me a secure job base as well. For the past year, I've had a job I like very much. My boss is very fair, and she has come to value my work enough to let me set my own work schedule. _____ (add a word or phrase), she lets me plan my work schedule around my class schedule. If I had moved away to attend college, I would have had to find a new job. _____ (add a word or phrase), I would have had a hard time finding a boss as understanding as the one I have now.

There are many good reasons to go to a college away from home. _____ (add a word or phrase), there are probably as many good reasons to go to one near home. I know that I'm happy with my decision. It has paid off financially and has helped me maintain a secure place to live and to work.

EXERCISE 13

RECOGNIZING SYNONYMS AND REPETITION USED TO LINK IDEAS IN AN ESSAY

In the following essay, underline all the synonyms and repetition (of words or phrases) that help remind the reader of the thesis sentence. (To help you, the thesis is underlined.)

Whenever I turn on the TV, I hear the story of an extraordinary act of courage. A firefighter, for example, rushes into a burning building to save an old man. Or a mother risks her own life to save her child from traffic. These are once-in-a-lifetime acts of courage, and they are indeed admirable. But <u>there is another, quiet kind of courage demonstrated all around us, every day.</u>

This kind of courage can be the fortitude of the person who has a terminal illness but who still carries on with living. I knew a person like that. He was the father of a family. When he found out he had a year to live, he did not waste much time in misery and despair. Instead, he used every moment to prepare his family for the time when he would no longer be there. He made financial arrangements. He spent time with his children, to show them how much he loved them. His bravery in the face of death was not unusual. Every day, there is someone who hears bad news from a doctor and quietly goes on. But because such people are so quiet in their courage, they are not given much credit.

Another example of quiet, everyday courage can be seen in people with the guts to try new and frightening things. The older person who decides to go to college, for instance, must be very scared. But he or she faces that fear and enters the classroom. And any student, of any age, who chooses the course that's supposed to be hard or the teacher who's supposed to be tough, instead of the easier one, shows a certain courage. Equally brave are the people who switch careers in middle age because they haven't found satisfaction in the workplace. It's frightening to start over at midlife, when starting over means trading job security and money for uncertainty and a lower starting salary. Yet many people make that trade, demonstrating real fortitude.

Sometimes we think that heroes are people who make the news. Granted, there are heroes splashed loudly across the papers and acclaimed on TV. Yet there are other, equally brave people who never make the news. They are the ones whose lives show a less dramatic form of courage. They are the ones who are all around us, and who deserve our admiration and respect.

FINAL LINES

PROOFREADING AND POLISHING: AN ESSAY

When you are satisfied with the final draft of your essay, you can begin preparing a good copy. Your essay will need a title. Try to think of a short title that is connected to your thesis. Since the title is the reader's first contact with your essay, an imaginative title can create a good first impression. If you can't think of anything clever, try using a key phrase from your essay.

The title is placed at the top of your essay, about 2.5 centimetres above the first paragraph. Always capitalize the first word of the title and all other words *except* articles ("the," "an," "a") or prepositions (like "of," "in," "with"). Do not underline or put quotation marks around your title.

The Final Version of an Essay

Below is the final version of the essay on working and going to college. When you compare it to the draft, you'll notice some changes:

- A title has been added.
- In the first paragraph, the words "I thought" have been added to make it clear that the statement is the writer's opinion.
- One topic sentence, in paragraph two, has been revised so that it includes the word "students" and the meaning is more precise.
- Words have been changed to sharpen the meaning.
- Transitions have been added.

ALONG THESE LINES/Pearson Education Canada

A Final Version of an Essay (*changes from the draft are underlined*)

Problems of the Working College Student

I work thirty hours a week at the front desk of a motel in Riverside. When I first <u>registered</u> for college classes, I figured college would be fairly easy to fit into my schedule. After all, <u>I thought,</u> college students are not in class all day, as high-school students are. So I <u>assumed</u> the twelve hours a week I'd spend in class wouldn't be too much of a load. But I was in for a big surprise. My first semester at college showed me that students who work while going to college face problems at school, at work, and at home.

First of all, <u>students who try</u> to juggle job and school responsibilities <u>find trouble at school.</u> Early-morning classes, for example, are particularly difficult for me. Because I work every weeknight from six to midnight, I don't get home until 1:00 a.m., and I can't fall asleep until 2:00 a.m. or later. <u>Consequently,</u> I am too tired to pay attention in my 8:00 a.m. class. Once, I even fell asleep in that class. My work hours create other conflicts. They cut into my study time, so I have little time to do all the assigned reading and papers. I get behind in the assignments, and I never seem to have enough time to catch up. <u>As a result,</u> my grades are not as good as they could be.

Because I both work and go to school, I have problems doing well at school. But work can also suffer when workers attend college. Students shouldn't bring school into the workplace. <u>I've been guilty of this practice and have paid the price.</u> One night I tried to study at work, but my boss caught me reading my biology textbook at the front desk. I was reprimanded, and now my boss doesn't trust me. Sometimes I come to work very tired, <u>creating another problem.</u> When I don't get enough sleep, I can be rude to motel guests who give me a hard time. Then the rudeness can get me into trouble. I remember one particular guest who reported me because I was sarcastic to her. She had spent half an hour complaining about her bill, and I had been too tired to be patient. Once again, my boss reprimanded me. Another time, school interfered with my job when I had to cut work to take a make-up test at school. I know my boss was unhappy with me then, too.

As a working student, I run into trouble on the job and at college. Working students also suffer outside of classes and the workplace. <u>My schedule illustrates the conflicts of trying to juggle too many duties.</u> Since I work nights during the week, the weekends are the only time I can study. Because I have to use my weekends to do schoolwork, I can't do other things. My apartment is a mess since I have no time to clean it. Worse, my girlfriend is ready to kill me because I have no social life. We never even go to the movies anymore. When she comes over, I am busy studying.

With responsibilities at home, at work, and at college, I face a cycle of stress. I am constantly racing around, and I can't break the cycle. I want a college

(continued)

ALONG THESE LINES/Pearson Education Canada

education, and I must have a job to pay my tuition. The only way I can manage is to learn to manage my time. <u>In my first semester at college, I've realized</u> that working students have to be very organized to cope with the responsibilities of college, work, and home.

Before you prepare the final copy of your essay, check your latest draft for errors in spelling and punctuation, and for any errors made in typing or recopying.

communication at work

Can't think of when you could possibly be asked to write anything as complex as an essay in the line of work you're planning? Think again. Technical reports, business cases, marketing descriptions, requests for proposals, and the like are all part of the job. For instance, if you are a computer technician, your employer may ask you to write a report comparing one operating system to another and recommending which should be implemented at your company. Your company may be asked to submit a "request for proposal," a written report of why your company would be the best to supply a given service. The Toronto Zoo (2008) recently tendered Requests for Proposals (RFPs) for the installation of a new skylight:

> You are invited to submit a written proposal, to the Purchasing & Supply of the Toronto Zoo, to provide Architectural/Engineering Design Services for the proposed Skylight Glazing Replacement and Exhibit Refurbishment at the African Rainforest Pavilion. Services to include review of existing facility and services, design, analysis with other consultants, and conformance of design to project budget, review and evaluation of tenders, and review during the construction of the project.

This kind of project demands focused writing and a clearly defined structure, skills that you practise when you write essays.

EXERCISE 14

PROOFREADING TO PREPARE THE FINAL VERSION

Below are two essays with the kinds of errors that are easy to overlook when you prepare the final version of an assignment. Correct the errors, writing above the lines. There are fourteen errors in the first essay and sixteen in the second.

Three Myths about Young People

Today, when a person says the word "teenager" or refers to "college kids," that person may be speaking with a little sneer. Young people have acquired a bad reputation. Some of the repution may be deserved, but some of it may not be. Young people are often judged according to myths—beliefs that are not true. Older people should not believe in three common myth's about the young.

We are always hearing that young people are irresponsable but their are many teens and people in their early twenties who disprove this statement. In every town, there are young people who hold full-time jobs and support a family. There are even more young people who work and go to school. All of my friends have been working since Grade Elven. The fact that not one of them has ever been fired from a job implies they must be pretty good workers. Furthermore, young people today are almost forced to be responsible they must learn to work and pay for their clothes and college tuition.

Another foolish belief is that all young people take drugs. Hollywood movies encourage this myth by including a drug-crazed teenager in almost every movie. Whenever television broadcasts a public service advertisement about drugs, the drug user shown is a young person. In reality, many young people have chosen not to take drugs. For every teen with a problem of abuse, there is probally another teen who has never taken drugs or who has conquered a drug problem. In my high scool, an anonymous student poll showed that more than half of the students had never experimented with drugs.

Some older adults label young people as irresponsible and addicted. Even more people are likely to say that the young are apathetic, but such critics are wrong. The young are criticized for not carring about political or social issues, for being unconscience of the problems we all face. yet high-school and college students are the ones who are out there, cleaning up the litter on the highways or beaches, whenever there is a local clean-up campaign. During the holidays, every school and college collects food, clothing, and toys for the needy students organize these drives, and students distributes these items. On many weekends, young people are out on the highways, collecting for charities.

Granted, there are apathetic, addicted, and irresponsible young people. But a whole group should not be judged by the actions of a few. Each young person deserve to be treated as an individual, not as an example of a myth.

Everyday Pleasures

As I hurry through each day, I focus on the demands and difficulties that face me. I thinks about driving in rush house; or studying for a quizz. I rarely stop to consider the many moments of enjoyment that fill each day. These simple pleasures compensate for all life's stressful moments.

Even as I get ready for the day ahead, I enjoy the sootheing comfort of a hot shower. The stream of hot waters soothes my aching muscles. I adjust the shower head so that warm needles of water masage my back. The rising steam surrounds me. I fill my body restoring itself and I never want to leave. Yet when I face the cold air outside the shower, drying off with the soft bath towels leaves me feeling clean and new

When I return home, my dogs greeting allways makes me smile. I hear him bark as I turn the key in the lock. Then he sees me and wriggles his entire body with joy. I feel a wet nose against my hand and look into two, deep brown eyes. He seems to be smiling at me. To my dog, my return means a long walk, some fun with a ball, and a good dinner. My dog's happiness makes me happy.

The evening has its own enjoyments. My couch is deep and wide with many pillows, perfect for laying in front of the television. I stretch out and turn on a movie, my dog at my feet. The movie is silly, but it does'nt matter. I burrow into the pillows. Soon my dog and me are both asleep on the couch.

As I face the irritations of my day, I forget the moments of pleasure, comfort, and happiness that I expereince. Because they are routine and ordinary, they are easy to forget, However stopping to remember these times makes me appreciate the good I have in my life.

Lines of Detail: A Walk-Through Assignment

Choose two radio stations popular with your age group. They can be two stations that broadcast music, or two stations that broadcast talk shows. Write a four-paragraph essay describing who listens to each station.

To write the essay, follow these steps:

Step 1: Begin with some investigation. Listen to two stations, talk or music, popular with your age group. Before you listen, prepare a list of at least six questions. The questions will help you gather details for your essay. For any radio station, you can ask:

> What kinds of products or services are advertised?
> Does the station offer any contests?
> Does the station sponsor any events?

For two music stations, your questions might include:

> What groups or individuals does the station play?
> What kind of music does it play?

For two talk-radio stations, your questions might include:

> What are the talk-show hosts like? Are they funny or insulting or serious?
> What topics are discussed?
> What kind of people call in?

Listen to the stations you chose and, as you listen, take notes. Answer your own questions, and write down anything about each station that catches your interest or that seems relevant.

Step 2: Survey your notes. Mark the related ideas with the same number. Then cluster the information you've gathered, and give each cluster a title.

Step 3: Focus all your clusters around one point. To find a focus, ask yourself whether the listeners of the two stations are people of the same social class, and with the same interests, the same educational background, and the same ethnic or racial background.

Try to focus your information with a thesis like one of these:

_____ (station name) and _____ (station name) appeal to the same audience.

_____ (station name) and _____ (station name) appeal to different audiences.

_____ (station name) and _____ (station name) use different strategies to appeal to the same kind of listeners.

_____ (station name) appeals to young people who _____, but _____ (station name) appeals to young people who _____.

While _____ (station name) is popular with middle-aged listeners interested in _____, _____ (station name) appeals to middle-aged listeners who like _____.

Step 4: Once you have a thesis and clustered details, draft an outline. Revise your draft outline until it is unified, expresses the ideas in a clear order, and has sufficient supporting detail.

Step 5: Write a draft of your essay. Revise the draft, checking it for balanced paragraphs, relevant and specific details, a strong conclusion, and smooth transitions.

Step 6: Before you prepare the final version of your essay, check for spelling, word choice, punctuation, and grammar errors. Also, give your essay a title.

Writing Your Own Essay

When you write on any of these topics, be sure to work through the stages of the writing process in preparing your essay.

1. Take any paragraph you wrote for this class and develop it into an essay of four or five paragraphs. If your instructor agrees, read the paragraph to a partner or group, and ask your listener(s) to suggest points inside the paragraph that could be developed into paragraphs of their own.

2. Write an essay using one of the following thesis statements:

    If I won a million dollars, I know what I would do with it.

    Most families waste our natural resources every day, simply by going through their daily routines.

    TV coverage of hockey (or basketball, or tennis, or other sport that you choose) could be improved by a few changes.

    The one place I'll never visit again is _____, because _____.

    All bad romances share certain characteristics.

    If I could be someone else, I'd like to be _____ for several reasons.

3. Write an essay on earliest childhood memories. Interview three classmates to gather details and to focus your essay. Ask each one to tell you about the earliest memory he or she has of childhood. Before you begin interviewing, make a list of questions, like these: What is your earliest memory? How old were you at the time of that recollection? What were you doing? Do you remember other people or events in that scene? If so, what were the others doing? Were you indoors? Outdoors? Is this a pleasant memory? Why do you think this memory has stayed with you?

    Use the details collected at the interviews to write a five-paragraph essay with a thesis sentence like one of the following:

    Childhood memories vary a great deal, from person to person.

    The childhood memories of different people are surprisingly similar.

    Although some people's first memories are painful, others remember a happy time.

    Some people claim to remember events from their infancy, but others can't remember anything before their third (or fourth, or fifth, etc.) birthday.

4. Freewrite for ten minutes on the two best days of your life. After you've completed the freewriting, review it. Do the two days have much in common? Or were they very different? Write a four-paragraph essay based on their similarities or differences, with a thesis like one of these:

    The two best days of my life were both _____. (Focus on similarities.)

    While one of the best days of my life was _____, the other great day was _____. (Fill in with differences.)

5. Write an essay on one of the following topics:

Three Careers for Me	The Three Worst Jobs
Three Workplace Hazards	Three Workplace Friends
Three Lucky People	Three Wishes
Three Family Traditions	Three Decisions for Me

6. Narrow one of the following topics and then write an essay on it.

nature	dreams	crime	music	celebrities
fears	family	lies	health	romance
habits	books	money	animals	travel
students	teachers	games	secrets	fashion

WRITING FROM READING: THE ESSAY

When Immigration Goes Awry

Daniel Stoffman

Daniel Stoffman is a writer who has written for most of Canada's major magazines.

Before you read this selection, consider these questions:

What are some of the most challenging issues—political, social, and economic— facing Canada today?

What are some of the challenges new immigrants face when settling in Canada?

What challenges do major urban centres face that smaller towns do not?

It's 2020 and, in Toronto, the days when everyone used the public health-care system are gone. So is the time when a majority of **affluent**, middle-class parents sent their kids to public schools. In 2020, vast tracts of suburban slums occupy what used to be good farmland on the city's outskirts.

affluent: well-off

Traffic congestion and air pollution are unbearable. Toronto's reputation as one of North America's most livable cities is a distant memory. It's now known as the "Sao Paulo of the north."

dystopian: bleak

This **dystopian** vision of the future of Canada's largest city is hardly far-fetched. Toronto is already suffering severe growing pains, the result of the federal government's insistence on maintaining the world's largest per capita annual immigration intake—around 250,000 people a year of whom about 43 per cent come to Toronto. That's more than 100,000 newcomers year after year after year.

infrastructure: facilities and systems that serve a city or community

It is impossible for any city to maintain its social and physical **infrastructure** in the face of such relentless population growth.

By 2020, Greater Toronto's population will have ballooned from 5 million to 7 million, or even more if immigration levels are raised higher still.

Every year Mercer Human Resource Consulting ranks world cities according to their livability. Vancouver always places at or near the top of the list while the other big Canadian cities are among the top 30. Most of the top-ranked cities are relatively small—places like Copenhagen (500,000) and Zurich (340,000).

agglomeration: a jumbled collection

amenity: any feature that provides comfort, convenience, or pleasure

megalopolis: very large city

irreparable: cannot be repaired

jurisdiction: authority

None of the world's vast urban **agglomerations** of 10 million or more, such as Sao Paulo and Seoul, is rated by Mercer as desirable places to live. Smaller big cities are more livable because their residents can enjoy the **amenities** of urban life without the congestion, crime, and pollution associated with sprawling **megalopolises**.

Canada's livable cities are an unsung national asset. One of the things that makes them special is the presence of immigrants from all over the world who have contributed new energy and cultural diversity. But, in immigration as in everything else, too much of a good thing isn't better. Ottawa's policy of mass immigration, for which no reasonable explanation has ever been offered, risks doing **irreparable** damage to our cities. This policy of rapid urban growth is being implemented by Ottawa even though it has no **jurisdiction** over urban affairs and even though the policy has never been stated explicitly.

Yet the impact is already evident.

Highway 401 across Toronto has become the busiest road in North America, the city can't find a place to put its garbage, and its public schools can't afford to provide the English instruction newly arrived children need. In Vancouver, meanwhile, controversy rages over the British Columbia government's plan to expand the Port Mann bridge that links the rapidly growing Fraser Valley suburbs to the city.

Amazingly, the local politicians who have to cope with the results never suggest that perhaps the immigration intake might be lowered from time to time as was standard practice until the late 1980s. To listen to their silence, one would think the relentless influx of huge numbers of new residents was a natural phenomenon like the weather rather than a deliberate federal policy that easily could be changed.

disingenuous: insincere

Ottawa might claim it is not to blame for unmanageable urban growth because it just lets the immigrants in, it doesn't tell them where to go. But this would be **disingenuous**, because Ottawa knows Toronto gets almost half of all immigrants while Vancouver gets 18 per cent and Montreal 12 per cent. Many of those who settle elsewhere at first also eventually wind up in one of the three biggest cities.

dispersion: spreading out

Attempts at **dispersion** are doomed because immigrants want to live where previous cohorts of the same ethnicity are already established. They also want to live in cities for the same reason Canadian-born people do—they are more likely to find jobs there.

The country most comparable to Canada is Australia. Like Canada, it is an English-speaking Commonwealth nation settled in relatively recent history. Like Canada, it has an organized immigration program and has used immigration effectively to

vigour: vitality

enhance population growth and increase the **vigour** and diversity of its major cities.

Australia's current net migration rate (immigration minus emigration per 1,000 of population) is 3.85. Canada's is 5.85. Before the Progressive Conservative government of Brian Mulroney increased immigration levels and made them permanent during the latter part of the 1980s, a policy continued by the Liberals under Jean Chrétien, Canada had an intake similar, on a per-capita basis, to Australia's.

There is no reason why Canada should have far more immigration than any other country. Canada's existing population is younger than those of most other developed countries and its ratio of working age people to retired ones is higher. If Canada reverted to its traditional, more moderate, immigration program, it could continue to enjoy the benefits of immigration while sparing its cities the problems of unmanageable growth. Immigrants would benefit too. Their economic performance has been in free fall over the past 15 years.

Previously the number of new immigrants varied according to labour market needs. Sometimes it would be cut to give the newly arrived a chance to be absorbed successfully into the economy without intense competition from more new arrivals. Not any more.

An endless stream of newcomers arrives in the big cities with few options but to work in poorly paid jobs such as cleaning houses and driving taxis. Wages of these jobs are thus kept low and the occupants of them have little chance to get ahead.

Previously, poverty levels among immigrants were about the same as those of the Canadian-born. Now they are much worse. According to a report by the Canadian Council on Social Development, whereas the poverty level of those who arrived before 1986 was 19.7 per cent, or slightly lower than that of the Canadian-born, the poverty level of those who came after 1991 was an alarming 52.1 per cent, while that of people born in Canada remained unchanged at around 20 per cent.

entrenched: firmly fixed

gentrification: revitalization of an older neighbourhood that often results in the displacement of lower-income residents by new higher-income residents

shrewdly: keenly

If this trend is not reversed, Toronto and Vancouver will by 2020 be home to an **entrenched** underclass living in slums. Because of **gentrification** and rising property values in the central cities, these slums will be located in the suburbs, requiring long commutes for those fortunate enough to have employment.

Fan Yang, a reader of the *Toronto Star*, **shrewdly** analyzed the impact of federal immigration policy in a letter to the newspaper in 2003. He accused the federal government of "dumping more cheaply acquired labour into the domestic labour pool, regardless of whether there is a healthy demand. Businesses welcome that enthusiastically as they bear no direct cost of unemployed immigrants and only garner the rewards of lower labour costs."

Even skilled workers are doing poorly. According to the 2001 census, male immigrants with a university degree who came to Ontario in the late 1990s were earning after six to 10 years in Canada only 54 per cent of what native-born Canadians with similar qualifications in that province earned.

Remarkably, immigrant labour market performance has declined during a time of increasing shortages of skilled workers. But, as the above data suggest, just bringing in huge numbers of people doesn't solve skills shortages. Mexico has a worse skills shortage than Canada yet it has no shortage of people. The trick is to match immigrants to jobs and our current immigration program doesn't do that well.

reinvent the wheel: start from the beginning

emulate: imitate

Luckily, Canada doesn't need to **reinvent the wheel**. It merely needs to **emulate** the solutions that Australia's more successful immigration program has already found, such as requiring the credentials of skilled immigrants to be approved before they come and imposing strict requirements for language skills.

cohort: group

In addition to creating poverty, mismanaged immigration is weakening our public health-care and education systems. By 2020, the huge baby boomer **cohort**

interminable: lengthy

of Canadians will be entering its stage of heaviest reliance on the health-care system. The boomers will not tolerate **interminable** waits for hip replacements and cancer treatment.

As if the challenge of caring for impatient boomers weren't enough, the presence of millions of new immigrants will intensify the demands on the system. Many of the newcomers will be old because Canada is the most generous country in allowing immigrants to sponsor elderly parents and grandparents.

There is no chance that our health-care system can survive in its current form given the demands on it from these demographic changes. As a result, by 2020 a full-fledged, parallel, private health-care system will be in operation in the major immigrant-receiving cities which are also where most of the boomers live. Private health care will be relied upon not just by the wealthy but by much of the middle class as well.

A similar transformation will occur in education. A report last January conducted for the Elementary Teachers of Toronto said teachers were spending the equivalent of one day a week trying to make up for the lack of English as a second language support for their immigrant students.

"The more time the regular classroom teacher is having to devote to ESL students . . . it detracts from the level of service we want for all of our students," union president Martin Long told *The Globe and Mail*.

rash: ill-considered

In other words, the lack of support for ESL students is hurting all students. This is certainly not the fault of the immigrant children. It is the fault of **rash** and ill-conceived federal policy. As a result, by 2020 most middle-class families will have abandoned the public system. This will be an unfortunate development because the public schools are where immigrants and Canadian-born get to know each other. They are an important force for social cohesion.

plausible: believable; workable

A seemingly **plausible** argument for boosting the population of at least one Canadian city to 10 million or more would be that the truly great cities of the world are very big. But London and Paris grew to their current size gradually over hundreds of years and their greatness is the result of the wealth of the empires of which they were the capitals.

You don't build London and Paris by adding millions of bodies over a short period of time. That's how you build Mumbai and Mexico City.

Ontario's environment commissioner, Gord Miller, issued a warning last year about what the future holds for Toronto given current trends:

"The environmental impacts of this magnitude of growth . . . will compromise the quality of our lifestyle to a stage where it will be unrecognizable," he said. "We already have trouble dealing with our waste right now . . . What about another 4 million tonnes a year? What about another 4 million cars?"

The new Conservative government's immigration minister, Monte Solberg, told a House of Commons committee in May that he was concerned about the "huge burden" high immigration levels place on our major cities. He thus became the first immigration minister in at least two decades to show any sensitivity to the impact of immigration policy on the urban environment.

ostrichlike: refusal to acknowledge reality

Now it's the turn of local officials to abandon their **ostrichlike** refusal even to mention immigration when discussing urban growth. Perhaps they fear being branded "anti-immigrant" if they do.

But Pierre Trudeau, in his last year as prime minister, cut immigration by 25 per cent and no one called him anti-immigrant. In that case, good management **trumped** politics. It's an example the Conservative government would do well to follow.

trump: surpass

UNDERSTANDING "WHEN IMMIGRATION GOES AWRY"

1. According to the article, why do "vast urban centres" often not make the list of most desirable places to live?

2. How does Stoffman envision the year 2020, should Canadian immigration policies not change?

3. What does Stoffman suggest as a possible solution to the situation? What do you think of this solution?

WRITING FROM READING "WHEN IMMIGRATION GOES AWRY"

1. Canada has often been called a "mosaic," whereas the United States has been called a "melting pot." What do you think this means? Write an essay in which you agree or disagree with this statement.

2. Often, immigrants settle in areas where there are higher concentrations of people who speak their language and share their customs. However, some critics have said that this prevents immigrants from learning a new language, learning about their new country, and meeting other citizens. Write an essay in which you agree or disagree with this position.

3. Are you a recent immigrant to Canada? Have your experiences been primarily positive or negative? Write an essay advising friends and family "back home" either to emigrate to Canada or stay home.

4. It has been suggested that the Canadian government provide incentives (i.e. financial bonuses, housing) to new immigrants to encourage them to settle in less populated areas. What do you think of this suggestion? Can you think of any other solutions to the problem of increased stress on our cities' infrastructure? Write an essay in which you explore some other options.

5. Margaret Atwood, one of Canada's most famous writers, once said that Canada is a "land of immigrants" because we are all from somewhere else. Write an essay in which you agree or disagree with this statement, and whether you think a "land of immigrants" is a positive or negative quality.

Joined in Jihad?

Adnan R. Khan

Adnan R. Khan is a Toronto writer who is currently on assignment for Maclean's.

Before you read this selection, consider these questions:

> *What is a stereotype? Are stereotypes always negative?*
>
> *Have you ever been in a public situation where you were intentionally targeted because of your gender, race, or age?*
>
> *How important is religion in your personal and family life?*
>
> *How do we as Canadians learn about other cultures and religions?*

trite: stale, common, used too many times

From now on, I've decided to wear a sign slung from my neck that reads: "Adnan R. Khan, non-Muslim." At the risk of sounding **trite**, it's not fun being a Muslim anymore, either at home in Canada or abroad in the Islamic world. I did fleetingly consider using "infidel" on my sign instead of "non-Muslim," but I felt the word was misleading. After all, "**fidelity**" is an **integral** part of who I am; Islam is not, at least not the Islam paraded across television screens, and definitely not the Islam screaming for retribution against the "evil invaders" of Iraq.

fidelity: faithfulness, loyalty

integral: essential, important

cringing: wincing, stepping back

My parents are probably **cringing** after reading that. So for their sake, and for the record, I must stress that I am not anti-Islam. I am proud of my Islamic heritage. Really. I regularly read works by the 13th-century Muslim visionary Rumi, and travel back to Pakistan whenever I can. I've even started to appreciate the immense musical value of **Koranic recitations**. It's the stereotypes that **gall** me. There's no escaping them these days, even in Islamic countries like Turkey where I am now, and had hoped to blend into the background. *Especially* in Islamic nations, actually, where being a Muslim in these trying times automatically aligns you with the **spiralling** communal hatred sweeping across the Arab world against **the West**. The logic is straightforward: you're brown and you have an Arabic name, therefore you must hate the West.

Koranic: from the Koran, the sacred book of Muslims

recitations: spoken lessons, lectures

gall: annoy

spiralling: escalating, getting bigger

the West: European/ North American cultures

refrain: repeated song or verse

"Adnan? Ah, a Muslim! Down with Bush!" The **refrain** has become a bad song haunting my sleepless nights. Worse still, it's not even confined to my head. (If it were only so simple.) I hear it everywhere I go, from Malaysia to Turkey: grizzly old Muslim men chafing my tender cheeks with a flurry of kisses; university students embracing me as a brother, for no other reason than an **appellation** over which I had no control. And since the onset of war in Iraq, the dilemma has intensified.

appellation: name, title

paradoxically: unexpectedly

divisiveness: disagreements that separate people

chasm: gap, ravine, gulf

Shias, Sunnis: different denominations within Islam

internecine: destructive behaviour within a group

erstwhile: former

Paradoxically, the growing sense of unity rising from the ashes of **divisiveness** is the most unsettling consequence of the current conflict in Iraq. As the **chasm** between the West and Islam continues to widen, the internal divisions that have plagued Muslims shrink proportionally. **Shias** and **Sunnis** have never been so agreeable with each other, Kurdish factions in northern Iraq fight side by side after nearly a decade of **internecine** warfare, and for **erstwhile** Muslims like myself, simply looking the part is as good as a pass-go card. Welcome to the club.

ALONG THESE LINES/Pearson Education Canada

dervishes: believers in poverty and strict morals

Sufi: another denomination within Islam

smithereens: little pieces, fragments

jihad: religious war against non-believers

martyrdom: death or suffering for a great cause

mullahs: scholars, religious leaders

tenuous: weak, questionable

nadir: lowest point

flux: constant change

fray: fight, conflict

profiling: identification using specific physical characteristics

At this rate, whirling **dervishes** and peaceful **Sufi** mystics, some of whom live in the hollowed-out trunks of trees in Pakistan, will soon be heading to Iraq for a piece of the action. Already, according to reports, Arabs from other countries have slipped into Iraq, many of them suicide bombers determined to blast themselves and anyone else nearby to **smithereens.**

The call to **jihad** against the West echoes throughout the Muslim world, travelling as far as Indonesia, where more than 20,000 men have reportedly lined up to volunteer for a chance at **martyrdom** in Iraq. **Mullahs** everywhere demand all Muslims fulfill their duty to Islam. "Kill the infidels where they stand," they often shout in their sermons to an audience increasingly receptive to that angry message.

Sadly, these so-called Islamic leaders have failed to recognize that alliances based on mutual hatred are always **tenuous** at best. Western culture is nowhere near its **nadir,** and one has to wonder whether Muslim unity can endure the calm after the storm. Will the stereotype of the "evil" West carry any currency once the clouds of war have cleared? The hearts and minds of Muslims are in a state of **flux,** easily swayed by impassioned pleas and distressing images coming from the brutal war in Iraq. For the moment, any non-Muslim is suspect, but suspicion has a tendency to evaporate in a climate of peace.

As a Canadian, I feel one step removed from the **fray.** But there are times when I feel saddled by the responsibilities imposed on me by my Muslim heritage. On the one hand, there's the pressure of correcting the misconceptions circulating about Islam in the Western consciousness. On the other, I've become increasingly disheartened by the myths perpetuated about Western culture in the Islamic world.

I've fallen victim to racial **profiling** since Sept. 11 in Canada, but I've also witnessed first-hand the same sort of profiling of Westerners by Muslims. Am I expected to join the chorus of anti-American sentiment, to despise this war for its hostility toward Islam? All because I have an Arabic name? The reality is I view the conflict in its political and economic dimensions. Does that make me anti-Islam?

It's all a bit confusing, really. I'd like to think I can play a role bridging the gap between the West and the Muslim world, but I find myself frustrated by the complete lack of openness to the Western perspective in Islamic culture—just as frustrated as I am with the inaccurate pictures being painted by the West of Muslims. There are times I wish I really could disappear into the background, become a non-entity, but the battle lines have been drawn and I'm told I must pick a side. "No real Muslim will abandon his brothers in this time of need," Newroz, a Kurdish Muslim in Turkey, told me. Real or not, I think I'll get to work on that sign.

UNDERSTANDING "JOINED IN JIHAD?"

1. Adnan R. Khan has travelled in many Islamic countries and "hoped to blend into the background." Instead, he finds that he is stereotyped. What do the people he meets automatically assume?

2. According to the author, what has been "the most unsettling consequence of the current conflict in Iraq"?

3. As a Canadian, Khan believes he has two responsibilities imposed on him. What are they?

4. Even though the author is proud of his Islamic heritage, why does he joke about wearing a sign that reads: "Adnan R. Khan, non-Muslim"?

WRITING FROM READING "JOINED IN JIHAD?"

1. Like Adnan R. Khan, many college students have balanced cultural and religious traditions from other countries with their Canadian lives. Interview three people in your class. Find out how long their families have been in Canada, how important their "old country" heritage is, how many languages they speak, and how they define themselves as Canadians. Based on your interviews, write an essay about the diverse backgrounds of college students.

2. Write a letter, several paragraphs long, to a person who misjudged or misunderstood you based on stereotyping. Explain what the misunderstanding was, why it hurt you, and how the person can avoid making the same mistake again.

3. Write an essay about a group that many people fear. In your essay, discuss whether the fear of this group is justified. You may write about such groups as homeless people, bikers, street gangs, or any other group that may be feared, misunderstood, or stereotyped.

4. A wise student once said, "It's easy to hate a whole group of people. It's harder to dislike an individual because you have to really get to know him before you can decide." Write an essay explaining how this quotation applies to stereotyping.

GRAMMAR FOR WRITERS:

The Bottom Line

INTRODUCTION

Overview

In this part of the book, you'll be working with "the bottom line," the basics of grammar that you need to be a clear writer. If you are willing to memorize certain rules and work through various activities, you'll be able to apply grammatical rules automatically as you write.

Using "Grammar for Writers"

Because this portion of the textbook is divided into several self-contained sections, it does not have to be read in sequence. Your instructor may suggest you review specific rules and examples, or you may be assigned various segments as either a class or a group. Several approaches are possible, and thus you can regard this section as a user-friendly grammar handbook for quick reference. Mastering the practical parts of grammar will improve your writing; you'll feel more confident because you'll know the bottom line.

Contents

The Simple Sentence

Identifying the crucial parts of a sentence is the first step in many writing decisions: how to punctuate, how to avoid sentence fragments, how to be sure that subjects and verbs "agree" (match). To move forward to these decisions requires a few steps backward—to basics.

RECOGNIZING A SENTENCE

Let's start with a few basic definitions. A basic unit of language is a **word**.

> **examples:** car, dog, sun

A group of words that relate to each other can be a **phrase**.

> **examples:** shiny sports car; welcoming, inclusive environment; in the bright sun

When a group of words contains a **subject** and a complete **predicate** (the verb, plus objects and phrases modifying the verb), it is called a **clause**. When the clause makes sense on its own, it is called a **sentence**, or an independent clause.

If you want to see whether you have written a complete sentence, and not just a group of words that relate to each other, you first have to check for a subject and a verb. It's often easier to locate the verbs first.

RECOGNIZING VERBS

Verbs are words that express some kind of action or being. Verbs about the five senses—sight, touch, smell, taste, and sound—are part of the group called **being verbs**. Look at some examples of verbs as they work in sentences:

action verbs:

We **take** two buses to work every day.

I **ran** from the subway to my class.

being verbs:

My mother **is** my role model.

The customer **seems** unhappy.

The soup **smells** delicious.

ALONG THESE LINES/Pearson Education Canada

EXERCISE 1	RECOGNIZING VERBS

Underline the verbs in each of the following sentences.

1. The truck stalled on the highway.
2. Early in the morning, he jogs around the park.
3. She looks anxious about the driving test.
4. My cousin Bill was the best player on the team.
5. The rain floods the street on stormy days.
6. Most people love long weekends.
7. Single parents face many challenges at home and at work.
8. The old blanket feels rough and scratchy.
9. My daughter lay in bed with a fever.
10. I went to three interviews before I got a job.

More on Verbs

The verb in a sentence can be more than one word. First of all, there can be **helping verbs** in front of the main verb, which is the action or being verb. Here is a list of some frequently used helping verbs: *am, are, can, could, do, have, is, may, might, must, shall, should, was, were, will, would.*

> I **was watching** the World Cup Finals. (The helping verb is *was.*)
>
> You **should have called** me. (The helping verbs are *should* and *have.*)
>
> The president **can select** his assistants. (The helping verb is *can.*)
>
> Leroy **will graduate** in May. (The helping verb is *will.*)

Helping verbs can make the verb in a sentence more than one word long. But a sentence can also have more than one main verb:

> Andrew **planned** and **practised** his speech.
>
> I **stumbled** over the rug, **grabbed** a chair, and **fell** on my face.

EXERCISE 2	WRITING SENTENCES WITH HELPING VERBS

Complete this exercise with a partner or with a group. First, ask one person to add at least one helping verb to the verb given. Then work together to write two sentences using the main verb and the helping verb(s). Appoint one spokesperson for your group to read all your sentences to the class. Notice how many combinations of main verb and helping verb you hear.

The first one is done as a sample.

1. verb: called

   verb with helping verb(s): has called

   sentence 1: Sam has called me twice this week.

   sentence 2: She has called him a hero.

2. verb: moving

    verb with helping verb(s): _____

    sentence 1: _____

    sentence 2: _____

3. verb: fly

    verb with helping verb(s): _____

    sentence 1: _____

    sentence 2: _____

4. verb: laughed

    verb with helping verb(s): _____

    sentence 1: _____

    sentence 2: _____

5. verb: spoken

    verb with helping verb(s): _____

    sentence 1: _____

    sentence 2: _____

RECOGNIZING SUBJECTS

After you learn to recognize verbs, it's easy to find the subjects of sentences because subjects and verbs are linked. If the verb is an action verb, for example, the subject will be the word or words that answer the question, "Who or what is doing that action?"

The truck stalled on the highway.

Step 1: Identify the verb: *stalled*

Step 2: Ask, "Who or what stalled?"

Step 3: The answer is the subject: The **truck** stalled on the highway. The *truck* is the subject.

If your verb expresses being, the same steps apply to finding the subject.

Deon is my best friend.

Step 1: Identify the verb: *is*

Step 2: Ask, "Who or what is my best friend?"

Step 3: The answer is the subject: **Deon** is my best friend. *Deon* is the subject.

Just as there can be more than one word to make up a verb, there can be more than one subject.

examples: **Rob** and **John-David** planned the surprise party.

My father and **I** worked in the yard yesterday.

EXERCISE **3**	RECOGNIZING SUBJECTS IN SENTENCES

Underline the subjects in the following sentences.

1. Maggie might have followed the directions more carefully.
2. They were stacking the records in neat piles.
3. Mike and Jordan will be coming over tomorrow.
4. Suddenly, a car appeared on the runway.
5. Happiness can come in many shapes and forms.
6. Complaining can sometimes make a situation worse.
7. Anticipation and tension filled the locker room.
8. Books and magazines covered every table and desk.
9. The manager will be contacting you about the job interview.
10. Somebody took the last piece of cake.

More about Recognizing Subjects and Verbs

When you look for the subject of a sentence, look for the core word or words; don't include descriptive words around the subject. The idea is to look for the subject, not for the words that describe it.

> The dark blue **dress** looked lovely on Anita.
>
> Dirty **streets** and grimy **houses** destroy a neighbourhood.

The simple subjects of the above sentences are the core words *dress, streets,* and *houses,* not the descriptive words *dark blue, dirty,* and *grimy.*

Prepositions and Prepositional Phrases

Prepositions are usually small words that often signal a kind of position or possession, as shown in the Infobox below.

INFOBOX	SOME COMMON PREPOSITIONS				
about	around	between	in	on	under
above	at	beyond	inside	onto	until
across	before	by	into	over	up
after	behind	during	like	since	upon
against	below	except	near	through	with
along	beneath	for	of	to	within
among	beside	from	off	toward	without

A prepositional phrase is made up of a preposition and its object. Here are some prepositional phrases. In each one, the first word is the preposition; the other words are the object of the preposition.

Prepositional Phrases

about the movie	of mice and men
around the corner	off the record
between two lanes	on the mark
during recess	up the wall
near my house	with my sister and brother

There's an old memory trick to help you remember prepositions. Think of a chair. Now, think of a series of words you can put *in front of* the word *chair*:

around the chair	**with** the chair
by the chair	**to** the chair
behind the chair	**near** the chair
between the chairs	**under** the chair
of the chair	**on** the chair
off the chair	**from** the chair

These words are prepositions.

You need to know about prepositions because they can help you identify the subject of a sentence. Here is an important grammar rule about prepositions:

Nothing in a prepositional phrase can ever be the subject of the sentence.

Prepositional phrases describe people, places, or things. They may describe the subject of a sentence, but they *never include* the subject. Whenever you are looking for the subject of a sentence, begin by putting parentheses around all the prepositional phrases.

> The restaurant (around the corner) makes the best fried chicken
> (in town.)

Notice that the prepositional phrases are in parentheses. Since *nothing* in them can be the subject, once you have eliminated the prepositional phrases you can follow the steps to find the subject of the sentence:

> What's the verb? *makes*
> Who or what makes the best fried chicken? The *restaurant*.
> *Restaurant* is the subject of the sentence.

By marking off the prepositional phrases, you are left with the *core* of the sentence. There is less to look at.

> (Behind the park), a **carousel** (with gilded horses) delighted children
> (from all the neighbourhoods).
> subject: *carousel*

> The **firm** (with flex hours) was named Company (of the Year).
> subject: *firm*

EXERCISE 4

RECOGNIZING PREPOSITIONAL PHRASES, SUBJECTS, AND VERBS

Put parentheses around all the prepositional phrases in the following sentences. Then underline the subject and verb, putting *S* above the subject and *V* above the verb.

1. The car in the parking lot near the bank has a huge dent in its fender.

2. Some of the people on my street like sitting on their front steps on a hot night.

3. Candidates can say amusing things in job interviews.

4. During my lunch hour, I often go to the park across the street from my office.

5. The true story beneath all his lies was a tale with some horrifying twists.

6. Team-building exercises are an important part of corporate culture.

7. The doctor in the emergency room dashed down the hall toward the trauma victim.

8. Many small towns in Canada are under boil-water advisories.

9. Seasonal Affective Disorder affects many people in northern climates.

10. A strong Canadian dollar often hinders tourism.

EXERCISE 5

WRITING SENTENCES WITH PREPOSITIONAL PHRASES

Complete this exercise with a partner. First, add one prepositional phrase to the core sentence given. Then ask your partner to add a second prepositional phrase to the same sentence. For the next sentence, let your partner add the first phrase; you add the second. Keep reversing the process throughout the exercise. When you have completed the exercise, be ready to read to the class the sentences with two prepositional phrases. The first one has been done for you as an example. **Hint:** Make sure you are adding *only* a prepositional phrase (preposition plus its object) rather than a new clause. For example, if in question 1 you write, "After the sun set, rain fell on the mountains," you will have added a new subject (*sun*) and a new verb (*set*) instead of just a prepositional phrase.

1. core sentence: Rain fell.

   add one prepositional phrase: Rain fell on the mountains.

   add another prepositional phrase: After dark, rain fell on the mountains.

2. core sentence: The school was closed.

   add one prepositional phrase: _____

   add another prepositional phrase: _____

3. core sentence: The canoe drifted.

   add one prepositional phrase: _____

   add another prepositional phrase: _____

4. core sentence: Parents must struggle.

add one prepositional phrase: _____

add another prepositional phrase: _____

5. core sentence: Raj chopped the onions.

add one prepositional phrase: _____

add another prepositional phrase: _____

WORD ORDER

When we speak, we often use a very simple word order: first, the subject; then, the verb. For example, someone would say, "I am going to the store." *I* is the subject that begins the sentence; *am going* is the verb that comes after the subject.

But not all sentences are in such a simple word order. Prepositional phrases, for example, can change the word order.

> **sentence:** Among the contestants was an older man.

> **Step 1:** Mark off the prepositional phrase(s) with parentheses:

> (Among the contestants) was an older man.

> Remember that nothing in a prepositional phrase can be the subject of a sentence.

> **Step 2:** Find the verb: *was*
> **Step 3:** Who or what was? An older **man** was. The subject of the sentence is *man*.

After you change the word order of this sentence, you can see the subject (*S*) and verb (*V*) more easily.

>   S   V
> An older **man was** among the contestants.

EXERCISE **6**	**FINDING PREPOSITIONAL PHRASES, SUBJECTS, AND VERBS IN COMPLICATED WORD ORDER**

Put parentheses around the prepositional phrases in the sentences below. Then underline the subjects and verbs, putting *S* above each subject and *V* above each verb.

1. Down the street from my apartment is an all-night supermarket.

2. Behind the counter is a cash register.

3. Inside the student union are video games and vending machines.

4. Among the workers lay a long and deep-seated resentment.

5. Above the rooftops of the houses stands the steeple of an old church.

6. From the back of the alley came a loud scream.

7. Between the houses was a fence with a clinging vine of red flowers.

8. On my laptop are stored all my work documents and family photos.

9. Among my fondest memories is a recollection of a day at the park.

10. With the man from Winnipeg came an officer in uniform.

More on Word Order

The expected word order of subject first, then verb changes when a sentence starts with *There is/are, There was/were, Here is/are, Here was/were.* In such cases, look for the subject after the verb.

There **are** a **bakery** and a **pharmacy** down the street.

Here **is** the **man** with the answers.

If it helps you to understand this pattern, change the word order:

A **bakery** and a **pharmacy are** there, down the street.

The **man** with the answers **is** here.

You should also note that even when the subject comes after the verb, the verb has to "match" the subject. For instance, if the subject refers to more than one thing, the verb must also refer to more than one thing.

There **are** a **bakery** and a **pharmacy** down the street.

(Two things, a bakery and a pharmacy, *are* down the street.)

Word Order in Questions

Questions may have a different word order. The main verb and the helping verb may not be next to each other.

question: Do you like pizza?

subject: you

verbs: *do, like*

If it helps you to understand this concept, think about answering the question. If someone accused you of not liking pizza, you might say, "I *do like* it." You'd use two words as verbs.

question: Will he think about it?

subject: he

verbs: will, think

question: Is Maria telling the truth?

subject: Maria

verbs: is, telling

| EXERCISE 7 | RECOGNIZING SUBJECTS AND VERBS IN A COMPLICATED WORD ORDER: A COMPREHENSIVE EXERCISE |

Underline the subjects and verbs and put an *S* above the subjects and *V* above the verbs.

1. Behind the fancy menu and the high prices was a restaurant with bad food.

2. Has Jimmy met the newest member of the team?

3. Near the bottom of the box was a jar of pennies.

4. Around the back of the house there were a porch and a garden shed.

5. Inside her heart was a longing for understanding.

6. Here are the cheques for the rent and the phone bill.

7. From three provinces came eager reporters with their cameras.

8. There were many questions about the disappearance of the man.

9. In my travel mug sits a day-old double double.

10. Will words in a prepositional phrase ever be the subject of the sentence?

Words That Can't Be Verbs

Some words look like they are part of the verb in a sentence, but they are not verbs. Such words include adverbs (words like *always, ever, nearly, never, not, often, rarely*) that are placed close to the verb, or between the helping verb and main verb, but are not verbs.

When you are looking for verbs in a sentence, be careful to eliminate words like *often* and *not*.

> He will not listen to me. (The verbs are **will listen**.)
> Althea can often find a bargain. (The verbs are **can find**.)

Be careful with contractions:

> They haven't raced in years. (The verbs are **have raced**. *Not* is not a part of the verb, even in contractions.)
> Don't you come from Alberta? (The verbs are **do come**.)
> Won't he ever learn? (The verbs are **will learn**. **Won't** is a contraction for **will not**.)

Recognizing Main Verbs

If you're checking to see if a word is a main verb, try the *pronoun test*. Combine your word with this simple list of pronouns: *I, you, he, she, it, we, they*.

A main verb is a word such as *drive* or *noticed* that can be combined with the words on this list. Now try the pronoun test.

> For the word **drive**: I drive, you drive, he drives, she drives, it drives, we drive, they drive

For the word ***noticed***: I noticed, you noticed, he noticed, she noticed, it noticed, we noticed, they noticed

But words like *never* can't be used, alone, with the pronouns:

~~I never, you never, he never, she never, it never, we never, they never~~ (Never did what?)

Never is not a verb. *Not* is not a verb either, as the pronoun test indicates:

~~I not, you not, he not, she not, it not, we not, you not, they not~~

Verb Forms That Can't Be Main Verbs

There are forms of verbs that can't be main verbs by themselves, either. The *-ing* form of a verb, by itself, cannot be the main verb, as the pronoun test shows.

For the word ***voting***: ~~I voting, you voting, he voting, she voting, we voting, they voting~~

If you see the *-ing* form of a verb by itself, correct the sentence by adding a helping verb.

Danny ~~riding~~ his motorcycle. (*Riding*, by itself, cannot be a main verb.)

correction: Danny **was riding** his motorcycle.

Another verb form, called an **infinitive**, also cannot be a main verb. An infinitive is the form of the verb that has *to* placed in front of it.

INFOBOX	**SOME SAMPLE INFINITIVES**	
to care	to play	to stumble
to feel	to reject	to view
to need	to repeat	to vote

Try the pronoun test and you'll see that infinitives can't be main verbs:

For the infinitive ***to vote***: ~~I to vote, you to vote, he to vote, she to vote, we to vote, they to vote~~

So if you see an infinitive being used as a verb, correct the sentence by adding a main verb.

We ~~to vote~~ in the election tomorrow. (There's no verb, just an infinitive.)

correction: We **are going** to vote in the election tomorrow. (Now there's a verb.)

The infinitives and the *-ing* forms of verbs just don't work as main verbs. You must put a verb with them to make a correct sentence.

EXERCISE	CORRECTING PROBLEMS WITH *-ING* OR INFINITIVE
8	**VERB FORMS**

Most—but not all—of the following sentences are faulty; an *-ing* form of a verb or an infinitive may be taking the place of a main verb. Rewrite the sentences that have errors. Write *C* beside sentences that are correct as written.

1. Everyone in the Human Resources department to visit the Mini-Golfing range on Friday.

   rewritten: _____

   _____

2. My husband paying no attention to the feud between his sisters.

   rewritten: _____

   _____

3. The tuner car ahead of me speeding out of control and into the median.

   rewritten: _____

   _____

4. Sylvia learned to care about her health after her bout with pneumonia.

   rewritten: _____

   _____

5. Among his other goals, Jason to hike the entire Bruce Trail.

   rewritten: _____

   _____

6. After all the discussion and deliberation, the committee taking a very conservative position on the question of tenants' rights.

   rewritten: _____

   _____

7. One of the most famous experts in the field of forensic science to speak to my criminal justice class tomorrow.

   rewritten: _____

   _____

8. My manager being away from work for almost a month.

   rewritten: _____

   _____

9. Ever since the accident, I have been picking tiny pieces of glass out of the carpet.

   rewritten: _____

   _____

10. In her lectures, the nutritionist emphasizing the importance of fibre in our diet.

rewritten: _____

_____

ALONG THESE LINES/Pearson Education Canada

EXERCISE 9

FINDING SUBJECTS AND VERBS: A COMPREHENSIVE EXERCISE

Underline the subjects and verbs in these sentences, putting *S* above the subjects and *V* above the verbs.

1. Do you ever visit your grandmother in Montreal?
2. I, along with my husband and son, am going to go to the Toronto Marlies game on Sunday.
3. Behind the mall is a huge parking lot.
4. Robert needs to improve his grades.
5. Won't you consider my suggestion?
6. Football players are often injured during the season.
7. I'll never ride that roller coaster again.
8. There are three reasons for the price hike.
9. Jackie should have been thinking about her boyfriend's feelings.
10. There are a Mazda, a Chrysler, and a Volkswagen in the used-car lot.
11. Lakeesha paid the bills and picked up her son from daycare.
12. Within the fenced yard is a lovely garden of tropical plants.
13. He and my father looked tired and dirty.
14. My classmates have had many amazing life experiences.
15. Swimming is easy on the joints.

EXERCISE 10

CREATE YOUR OWN TEXT

Complete this activity with two partners. Below is a list of rules you've just studied. Each member of the group should write one example for each rule. When your group has completed three examples for each rule, trade your completed exercise with another group, and check their examples while they check yours.

The first rule has been done for you, as a sample.

Rule 1: The verb in a sentence can express some kind of action.

examples: **a.** Janelle drives to work every day.

           b. Last week my brother quit his job.

           c. My little sister dyed her hair with Kool-Aid.

Rule 2: The verb in a sentence can represent some state of being or the perceptions of one of the five senses.

examples: a. _____

b. _____

c. _____

Rule 3: The verb in a sentence can consist of more than one word.

examples: a. _____

b. _____

c. _____

Rule 4: There can be more than one subject of a sentence.

examples: a. _____

b. _____

c. _____

Rule 5: If you take out the prepositional phrases, it's easier to identify the subject of a sentence, because nothing in a prepositional phrase can be the subject of a sentence.

examples: (For examples, write sentences with at least one prepositional phrase in them; put parentheses around the prepositional phrases.)

a. _____

b. _____

c. _____

Rule 6: Not all sentences have the simple word order of subject first, then verb.

examples: (Give examples of a more complicated word order.)

a. _____

b. _____

c. _____

Rule 7: Words like *not, never, often, always, ever* are not verbs.

examples: (Write sentences using those words, but underline the correct verb.)

a. _____

b. _____

c. _____

Rule 8: An *-ing* verb form by itself or an infinitive (*to* preceding the verb) cannot be a main verb.

examples: (Write sentences with *-ing* verb forms or infinitives, but underline the main verb.)

a. _____

b. _____

c. _____

EXERCISE **11**	RECOGNIZING SUBJECTS AND VERBS IN A PARAGRAPH

Underline the subjects and verbs in the paragraph and put an *S* above each subject and a *V* above each verb.

Writing with a felt-tipped pen can be hazardous to a person's skin and possessions. Many people use felt-tipped pens for their smooth, gliding stroke. However, there are some drawbacks to these pens. The ink in them is runny, and it stains. It has been known to smear on the writer's fingers or wrists and to leave a bright slash of colour. A careless writer may also leave an ink smear across a page. The pens have a tendency to leak. Leaving an uncapped pen on the page of an open book can produce an ink blob on the paper. The uncapped pen can leak onto a shirt or pants and destroy the clothes in a minute. Felt-tipped pens are easy to use. On the other hand, isn't a pencil safer?

CHAPTER 13
The Compound Sentence: Coordination

A group of words containing a subject and a complete predicate is called a clause. When that group makes sense on its own, it is called a sentence, or an **independent clause**.

A sentence that has *one independent clause* is called a **simple sentence**. If you rely too heavily on a sentence pattern of simple sentences, you risk writing paragraphs like

> I am a college student. I am also a salesperson in a mall. I am always busy. School is time-consuming. Studying is time-consuming. Working makes me tired. Balancing these activities is hard. I work too many hours. Work is important. It pays for school.

Here is a better version:

> I am a college student and a salesperson at a mall, so I am always busy. School and study are time-consuming, and working makes me tired. Balancing these activities is hard. I work too many hours, but that work is important. It pays for school.

OPTIONS FOR COMBINING SIMPLE SENTENCES

Good writing involves sentence variety. This means mixing a simple sentence with a more complicated one, or a short sentence with a long one. Sentence variety is easier to achieve if you can combine related, short sentences into one.

Some students avoid such combining because they're not sure how to do it. They don't know how to punctuate the new combinations. It's true that punctuation involves memorizing a few rules, but once you know them you'll be able to use them automatically and write with more confidence. Here are three options for combining simple sentences followed by the punctuation rules you need to use in each case.

OPTION 1: USING A COMMA WITH A COORDINATING CONJUNCTION

You can combine two simple sentences with a **comma** and a coordinating conjunction. The coordinating conjunctions are *for, and, nor, but, or, yet,* and *so.* You need to memorize these seven coordinating conjunctions so that you can make a decision about punctuating your combined sentences. An easy way to remember them is to think of the acronym *FANBOYS: For, And, Nor, But, Or, Yet, So.*

ALONG THESE LINES/Pearson Education Canada

To coordinate means to join equals. When you join two simple sentences with a comma and a coordinating conjunction (*CC*), each half of the combination remains an independent clause, with its own subject (*S*) and verb (*V*).

Here are two simple sentences:

> S   V   S   V
> **He cooked** the dinner. **She washed** the dishes.

Here are the two simple sentences combined with a comma, and with the word *and*, a coordinating conjunction (*CC*):

> S   V   , CC S   V
> **He cooked** the dinner, **and she washed** the dishes.

The combined sentences keep the form they had as separate sentences; that is, they are still both independent clauses, with a subject and a verb and with the ability to stand alone.

The word that joins them is the **coordinating conjunction**. It is used to join *equals*. Look at some more examples. These examples use a variety of coordinating conjunctions to join two simple sentences:

sentences combined with *but*:

> S   V   , CC S V
> **I rushed** to the bank, **but I was** too late.

sentences combined with *or*:

> S   V   , CC S V
> **She can email** Jim, **or she can call** him.

sentences combined with *nor*:

> S   V   , CC V S V
> **I didn't like** the book, **nor did I like** the movie based on the book.
> (Notice what happens to the word order when you use *nor*.)

sentences combined with *for*:

> S   V   , CC S V
> **Sam worried** about the job interview, **for he saw** many qualified applicants in the waiting room.

sentences combined with *yet*:

> S   V   , CC S   V
> **Leo tried** to please his manager, **yet she** never **seemed** appreciative of his efforts.

sentences combined with *so*:

> S V   , CC S V
> **I was** the first in line for the concert tickets, **so I got** the best seats in the stadium.

Where Does the Comma Go?

Notice that the comma comes *before* the coordinating conjunction (*for, and, nor, but, or, yet, so*). It comes before the new idea—the second independent clause.

It goes where the first independent clause ends. Try this punctuation check: after you've placed the comma, look at the combined sentences. For example:

> She joined the armed forces, and she travelled overseas.

Now split it into two sentences at the comma:

> She joined the armed forces. And she travelled overseas.

(The split makes sense.)

If you put the comma in the wrong place, after the coordinating conjunction, your split sentences would be

> She joined the armed forces and. She travelled overseas.

(The split doesn't make sense.)

This test helps you see whether the comma has been placed correctly—*where the first independent clause ends.* (Notice that you can begin a sentence with *and.* You can also begin a sentence with the other coordinating conjunctions *for*, *nor*, *but*, *or*, *yet*, and *so*—as long as you're writing a complete sentence.)

If the subject is the *same* in the two simple sentences, you could write them either as two independent clauses joined by a coordinating conjunction *or* as a simple sentence with one subject and two verbs:

> **She joined** the armed forces**, and she travelled** overseas.

or

> **She joined** the armed forces **and travelled** overseas.

(In this case you don't need a comma.)

Caution: Do *not* put a comma every time you use the words *for*, *and*, *nor*, *but*, *or*, *yet*, and *so*; use it only when the coordinating conjunction joins independent clauses. Do not use a comma when the coordinating conjunction joins two words:

> blue and gold   tired but happy   hot or cold

Do not use a comma when the coordinating conjunction joins two phrases:

> on the chair or under the table
>
> in the water and by the shore
>
> with a smile but without an apology

The comma is used when the coordinating conjunction joins two independent clauses. Another way to say the same rule is to say that the comma is used when the coordinating conjunction joins two simple sentences.

Placing the Comma by Using S–V Patterns

An independent clause, or simple sentence, follows this basic pattern:

> S   V
> **He ran.**

> S   S V
> **He** and **I ran.**

S   V   V
He ran and **swam**.

S   S V   V
He and **I ran** and **swam**.

Study all four patterns for the simple sentence, and you'll notice that you can draw a line separating the subjects on one side and the verbs on the other:

S | V
SS | V
S | V V
SS | V V

Whether the simple sentence has one or more subjects and one or more verbs, the pattern is subject(s) followed by verb(s) (or sometimes verbs followed by subject(s), when sentence is in inverted word order).

When you combine two simple sentences, the pattern changes:

S   V   S V
two simple sentences: He swam. I ran.

S   V   S V
two simple sentences combined: He swam, but **I ran**.

In the new pattern, *SVSV*, you can't draw a line separating all the subjects on one side and all the verbs on the other. This new pattern is called a **compound sentence**: two simple sentences, or independent clauses, joined into one.

Recognizing the *SVSV* pattern will help you place the comma for compound sentences. Here's another way to remember this rule. When you have this pattern,

SV   SV

use a comma in front of the coordinating conjunction. Do not use a comma in front of the coordinating conjunctions with these patterns:

S | V
SS | V
S | V V
SS | V V

For example, use a comma for this pattern:

S   V   S V
Jane followed directions, but **I rushed** ahead.

but do not use a comma for this pattern:

S   V   V
Carol cleans her kitchen every week but never **wipes** the top of the refrigerator.

You've just studied one way to combine simple sentences. If you are going to take advantage of this method, you need to memorize the seven coordinating conjunctions—*for, and, nor, but, or, yet, so*—so that your use of them, with the correct punctuation, will become automatic.

EXERCISE 1	RECOGNIZING COMPOUND SENTENCES AND ADDING COMMAS

Add commas only where they are needed in the following sentences. Do not add words.

1. I came to see the play but the theatre was closed.

2. The waiter at the crowded restaurant rushed from table to table and tried to pacify the impatient customers.

3. Before my trip I read everything in the library about Hong Kong and I took a Cantonese class in night school.

4. The college students are planning to save their money and are hoping to buy a small house near campus.

5. I took a part-time job so I found it difficult to find time to study.

6. Rosa showed signs of nervousness in her speech yet her words carried conviction and power.

7. I looked in three stores for masala but couldn't find it anywhere.

8. You have to prepare for a marathon or you might do serious damage to your body.

9. She deserved to win first prize for she had spent years practising her skills.

10. The customers were not interested in my excuses nor were they sympathetic to my problems.

EXERCISE 2	MORE ON RECOGNIZING COMPOUND SENTENCES AND ADDING COMMAS

Add commas only where they are needed in the following sentences. Do not add words.

1. Sameer drove to the airport in twenty minutes but he couldn't find the right terminal for his flight.

2. A few of my co-workers bought a get-well card and sent it to our manager.

3. The mall was crowded so Anthony decided to come back later.

4. Love stories in movies are unrealistic yet romantic movies provide an escape from everyday life.

5. Stella wrote the bibliography and Brian prepared the charts.

6. Stella and Brian wrote the bibliography and prepared the charts.

7. Lara appears to be outgoing yet is rarely seen at parties or other gatherings.

8. Next week the supervisor will meet with the safety committee or he will speak to them individually.

9. The apartment has high ceilings and a kitchen with room for a small table.

10. The entrance to our apartment complex is neither lighted nor clearly marked with a large sign.

OPTION 2: USING A SEMICOLON BETWEEN TWO SIMPLE SENTENCES

Sometimes you want to combine two simple sentences (independent clauses), but you don't want to use a coordinating conjunction. If you want to join two simple sentences that are related in their ideas and you don't use a coordinating conjunction, you can combine them with a **semicolon**.

two simple sentences:

S   V   S   V
I **cooked** the turkey. **She made** the stuffing.

two simple sentences combined with a semicolon:

S   V   ; S   V
I **cooked** the turkey; **she made** the stuffing.

Here's another example of this option in use:

S   V   V   ; S   V
Rain can be dangerous; **it makes** the roads slippery.

Notice that when you join two simple sentences with a semicolon, the second sentence begins with a lower-case letter, not a capital letter.

Remember these rules for punctuating combined simple sentences:

- If a coordinating conjunction joins the combined sentences (remember option 1), put a comma in front of the coordinating conjunction.

S   V   ,   S   V
Tom had a barbecue in his backyard, and the **food was** delicious.

- If there is no coordinating conjunction, put a semicolon in front of the second independent clause (option 2).

S   V   ;   S   V
Tom had a barbecue in his backyard; the **food was** delicious.

OPTION 3: USING A SEMICOLON AND A CONJUNCTIVE ADVERB

Sometimes you want to join two simple sentences (independent clauses) with a connecting word called a **conjunctive adverb**. This word points out or clarifies a relationship between sentences. The Infobox provides a list of some conjunctive adverbs.

INFOBOX	SOME COMMON CONJUNCTIVE ADVERBS			
also	furthermore	likewise	otherwise
anyway	however	meanwhile	similarly
as a result	in addition	moreover	still
besides	incidentally	nevertheless	then
certainly	indeed	next	therefore
consequently	in fact	now	thus
finally	instead	on the other hand	undoubtedly

You can use a conjunctive adverb (*CA*) to join simple sentences, but when you do, you still need a semicolon in front of the adverb.

two simple sentences:

S   V   S V

My **parents checked** my homework every night. **I did** well in math.

two simple sentences joined by a conjunctive adverb and a semicolon:

S   V   ; CA S V

My **parents checked** my homework every night; **thus I did** well in math.

S   V   ;   CA   S   V

She gave me good advice; **moreover, she helped** me follow it.

Punctuating after a Conjunctive Adverb

Notice the comma *after* the conjunctive adverb in the preceding sentence. Here's the generally accepted rule:

Put a comma after the conjunctive adverb if the conjunctive adverb is more than one syllable long.

For example, if the conjunctive adverb is a word like *consequently*, *furthermore*, or *moreover*, you use a comma. If the conjunctive adverb is one syllable, you do not have to put a comma after the conjunctive adverb. One-syllable conjunctive adverbs are words like *then* or *thus*.

We worked on the project all weekend; **consequently**, we finished a week ahead of the deadline.

I saw her cruel behaviour to her staff; **then** I lost respect for her.

EXERCISE **3**	COMBINING SIMPLE SENTENCES THREE WAYS

Add a comma, or a semicolon, or a semicolon and a comma to the following sentences. Don't add, change, or delete any words; just add the correct punctuation.

1. Samira has been cooking all day soon it will be time for dinner.

2. All-terrain vehicles are fun to drive but they are not for children.

3. It was the best party of the summer moreover it was the best party of the year.

4. Jeans are popular in all countries Levis cost a fortune in Europe.

5. Renovating a house is a big project furthermore it's an expensive undertaking.

6. The crowd in the arena cheered wildly and the team felt enormously proud.

7. The crowd in the arena cheered wildly the team felt enormously proud.

8. You can plan your future carefully however you can't avoid surprises.

9. The surfer got up at dawn then he checked the local weather report.

10. Bill forgot to pack his camera consequently he has no pictures of his trip.

EXERCISE **4**	**MORE ON COMBINING SIMPLE SENTENCES THREE WAYS**

Add a comma, or a semicolon, or a semicolon and a comma to the following sentences. Don't add, change, or delete any words; just add the correct punctuation.

1. Kim was disappointed at the turnout she had expected a larger crowd at the last game of the season.

2. We sat in front of the fireplace roasting chestnuts meanwhile the snow swirled against the windows.

3. He sat right next to me yet he ignored me all evening.

4. Driving across the country can be boring instead you can look for a cheap airfare.

5. First he showed us the basic scuba equipment next he stressed the importance of safety.

6. It is not easy for me to work at home nor is it any easier to work from the office.

7. I used to wait for hours at the passport office now I simply submit my application online.

8. I am sick of eating fast food still it beats cooking for myself.

9. The doctor's office kept putting me on hold so I got angry and hung up.

10. The quarrel was partly his fault he could have been more tactful in asking for his money back.

EXERCISE

5

COMBINING SIMPLE SENTENCES

Below are pairs of simple sentences. Working with a partner or partners, combine each pair into one sentence. Use any of the three combining options discussed in this section: (1) a comma and a coordinating conjunction, (2) a semicolon, (3) a semicolon and a conjunctive adverb (with a comma, if it is needed). Then use a different option to create a second combination. The first one has been done for you.

Pick the options that make the most sense for each sentence.

1. Jim missed the beginning of the movie.

   I had to explain the story to him.

   combinations:

   a. Jim missed the beginning of the movie, so I had to explain the story to him.

   b. Jim missed the beginning of the movie; therefore, I had to explain the story to him.

2. The meal was very expensive.

   It was worth the price.

   combinations:

   a. _____

   _____

   b. _____

   _____

3. Kishan will never get the job he wants.

   He has a terrible work ethic.

   combinations:

   a. _____

   _____

   b. _____

   _____

4. He forgot to check the oil regularly.

   He had to pay for major car repairs.

   combinations:

   a. _____

   _____

   b. _____

   _____

5. The bank was closed.

The automatic teller was available.

combinations:

a. _____

_____

b. _____

_____

EXERCISE

6

EDITING A PARAGRAPH FOR ERRORS IN COORDINATION

Edit the following paragraph for errors in coordination. Do not add or change words; just add, delete, or change punctuation. There are six errors in the paragraph.

A bad cold is a minor illness but it can be one of the most miserable ailments in the world. Most people soon forget their own colds, and don't sympathize with someone else's bad cold. A cold is supposed to be a silly, sniffling disturbance in the head however, the person with a cold feels very sick. He or she is sneezing, wheezing, and grabbing at tissues. Fever, headache, and stuffiness suddenly attack the sufferer and no remedy seems to work. Cold pills cannot make a person feel less congested nor can chicken soup clear up a headache. The victim of a cold can only wait for the misery to pass then the cold bug brings its nasty symptoms to a new victim.

CHAPTER 14
The Complex Sentence: Subordination

MORE OPTIONS FOR COMBINING SIMPLE SENTENCES

Before you go any further, look back. Review the following:

- A clause has a subject and a complete predicate (the verb, plus the objects and phrases modifying the verb).
- An independent clause is a simple sentence; it is a group of words, with a subject and verb, that makes sense on its own.
- Independent clauses can be combined in various ways to make compound sentences.

There is another kind of clause, called a **dependent clause**. It has a subject and a verb, but it doesn't make sense by itself. It can't stand alone. It isn't complete by itself. That is, it *depends* on the rest of the sentence to give it meaning. You can use a dependent clause in combining simple sentences.

Using a Subordinating Conjunction

Changing an independent clause to a dependent one is called subordinating. How do you do it? You add a certain word, called a **subordinating conjunction**, to an independent clause, which makes it dependent, less important, or subordinate in the new sentence.

Keep in mind that the subordinate clause is still a clause; it has a subject and a complete predicate, but it doesn't make sense on its own. For example, here is an independent clause:

S   V

Caroline studies.

Somebody (*Caroline*) does something (*studies*). The statement makes sense by itself. But if you add a subordinating conjunction to the independent clause, the clause becomes dependent, incomplete, and unfinished, like this:

When Caroline studies. (When she studies, what happens?)
Unless Caroline studies. (Unless she studies, what will happen?)
If Caroline studies. (If Caroline studies, what will happen?)

Now, each dependent clause needs an independent clause to finish the idea:

dependent clause   independent clause
When Caroline studies, she gets good grades.

dependent clause   independent clause
Unless Caroline studies, she forgets key ideas.

dependent clause independent clause

If Caroline studies, she will pass the course.

There are many subordinating conjunctions. When you put any of these words in front of an independent clause, you make that clause dependent. The Infobox provides a list of some common subordinating conjunctions.

INFOBOX	SOME COMMON SUBORDINATING CONJUNCTIONS		
after	because	in order that	whatever
although	before	since	when
as	even if	though	whenever
as if	even though	unless	whereas
as soon as	if	until	while

You can use these subordinating conjunctions to create dependent clauses for two more options for combining simple sentences.

OPTION 4: USING A DEPENDENT CLAUSE TO BEGIN A SENTENCE

Often, you can combine simple sentences by changing the independent clause from one sentence into a dependent clause and placing it at the beginning of the new sentence.

two simple sentences:

S V   S V

I was late for work. My **car had** a flat tire.

changing one simple sentence into a beginning dependent clause:

S V   S V

Because my **car had** a flat tire, **I was** late for work.

Note that you can begin a sentence with a subordinating conjunction such as *because* as long as you follow it with an independent clause to make a complete sentence.

OPTION 5: USING A DEPENDENT CLAUSE TO END A SENTENCE

You can also combine simple sentences by changing an independent clause into a dependent clause and placing it at the end of the new sentence:

the same two simple sentences as above:

S V   S V

I was late for work. My **car had** a flat tire.

ALONG THESE LINES/Pearson Education Canada

changing one simple sentence into a dependent clause at the end:

S V   S V
I **was** late for work because my **car had** a flat tire.

Choosing a Subordinating Conjunction

If you pick the right subordinating conjunction, you can effectively combine simple sentences (independent clauses) into a more sophisticated sentence pattern. Such combining helps you add sentence variety to your writing and helps to explain relationships between ideas.

simple sentences:

S V   V   S   V
Leo could not **read** music. His **performance was** exciting.

new combination:

dependent clause   independent clause
Although Leo could not read music, his performance was exciting.

simple sentences:

S V   S V
I **caught** a bad cold last night. I **forgot** to bring a sweater to the baseball game.

new combination:

independent clause   dependent clause
I caught a bad cold last night because I forgot to bring a sweater to the baseball game.

Punctuating Complex Sentences

A sentence that has one independent clause and one or more dependent clauses is called a **complex sentence**. Complex sentences are very easy to punctuate. See if you can figure out the usual rule for punctuating by yourself. Look at the following examples. All are punctuated correctly.

example 1:

dependent clause   independent clause
Whenever the baby smiles, his mother is delighted.

independent clause   dependent clause
His mother is delighted **whenever the baby smiles.**

example 2:

dependent clause   independent clause
While you were away, I saved your mail for you.

independent clause   dependent clause
I saved your mail for you **while you were away.**

ALONG THESE LINES/Pearson Education Canada

In the above examples, look at the sentences that have a comma. Now look at the ones that don't have a comma. Both kinds of sentences are punctuated correctly. Do you see the rule?

Rule: When a dependent clause comes at the beginning of a sentence, the clause is followed by a comma. When a dependent clause comes at the end of a sentence, the clause usually does not need a comma.

Using a Relative Pronoun

Another type of dependent clause can be created by adding a **relative pronoun** such as *that, who, whoever, whom, what, which,* and *whose.*

This **relative clause** can be used as an adjective or a noun:

used as a noun (subject):

Whoever eats with us will enjoy a terrific meal. (Note that the clause actually forms the subject of the sentence—the subject of the independent clause.)

used as a noun (object of the verb):

She wanted to know **whom he would be visiting.** (answers the question "to know what"?)

used as an adjective:

John recorded the game **that was played last night.** (describes what game)

The previous examples of complex sentences have one independent clause and one dependent clause. A complex sentence can have one independent clause and *one or more* dependent clauses. Note the following example of a complex sentence with one independent clause and *two* dependent clauses:

independent clause	dependent clause	dependent clause

He tried to call her at home before she left with the man whose background was a mystery.

EXERCISE 1	**PUNCTUATING COMPLEX SENTENCES**

All of the following sentences are complex sentences; that is, they have one independent clause and one or more dependent clauses. Add a comma to the sentences that need one.

1. Until I became a parent I never realized that parenting could be so difficult.

2. Because they wanted me to have the best education my parents each worked two jobs.

3. My mother worked full-time as a teacher while she cleaned offices at night.

4. I knew how stressed my parents were even though they thought that they were hiding their worries from me.

5. When I am dealing with my own concerns I try to shelter my son from them.

6. I want my son to enjoy his childhood until he is old enough to have his own responsibilities.

7. My husband and I try to take our son on family outings whenever we can.

8. Although I would like to give my son everything that he wants, I know that would spoil him.

9. I want to raise a healthy, well-adjusted child as my parents did.

10. Whereas I didn't have many luxuries growing up my son will have an easier life.

EXERCISE 2 MORE ON PUNCTUATING COMPLEX SENTENCES

All the sentences below are complex sentences; that is, they have one independent clause and one or more dependent clauses. Add a comma to each sentence that needs one.

1. It amazes me that my wife and I get along so well because we are two entirely different people.

2. Whereas my dream vacation involves a five-star hotel my wife's dream vacation means hiking and camping.

3 Even though she would like to visit Gros Morne National Park before the end of the summer I have other plans.

4. I would prefer to spend a week on a beach somewhere though my wife insists it would be a nice change to go camping.

5. Why would I want to sleep on the rocky ground while I am being bitten by mosquitoes?

6. My wife would like to take our son camping before he goes back to school.

7. While we do have our differences I love my wife.

8. We will go camping this summer as long as we can go to the beach next year.

9. If I remember to bring mosquito repellant I might just have a good time.

10. As I write this my wife is already packing the tent.

COMBINING SENTENCES: A REVIEW OF YOUR OPTIONS

You've seen several ways to combine simple sentences. The following chart will help you to see them all, at a glance:

| INFOBOX | OPTIONS FOR COMBINING SENTENCES |

Coordination

Option 1:

Independent clause + comma + coordinating conjunction + independent clause.

> , for
> , and
> , nor
> , but
> , or
> , yet
> , so

Option 2:

Independent clause + semicolon + independent clause.

Option 3:

Independent clause + semicolon + conjunctive adverb + independent clause.

> ; also,
> ; anyway,
> ; as a result,
> ; besides,
> ; certainly,
> ; consequently,
> ; finally,
> ; furthermore,
> ; however,
> ; incidentally,
> ; in addition,
> ; in fact,
> ; indeed,
> ; instead,
> ; likewise,
> ; meanwhile,
> ; moreover,
> ; nevertheless,
> ; next
> ; now
> ; on the other hand,
> ; otherwise,
> ; similarly,
> ; still
> ; then
> ; therefore,
> ; thus
> ; undoubtedly,

(continued)

Subordination

Option 4:

Subordinating conjunction + dependent clause + comma + independent clause.

After
Although
As
As if
As soon as
Because
Before
Even if
Even though
If
In order that   (Put a comma at
Since   the end of the
So that   dependent clause.)
Though
Unless
Until
Whatever
When
Whenever
Whereas
Whether
While

Option 5:

Independent clause + subordinating conjunction + dependent clause.

after
although
as
as if
as soon as
because
before
even if
even though
if
in order that
since
so that
though
unless
until
whatever
when
whenever
whereas
whether
while

ALONG THESE LINES/Pearson Education Canada

Note: In Option 4, words are capitalized because the dependent clause will begin your complete sentence.

Creating Compound-Complex Sentences

Another type of sentence is the **compound-complex sentence**. This type of sentence has *two or more* independent clauses and *one or more* dependent clauses. You can join simple sentences to create the compound-complex sentence by using the same punctuation and conjunctions that you've already learned.

dependent clause   independent clause   dependent clause   CA

When we left for school, we knew that we were already late; however,

independent clause

the instructor was late too.

independent clause   dependent clause   CA   independent clause

Stefan tried to tell her that she shouldn't go; however, she wanted to make

independent clause dependent clause

her own decision, so she left before anyone else awoke.

EXERCISE 3	USING THE FIVE OPTIONS FOR COMBINING SENTENCES

Add the missing commas and/or semicolons to the following compound, complex, or compound-complex sentences. Some sentences are correct as written.

1. People can be more environmentally friendly if they make just a few simple changes.

2. My family has long been environmentally aware so I have always conserved energy.

3. Don't use incandescent light bulbs instead replace them with compact fluorescent ones.

4. My family always turns off the lights when they leave a room.

5. We don't run the dishwasher unless it is completely full.

6. We hang our clothes up to dry even if it is raining we just hang them up in the basement.

7. We bought a programmable thermostat so the furnace turns itself off when we aren't home.

8. Before the cold weather set in we added insulation to our house.

9. Even though we live in the suburbs we have only one car and it is fuel-efficient.

10. We buy our groceries in bulk and don't use plastic bags.

11. My son and I plant vegetables in our garden when the threat of frost has passed.

12. We use our composter regularly so we have very little trash to put out every two weeks.

13. We put out one bag of trash however we usually put out three recycling bins.

14. Even though we live in the suburbs I take the bus whenever I can.

15. There is a rain barrel in our backyard we use the water in the garden.

16. Because native plants require less watering I have replaced the non-native plants in our garden with native ones.

17. When the leaves appear on the large tree in our garden the tree shades our house in the summer.

18. Often we don't have to turn on the air conditioner in the summer because we are shaded by the tree.

19. We water the garden first thing in the morning and for just 20 minutes at a time.

20. I like to think that I am helping the environment and teaching my son about environmental responsibility.

EXERCISE 4

COMBINING SENTENCES

Do this exercise with a partner or with a group. Combine each pair of sentences below into one clear, smooth sentence in two different ways. You can add words as well as punctuation. The first pair of sentences is done for you.

1. I love the café on the corner of my street.
   The owners let me work on my laptop for hours.

   combination 1: I love the café on the corner of my street because the owners let me work on my laptop for hours.

   combination 2: I love the café on the corner of my street; the owners let me work on my laptop for hours.

2. I had never been to the Rockies.
   I wasn't prepared for their beauty.

   combination 1: _____

   _____

   combination 2: _____

   _____

3. Jack was falling asleep at the wheel of his car.
   He ran a red light.

   combination 1: _____

   _____

   combination 2: _____

   _____

4. I need to maintain a 3.5 GPA to keep my scholarship.
   I should study for the final exam.

   combination 1: _____

   _____

   combination 2: _____

   _____

5. Several of my cousins are planning a family reunion.
   Not all family members are enthusiastic about the plan.

   combination 1: _____

   _____

   combination 2: _____

   _____

6. Mario needs a down payment for the house.
   He is saving money and working overtime.

   combination 1: _____

   _____

   combination 2: _____

   _____

7. The air gets damp and chilly in the winter.
   I can feel the change in my bones.

   combination 1: _____

   _____

   combination 2: _____

   _____

8. My father and brother watch football together.
   They always argue about the fine points of the game.

   combination 1: _____

   _____

   combination 2: _____

   _____

9. I love Japanese food.
   I've never tried to cook it.

   combination 1: _____

   _____

   combination 2: _____

   _____

EXERCISE
5

CREATE YOUR OWN TEXT ON COMBINING SENTENCES

Below is a list of rules for coordinating and subordinating sentences. Working with a group, create two examples of each rule.

Option 1: You can join two simple sentences (two independent clauses) into a compound sentence with a coordinating conjunction and a comma in front of it.

The coordinating conjunctions are *for, and, nor, but, or, yet,* and *so.*

example 1: _____

_____

example 2: _____

_____

Option 2: You can combine two simple sentences (two independent clauses) into a compound sentence with a semicolon between independent clauses.

example 1: _____

_____

example 2: _____

_____

Option 3: You can join two simple sentences (two independent clauses) into a compound sentence with a semicolon and a conjunctive adverb between independent clauses.

Some conjunctive adverbs are *also, anyway, as a result, besides, certainly, consequently, finally, furthermore, however, incidentally, in addition, in fact, indeed, instead, likewise, meanwhile, moreover, nevertheless, next, now, on the other hand, otherwise, similarly, still, then, therefore, thus, undoubtedly.*

example 1: _____

_____

example 2: _____

_____

Option 4: You can combine two simple sentences (two independent clauses) into a complex sentence by making one clause dependent. The dependent clause starts with a subordinating conjunction. Then, if the dependent clause begins the sentence, the clause ends with a comma.

Some common subordinating conjunctions are *after, although, as, as if, as soon as, because, before, even if, even though, if, in order that, since, though, unless, until, whatever, when, whenever, whereas, whether, while.*

example 1: _____

_____

example 2: _____

_____

Option 5: You can combine two simple sentences (two independent clauses) into a compound sentence by making one clause independent. Then, if the dependent clause comes after the independent clause, usually no comma is needed.

example 1: _____

_____

example 2: _____

_____

EXERCISE
6

EDITING A PARAGRAPH FOR ERRORS IN COORDINATION AND SUBORDINATION

Edit the following paragraph for errors in coordination and subordination. Do not add words to the paragraph; just add, delete, or change punctuation. There are ten errors.

I am beginning to realize the importance of punctuality. This lesson came to me the hard way when I almost lost my job at a small, friendly insurance office certainly, I felt at ease with its casual and open atmosphere. I think I confused friendliness with slackness and soon found trouble. Since my boss and the other agents are often busy they rely on me to open up in the morning. I usually arrive on time at least I try to get there on time. I figured it didn't matter if I was ten or fifteen minutes late. When I arrived late last Friday it did matter. My boss came in thirty minutes after I did so I figured everything was fine. As soon as she took one call she came up to my desk and started shouting. The call was a customer with an emergency. That customer had called the office six times early in the morning no one had answered. Of course, I had not yet opened the office. My boss explained the seriousness of the problem finally, she gave me one more chance. I'll be on time from now on for I will not risk losing that chance.

CHAPTER 15
Avoiding Run-on Sentences and Comma Splices

RUN-ON SENTENCES

Run-on sentences are independent clauses that have not been joined correctly. This error, also called a **fused sentence**, is a major grammar error.

run-on sentence error:

I studied for the test all weekend I am well prepared for it.

run-on sentence error corrected:

I studied for the test all weekend, so I am well prepared for it.

run-on sentence error:

Technology has changed today's lifestyles social networking programs have replaced face-to-face socializing.

run-on sentence error corrected:

Technology has changed today's lifestyles; social networking programs have replaced face-to-face socializing.

run-on sentence error:

The causes of many illnesses have been found scientists have done much research.

run-on sentence error corrected:

The causes of many illnesses have been found because scientists have done much research.

Note: Two independent clauses could also be punctuated correctly as two separate sentences.

I studied for the test all weekend. I am well prepared for it.

CORRECTING RUN-ON SENTENCES

When you edit your writing, you can correct run-on sentences by following these steps:

INFOBOX	TWO STEPS IN CORRECTING RUN-ON SENTENCES

Step 1: Check for two independent clauses.
Step 2: Check that the clauses are separated by a comma and coordinating conjunction, by a semicolon, or by a subordinating conjunction.

ALONG THESE LINES/Pearson Education Canada

Follow the steps in checking this sentence:

The meeting was a waste of time the councillors argued about silly issues.

Step 1: Check for two independent clauses. You can do this by checking for the subject–verb, subject–verb pattern that indicates two independent clauses:

   S   V   S   V

The **meeting was** a waste of time the **councillors argued** about silly issues.

The pattern indicates that you have two independent clauses.

Step 2: Check that the clauses are separated either by a comma and coordinating conjunction (*for, and, nor, but, or, yet,* and *so*), by a semicolon, or by a subordinating conjunction.

The independent clauses are not separated by any of those options, so you have a run-on sentence. You can correct the run-on sentence three ways:

run-on sentence corrected with a comma and a coordinating conjunction:

The meeting was a waste of time, **for** the councillors argued about silly issues.

run-on sentence corrected with a semicolon:

The meeting was a waste of time; the councillors argued about silly issues.

run-on sentence corrected with a subordinating conjunction:

The meeting was a waste of time **since** the councillors argued about silly issues.

or

Since the councillors argued about silly issues, the meeting was a waste of time.

Follow the steps, once more, as you check this sentence:

I had the flu I missed class last week.

Step 1: Check for two independent clauses. Do this by checking the subject–verb, subject–verb pattern:

S V   S V

I had the flu **I missed** class last week.

Step 2: Check that the clauses are separated either by a comma and coordinating conjunction (*for, and, nor, but, or, yet, so*), by a semicolon, or by a subordinating conjunction.

The independent clauses are not separated by any of those options, so you have a run-on sentence. You can correct the run-on sentence three ways:

run-on sentence corrected with a comma and coordinating conjunction:

I had the flu, **so** I missed class last week.

run-on sentence corrected with a semicolon:

I had the flu; I missed class last week.

run-on sentence corrected with a subordinating conjunction:

Because I had the flu, I missed class last week.

Using the steps to check the run-on sentences can also help you avoid unnecessary punctuation. Consider this sentence:

The manager gave me my schedule for next week, and told me about a special sales promotion.

> Step 1: Check for two independent clauses. Do this by checking the subject–verb, subject–verb pattern:

S V   V

The **manager gave** me my schedule for next week, and **told** me about a special sales promotion.

The pattern is *SVV*, not *SV, SV*. The sentence is not made up of two independent clauses, so it does not need a comma before the coordinating conjunction. The sentence should read as follows:

The **manager gave** me my schedule for next week and **told** me about a special sales promotion.

Following the steps in correcting run-on sentences can help you combine sentences effectively.

EXERCISE 1 — CORRECTING RUN-ON (FUSED) SENTENCES

Some of the sentences below are correctly punctuated. Some are run-on (fused) sentences; that is, they are two simple sentences run together without any punctuation. If a sentence is correctly punctuated, write *OK* in the space provided. If it is a run-on sentence, put an *X* in the space provided and correct the sentence above the lines.

1. _____ Kameron took me to the dentist yesterday. I had a sharp pain in my lower jaw.

2. _____ I never liked science fiction movies then Marisol dragged me to a great one yesterday.

3. _____ From the top of the mountain came a cry for help rescuers rushed toward the stranded climbers.

4. _____ The most famous stars in action films use a stunt double for their most dangerous scenes or rely on computerized special effects.

5. _____ The refugee's account of her escape was startling it revealed the danger and horror around her.

6. _____ Omid is a full-time student he works 30 hours a week.

7. _____ Many people work downtown they live in the suburbs.

8. _____ I love all kinds of Latin music yet don't know many words of Spanish.

9. _____ Daniel makes a good salary he never worries about money.

10. _____ With the help of computers and wireless technology many people can work from home employers are granting many more flex hours.

EXERCISE 2

MORE ON CORRECTING RUN-ON (FUSED) SENTENCES

Some of the sentences below are correctly punctuated. Some are run-on (fused) sentences; that is, they are two simple sentences run together without any punctuation. If a sentence is correctly punctuated, write *OK* in the space provided. If it is a run-on sentence, put an *X* in the space provided and correct the sentence above the lines.

1. _____ Sam wanted some time with his family now he wants some time alone.

2. _____ Many people are beginning to recognize the benefits of meditation classes have even begun at my local gym.

3. _____ Commuters on subways and passengers in airplanes share the stresses of crowded spaces and unhealthy air.

4. _____ A membership in a health club was the perfect gift for my grandmother she loves her aerobics and swimming classes.

5. _____ Swimming and weight training are good activities to help prevent osteoporosis I have recommended my mom take them up.

6. _____ So many cooking shows have appeared on television; many people now think working in a professional kitchen is glamorous.

7. _____ First the long-distance company called at dinner time next it called in the early morning.

8. _____ The carpenters worked with the finest wood the panels looked rich and elegant.

9. _____   Companies concerned with the well-being of their employees offer specially designed chairs and other office equipment my employer doesn't do any of that.

10. _____   I am planning a small wedding at a local park instead of a big celebration with hundreds of people in a big hall.

COMMA SPLICES

A **comma splice** is an error that occurs when you punctuate with a comma but should use either a comma plus coordinating conjunction (*for, and, nor, but, or, yet, so*) or a semicolon. A comma alone is not enough.

comma splice error:

The crowd pushed forward, people began to panic.

comma splice error corrected:

The crowd pushed forward, and people began to panic.

or

The crowd pushed forward; people began to panic.

comma splice error:

I forgot my glasses, I couldn't read the small print in the contract.

comma splice error corrected:

I forgot my glasses, so I couldn't read the small print in the contract.

or

I forgot my glasses; I couldn't read the small print in the contract.

CORRECTING COMMA SPLICES

When you edit your writing, you can correct splices by following these steps:

INFOBOX	TWO STEPS IN CORRECTING COMMA SPLICES

Step 1: Check for two independent clauses.

Step 2: Check that the clauses are separated by a coordinating conjunction (FANBOYS: *for, and, nor, but, or, yet, so*) after the comma. If they are, then a comma is sufficient. If they are not separated by a coordinating conjunction, you have a comma splice. Correct the comma splice by adding a coordinating conjunction after the comma or by changing the comma to a semicolon.

Follow the steps to check for a comma splice in this sentence:

> I dropped the glass, it shattered on the tile floor.

Step 1: Check for two independent clauses. You can do this by checking for the subject–verb, subject–verb pattern that indicates two independent clauses.

> S   V   S   V
> **I dropped** the glass, **it shattered** on the tile floor.

The pattern indicates that you have two independent clauses.

Step 2: Check that the clauses are separated by a coordinating conjunction after the comma.

There is no coordinating conjunction. To correct the comma-splice error, you must add a coordinating conjunction or use a semicolon instead of a comma.

comma-splice error corrected:

> I dropped the glass, and it shattered on the tile floor.

or

> I dropped the glass; it shattered on the tile floor.

Be careful not to mistake a short word like *then* or *thus* for a coordinating conjunction. Only the seven coordinating conjunctions (*for*, *and*, *nor*, *but*, *or*, *yet*, *so*) can join independent clauses with a comma. *Then* is not a coordinating conjunction; it is a conjunctive adverb. When it joins two independent clauses, it needs a semicolon in front of it.

comma-splice error:

> Susie prepared her résumé, then she applied for the job.

comma-splice error corrected:

> Susie prepared her résumé; then she applied for the job.

Also remember that conjunctive adverbs that are two or more syllables long (like *consequently*, *however*, and *therefore*) need a comma after them as well as a semicolon in front of them when they join independent clauses:

> Harry has been researching plane fares to Vancouver; consequently, he knows how to spot a cheap flight.

(For a list of some common conjunctive adverbs, see Chapter 13.)

Sometimes writers see commas before and after a conjunctive adverb and think the commas are sufficient. Check this sentence for a comma splice by following the steps:

> Jonathan loves his job, however, it pays very little.

Step 1: Check for two independent clauses by checking for the subject–verb, subject–verb pattern.

S   V   S V

Jonathan loves his job, however, **it pays** very little.

The pattern indicates that you have two independent clauses.

Step 2: Check for a coordinating conjunction.

There is no coordinating conjunction. *However* is a conjunctive adverb, not a coordinating conjunction. Because there is no coordinating conjunction, you need a semicolon between the two independent clauses.

comma splice error corrected:

Jonathan loves his job; however, it pays very little.

EXERCISE **3**	**CORRECTING COMMA SPLICES**

Some of the sentences below are correctly punctuated. Some contain comma splices. If the sentence is correctly punctuated, write *OK* in the space provided. If it contains a comma splice, put an *X* in the space provided and correct the sentence above the lines. To correct a sentence, add the necessary punctuation. Do not add any words.

1. _____ Aloo Gobi is delicious, it contains cauliflower, potatoes, and spices.

2. _____ It is important to protect your personal information, never respond to emails asking for your bank account information or credit card number.

3. _____ You should also be careful at the ATM, thieves have been known to hide cameras there.

4. _____ The cameras record you as you enter your PIN, then the thieves use that number to access your bank account and to drain your funds.

5. _____ Try to cover the keypad with your hand as you enter your PIN, in addition never write your PIN down.

6. _____ I had to wait four hours for those tickets, nevertheless, the wait was worth it.

7. _____ Sheila had to borrow money from her father, otherwise she would have had to drop out of college.

8. _____ George is not particularly good-looking or smart, yet all the ladies like him.

9. _____ Kendra kicked the back of the driver's seat for an hour, then she began to pull her little sister's hair.

10. _____ Some people think of graffiti as vandalism, however, I think many pieces are works of art.

EXERCISE 4

MORE ON CORRECTING COMMA SPLICES

Some of the sentences below are correctly punctuated. Some contain comma splices. If the sentence is correctly punctuated, write *OK* in the space provided. If it contains a comma splice, put an *X* in the space provided and correct the sentence above the line. To correct a sentence, add the necessary punctuation. Do not add any words.

1. _____ The carpenter used nails instead of screws to lay the floor, as a result, the floor creaked.
2. _____ Freshteh loves children, so she got her Early Childhood Education diploma.
3. _____ Our seats were at the back, I could barely see the stage.
4. _____ Ben loves chocolate, but he will not eat anything with white chocolate in it.
5. _____ One kind of computer uses a dual-core processor, another does not.
6. _____ One good thing about the class is the time period, and another is the teacher.
7. _____ We can still get to work on time, anyway, we can try.
8. _____ Christine makes all her own clothes, and she always has her own style.
9. _____ There is much demand for dental hygienists, therefore I think I may apply to the hygienist program next semester.
10. _____ Here comes the bill, I will pay it.

EXERCISE 5

COMPLETING SENTENCES

With a partner or group, write the first part of each of the following incomplete sentences. Make your addition an independent clause. Be sure to punctuate your completed sentences correctly. The first one is done for you.

1. <u>The driver ignored the railroad warning signals,</u> and his car was hit by the train.
2. _____ then Kayla heard a mysterious noise.
3. _____ furthermore, you are constantly complaining.
4. _____ or the food will get cold.
5. _____ now I need a long vacation.
6. _____ somebody took it.
7. _____ however, it lasted too long.
8. _____ but I learned from the experience.
9. _____ Carlos refused to apologize to her.
10. _____ otherwise, we will miss the exam.

ALONG THESE LINES/Pearson Education Canada

| EXERCISE
6 | **EDITING A PARAGRAPH FOR RUN-ON
SENTENCES AND COMMA SPLICES** |

Edit the following paragraph for run-on sentences and comma splices. There are seven errors.

Choosing a career is difficult I am torn between two fields. My best grades have been in my math classes and my father wants me to be an accountant. Accountants make a good salary in addition, they are always in demand. My uncle is an accountant and has found good jobs in four exciting cities. I would like the security and opportunity of such employment on the other hand, I dream of a different career. I have been working at a restaurant for four years as a result, I have learned about the inner workings of the restaurant business. The job is tough nevertheless, I would love to have my own restaurant. Everyone warns me about the huge financial risks and long hours yet these challenges can be exciting. Someday I will have to choose between a risky venture in the restaurant business and a safe, well-paying career in accounting.

CHAPTER 16
Avoiding Sentence Fragments

A **sentence fragment** is a group of words that looks like a sentence and is punctuated like a sentence but isn't a sentence. Writing a sentence fragment is a major error in grammar because it reveals that the writer isn't sure what a sentence is.

The following groups of words are all fragments:

> Because customers are often in a hurry and have little time to look for bargains.
>
> My job being very stressful and fast-paced.
>
> For example, the trend of "Tapas," or serving appetizer-sized portions.

Two simple steps that can help you check your writing for sentence fragments are provided in the Infobox.

INFOBOX	TWO STEPS IN RECOGNIZING SENTENCE FRAGMENTS

Step 1: Check each group of words punctuated like a sentence; look for a subject and a complete predicate.

Step 2: If you find a subject and a complete predicate, check that the group of words makes a complete statement.

RECOGNIZING FRAGMENTS: STEP 1

Check for a subject and a complete predicate (verb plus object and modifiers). Some groups of words that look like sentences may actually have a subject, but no complete predicate; or they may have a complete predicate, but no subject; or they may have neither a subject *nor* a complete predicate.

> The customer by the cashmere sweaters. (***Customer*** could be the subject of a sentence, but there's no complete predicate.)
>
> Doesn't matter to me one way or the other. (There is a complete predicate, ***does matter***, but there is no subject.)
>
> In the back of my mind. (There are two prepositional phrases, ***In the back*** and ***of my mind***, but there is no subject or complete predicate.)

Remember that the -*ing* form of a verb by itself cannot be the main verb in a sentence (see Chapter 12). Therefore, groups of words like the ones below may look like sentences, but they are missing a complete predicate and are really fragments:

> Your sister having all the skills required of a good salesperson.
>
> The two top tennis players struggling with exhaustion and the stress
>
> of a highly competitive tournament.
>
> Jack being the only one in the room with a piece of paper.

An infinitive (*to* plus a verb) can't be a main verb in a sentence, either. The following groups of words are also fragments:

> The manager of the store to attend the meeting of regional managers next
>
> month in Brampton.
>
> The purpose to explain the fine points of the game to new players.

Groups of words beginning with words like *also, especially, except, for example, in addition,* and *such as* need subjects and complete predicates, too. Without subjects and complete predicates, these groups can be fragments, like the ones below:

> Also a good place to grow up.
>
> Especially the youngest member of the family.
>
> For example, a person without a high-school diploma.

Note that there is one type of sentence that may look as if it has no subject but in fact is complete. With a verb that gives a direct command or instruction, the subject *you* is understood. Thus, the following are complete sentences:

> Hang up your coat.
>
> Don't be afraid of the dog.
>
> Please sit down.

EXERCISE 1	CHECKING GROUPS OF WORDS FOR SUBJECTS AND COMPLETE PREDICATES

Check the following groups of words for subjects and complete predicates. Some have subjects and complete predicates and are sentences. Some are missing subjects or complete predicates or both: they are fragments. Put an *S* by the ones that are sentences; put an *F* by the ones that are fragments.

1. _____ For example, candy wrappers and pop cans litter the park.
2. _____ Across the street from her house was an empty lot.
3. _____ The rock musician strutting across the stage, rhythmically swinging the microphone toward the audience and back again.
4. _____ Can't possibly be the person with the best chance of getting the job.
5. _____ Especially a small child afraid of the water.

6. _____ The child was skipping across the sidewalk and trying hard not to step on a crack.
7. _____ In the darkest part of the forest with no flashlight.
8. _____ In addition, the pizza was stale and soggy.
9. _____ Daniel being the brightest of the boys in the family.
10. _____ For instance, another tie for my father on his birthday.

EXERCISE 2

MORE ON CHECKING GROUPS OF WORDS FOR SUBJECTS AND COMPLETE PREDICATES

Some of the following groups of words have subjects and complete predicates; these are sentences. Some are missing subjects, complete predicates, or both; these are fragments. Put an *S* by each sentence; put an *F* by each fragment.

1. _____ Mayor Noda to consider running for prime minister.
2. _____ Anyone with an ounce of common sense and some patience.
3. _____ One possible motive being revenge against a rival leader.
4. _____ The roast from the oven needs to rest for ten minutes.
5. _____ Should have been more careful with the valuable antique.
6. _____ Vinnie giving me encouragement from the sidelines and Elena cheering me on.
7. _____ The child pulling back from the little boy with a frog in his pocket.
8. _____ Except the apartments on the third floor of the building.
9. _____ At the door was a smiling salesperson.
10. _____ Will think about the chances of getting a job in engineering.

RECOGNIZING FRAGMENTS: STEP 2

If you find a subject and a complete predicate, check that the group of words makes a complete statement. Many groups of words have both a subject and a verb, but they don't make sense by themselves. They are **dependent clauses.**

How can you tell if a clause is dependent? After you've checked each group of words for a subject and complete predicate, check to see if it begins with one of the **subordinating conjunctions** that start dependent clauses. (Here again are some common subordinating conjunctions: *after, although, as, because, before, even if, even though, if, in order that, since, though, unless, until, when, whereas, while*).

A clause that begins with a subordinating conjunction is a dependent clause. When you punctuate a dependent clause as if it were a sentence, you have a kind of fragment called a **dependent clause fragment:**

> After I woke up this morning.
>
> Because he liked cricket better than soccer.
>
> Unless it stops raining by lunchtime.

It's important to remember both steps in checking for fragments:

Step 1: Check for a subject and a complete predicate.

Step 2: If you find a subject and a complete predicate, check that the group of words makes a complete statement.

EXERCISE 3

CHECKING FOR DEPENDENT CLAUSE FRAGMENTS

Some of the following groups of words are sentences. Some are dependent clauses punctuated like sentences; these are sentence fragments. Put an *S* by the sentences and an *F* by the fragments.

1. _____ As he carefully washed the outside of the car and polished the chrome trim with a special cloth.

2. _____ Commuters rushed past the ticket windows and slipped into the train at the last possible minute.

3. _____ Because no one in the class had been able to buy a copy of the required text in the campus bookstore.

4. _____ Even though many people expect to own their own home and to be able to meet the mortgage payments.

5. _____ Most of the movies were sequels to the popular movies of last summer.

6. _____ While I wanted to go to a place in the desert with dry air and bright sunshine.

7. _____ Although defendants in some countries are considered guilty until they prove their innocence.

8. _____ If people in our community were more serious about conserving water.

9. _____ Ever since Ron began taking martial arts classes.

10. _____ When women are afraid to leave their homes at night.

EXERCISE 4

MORE ON CHECKING FOR DEPENDENT CLAUSE FRAGMENTS

Some of the following groups of words are sentences. Some are dependent clauses punctuated like sentences; these are sentence fragments. Put an *S* by each sentence and an *F* by each fragment.

1. _____ After I finish my shift at work.

2. _____ Down the ladder came a firefighter with a child in his arms.

3. _____ Since we met at the student centre for a cup of coffee.

4. _____ Near the hospital is a huge medical building.

5. _____ Before I had a chance to put the key in the door.

6. _____ Because anyone could have broken into the gym.

7. _____ While Sergei painted the green trim on the outside of the house.

8. _____ Suddenly my car alarm sounded.
9. _____ Unless you can give me a better deal on this
DVD player.
10. _____ Whenever Tanya borrows my USB drive.

EXERCISE 5	USING TWO STEPS TO RECOGNIZE SENTENCE FRAGMENTS

Some of the following are complete sentences; some are fragments. To recognize the fragments, check each group of words by using the two-step process:

Step 1: Check for a subject and a complete predicate.
Step 2: If you find a subject and a complete predicate, check that the group of words makes a complete statement.

After you've used both steps, put an *S* by the groups of words that are sentences and an *F* by the ones that are fragments.

1. _____ The reason being a computer error on the bill from the telephone company.
2. _____ As the graduates lined up for their march into the auditorium.
3. _____ Christopher was being very stubborn about apologizing to his uncle.
4. _____ Whenever it is cold and dreary outside and my bed seems warm and cozy.
5. _____ Without a single word of explanation for her rude behaviour.
6. _____ In the curb lane sat a stalled truck.
7. _____ Without a comfortable pair of shoes, you'll have trouble walking that distance.
8. _____ Because of their lack of education and inability to compete with others in the workforce.
9. _____ Expensive cars representing the height of success to him.
10. _____ Which was precisely the wrong thing to say to her.
11. _____ Armand feeling lost and alone without his family in Jamaica.
12. _____ For example, a child with no self-esteem or confidence.
13. _____ Although I'd never thought much about it, one way or another.
14. _____ The expensive gift to be sent Priority Courier to the girl from Thunder Bay.
15. _____ Oranges providing a good source of Vitamin C in the winter.
16. _____ While he did all the paperwork and paid all the bills.
17. _____ From the first day of school to the last, she enjoyed her math class.
18. _____ When I'd spent hours pleading with her to keep it a secret.
19. _____ The answer came to me all of a sudden.
20. _____ The reason being a resistance to facing the truth about herself.

CORRECTING FRAGMENTS

You can correct fragments easily if you follow the two steps for identifying them.

Step 1: Check for a subject and a complete predicate. Then, if a group of words is a fragment because it lacks a subject or a complete predicate, or both, *add what's missing*.

fragment: My father being a very strong person.

(This fragment lacks a main verb, since an *-ing* form by itself is not a main verb.)

corrected: My father is a very strong person.

(The verb *is* replaces the *-ing* form **being**.)

fragment: Doesn't care about the party. (This fragment lacks a subject.)

corrected: Alicia doesn't care about the party. (A subject, **Alicia**, is added.)

fragment: Especially on dark winter days. (This fragment has neither a subject nor a verb.)

corrected: I love hot chocolate, especially on dark winter days. (A subject, **I**, and a verb, **love**, are added.)

Step 2: If you find a subject and a verb, check that the group of words makes a complete statement. Then, to correct the fragment, (a) you can turn a dependent clause into an independent one by removing the subordinating conjunction, *or* (b) you can add an independent clause to the dependent one to create a statement that makes sense by itself.

fragment: When the rain beat against the windows. (The statement does not make sense by itself. The subordinating conjunction **when** leads the reader to ask, "What happened when the rain beat against the windows?" The subordinating conjunction makes this a dependent clause, not a sentence.)

corrected using (a): The rain beat against the windows. (Removing the subordinating conjunction makes this an independent clause, a sentence.)

corrected using (b): When the rain beat against the windows, I reconsidered my plans for the picnic. (Adding an independent clause turns this into something that makes sense.)

Note: Sometimes you can correct a fragment by linking it to the sentence before it or after it.

fragment (underlined):

I have always enjoyed outdoor concerts. <u>Like the ones at Pioneer Park.</u>

corrected:

I have always enjoyed outdoor concerts like the ones at Pioneer Park.

fragment (underlined): <u>Even if she apologizes for that nasty remark.</u>
I will never trust her again.

corrected: Even if she apologizes for that nasty remark, I will never trust her again.

You have several choices for correcting fragments: you can add words, phrases, or clauses; you can take words out; or you can combine independent and dependent clauses. You can transform fragments into simple sentences or create compound (see Chapter 13) or complex sentences (see Chapter 14). To punctuate your new sentences, remember the options for combining sentences (see Infobox in Chapter 14, pages 335–36).

EXERCISE **6**	**CORRECTING FRAGMENTS**

Correct each sentence fragment below in the most appropriate way.

1. It can be difficult to learn the finer points of grammar. Such as identifying comma splices, run-on sentences, and sentence fragments.

   corrected: _____

   _____

2. If you pay attention in class and do all the practice exercises. You will probably find it easier to identify grammatical errors.

   corrected: _____

   _____

3. Writing my draft at the last minute. I had the feeling I missed some details in my paragraph.

   corrected: _____

   _____

4. I find some of the elements of the essay difficult to write. Especially the conclusion.

   corrected: _____

   _____

5. Because the topic sentence is so important. Sometimes I get writer's block.

   corrected: _____

   _____

6. Brainstorming being the best way to overcome writer's block.

   corrected: _____

   _____

7. I have lots of ideas. Once I get started.

corrected: _____

_____

8. After taking four weeks of this course. I feel more confident organizing my ideas.

corrected: _____

_____

9. Students editing their writing. Write more effective paragraphs.

corrected: _____

_____

10. Effective writing important for success in college.

corrected: _____

_____

<table>
<tr><td>EXERCISE
7
</td><td>## MORE ON CORRECTING FRAGMENTS</td></tr>
</table>

With a partner or a group, correct each fragment below in two ways. The first one is done for you.

1. Whenever I am waiting for an important phone call.

corrected: <u>I am waiting for an important phone call.</u>

corrected: <u>Whenever I am waiting for an important phone call, I am extremely impatient and anxious.</u>

2. Christina took the customers' orders. While Robert worked in the kitchen.

corrected: _____

_____

corrected: _____

_____

3. When we get together on Sundays. We have an enormous dinner.

corrected: _____

_____

corrected: _____

_____

4. Jason being more talented than any of the professional hockey players.
    corrected: _____

    _____

    corrected: _____

    _____

5. With a great deal of enthusiasm for his subject. He began his lecture.
    corrected: _____

    _____

    corrected: _____

    _____

6. Although no one could tell him how to get to the gas station.
    corrected: _____

    _____

    corrected: _____

    _____

7. In the forest, where the fire had originally broken out.
    corrected: _____

    _____

    corrected: _____

    _____

8. He'll never make friends. Unless he learns to control his temper.
    corrected: _____

    _____

    corrected: _____

    _____

9. I was beginning to feel sick. As the boat rocked from side to side.
    corrected: _____

    _____

    corrected: _____

    _____

10. Which is one place I'd like to visit.
    corrected: _____

    _____

    corrected: _____

    _____

EXERCISE	EDITING A PARAGRAPH FOR SENTENCE
8	**FRAGMENTS**

Correct the sentence fragments in the following paragraph. There are six fragments.

Nick would love to meet a celebrity. Like a famous athlete. He sees these celebrities on television. Where they drive expensive cars and wear wild clothes. They seem to have it all. Talent, looks, money, and fame. These things all appear to come easily to celebrities. They can live anywhere they want and buy anything they desire. These famous people filling Nick's dreams. To talk to one basketball or music star and get the person's photograph. Being close to a celebrity would make Nick feel important. Since Nick is only six years old. He has plenty of time to find other dreams.

CHAPTER 17
Using Parallelism in Sentences

Parallelism means balance in a sentence. To create sentences with parallelism, remember this rule:

Similar points should be written with a similar structure.

Often, you will include two or three (or more) related ideas, examples, or details in one sentence. If you express these ideas in a parallel structure, they will be clearer, smoother, and more convincing. In fact, speech writers frequently use parallel structure in their speeches, as it makes for a more powerful and memorable speech. Some examples of parallel structures in famous speeches include:

- "Veni, vidi, vinci" or, "I came, I saw, I conquered" ~ *Julius Caesar*
- "If some countries have too much history, we have too much geography." ~ *Mackenzie King*
- "We shall fight on the beaches. We shall fight on the landing grounds. We shall fight in the fields and in the streets. We shall fight in the hills. We shall never surrender." ~ *Winston Churchill*

Here are some pairs of sentences with and without parallelism:

not parallel: Of all the sports I've played, I prefer tennis, handball, and playing golf.

parallel: Of all the sports I've played, I prefer **tennis, handball, and golf**. (Three words are parallel.)

not parallel: If you're looking for the car keys, you should look under the table, the kitchen counter, and they might be behind the refrigerator.

parallel: If you're looking for the car keys, you should look **under the table, on the kitchen counter, and behind the refrigerator**. (Three prepositional phrases are parallel.)

not parallel: He is a good choice for manager because he works hard, he keeps calm, and well-liked.

parallel: He is a good choice for manager because **he works hard, he keeps calm, and he is well-liked**. (Three clauses are parallel.)

From these examples you can see that parallelism involves matching the structures of parts of your sentence.

ALONG THESE LINES/Pearson Education Canada

ACHIEVING PARALLELISM

There are two steps that can help you check your writing for parallelism, shown in the following Infobox:

INFOBOX	**TWO STEPS IN CHECKING A SENTENCE FOR PARALLEL STRUCTURE**

Step 1: Look for the list in the sentence.
Step 2: Put the parts of the list into a similar structure.

(You may have to change or add something to get a parallel structure.)

Let's correct the parallelism of the following sentence:

> **sample sentence:** The committee for neighbourhood safety met to set up a schedule for patrols, coordinating teams of volunteers, and also for the purpose of creating new rules.

To correct this sentence, we'll follow the steps.

Step 1: Look for the list. The committee met to do three things. Here's the list:

1. to set up a schedule for patrols
2. coordinating teams of volunteers
3. for the purpose of creating new rules

Step 2: Put the parts of the list into a similar structure:

1. *to set up* a schedule for patrols
2. *to coordinate* teams of volunteers
3. *to create* new rules

Now revise to get a parallel sentence.

> **parallel:** The committee for neighbourhood safety met **to set up** a schedule for patrols, **to coordinate** teams of volunteers, and **to create** new rules.

When writing a parallel list with an infinitive (*to* plus the verb), either use *to* with every item in the list (*to* set up . . . *to* coordinate . . . and *to* create) or use it just once at the beginning of the list (*to* set up . . . coordinate . . . and create). Don't write an unbalanced list (*to* set up . . . coordinate . . . and *to* create).

Caution: Sometimes making ideas parallel means adding something to a sentence because all the parts of the list can't match exactly.

> **sample sentence:** In his pocket the little boy had a ruler, rubber band, baseball card, and apple.

ALONG THESE LINES/Pearson Education Canada

Step 1: Look for the list.

In his pocket the little boy had a

1. ruler
2. rubber band
3. baseball card
4. apple

As the sentence is written, the *a* goes with *a ruler*, *a rubber band*, *a baseball card*, and *a apple*. But *a* isn't the right word to put in front of apple. Words beginning with vowels (a, e, i, o, u) need *an* in front of them: *an apple*. So to make the sentence parallel, you have to change something in the sentence.

Step 2: Put the parts of the list into a parallel structure.

parallel: In his pocket the little boy had **a ruler, a rubber band, a baseball card**, and **an apple**.

Here's another example:

sample sentence: She was amused and interested in the silly plot of the movie.

Step 1: Look for the list.

She was

1. amused
2. interested in

the silly plot of the movie.

Check the sense of this sentence by looking at each part of the list and determining how it is working in the sentence: "She was *interested in* the silly plot of the movie." That part of the list seems clear. But "She was *amused* the silly plot of the movie"? Or "She was *amused in* the silly plot of the movie"? Neither sentence is right. People are not *amused in*.

Step 2: Put the parts of the list into a parallel structure. In this case, the sentence needs a word added to make the structure parallel.

parallel: She was **amused by** and **interested in** the silly plot of the movie.

Sometimes the clauses in a compound or complex sentence are not written in a parallel structure. You may need to change the subject of one of the clauses or reorder the words in the sentence so the clauses are parallel:

sample sentence: Adarsh carried three books in his knapsack; **Lael's knapsack held** five.

parallel: Adarsh carried three books in his knapsack; **Lael carried** five in hers.

sample sentence: Before **you write** an essay, **research needs** to be done.

parallel: Before **you write** an essay, **you need** to do research.

When you follow the two steps to check for parallelism, you can write clear sentences and improve your style.

ALONG THESE LINES/Pearson Education Canada

EXERCISE	REVISING SENTENCES FOR PARALLELISM
1	

Some of the following sentences need to be revised so they have parallel structures. Revise the ones that need parallelism. Write C for the sentences that are already correct.

1. The road begins at the beach; the city centre is where it ends.

   revised: _____

   _____

2. The restaurant is very popular, noisy, and has crowds.

   revised: _____

   _____

3. My work day is so busy with activities that I have to shop for groceries, washing and ironing my clothes, and clean my room at night.

   revised: _____

   _____

4. You can get to the carnival by chartered bus or by special train.

   revised: _____

   _____

5. He is a player with great energy and who is ambitious.

   revised: _____

   _____

6. When we meet tomorrow, I'd like to discuss your job description, explaining your health benefits, and a description of the package of retirement options you will have.

   revised: _____

   _____

7. The location of the house, its size, and how much it cost made it the best choice for the family.

   revised: _____

   _____

8. Going to college is not the same as when you go to high school.

   revised: _____

   _____

9. Jim was the friendliest person she met at school, also the most helpful person and the most funny.

   revised: _____

   _____

10. Ramona would rather sew her own wedding gown than paying a fortune to buy one.

    revised: _____

    _____

EXERCISE 2

WRITING SENTENCES WITH PARALLELISM

With a partner or with a group, complete each sentence. Begin by brainstorming a draft list; then revise the list for parallelism. Finally, complete the sentence in parallel structure. (Note: A colon is not necessary before the list of items in the sentences in this exercise; see Chapter 24 on the correct use of a colon). You may want to assign one task (brainstorming a draft list, revising it, etc.) to each group member, then switch tasks on the next sentence. The first one is done for you:

1. Three habits I'd like to break are

   draft list: **revised list:**

   a. *worry too much*   a. *worrying too much*

   b. *talking on the phone for hours*   b. *talking on the phone for hours*

   c. *lose my temper*   c. *losing my temper*

   sentence: *Three habits I'd like to break are worrying too much, talking on the phone for hours, and losing my temper.*

2. Three ways to spend a rainy Sunday are

   draft list: **revised list:**

   a. _____   a. _____

   b. _____   b. _____

   c. _____   c. _____

   sentence: _____

   _____

3. Two reasons to stop smoking are

   draft list: **revised list:**

   a. _____   a. _____

   b. _____   b. _____

   sentence: _____

   _____

4. Three irritations in my daily life are

   draft list: **revised list:**

   a. _____   a. _____

   b. _____   b. _____

   c. _____   c. _____

   sentence: _____

   _____

5. Exercise is good for you because (add three reasons)

   draft list: **revised list:**

   a. _____   a. _____

   b. _____   b. _____

   c. _____   c. _____

sentence: _____

_____

6. Getting enough sleep is important because (add three reasons)

   draft list: **revised list:**

   a. _____   a. _____

   b. _____   b. _____

   c. _____   c. _____

   sentence: _____

   _____

7. Five years from now, I want to (add two goals)

   draft list: **revised list:**

   a. _____   a. _____

   b. _____   b. _____

   sentence: _____

   _____

8. Ending a relationship can be stressful because (add three reasons)

   draft list: **revised list:**

   a. _____   a. _____

   b. _____   b. _____

   c. _____   c. _____

   sentence: _____

   _____

9. I am most carefree when (add two times or occasions)

   draft list: **revised list:**

   a. _____   a. _____

   b. _____   b. _____

   sentence: _____

   _____

10. Three characteristics of a good parent are

   draft list: **revised list:**

   a. _____   a. _____

   b. _____   b. _____

   c. _____   c. _____

sentence: _____

_____

11. Two experiences most people dread are

draft list: revised list:

a. _____   a. _____

b. _____   b. _____

c. _____   c. _____

sentence: _____

_____

| EXERCISE **3** | **COMBINING SENTENCES AND CREATING A PARALLEL STRUCTURE** |

Combine each of the following clusters of sentences into one clear, smooth sentence. The first one is done for you:

1. Before you buy a used car, you should research what similar models are selling for.
   It would be a good idea to have a mechanic examine the car.
   Also, how much mileage it has racked up is a consideration.

   combination: *Before you buy a used car, you should compare prices of similar models, get a mechanic to examine the car, and think carefully about the mileage.*

2. The service at Cyber Barn was excellent.
   The sales representative was patient and friendly.
   The fact that there was a full three-year warranty on my MP3 player was a bonus too.

   combination: _____

   _____

3. If you want to lose weight, you should limit the amount of fat in your diet.
   Cutting back on junk food is also a good idea.
   Regular exercise is important, too.

   combination: _____

   _____

4. Business people advertise by computer.
    Children use computers to play video games.
    Computers are used by teachers to teach basic skills.

    combination: _____

    _____

5. He was a dynamic professor.
    He had energy.
    He had enthusiasm.

    combination: _____

    _____

6. As a friend, he was extremely loyal.
    As a friend, he also told the truth.
    He was also a compassionate friend.

    combination: _____

    _____

7. Richard joined the conversation club.
    Richard spoke with other members three times a week.
    Richard's pronunciation improved significantly.

    combination: _____

    _____

8. The demonstrators came from small towns.
    The demonstrators came from major cities.
    The demonstrators came from farms.
    The demonstrators came from factories.
    The demonstrators came to express their concern about the environment.

    combination: _____

    _____

9. People crowded the entrances to the department store.
    They hoped to be the first inside the store.
    Their goal was to find a bargain at the sale.

    combination: _____

    _____

10. The city was well-planned.
    It had wide sidewalks.
    It had many mixed-use areas.

It had lots of community centres.
The city was a welcoming place to live.

combination: _____

_____

11. People don't swim at the lake anymore.
    The shore is littered with garbage.
    Chemicals pollute the water.
    City officials had the picnic tables removed.

    combination: _____

    _____

12. The federal government should provide more funding to the arts.
    An appreciation of the arts can build a sense of community.
    Exposure to the arts encourages children to become more flexible thinkers.
    More independent local artists are supported.

    combination: _____

    _____

EXERCISE 4

EDITING A PARAGRAPH FOR ERRORS IN PARALLELISM

Correct any errors in parallelism in the following paragraph. There are six errors.

    I cannot understand why my brother is a big baseball fan; I think the game is slow, causes me to get bored, and it's outdated. My brother always drags me to baseball games where he pays close attention to every minute of the game. Meanwhile, I am waiting for the action to begin. I can see only men standing around the field, talking to each other, chew gum, or they spit tobacco juice. I don't see why this behaviour is exciting. In addition, there are the boring moments when the game seems to stop completely. Then the coaches or the umpire or the players seem to be having a conference on the field. These little talks seem endless. My last complaint is about the atmosphere of a ball game. Even the big, nationally televised games seem old-fashioned. The games feature the same kinds of uniforms, music playing, and fans as a baseball game in a 50-year-old movie. While my brother enjoys this slow, traditional game, I want the action, excitement, and sense of aggression of modern football or basketball.

CHAPTER 18
Correcting Problems with Modifiers

Modifiers are words, phrases, or clauses that describe or *modify* something in a sentence. The following words, phrases, and clauses that appear in bold are modifiers.

the **blue** van (word)
the van **in the garage** (phrase)
the van **that she bought** (clause)
foreign tourists (word)
tourists **coming to Charlottetown** (phrase)
Coming to Charlottetown, tourists . . . (phrase)
To meet friends, she (phrase)
tourists **who visit the province** (clause)

Modifiers limit another word and make another word (or words) more specific.

the girl **in the corner** (tells exactly which girl)
fifty metres (tells exactly how many metres)
the movie **that I liked best** (tells which movie)
He **never** calls. (tells how often)

EXERCISE 1	RECOGNIZING MODIFIERS

In each of the following sentences, underline the modifiers (words, phrases, or clauses) that describe the italicized word or phrase.

1. *The movie* starring Julie Christie and Omar Sharif is my favourite.

2. I saw *a woman* driving a beautifully restored Corvette.

3. *The people* who were standing in the long lines showed great patience.

4. The fisherman reeled in *a fish* which fought every inch of the way.

5. Julie and Sabina always write thank-you *notes*.

6. To learn a new trade, my *father* enrolled in college.

7. Flashing its pink neon message, *the sign* attracted many new customers.

8. *The* teenage *girl* dressed in the Harajuku outfit drew many looks.

9. Jumping across the sidewalk, *the frog* startled me.

10. The battered old denim *jacket*, with its frayed sleeves and torn pocket, finally had to be thrown out.

ALONG THESE LINES/Pearson Education Canada

CORRECTING MODIFIER PROBLEMS

Modifiers can make your writing more specific and more concrete. Used effectively and correctly, modifiers give the reader a clear, exact picture of what you want to say, and they help you to say it precisely. But modifiers have to be used correctly. You can check for errors with modifiers as you revise your sentences.

INFOBOX	THREE STEPS IN CHECKING FOR SENTENCE ERRORS WITH MODIFIERS

Step 1: Find the modifier.
Step 2: Ask, "Does the modifier have something to modify?"
Step 3: Ask, "Is the modifier in the right place, as close as possible to the word, phrase, or clause it modifies?"

If you answer *No* to either Step 2 or Step 3, you need to revise your sentence.

Correcting Misplaced Modifiers

Let's use the steps in the following example.

sample sentence: I saw a woman driving a Porsche wearing a bikini.

Step 1:   Find the modifier. The modifiers are *driving a Porsche*, *wearing a bikini*.

Step 2:   Ask, "Does the modifier have something to modify?" The answer is yes. A woman is driving a Porsche. A woman is wearing a bikini. Both modifiers go with *a woman*.

Step 3:   Ask, "Is the modifier in the right place?" The answer is *yes* and *no*. One modifier is in the right place:

I saw **a woman driving a Porsche**

The other modifier is *not* in the right place:

a Porsche wearing a bikini

The Porsche is not wearing a bikini.

revised: I saw a woman **wearing a bikini** and **driving a Porsche**.

Let's work through the steps once more:

sample sentence: Hurriedly taking orders, the diners motioned to the harried server.

Step 1:   Find the modifier. The modifiers are *hurriedly taking orders*, and *harried*.

Step 2:   Ask, "Does the modifier have something to modify?" The answer is yes. There is the *harried server*. The *harried server* is *hurriedly taking orders*. Both modifiers go with *server*.

Step 3:   Ask, "Is the modifier in the right place?" The answer is *yes* and *no*. The word *harried* is in the right place:

harried server

But *Hurriedly taking orders* is in the wrong place:

Hurriedly taking orders, the diners

The diners are not hurriedly taking orders. The server is.

revised: The diners motioned to the harried server **hurriedly taking orders**.

Caution: Be sure to put words like *almost, even, exactly, hardly, just, merely, nearly, only, scarcely,* and *simply* as close as possible to what they modify. If you put them in the wrong place, you may write a confusing sentence.

sample sentence: Etienne **only wants** to grow carrots and zucchini.

The modifier that creates confusion here is *only*. Does Etienne have only one goal in life—to grow carrots and zucchini? Or are these the *only* vegetables he wants to grow? To create a clearer sentence, move the modifier.

possible revision: Etienne wants **only to grow** carrots and zucchini.

This still could be confusing. Does Etienne want only *to grow* the carrots and zucchini but not to harvest them, market them, etc.?

further revision (and probably most accurate): Etienne wants to grow **only carrots and zucchini**.

The examples you have just worked through show one common error in using modifiers. This error involves **misplaced modifiers**, words that describe something but are not where they should be in the sentence. Here is the rule to remember:

Put the modifier as close as possible to the word, phrase, or clause it modifies.

EXERCISE 2

CORRECTING SENTENCES WITH MISPLACED MODIFIERS

Some of the following sentences contain misplaced modifiers. Revise any sentence that has a misplaced modifier by putting the modifier as close as possible to whatever it modifies. Write C beside any sentences that are already correct.

1. Falling from the top of my refrigerator, I saw my best glass dish.

   revised: _____

   _____

2. When we criticized her performance, the actress was ready to nearly cry.

   revised: _____

   _____

3. When we go out for dinner, we only want to eat Indian food.

   revised: _____

   _____

ALONG THESE LINES/Pearson Education Canada

4. Wrapped in shiny paper, I accepted the tiny gift.

   revised: _____

   _____

5. The doctor gave the prescription for sedatives to the nervous patient.

   revised: _____

   _____

6. When he starts college next fall, he wants to take only business courses.

   revised: _____

   _____

7. Cracked in two places, she was sure the window would have to be replaced.

   revised: _____

   _____

8. The team doesn't like the umpire who lost the game.

   revised: _____

   _____

9. Soaked in brandy, she tasted the fruitcake.

   revised: _____

   _____

10. Flailing wildly, Jim avoided the downed electrical wire.

   revised: _____

   _____

Correcting Dangling Modifiers

The three steps for correcting modifier problems can help you to recognize another kind of error. For example, let's use the steps to check the following sentence.

> **sample sentence:** Strolling through the tropical paradise, many colourful birds could be seen.

Step 1: Find the modifier. The modifiers are *Strolling through the tropical paradise* and *many colourful.*

Step 2: Ask, "Does the modifier have something to modify?" The answer is *yes* and *no*. The words *many* and *colourful* modify birds. But who or what is *Strolling through the tropical paradise*? There is no person mentioned in this sentence. The birds are not strolling.

This kind of error is called a **dangling modifier**. It means that the modifier does not have anything to modify; it just dangles in the sentence. To correct this kind of error, you can't just move the modifier:

> **still incorrect:** Many colourful birds could be seen strolling through the tropical paradise.

(There is still no person strolling.)

The way to correct this kind of error is to add something to the sentence. If you gave the modifier something to modify (let's use *the tourists*), you might come up with several different revised sentences:

> **Strolling through the tropical paradise, the tourists** could see many colourful birds.

(Keep the structure of the sentence the same as in the sample, but add the appropriate words *the tourists* to the sentence in the subject position.)

> or

> **The tourists strolling through the tropical paradise** could see many colourful birds.

(Move the phrase *strolling through the tropical paradise* so that it is clearly modifying *tourists*.)

> or

> **As the tourists were strolling through the tropical paradise,** many colourful birds could be seen.

(Change the phrase *strolling through the tropical paradise* to a dependent clause with its own subject; then the subject of the independent clause [*many colourful birds*] can remain the same.)

> or (better)

> **As the tourists were strolling through the tropical paradise, they** could see many colourful birds.

(Avoid the wordier passive structure [see Chapter 20] of *many colourful birds could be seen.*)

> or

> Many colourful birds could be seen **as the tourists were strolling through the tropical paradise**.

(As in the previous revision, change the phrase *strolling through the tropical paradise* to a dependent clause; then place it at the end of the sentence.)

Be careful with this revision: The **tourists** could see many colourful birds **as they were strolling through the tropical paradise.**

(This one could create a pronoun reference problem because *they* in the second clause of the sentence could refer to either tourists or birds.)

Try the process for correcting dangling modifiers once more:

> **sample sentence:** Ascending in the glass elevator, her eyes needed to be closed because of her terrible fear of heights.

Step 1: Find the modifier. The modifiers are *Ascending in the glass elevator* and *terrible.*

Step 2: Ask, "Does the modifier have anything to modify?" The answer is *yes—terrible* modifies *fear,* and *no—Ascending in the glass elevator* doesn't modify anything. Who or what is ascending in the elevator? *Her eyes* are mentioned, but not the person herself. To revise this sentence, put somebody or something in the sentence for the modifier to describe.

revised sentences: Ascending in the glass elevator, the guest needed to close her eyes because of her terrible fear of heights.

or

As the guest ascended in the glass elevator, she needed to close her eyes because of her terrible fear of heights.

Remember that you can't correct a dangling modifier just by moving the modifier. You have to give the modifier something to modify; you have to add something to the sentence.

EXERCISE 3

CORRECTING SENTENCES WITH DANGLING MODIFIERS

Some of the following sentences use modifiers correctly. Some sentences have dangling modifiers. Revise the sentences with dangling modifiers. To revise, you will have to add and change words. Write *C* beside the sentences that are already correct.

1. Racing across the station, the train was reached before the doors closed.

   revised: _____

   _____

2. Breaking into the house at night, the homeowners lost their most valuable possessions.

   revised: _____

   _____

3. At the age of five, my family moved to Regina.

   revised: _____

   _____

4. Lost in the fog, the lighthouse could not be seen.

   revised: _____

   _____

5. Stumbling across the finish line, the runner gasped for breath.

   revised: _____

   _____

6. When taking the geometry exam, an argument between the teacher and a student began.

revised: _____

_____

7. While mowing the lawn, a wasp stung him.

revised: _____

_____

8. Tired and irritable, the work day seemed endless.

revised: _____

_____

9. Visiting Mexico for the first time, I thought the country was strange and exciting.

revised: _____

_____

10. To enter that contest, an entry fee of $50 is needed.

revised: _____

_____

REVIEWING THE STEPS AND THE SOLUTIONS

It's important to recognize problems with modifiers and to correct these problems. Modifier problems can result in confusing or even silly sentences. And when you confuse or unintentionally amuse your reader, you're not making your point.

Remember to check for modifier problems by using three steps, and to correct each kind of problem in the appropriate way.

INFOBOX   **A SUMMARY OF MODIFIER PROBLEMS**

Checking for Modifier Problems

Step 1: Find the modifier.
Step 2: Ask, "Does the modifier have something to modify?"
Step 3: Ask, "Is the modifier in the right place?"

Correcting Modifier Problems

- If a modifier is in the wrong place (a misplaced modifier), put it as close as possible to the word, phrase, or clause it modifies.
- If a modifier has nothing to modify (a dangling modifier), add or change words so that it has something to modify.

EXERCISE 4   REVISING SENTENCES WITH MODIFIER PROBLEMS

All of the following sentences have some kind of modifier problem. Write a new, correct sentence for each one. You can move words, add words, change words, or remove words. The first one is done for you.

1. Stopping suddenly, the box with the cake in it fell from the seat of the car.

   revised: When I had to stop suddenly, the box with the cake in it fell from the seat of the car.

2. Without a trace of bitterness, the argument between the neighbours was settled.

   revised: _____

   _____

3. Staring into space, the teacher scolded the student.

   revised: _____

   _____

4. After considering the alternatives, a compromise was reached by the two sides.

   revised: _____

   _____

5. After drag racing down the street until 3 a.m., the neighbours decided to complain to the teenagers' parents.

   revised: _____

   _____

6. Shivering from the cold, the winter took its toll on the homeless man.

   revised: _____

   _____

7. Susan nearly missed all the multiple-choice questions on the test.

   revised: _____

   _____

8. Taking every precaution, safety was a priority at the machining shop.

   revised: _____

   _____

9. To make friends at school, an outgoing personality is necessary.

   revised: _____

   _____

10. When packing a suitcase for a trip, a little ingenuity and planning go a long way.

    revised: _____

    _____

EXERCISE 5

EDITING A PARAGRAPH FOR MODIFIER PROBLEMS

Correct any errors in modifiers in the following paragraph. There are four errors. Write your corrections above the lines.

When entering a new school, it is difficult to make new friends. If the school is a college, the process can be especially hard. Colleges have students of all ages, and new students may think they can only see a few people of their own age. Everyone else may look much younger or older. College also seems to be a more serious place than high school, so students may feel shy about starting a conversation. Standing alone in the hall before class, nervousness paralyzes a newcomer. It may seem as if everyone else has a close friend to talk to. Then, when the newcomer starts to meet one or two people, another problem arises. A new student may hesitate before giving a phone number or email address to a classmate fearing too much intimacy too soon. Fortunately, time passes, and new students become a part of school and of new friendships.

CHAPTER 19
Using Verbs Correctly

USING STANDARD VERB FORMS

Many people use nonstandard verb forms in everyday conversation. But everyone who wants to write and speak effectively should know the difference between the slang and dialect you might hear in everyday conversation and the **standard English** of college, business, and professional environments.

In everyday conversation, you might hear nonstandard forms like

I goes	he don't	we was
you was	it don't	she smile
you be	I be	they walks

But these are not correct forms in standard English.

Verbs are words that show some kind of action or being. These verbs show action.

>   verb
> He **runs** to the park.

>   verb
> Ashraf **tastes** the pizza.

These verbs show being.

>   verb
> Melanie **is** my best friend.

>   verb
> The pizza **tastes** delicious.

(The verb *tastes* in this sentence shows "being" rather than action because the pizza is not actually tasting something. Instead, the verb is used in this sentence to tell about the pizza's condition.)

Verbs also tell about when something takes place (time).

> He **will run** to the park. (The time is future.)
> Melanie **was** my best friend. (The time is past.)
> The pizza **tastes** delicious. (The time is present.)

The time of a verb is called its *tense*. You can say a verb is in the *future tense*, the *past tense*, the *present tense*, or many other tenses.

Using verbs correctly involves knowing which form of the verb to use, choosing the right verb tense, and being consistent in verb tense.

ALONG THESE LINES/Pearson Education Canada

THE PRESENT TENSE

Look at the standard verb forms for the **present tense** of *to listen*.

verb: to listen

I listen	we listen
you listen	you listen
he, she, it listens	they listen

Take a closer look at the standard verb forms. Only one form is different:

he, she, it *listens*

This is the only form that ends in *s* in the present tense.

INFOBOX	**PRESENT TENSE ENDINGS**

In the present tense, use an *s* or *es* ending on the verb only when the subject is *he*, *she*, or *it*, or the equivalent of *he*, *she*, or *it*.

Notice how the *s* is used on the end of the verb forms in each of the following examples because the subject is *he*, *she*, or *it* or the equivalent:

He calls his mother every day.
She watches television after she puts her children to bed.
It runs like a new car.
Lane calls his mother every day.
Jie watches television after she puts her children to bed.
The jalopy runs like a new car.

Take another look at the present tense. If the verb is a regular verb, it will follow this form in the present tense.

I attend every lecture.
You care about the truth.
He visits his grandfather regularly.
She drives a new car.
The new album sounds great.
We follow that team.
You work well when you both compromise.
They buy the store brand of cereal.

In the list above, the only forms that end in *s* are those used with *he*, *she*, and *the new album* (the equivalent of *it*).

EXERCISE 1	**CHOOSING THE RIGHT VERB IN THE PRESENT TENSE**

Underline the subject and circle the correct verb form in parentheses in each of the following sentences.

1. The dress in the discount store (look/looks) better to me than the one in the boutique.

2. I (work/works) in a dirty part of the city.

3. Grocery shopping (take/takes) a good part of the morning.

4. The raccoon in the yard (frighten/frightens) my sister.

5. She sometimes (travel/travels) for three days without calling home.

6. Ipinder (concentrate/concentrates) better with the radio on.

7. Down the street by the vendors (stand/stands) a statue of Sir Wilfrid Laurier.

8. With great determination, Carla and Leon (exercise/exercises) every day.

9. A meal in a restaurant (cost/costs) more than a meal at home.

10. It (seem/seems) like a good idea.

EXERCISE 2

MORE ON CHOOSING THE RIGHT VERB IN THE PRESENT TENSE

Underline the subject and circle the correct verb form in parentheses in each sentence below.

1. On warm days, our neighbour (relax/relaxes) on the patio.

2. You (talk/talks) about yourself too much.

3. The chief of detectives (drive/drives) an unmarked car.

4. A clean house (make/makes) a good impression.

5. Behind the factories (sit/sits) a small stone house.

6. Some of my friends (post/posts) everyday on Facebook.

7. Every Saturday night, they (rent/rents) an old horror movie.

8. Humour (get/gets) people through tough situations.

9. A representative of the student government (attend/attends) the conference.

10. At that price, it (sound/sounds) like a bargain.

THE PAST TENSE

The **past tense** of most verbs is formed by adding *d* or *ed* to the verb.

verb: to listen

I listened	we listened
you listened	you listened
he, she, it listened	they listened

Add *ed* to *listen* to form the past tense. For some verbs that already end in *e*, you will add just *d*:

The sun **faded** from the sky.
He **quaked** with fear.
She **crumpled** the paper into a ball.

EXERCISE	WRITING THE CORRECT FORM OF THE PAST TENSE
3	Write *d* or *ed* in the blank to create the correct past-tense form of each verb in parentheses in the sentences below.

1. Last week, he and I (remove__) the stain from the counter.
2. The coach in high school (warn__) some players to pay attention to the game.
3. As a child, I (perform__) in an annual piano recital.
4. After doing some research into the company, I (reject__) its offer of a job.
5. Last night, we (compromise__) on the issue of where to build the park.
6. Yesterday, Christine (call__) me about driving to the party.
7. Reporters at the scene of last night's train accident (interview__) a witness.
8. Fifteen years ago, Arnold and Bruce (start__) a climb to success in Hollywood.
9. The girl at the desk (wave__) at me.
10. You (waste__) too much time on it yesterday.

THE FOUR MAIN VERB FORMS: PRESENT, PAST, PRESENT PARTICIPLE, AND PAST PARTICIPLE

When you are deciding what form of a verb to use, you will probably rely on one of four forms: the present tense, the past tense, the present participle, or the past participle. Most of the time, you will use one of these forms or add a helping verb to it. As an example, look at the four main forms of the verb *to listen*.

Present	Past	Present Participle	Past Participle
listen	listened	listening	listened

When a verb is regular, like *fade* or *listen*, the past form is created by adding *d* or *ed* to the present form. The present participle is formed by adding *ing* to the present form, and the past participle is the same as the past form.

You use the four verb forms—present, past, present participle, past participle—alone or with helping verbs to express time (tense). They are very easy to remember when a verb is a **regular verb**, like *listen*. Use the present form for the present tense:

We **listen** to the news on the radio.

The past form expresses past tense:

I **listened** to language tapes for three hours yesterday.

The present participle, or *-ing* form, is used with helping verbs:

I **am listening** to you.
He **was listening** to me.
You **should have been listening** more carefully.

Notice from the above examples that the *-ing* form plus helping verb(s) can be used to discuss events in the present, in the past, or in other situations.

ALONG THESE LINES/Pearson Education Canada

The past participle of regular verbs is the *-d* or *-ed* form used with helping verbs:

I **have listened** for hours.
She **has listened** to the tape.
We **could have listened** to the tape before we bought it.

Of course, you can also add many helping verbs to the present tense:

present tense:
We **listen** to the news on the car radio.

add helping verbs:
We **will** listen to the news on the car radio.
We **should** listen to the news on the car radio.
We **can** listen to the news on the car radio.

INFOBOX	FREQUENTLY USED HELPING VERBS			
am	do	might	was
are	have	must	were
can	is	shall	will
could	may	should	would

IRREGULAR VERBS

The Present Tense of *Be, Have,* and *Do*

Irregular verbs don't follow the same rules for creating verb forms that regular verbs do. Three verbs that we use all the time—*be, have,* and *do*—are irregular verbs. You need to study them closely. Look at the present-tense forms for all three, and compare the standard present-tense forms to the nonstandard ones you might hear in everyday conversation. *Remember always to use the standard forms when speaking or writing in college, business, and professional environments.*

verb: to be

Nonstandard	Standard
I be or I is	I am
you be	you are
he, she, it be	he, she, it is
we be	we are
you be	you are
they be	they are

verb: to have

Nonstandard	Standard
I has	I have
you has	you have
he, she, it have	he, she, it has
we has	we have
you has	you have
they has	they have

verb: to do

Nonstandard	Standard
I does	I do
you does	you do

he, she, it do	he, she, it does
we does	we do
you does	you do
they does	they do

Caution: Be careful when you add *not* to *does*. If you're writing a contraction of *does not*, be sure you write *doesn't* instead of *don't*.

not this: The light *don't* work.

but this: The light *doesn't* work.

EXERCISE 4

CHOOSING THE CORRECT FORM OF *BE, HAVE,* OR *DO* IN THE PRESENT TENSE

Circle the correct form of the verb in parentheses in each sentence below.

1. Two of the salesmen (is/are/am) meeting at the branch office.
2. I am sure the dancers (has/have) the ability to reach the top.
3. My mother (don't/doesn't) need another set of earrings for her birthday.
4. The winner of the contest (do/does) whatever he wants with the money.
5. Without an excuse, he (has/have) no choice but to apologize.
6. Every weekend, I (do/does) the laundry for the whole family.
7. The musicians (has/have) a huge bus equipped for travelling long distances.
8. I (is/am/are) very embarrassed.
9. They know he (do/does) his exercises early in the morning.
10. Amin and Lee (be/are/is) coming over in half an hour.

EXERCISE 5

MORE ON CHOOSING THE CORRECT FORM OF *BE, HAVE,* OR *DO* IN THE PRESENT TENSE

Circle the correct form of the verb in parentheses in each sentence below.

1. Consequently, her son (do/does) nothing about the arguments.
2. Today I (be/am/is) the youngest member of the cricket team.
3. Lamont (has/have) nothing but praise for his boss.
4. Regular exercise is important; it (do/does) affect your health.
5. Even though you pretend to be carefree, you (do/does) too much worrying.
6. Most of the time, a paperback book (don't/doesn't) cost as much as a hardcover book.
7. At New Year's, we (has/have) a traditional meal.
8. My shifts (be/are/is) too long; I never have enough time to see my friends.
9. The new gym (has/have) great air conditioning.
10. If you (has/have) a student ID, you can get a discount.

The Past Tense of *Be, Have,* and *Do*

The past-tense forms of these irregular verbs can be confusing. Again, compare the nonstandard forms to the standard forms. *Remember always to use the standard forms when speaking or writing in college, business, and professional environments.*

verb: to be

Nonstandard	Standard
I were	I was
you was	you were
he, she, it were	he, she, it was
we was	we were
you was	you were
they was	they were

verb: to have

Nonstandard	Standard
I has	I had
you has	you had
he, she, it have	he, she, it had
we has	we had
you has	you had
they has	they had

verb: to do

Nonstandard	Standard
I done	I did
you done	you did
he, she, it done	he, she, it did
we done	we did
you done	you did
they done	they did

In college and professional writing, you sometimes need to express doubtful ideas or unproven facts. For example,

Manpreet eats very little. (expresses a fact)

If she were fat, she could easily lose weight. (expresses an idea that is not necessarily true)

I am already two hours late for the class. (expresses a fact)

If I were two minutes earlier, I could catch the 7:42 train to Union Station. (expresses an idea that is possible but not probable)

Note that the verb tenses *she were* and *I were* appear to be nonstandard English. However, the choices are correct *if you wish to show a doubtful condition.*

EXERCISE

6

CHOOSING THE CORRECT FORM OF *BE, HAVE,* OR *DO* IN THE PAST TENSE

Circle the correct verb form in parentheses in each sentence.

1. The people next door (was/were) mysterious in their habits.

2. Last night, Alonzo (done/did) the decorating for the Grey Cup party.

3. In spite of the rain, the club (had/have) a large turnout for the picnic.

4. Three hours after the deadline, we (was/were) still busy.

5. Yesterday, at that intersection, I (had/have) a minor car accident.

6. As a little girl, Shireen (was/were) quiet and shy around strangers.

7. Believing in helping others, the volunteers (done/did) a good deed for two lost people.

8. I (was/were) unhappy with the grade on my math test.

9. Two years ago, you (was/were) the most valuable player on the team.

10. Her class in music appreciation (done/did) the most to interest her in music.

EXERCISE 7

MORE ON CHOOSING THE CORRECT FORM OF *BE, HAVE,* OR *DO* IN THE PAST TENSE

Circle the correct verb form in parentheses in each sentence below.

1. Lorenzo and I (was/were) once clerks at the same bank.

2. Last winter, my sister (had/have) an encounter with a black bear.

3. I learned Portuguese when I (was/were) a student in Brazil.

4. Brendan (done/did) what he could to help his parents find a place to live.

5. We (was/were) minding our own business when the robbery occurred.

6. Last month, my cousin Raj (had/have) a job interview with the parks department.

7. Yesterday, you and I (was/were) calm and confident.

8. After the car accident, Monica (had/have) to fill out a statement for the police.

9. I have the evening free because I (done/did) the laundry and the ironing yesterday.

10. The student lounge at the college (had/have) comfortable chairs.

More Irregular Verb Forms

Be, *have,* and *do* are not the only verbs with irregular forms. There are many such verbs, and everybody who writes uses some form of an irregular verb. When you write and you are not certain if you are using the correct form of a verb, check the following list of irregular verbs.

For each irregular verb listed, the *present*, the *past*, and the *past participle* forms are given. The present participle isn't included because it is always formed by adding *ing* to the present form.

Irregular Verb Forms

Present	Past	Past Participle
(Today I *arise*.)	(Yesterday I *arose*.)	(I have/had *arisen*.)
arise	arose	arisen
awake	awoke, awaked	awoken, awaked

bear	bore	borne, born
beat	beat	beaten
become	became	become
begin	began	begun
bend	bent	bent
bite	bit	bitten
bleed	bled	bled
blow	blew	blown
break	broke	broken
bring	brought	brought
build	built	built
burst	burst	burst
buy	bought	bought
catch	caught	caught
choose	chose	chosen
cling	clung	clung
come	came	come
cost	cost	cost
creep	crept	crept
cut	cut	cut
deal	dealt	dealt
draw	drew	drawn
dream	dreamt, dreamed	dreamt, dreamed
drink	drank	drunk
drive	drove	driven
eat	ate	eaten
fall	fell	fallen
feed	fed	fed
feel	felt	felt
fight	fought	fought
find	found	found
fling	flung	flung
fly	flew	flown
freeze	froze	frozen
get	got	got, gotten
give	gave	given
go	went	gone
grow	grew	grown
hear	heard	heard
hide	hid	hidden
hit	hit	hit
hold	held	held
hurt	hurt	hurt
keep	kept	kept
know	knew	known
lay (means to put)	laid	laid
lead	led	led
leave	left	left
lend	lent	lent
let	let	let
lie (means to recline)	lay	lain
light	lit, lighted	lit, lighted
lose	lost	lost

make	made	made
mean	meant	meant
meet	met	met
pay	paid	paid
ride	rode	ridden
ring	rang	rung
rise	rose	risen
run	ran	run
say	said	said
see	saw	seen
sell	sold	sold
send	sent	sent
sew	sewed	sewn, sewed
shake	shook	shaken
shine	shone, shined	shone, shined
shrink	shrank	shrunk
shut	shut	shut
sing	sang	sung
sit	sat	sat
sleep	slept	slept
slide	slid	slid
sling	slung	slung
speak	spoke	spoken
spend	spent	spent
stand	stood	stood
steal	stole	stolen
stick	stuck	stuck
sting	stung	stung
stink	stank, stunk	stunk
string	strung	strung
swear	swore	sworn
swim	swam	swum
teach	taught	taught
tear	tore	torn
tell	told	told
think	thought	thought
throw	threw	thrown
wake	woke, waked	woken, waked
wear	wore	worn
win	won	won
write	wrote	written

EXERCISE 8 — CHOOSING THE CORRECT FORM OF IRREGULAR VERBS

Write the correct form of the verb in parentheses in the following sentences. Be sure to check the list of irregular verbs.

1. I bought a huge bag of potato chips last night, and by midnight, I had _____ (eat) the whole thing.

2. Patty and Tom should have _____ (know) how to get to the store; they've been there before.

ALONG THESE LINES/Pearson Education Canada

3. Last night, I had _____ (lie) awake for three hours before I finally fell asleep.

4. I bought my five-year-old a new pair of blue jeans yesterday, but she has _____ (tear) them already.

5. I don't know what he _____ (mean) when he said, "I'm not interested."

6. Virginia asked Jack if he had ever _____ (lend) money to a friend.

7. Normally my teacher begins the class with "Good morning," but yesterday she_____ (lay) her books on the table and said, "Today we're doing something different."

8. For years, that pawnbroker has _____ (deal) in stolen merchandise, but now he is being investigated.

9. The children have _____ (drink) all the milk in the refrigerator.

10. The child was hoping to get toys for his birthday, but instead his uncle _____ (bring) a sweater.

EXERCISE 9

WRITING SENTENCES WITH CORRECT VERB FORMS

With a partner or with a group, write two sentences that correctly use each of the following verb forms. In writing these sentences, you may add helping verbs to the verb forms, but you may *not* change the verb form itself. The first one is done for you.

1. sent

   a. He sent her a dozen roses on Valentine's Day.

   b. I have sent him all the information he needs.

2. seen

   a. _____

   b. _____

3. cost

   a. _____

   b. _____

4. drew

   a. _____

   b. _____

5. lain

a. _____

b. _____

6. felt

a. _____

b. _____

7. hurt

a. _____

b. _____

8. laid

a. _____

b. _____

9. got

a. _____

b. _____

10. eaten

a. _____

b. _____

EXERCISE 10

EDITING A PARAGRAPH FOR CORRECT VERB FORMS

Correct the errors in verb forms in the following paragraph. There are seven errors.

My responsibilities at home often interferes with my responsibilities at school. I am not a parent, but I live with my parents and my two younger brothers. Because my mother and father work full-time, they turn to me when they has a family emergency. Last week, my five-year-old brother was sick and feverish. My mother thought he had catched a cold and wanted to keep him out of school. That meant I had to stay out of school, too. I missed a quiz in my English class because I was stuck in the house with my sick brother. Something similar happened yesterday. My father's car breaked down on the highway, so he called me at school on my cell-phone. He needed help, so I leaved my math class and picked him up on the road. Some students skip class because they have sleeped through the alarm or spent all night at a party, but I miss class because I be busy with my family.

ALONG THESE LINES/Pearson Education Canada

CHAPTER 20
More on Verbs: Consistency and Voice

Remember that your choice of verb form indicates the time (tense) of your statements. Be careful not to shift from one tense to another unless you have a reason to change the time.

CONSISTENT VERB TENSES

Staying in one tense (unless you have a reason to change tenses) is called **consistency of verb tense**.

> **incorrect shifts in tense:**
> The waitress **ran** to the kitchen with the order in her hand, **raced** back to her customers with glasses of water, and **smiles** calmly.
>
> He **grins** at me from the ticket booth and **closed** the ticket window.

You can correct these errors by putting all the verbs in the same tense.

> **consistent present tense:**
> The waitress **runs** to the kitchen with the order in her hand, **races** back to her customers with glasses of water, and **smiles** calmly.

or

> The waitress **ran** to the kitchen with the order in her hand, **raced** back to her customers with glasses of water, and **smiled** calmly.

> **consistent past tense:**
> He **grins** at me from the ticket booth and **closes** the ticket window.

or

> He **grinned** at me from the ticket booth and **closed** the ticket window.

Whether you correct by changing all the verbs to the present tense or to the past tense, you are making the tenses consistent. Consistency of tense is important in the events you are describing because it helps the reader understand what happened and when it happened.

EXERCISE 1	CORRECTING SENTENCES THAT ARE INCONSISTENT IN TENSE

In each sentence below, one verb is inconsistent in tense. Cross it out and write the correct tense above.

1. Every month I stack all the household bills in a pile and drive to the ATM; then I paid all the bills at one time.

2. On the news, the reporter described the scene of the accident and interviewed a witness, but the reporter never explains how the accident happened.

3. When my father comes home from work, he sits in his recliner and turns on the television because he was too tired to talk.

4. Hundreds of pieces of junk mail come to our house every year and offered us magazine subscriptions, gifts, clothes, and fabulous prizes, but I throw all that junk mail in the garbage.

5. They were the top athletes in their class because they trained rigorously and follow a strict exercise routine.

6. In the kitchen, Adam struggled with the pipes under the sink and swore loudly; meanwhile, his wife calls a plumber.

7. Whenever she is depressed, she buys something chocolate and devoured it.

8. Because the parking lot at the supermarket is always crowded, people parked next door and walk the extra distance.

9. Working nights is hard for me because I had to get up early for classes and I have to find time for my family.

10. Although my friend says he's not afraid of heights, he shrank whenever he is at the edge of a balcony or apartment railing.

EXERCISE 2	EDITING PARAGRAPHS FOR CONSISTENCY OF TENSE

Read the following paragraphs. Then cross out any verbs that are inconsistent in tense and write the correction above. There are four errors in the first paragraph and four errors in the second paragraph.

1.   The rain came suddenly and pelts the holiday crowd with hail-sized nuggets. The storm transformed the scene. People grabbed their blankets and picnic baskets and run for cover. Several people congregated under nearby trees, but the lightning flashed nearby and worried them. Others sit under a picnic table while some raced to their cars. Everyone was soaking wet, and the picnic area becomes a scene of sopping paper plates and waterlogged barbecue grills.

2.   The alarm clock blasted into my ear. I cringed, crawled out from under the covers, and reached my arm across the nightstand. I fling the stupid clock across the room and burrowed back under the covers. The bed feels warm and cozy. I tried to fall back into my dream. But soon my dog leaped into the room, jumped onto the bed, and plants kisses all over my face. In spite of all my attempts to go back to sleep, all the signs told me it is time to get up.

EXERCISE 3	WRITING A PARAGRAPH WITH CONSISTENT VERB TENSES

The following paragraph has many inconsistencies in verb tense; it shifts between past and present tenses. Working with a group, write two versions of the paragraph: one in the present tense and one in the past tense. Half the group can record the present tense version; then the other half can record the past tense version. After both rewrites are complete, read the new paragraph aloud to the whole group.

The day starts off well, but it doesn't end that way. At first, I am confident about taking my driving test and getting my driver's licence. Then I got into the car with the examiner and wait for him to tell me to start. When he does, I turned the key in the ignition and slowly pull out of the parking lot. For some reason, I am sweating with fear, but I tried not to show it. I managed to drive without hitting another car. I remember to stop at a stop sign. But when it came to parallel parking, I knocked down all those orange markers! My driving examiner never cracks a smile or even talked to me. He just gives instructions. But I knew what he was thinking, and I know I won't get a licence. I feel like the worst driver in the world.

ALONG THESE LINES/Pearson Education Canada

Paragraph Revised for Consistent Tenses:

_____

_____

_____

_____

_____

_____

_____

_____

_____

_____

_____

_____

_____

THE PERFECT TENSES

When you are choosing the right verb tense, you need to know about two verb tenses that can make your meaning clear: the present perfect and the past perfect.

The Present Perfect Tense

The **present perfect tense** is made up of the past participle form of the verb plus *have* or *has* as a helping verb. It is used to show an action that started in the past but is still going on in the present.

> **past tense:** My father **drove** a truck for five months. (He doesn't drive a truck anymore, but he did drive one in the past.)

> **present perfect tense:** My father **has driven** a truck for five months. (He started driving a truck five months ago; he is still driving a truck.)

> **past tense:** For years, I **studied** ballet. (I don't study ballet now; I used to.)

> **present perfect tense:** For years, I **have studied** ballet. (I still study ballet.)

Remember, use the present perfect tense to show that an action started in the past and is still going on.

ALONG THESE LINES/Pearson Education Canada

<table>
<tr><td>EXERCISE
4</td><td>DISTINGUISHING BETWEEN THE PAST TENSE
AND THE PRESENT PERFECT TENSE</td></tr>
</table>

Circle the correct verb tense in parentheses in each of the following sentences. Be sure to look carefully at the meaning of the sentence.

1. Parvi (has borrowed/borrowed) my marketing textbook last night.

2. William (sang/has sung) in the choir for many years now.

3. The old car (was/has been) having mechanical problems, but no one wants to get rid of it.

4. I called the office and (have asked/asked) for the supervisor.

5. The comedians (performed/have performed) together for two years and are now appearing at our campus theatre.

6. Two of my best friends (were/have been) musicians but gave music up for business careers.

7. Music videos (were/have been) influencing teenagers for years now.

8. While he was in basic training, he (has written/wrote) many letters home.

9. He (sent/has sent) his resume to fifty companies and accepted a job from the first company that responded.

10. Melissa (lost/has lost) that bracelet three weeks ago.

The Past Perfect Tense

The **past perfect tense** is made up of the past participle form of the verb plus *had* as a helping verb. You can use the past perfect tense to show more than one event occurring in the past; that is, when more than one thing happened in the past but at different times.

> **past tense:** He **washed** the dishes.

> **past perfect tense:** He **had washed** the dishes by the time I came home.
> (He washed the dishes before I came home. Both actions happened in the past, but one happened earlier than the other.)

> **past tense:** Susan **waited** for an hour.

> **past perfect tense:** Susan **had waited** for an hour when she gave up on him.
> (Waiting came first; giving up came second. Both actions are in the past.)

The past perfect tense is especially useful because you write most of your essays in the past tense, and you often need to get further back into the past. Just remember to use *had* with the past participle of the verb, and you'll have the past perfect tense.

| EXERCISE 5 | DISTINGUISHING BETWEEN THE PAST TENSE AND THE PAST PERFECT TENSE |

Circle the correct verb tense in parentheses in the following sentences. Be sure to look carefully at the meaning of the sentence.

1. The child (had hidden/hid) the shattered vase just minutes before his aunt entered the living room.

2. My father drove a rental car last week because he (had wrecked/wrecked) his own car last month.

3. Bernie bought a new laptop yesterday; he (had saved/saved) for it for months.

4. Every weekend, I (had run/ran) errands and ironed my clothes.

5. The salesman asked whether we (had received/received) the merchandise yet.

6. As I (had cut/cut) the pattern for another dress, I thought about becoming a dress designer.

7. They (had left/left) for the party by the time we came to pick them up.

8. She (threw/had thrown) the candy wrapper on the grass and ignored a nearby trash bin.

9. I was not sure if he (had returned/returned) my tools earlier in the day.

10. When the little boy screamed, the mother (had jumped/jumped) up with a worried look on her face.

PASSIVE AND ACTIVE VOICE

Not only do verbs have tenses, but they also have voices. When the subject in the sentence is doing something, the verb is in the **active voice**. When something is done to the subject—when it receives the action of the verb—the verb is in the **passive voice**.

> **active voice:** I painted the house. (**I**, the subject, did it.)
>
> The people on the corner made a donation to the emergency fund.
> (The **people**, the subject, did it.)
>
> **passive voice:** The house was painted by me. (The **house**, the subject, didn't do anything. It received the action—it was painted.)
>
> A donation to the emergency fund was made by the people on the corner.
> (The **donation**, the subject, didn't do anything. It received the action— it was given.)

Notice what happens when you use the passive voice instead of the active:

> **active voice:** I painted the house.
>
> **passive voice:** The house was painted by me.

ALONG THESE LINES/Pearson Education Canada

The sentence in the passive voice is two words longer than the one in the active voice. Yet the sentence using the passive voice doesn't say anything different, and it doesn't say it more clearly than the one using the active voice does.

Using the passive voice can make your sentences wordy, it can slow them down, and it can make them boring. The passive voice can also confuse readers. When the subject of the sentence isn't doing anything, readers may have to look carefully to see who or what *is* doing something. Look at this sentence, for example:

> A decision to fire you was reached.

Who decided to fire you? In this sentence, it's hard to find the answer to that question.

Of course, there will be times when you have to use the passive voice. For example, you may have to use it when you don't know who did something:

> Our house was broken into last night.

> A leather jacket was left behind in the classroom.

But in general, you should avoid using the passive voice and rewrite sentences so they are in the active voice.

EXERCISE 6

REWRITING SENTENCES, CHANGING THE PASSIVE VOICE TO THE ACTIVE VOICE

In the following sentences, change the passive voice to the active voice. If the original sentence doesn't tell you who or what performed the action, add words that tell who or what did it. An example is done for you.

example: He was appointed chief negotiator last night.

rewritten: The union leaders appointed him chief negotiator last night.

1. The scholarship was won by the student with the highest GPA.

   rewritten: _____

   _____

2. A compromise has been reached by the lawyers on both sides.

   rewritten: _____

   _____

3. The wrong number was called several times.

   rewritten: _____

   _____

4. Finally, a candidate was selected by the hiring committee.

   rewritten: _____

   _____

5. Great care was taken to protect the fragile package.

    rewritten: _____

    _____

6. Honorary degrees are conferred every year by universities across the country.

    rewritten: _____

    _____

7. Every day, the park is patrolled by a security guard.

    rewritten: _____

    _____

8. Last week, I was called on by an insurance agent.

    rewritten: _____

    _____

9. The real reason for his tardiness was not known by his teacher.

    rewritten: _____

    _____

10. The murder is being investigated by the police.

    rewritten: _____

    _____

Avoiding Unnecessary Shifts in Voice

Just as you should be consistent in the tense of verbs, you should be consistent in the voice of verbs. Don't shift from active voice to passive voice, or vice versa, without a good reason to do so.

                    active   passive
shift: I **designed** the decorations for the dance; **they were hung** by Chuck.

                    active   active
rewritten: I **designed** the decorations for the dance; **Chuck hung them**.

                         passive   active
shift: Many **problems were discussed** by the council members, but **they found** no easy answers.

                              active   active
rewritten: The council **members discussed** many problems, but **they found** no easy answers.

Being consistent in voice can help you to write clearly and smoothly.

ALONG THESE LINES/Pearson Education Canada

EXERCISE 7	REWRITING SENTENCES TO CORRECT SHIFTS IN VOICE

Rewrite the following sentences so that all the verbs are in the active voice. You may change the wording to make the sentences clear, smooth, and consistent in voice.

1. Christine called Jack yesterday, but I was called by Tom today.

   rewritten: _____

   _____

2. A revised set of rules is being written by the disciplinary committee; the committee is also writing a list of penalties.

   rewritten: _____

   _____

3. That girl can be helped by your advice because you know her problems.

   rewritten: _____

   _____

4. The windows were opened by the office workers as the temperature soared above thirty degrees.

   rewritten: _____

   _____

5. It was decided by a team of experts that the water contains harmful bacteria.

   rewritten: _____

   _____

6. Some people worship celebrities; musicians, actors, and athletes are regarded as superhuman.

   rewritten: _____

   _____

7. Parvinder showed his dismay when his brother Sikander was rejected by the admissions committee.

   rewritten: _____

   _____

8. If a deal was made by the officers, I never knew about it.

   rewritten: _____

   _____

9. When the crime was committed by my brothers, they didn't tell me about it.

    rewritten: _____

    _____

10. Denise expressed her happiness when her father was praised by the mayor.

    rewritten: _____

    _____

Small Reminders about Verbs

There are a few errors that people tend to make with verbs. If you are aware of these errors, you'll be on the lookout for them as you edit your writing.

Used To Be careful when you write that someone *used to* do, say, or feel something. It is incorrect to write *use to*.

> **not this:** Janine ~~use to~~ visit her mother every week. They ~~use to~~ like Thai food.

> **but this:** Janine **used to** visit her mother every week. They **used to** like Thai food.

Could Have, Should Have, Would Have Using *of* instead of *have* with *could*, *should*, and *would* is another error with verbs.

> **not this:** I ~~could of~~ done better on the test.

> **but this:** I **could have** done better on the test.

> **not this:** He ~~should of~~ been paying attention.

> **but this:** He **should have** been paying attention.

> **not this:** The girls ~~would of~~ liked to visit Ottawa.

> **but this:** The girls **would have** liked to visit Ottawa.

Would Have/Had If you are writing about something that might have been possible, but that did not happen, use *had* as the helping verb.

> **not this:** If I ~~would have~~ taken a foreign language in high school, I wouldn't have to take one now.

> **but this:** If I **had** taken a foreign language in high school, I wouldn't have to take one now.

> **not this:** I wish they ~~would have~~ won the game.

> **but this:** I wish they **had** won the game.

> **not this:** If she ~~would have~~ been smart, she would have called a plumber.

> **but this:** If she **had** been smart, she would have called a plumber.

EXERCISE 8

WRITING SENTENCES WITH THE CORRECT VERB FORMS

Complete this exercise with a partner or with a group. Follow directions to write or complete each of the following sentences.

1. Complete this sentence and add a verb in the correct tense: I had cleaned the whole house by the time

   _____

   _____

   _____

2. Write a sentence that is more than six words long and that uses the words *has studied karate* in the middle of the sentence.

   _____

   _____

   _____

3. Write a sentence that uses the past-tense form of both these words: *run, stumble.*

   _____

   _____

   _____

4. Write a sentence in the passive voice.

   _____

   _____

   _____

5. Write a sentence in the active voice.

   _____

   _____

   _____

6. Write a sentence that uses *would have* and *had*.

   _____

   _____

   _____

7. Write a sentence that is more than six words long and that uses the words *had prepared* and *before*.

   _____

   _____

   _____

8. Write a sentence of more than six words that uses the words *used to.*

_____

_____

_____

9. Write a sentence that contains two verbs in the same tense.

_____

_____

_____

10. Write a sentence that uses the words *should have.*

_____

_____

_____

EXERCISE

9

EDITING A PARAGRAPH FOR ERRORS IN VERBS: CONSISTENCY, CORRECT TENSES, AND VOICE

Edit the following paragraph for errors in verb consistency, tense, or voice. There are eight errors.

Last week, a tragedy struck our town, and it was particularly terrible because it was so senseless. Two cars sped down a dark country road, one driver loses control, and four high-school students died. The dangers of that road were known by everyone at the high school; two accidents already occurred there earlier in the year. It was a notoriously unsafe road for years, yet nothing was done by the local police. More and better enforcement could of saved lives. Even speed bumps could have helped. Of course, the two drivers who drove down that stretch of concrete at more than 140 kilometres per hour do not use their heads. They choose to risk their lives long before they crashed. If they were more rational and less in love with street racing, four people would be alive today.

CHAPTER 21
Making Subjects and Verbs Agree

Subjects and verbs must *agree in number*. **Subject–verb agreement** means a singular subject must be matched with a singular verb form; a plural subject must be matched with a plural verb form.

singular subject singular verb

My **sister walks** to work every morning.

plural subject   plural verb

Nadeer, Myoungok, and Joel study hard.

singular subject singular verb

That **movie is** too violent for me.

plural subject   plural verb

Bulky **packages are** difficult to carry.

Caution: Remember that a *regular verb* has an *s* ending in one singular form in the present tense—the form that goes with *he*, *she*, *it*, or their equivalent.

He **makes** me feel confident.

She **appreciates** intelligent conversation.

It **seems** like a good buy.

Raheel **runs** every day.

That girl **swims** well.

The machine **breaks** down too often.

EXERCISE 1	SUBJECT–VERB AGREEMENT: SELECTING THE CORRECT VERB FORM

Select the correct form of the verb in parentheses in each sentence below.

1. My sisters (spend/spends) too much time writing and reading email.
2. If the weather is cold, I (like/likes) to drink coffee with double cream and double sugar.
3. Shyness (keep/keeps) many people from making friends.
4. Interesting conversations always (start/starts) at the end of our psychology class.
5. When he (want/wants) something done right, Ayez can be very demanding.

6. The basement and attic (need/needs) a good cleaning.

7. I see that cat every night; it (belong/belongs) to the people across the hall.

8. I have to get away from my manager because his lack of leadership (make/makes) me want to scream.

9. An alarm system (cost/costs) more than I want to pay.

10. You (is/are) my best friend, and I trust you with my secrets.

EXERCISE **2**	CORRECTING ERRORS IN SUBJECT–VERB AGREEMENT IN A PARAGRAPH

There are errors in subject–verb agreement in the following paragraph. If a verb does not agree with its subject, change the verb form. Cross out the incorrect verb form and write the correct one above. There are four errors in agreement in the paragraph.

Every night, my sister follows the same routine. She pours a big glass of diet cola, sit down in an old easy chair, and settles down for a night on the telephone. My sister always call the same person, her best friend Irene. She and Irene talks for hours about the most trivial subjects. The two girls gossip about their friends, about their enemies, about what happened that day, and about what will happen the next day. My brother says men never spend as much time on the phone. But he always say that while he is trying to get the phone from my sister so he can make his evening calls!

PRONOUNS AS SUBJECTS

Pronouns can be used as subjects. Pronouns are words that take the place of nouns. When pronouns are used as subjects, pronouns and verbs must *agree in number*.

The Infobox provides a list of personal pronouns (those referring specifically to a person or thing) and the regular verb forms that agree with them in the present tense.

INFOBOX	SUBJECTIVE PRONOUNS AND A PRESENT-TENSE REGULAR VERB

pronoun	verb	
I	listen	
you	listen	all singular forms
he, she, it	listens	
we	listen	
you	listen	all plural forms
they	listen	

ALONG THESE LINES/Pearson Education Canada

In all of the following sentences, the pronoun used as the subject of the sentence agrees in number with the verb.

singular pronoun singular verb
I make the best lassi in town.

singular pronoun singular verb
You dance very well.

singular pronoun singular verb
She performs like a trained athlete.

plural pronoun plural verb
We need a new refrigerator.

plural pronoun plural verb
They understand the situation.

SPECIAL PROBLEMS WITH AGREEMENT

Agreement seems fairly simple: If a subject is singular, use a singular verb form. If a subject is plural, use a plural verb form. However, there are special problems with agreement that will come up in your writing. Sometimes it's hard to find the subject of a sentence; at other times, it's hard to determine whether a subject is singular or plural.

Finding the Subject

When you are checking for subject–verb agreement, you can find the real subject of the sentence by first eliminating the prepositional phrases. To find the real subject, put parentheses around the prepositional phrases. Then it's easy to find the subject, because nothing in a prepositional phrase can ever be the subject of a sentence (see Chapter 12). In the sentences below, the prepositional phrases have been placed in parentheses to reveal the subject and verb.

S   V
One (of my oldest friends) **became** a social worker.

S   V
A **student** (from one)(of the nearby school districts) **has won** the championship.

S   V
The **stores** (across the street) (from my house) **open** early in the morning.

S   V
You, (with all your silly jokes), **are** a nice person.

EXERCISE

3

FINDING THE REAL SUBJECT BY RECOGNIZING PREPOSITIONAL PHRASES

Put parentheses around all the prepositional phrases in the following sentences. Put an *S* above each subject and a *V* above each verb.

1. Two of my favourite television shows are crime dramas with lots of action scenes.

2. The cellphone with MP3 capacity is the best choice.

3. One of the three people on the decorations committee works as a professional artist.

4. The clerk in the "Geek Squad" T-shirt became a new employee.

5. A representative of the company from the proposed site has presented a convincing proposal.

6. The tree behind the house is 100 years old.

7. The elementary school with the modern architecture was built down the road from my house.

8. With a great deal of poise, she took the termination notice from her employer's hand.

9. The coat in the downstairs closet has my keys in its pocket.

10. The house with the solar panels contributes to the city's power source.

EXERCISE

4

SELECTING THE CORRECT VERB FORM BY IDENTIFYING PREPOSITIONAL PHRASES

In the following sentences, put parentheses around all the prepositional phrases; then circle the correct verb form in parentheses in each sentence.

1. A speaker from The Council of Cities (is/are) lecturing in our anthropology class today.

2. Several of the biggest bargains in the shop (lie/lies) stashed in the back room.

3. One of the contestants from the semifinal rounds (face/faces) the winner of this round.

4. The consequences of her argument with her father (seem/seems) severe.

5. A salesperson with a background in communications (has/have) a competitive advantage.

6. With a brand-new backpack and new shoes, the little girl on the bus (look/looks) excited on the first day of school.

7. A friend of mine from the Queen Charlotte Islands (love/loves) the West Edmonton Mall.

8. A change of plans (is/are) no reason for a change in your attitude.

9. An honest statement of the facts (is/are) behind the mayor's popularity in this city.

10. A person with energy, intelligence, and drive (meet/meets) the requirements for this job.

Changed Word Order

You are probably used to looking for the subject of a sentence in front of the verb, but not all sentences follow this pattern. Questions, sentences beginning with words like *here* or *there*, and other sentence patterns change the word order. So you have to look carefully to check for subject–verb agreement.

          V   S

Where **are** my **homework assignments?**

          V S V

When **is he going** to work?

                    V   S

Behind the courthouse **stands** a huge **statue.**

          V   S

There **are potholes** in the road.

          V   S

Here **is** the **reason** for his impatience.

EXERCISE 5

MAKING SUBJECTS AND VERBS AGREE IN SENTENCES WITH CHANGED WORD ORDER

In each of the following sentences, underline the subject; then circle the correct verb form in parentheses.

1. Included in the package of coupons (was/were) a coupon for a free breakfast.

2. Among my happiest memories (is/are) the memory of a day at the beach.

3. Along the side of the road (sit/sits) a fruit stand and a gas station.

4. There (was/were) several explanations for his tantrum.

5. Here (is/are) my brother and sister, in the midst of an argument about my birthday party.

6. Behind the fence (wait/waits) a fierce and evil dog.

7. There (was/were) a sudden increase in the price of groceries.

8. Under the porch (scurry/scurries) a mound of termites.

9. Where (was/were) the photographs of your trip to Mexico?

10. Here (is/are) the insurance policy for the car.

EXERCISE 6

MORE ON SELECTING THE CORRECT VERB FORM BY IDENTIFYING PREPOSITIONAL PHRASES

Put parentheses around all the prepositional phrases in the sentences below. Then circle the correct verb form in parentheses in each sentence.

1. A volunteer from Citizens for a Green Earth (speak/speaks) at the city council meeting on Wednesdays.

2. Several of the winners of the provincial semifinals (is/are) at the opening ceremonies.

3. One of the photographs from Mr. Khouri's portfolio (hang/hangs) on exhibit at the Photography Centre.

4. The protestors at the G8 trade conference (comes/come) from all parts of the world.

5. A person with weak managerial skills (has/have) little chance of success in business.

6. With his experience and hours of training, the Canadian swimmer (ranks/rank) far above the other swimmers at the meet.

7. One of the bushes at the edge of the fields (is/are) a rare type of wildflower from England.

8. Spending beyond your means (leads/lead) to money problems.

9. Her impressive background in medicine (makes/make) Dr. Baimel the most respected doctor at the clinic.

10. A college with a diverse student body, good teachers, and small classes (is/are) located within ten kilometres of your house.

COMPOUND SUBJECTS

A **compound subject** is two or more subjects joined by *and*, *or*, or *nor*. When subjects are joined by *and*, they are usually plural.

S   S   V
Jermaine and **Lisa are** bargain hunters.

S   S   V
The **house** and the **garden need** attention.

S   S   V
A **wireless card** and a **fingerprint reader are** in the box with the laptop.

ALONG THESE LINES/Pearson Education Canada

Caution: Be careful to check for a compound subject when the word order changes.

                      V   S   S

In the box with the laptop **are** a **wireless card** and a **fingerprint reader**. (Two things, a **wireless card** and a **fingerprint reader**, are in the box with the laptop.)

        V   S   S

Here **are** a **picture** of your father and a **copy** of his birth certificate. (Two things, a **picture** and a **copy**, are here.)

When subjects are joined by *or, either/or, neither/nor,* or *not only/but also,* the verb form agrees with the subject closer to the verb.

                singular S   plural S plural V

Not only the restaurant **manager** but also the **waiters were** pleased with the new policy.

           plural S   singular S   singular V

Not only the **waiters** but also the restaurant **manager was** pleased with the new policy.

           plural S singular S   singular V

Either the **parents** or the **boy walks** the dog every morning.

           singular S   plural S   plural V

Either the **boy** or the **parents walk** the dog every morning.

Caution: Sometimes a connecting word or phrase will come between the subject and the verb. Connectors such as *as well as, along with, in addition to, including, together with, plus,* and *with* are prepositions rather than coordinating conjunctions, so they don't form compound subjects.

        S   V

Her **sister** as well as her brothers **comes** home every weekend. (The subject is *sister*, so it takes a singular verb form.)

             S   V

My favourite **movies** as well as my novel **were taken** from me until my assignment was finished. (The subject is *movies*, so it takes a plural verb form.)

EXERCISE **7**	MAKING SUBJECTS AND VERBS AGREE: COMPOUND SUBJECTS

Circle the correct form of the verb in parentheses in each of the following sentences.

1. Neither my sisters nor my cousin (excels/excel) at sports.

2. When they came to this country, Aziz and Omid (was/were) eager to find employment.

3. Here (sits/sit) the guest of honour and her husband.

4. Either Kevin or his sisters (takes/take) out the garbage on Saturdays.

5. Either his sisters or Kevin (takes/take) out the garbage on Saturdays.

6. A coffee cake as well as doughnuts (was/were) in the bag.

7. Under the sofa there (is/are) an old ragged slipper and a shrivelled apple.

8. Her impressive background in medicine, together with her calm and soothing bedside manner, (makes/make) Dr. Baimel the most respected doctor at the clinic.

9. Not only the teacher but also the students (like/likes) the new classroom.

10. Hanging out with my friends and complaining about my parents (was/were) my principal activities in high school.

EXERCISE 8

MORE ON MAKING SUBJECTS AND VERBS AGREE: COMPOUND SUBJECTS

Circle the correct form of the verb in parentheses in each of the following sentences.

1. Not only the sausages but also the garlic bread (was/were) dripping with olive oil.

2. Neither the tire nor the shock absorbers (is/are) in good shape.

3. There (stands/stand) a small boy and his parents waiting at the end of the line.

4. Certainly, either Mr. Lopez or Mr. Woo (qualifies/qualify) for the position.

5. Here (was/were) my parents, tired after the long trip.

6. Kindness and generosity (make/makes) a person welcome in any group.

7. Here (is/are) a video of the crime and eyewitness testimony from a neighbour.

8. Whenever I come home for a visit, either my father or my brother (says/say) I look tired.

9. Within weeks of Mela's graduation, there (was/were) a family crisis as well as an accident facing her.

10. On Fridays, neither crazy drivers nor my nasty boss (spoils/spoil) my good mood.

INDEFINITE PRONOUNS

Indefinite pronouns, unlike personal pronouns, do not refer to a specific person or thing. Some indefinite pronouns always take a singular verb.

INFOBOX	**INDEFINITE PRONOUNS THAT TAKE SINGULAR VERBS**		
anybody	either	neither	somebody
anyone	everybody	nobody	someone
anything	everyone	nothing	something
each	everything	one	

If you want to write clearly and correctly, you must memorize these words and remember that they always take a singular verb. Using your common sense isn't enough because some of these words seem plural: for example, *everybody* seems to mean more than one person, but in grammatically correct English it takes a singular verb. Here are some examples of the pronouns used with singular verbs:

> singular S   singular V
> **Everyone** in town **is talking** about the scandal.

> singular S   singular V
> **Each** of the boys **is** talented.

> singular S   singular V
> **One** of their biggest concerns **is** crime in the streets.

> singular S   singular V
> **Neither** of the cats **is** mine.

Hint: You can memorize the indefinite pronouns as the *-one, -thing,* and *-body* words—every*one,* every*thing,* every*body,* and so forth—plus *each, either,* and *neither.*

Other indefinite pronouns such as *some, most,* and *all* can take either singular or plural verbs, depending on the sentence. If the sentence is talking about something you can count, then the verb must be plural; if the sentence is talking about something you cannot count, then the verb must be singular.

> All of the students *are going* to graduation. (You can count the number of students.)
>
> All of my flour *is* whole wheat. (You can't count flour.)

EXERCISE **9**	**MAKING SUBJECTS AND VERBS AGREE: USING INDEFINITE PRONOUNS**

Circle the correct verb form in parentheses in the following sentences.

1. Anybody in the suburbs (knows/know) the way to that freeway exit.

2. Nothing in the sales racks (is/are) sufficiently marked down.

3. Somebody (has/have) painted graffiti all over the walls.

4. All of the jewellery from that store (was/were) stolen.

5. (Has/Have) some of the toddlers had lunch?

6. Everybody in both schools (listens/listen) to the same radio station.

7. Nobody from the service clubs (volunteers/volunteer) for this project.

8. (Is/Are) some of these houses more environmentally friendly than others?

9. One of my most foolish decisions (was/were) to call in sick last week.

10. Here (is/are) someone who has come to see you.

EXERCISE 10

MORE ON MAKING SUBJECTS AND VERBS AGREE: USING INDEFINITE PRONOUNS

Circle the correct verb form in parentheses in the following sentences.

1. After the graduation ceremony, most of the guests (is/are) invited to a reception in the lobby.

2. Either of the applicants for the job (satisfies/satisfy) the criteria for hiring.

3. Someone (deliver/delivers) the paper very early in the morning.

4. Each of Michael's business trips (costs/cost) the office thousands of dollars.

5. Neither of my parents (like/likes) the same hockey team as I.

6. On Canada Day, everyone in the neighbourhood (goes/go) to see the fireworks at the marina.

7. Something in the stranger's explanation (hint/hints) at a mystery.

8. Beneath the stack of documents, there (was/were) nothing except a rusty nail.

9. At the end of the movie, (was/were) anyone crying?

10. Everything about cricket (confuse/confuses) me.

COLLECTIVE NOUNS

Collective nouns refer to more than one person or thing.

INFOBOX	SOME COLLECTIVE NOUNS	
audience	corporation	government
board	council	group
class	couple	jury
committee	crowd	staff
company	family	team

Collective nouns usually take a singular verb.

singular S singular V

The **committee is sponsoring** a fundraiser.

singular S singular V

The **audience was** impatient.

singular S singular V

The **jury has reached** a verdict.

The singular verb is used because the group is sponsoring, or getting impatient, or reaching a verdict, *as one unit*. Collective nouns take a plural verb only when the members of the group are acting individually, not as a unit.

The senior **class are fighting** among themselves. (The phrase *among themselves* shows that the class is not acting as one unit.)

EXERCISE **11**	MAKING SUBJECTS AND VERBS AGREE: USING COLLECTIVE NOUNS

Circle the correct verb form in parentheses in each of the following sentences.

1. My family (is/are) moving to another province next month.
2. The company with the safest work environment (receives/receive) an award tomorrow.
3. Our class (has/have) less school spirit than other classes.
4. The student council (meet/meets) every Tuesday afternoon.
5. My group of friends (is/are) attending two different colleges.
6. A team from the Philippines (was/were) competing in the international contest.
7. After Labour Day, the crowd at the beach (isn't/aren't) so large.
8. A truly enthusiastic audience (help/helps) the performers.
9. The governing board (vote/votes) on the annual budget tomorrow night.
10. The men's club (has/have) never endorsed candidates for political office.

MAKING SUBJECTS AND VERBS AGREE: THE BOTTOM LINE

As you've probably realized, making subjects and verbs agree is not as simple as it first appears. But if you can remember the basic ideas in this section, you will be able to apply them automatically as you edit your own writing. The Infobox below provides a quick summary of subject–verb agreement.

INFOBOX	MAKING SUBJECTS AND VERBS AGREE: A SUMMARY

1. Subjects and verbs should agree in number: singular subjects take singular verb forms; plural subjects take plural verb forms.
2. When pronouns are used as subjects, they must agree in number with verbs.
3. Nothing in a prepositional phrase can be the subject of the sentence.
4. Word order can change in questions, sentences beginning with *here* or *there*, and other sentences, so look carefully for the subject.
5. When subjects are joined by *and*, they are usually plural.
6. When subjects are joined by *or, either/or, neither/nor*, or *not only/but also*, the verb form agrees with the subject closer to the verb.
7. Many indefinite pronouns take singular verbs.
8. Collective nouns usually take singular verbs unless the members of the group are acting individually.

EXERCISE 12	A COMPREHENSIVE EXERCISE ON SUBJECT–VERB AGREEMENT

Circle the correct verb form in parentheses in the following sentences.

1. Some of the cooks at the restaurant (was/were) in my math class last year.
2. Anybody from Saskatchewan (know/knows) how to stay cool in the summer.
3. When (was/were) the packages delivered?
4. Each of the cars on the showroom floor (was/were) polished to a dazzling brightness.
5. Within the circle of diamonds (sit/sits) a deep red stone.
6. Neither my cousin nor his parents ever (think/thinks) about home security.
7. Every day, apathy and pessimism (grow/grows) stronger in the city.
8. Nothing in ten years (has/have) pleased her more than that party.
9. The candidate with a strong background in liberal arts and good leadership skills (remain/remains) my first choice for the position.
10. Behind the refrigerator (sit/sits) a giant cockroach.
11. Everything in the Botanical Gardens (seem/seems) rare and exotic.
12. Down the street from the bank there (is/are) a Chinese restaurant and an Italian deli.
13. Because of the lateness of the hour, the jury (is/are) adjourning until tomorrow.
14. The company (was/were) not eager to recruit college graduates.
15. Clearly defined steps and a realistic schedule (help/helps) you complete a difficult project.
16. If the city doesn't fix that road soon, someone (is/are) going to have an accident.

ALONG THESE LINES/Pearson Education Canada

17. Last year there (was/were) a shooting and two muggings in the parking lot by the club.

18. Neither of my parents (is/are) anxious about my decision.

19. In spite of the rejection letters, Julie still (try/tries) to get her books published

20. Here (is/are) your final marks.

<table>
<tr><td>

EXERCISE

13

</td><td>

WRITING SENTENCES WITH SUBJECT–VERB AGREEMENT

With a partner or with a group, write two sentences for each of the following phrases. Use a verb that fits and put it in the present tense. Be sure that the verb agrees with the subject.

</td></tr>
</table>

1. A crate of oranges _____

_____

A crate of oranges _____

_____

2. Either Superman or Batman _____

_____

Either Superman or Batman _____

_____

3. The committee _____

_____

The committee _____

_____

4. Thelma and Jody _____

_____

Thelma and Jody _____

_____

5. Everything in my closet _____

_____

Everything in my closet _____

_____

6. Someone from the suburbs _____

_____

Someone from the suburbs _____

_____

7. Not only the child but also his parents _____

_____

Not only the child but also his parents _____

_____

8. Anybody in town _____

_____

Anybody in town _____

_____

9. One of my greatest fears _____

_____

One of my greatest fears _____

_____

10. Everyone in the office _____

_____

Everyone in the office _____

_____

EXERCISE

14

👤+👤

CREATE YOUR OWN TEXT ON SUBJECT–VERB AGREEMENT

Working with a partner or with a group, create your own grammar handbook. Below is a list of rules on subject–verb agreement. Write one sentence that is an example of each rule. The first one is done for you.

Rule 1: Subjects and verbs should agree in number: singular subjects take singular verb forms; plural subjects take plural verb forms.

example: A battered old car stands in the front yard. _____

Rule 2: When pronouns are used as subjects, they must agree in number with verbs.

example: _____

_____

Rule 3: Nothing in a prepositional phrase can be the subject of the sentence.

example: _____

_____

Rule 4: Word order can change in questions, sentences beginning with *here* or *there*, and other sentences, so look carefully for the subject.

ALONG THESE LINES/Pearson Education Canada

example: _____

_____

Rule 5: When subjects are joined by *and*, they are usually plural.

example: _____

_____

Rule 6: When subjects are joined by *or, either/or, neither/nor,* or *not only/ but also,* the verb form agrees with the subject closer to the verb.

example: _____

_____

Rule 7: Many indefinite pronouns take singular verbs.

example: _____

_____

Rule 8: Collective nouns usually take singular verbs unless the members of the group are acting individually.

example: _____

_____

EXERCISE 15

EDITING A PARAGRAPH FOR ERRORS IN SUBJECT–VERB AGREEMENT

Edit the following paragraph by correcting any verbs that do not agree with their subjects. Write your corrections above the lines. There are five errors.

There is two simple lessons adults could learn from very young children. First of all, have anybody ever seen a toddler hesitate to have fun? Small children do not hold back; they run directly toward the joy of a bright flower or a pet or a parent's embrace. Yet everybody over the age of fifteen seem to worry about enjoying a moment of happiness. People debate whether they have time to enjoy the flower or play with the dog. They think hugging a child can be done later, after they have gone to work and made money to support the child. Toddlers, in contrast, lives fully in the moment, and that is the second lesson we can learn from them. When small children are building a house with their plastic blocks, they are fully focused on that project. Adults may be building a patio out of real bricks, but at the same time they are also talking on their cell phones and obsessing about tomorrow's workload. The adults have lost their ability to enjoy and to focus on a single, present moment. A group of children are often wiser than stressed and anxious adults.

CHAPTER 22
Using Pronouns Correctly: Agreement and Reference

NOUNS AND PERSONAL PRONOUNS

Nouns are the names of persons, places, or things:

> **Jack** is a good friend. (**Jack** is the name of a person.)
>
> The band is from **Winnipeg**. (**Winnipeg** is the name of a place.)
>
> I hate the **movie**. (**Movie** is the name of a thing.)

Pronouns are words that substitute for nouns. A pronoun's **antecedent** is the word or words the pronoun replaces. Personal pronouns refer to specific persons (or animals or objects); they can act as subjects or objects, or can show possession (see Chapter 23).

>   antecedent   pronoun
>
> **Jack** is a good friend; **he** is very trustworthy.

>   antecedent   pronoun
>
> I wasn't interested in **the movies** but my friend made me watch **them**.

>   antecedent   pronoun
>
> **Playing hockey** was fun, but **it** started to take up too much of my time.

>   antecedent   pronoun
>
> **Mike and Michelle** are sure that the money is **theirs** to enjoy.

>   antecedent   pronoun
>
> **Anya and I** gave away **our** old clothes.

>   antecedent   pronoun
>
> **The car** almost lost **its** muffler; it was dragging on the ground.

EXERCISE 1

IDENTIFYING THE ANTECEDENTS OF PRONOUNS

In each of the following sentences, a pronoun is underlined. Underline the word or words that are the antecedents of the underlined pronoun. Note that the sentences may contain other pronouns that are not underlined.

1. Kim and I are quitting tomorrow because <u>we</u> can't make enough money at the job.

2. Riding a stationary bike is good exercise because <u>it</u> strengthens leg muscles.

ALONG THESE LINES/Pearson Education Canada

3. My parents said <u>they</u> couldn't afford to send me to college.

4. The museum presented <u>its</u> best collection last week.

5. David, can <u>you</u> ever forgive me?

6. A small boy learns a great deal by observing <u>his</u> father.

7. Alan loves swimming, but I am not fond of <u>it</u>.

8. We told the security guard we had lost our tickets, but <u>he</u> wouldn't let us in.

9. The musicians at the club play <u>their</u> last set at midnight.

10. Constant criticism is dangerous; in fact, <u>it</u> can destroy a person's confidence.

AGREEMENT OF A PRONOUN AND ITS ANTECEDENT

A pronoun must agree in number with its antecedent. If the antecedent is singular, the pronoun must be singular. If the antecedent is plural, then the pronoun must be plural.

> singular antecedent   singular pronoun
> **Susan** tried to arrive on time, but **she** got caught in traffic.

> plural antecedent   plural pronoun
> **Susan and Ray** tried to arrive on time, but **they** got caught in traffic.

> plural antecedent   plural pronoun
> **The visitors** tried to arrive on time, but **they** got caught in traffic.

Agreement of pronoun and antecedent seems fairly simple. If an antecedent is singular, use a singular pronoun. If an antecedent is plural, use a plural pronoun. There are, however, some special problems with agreement of pronouns, and these problems will come up in your writing. If you become familiar with the explanations, examples, and exercises that follow, you'll be ready to handle the special problems.

INDEFINITE PRONOUNS

As we discussed in Chapter 21, certain words, called **indefinite pronouns**, are always singular. Therefore, if an indefinite pronoun is the antecedent, the pronoun that replaces it must be singular. Some examples of indefinite pronouns are listed in an Infobox in Chapter 21, page 411.

You may think that *everybody* is plural, but in grammatically correct English it is a singular word. Therefore, if you want to write clearly and correctly, memorize these words as the *-one*, *-thing*, and *-body* words—every*one*, every*thing*, every*body*, and so forth—plus *each*, *either*, *neither*. If any of these words is an antecedent, the pronoun that refers to it must be singular.

singular antecedent   singular pronoun

Each of the Boy Scouts received **his** merit badge.

singular antecedent   singular pronoun

Everyone on the girls' volleyball team donated **her** time to the project.

Using Gender-Neutral Language

Consider this sentence:

Everybody in the math class brought _____ own calculator.

How do you choose the correct pronoun to fill in the blank? If everybody in the class is male, you can write

Everybody in the math class brought **his** own calculator.

Or, if everybody in the class is female, you can write

Everybody in the math class brought **her** own calculator.

Or, if the class has students of both sexes, you can write

Everybody in the math class brought **his or her** own calculator.

In the past, most writers used the pronoun *his* to refer to both men and women. Today, many writers try to use *his or her* to avoid sexual bias. If you find using *his or her* is getting awkward or repetitive, you can rewrite the sentence and *make the antecedent plural*:

correct: **The students** in the math class brought **their** own calculators.

But you can't shift from singular to plural. You can't write

incorrect: **Everybody** in the math class brought **their** own calculators.

EXERCISE **2**	**MAKING PRONOUNS AND ANTECEDENTS AGREE**

Write the appropriate pronoun in the blank space in each of the following sentences. Look carefully for the antecedent before you choose the pronoun.

1. My essay is disorganized and confusing; I really should edit
   _____.

2. Years ago, most people were careful with their cash;
   _____ were taught to save money, not to spend it.

3. I noticed that a woman was advertising a reward for the return of
   _____ BlackBerry.

4. The restaurant was very luxurious; all of _____
   glassware was made of crystal.

5. When the little girl had a birthday party, _____ wanted to invite the whole neighbourhood.

6. Children with nothing to do all summer may wind up getting into trouble with _____ friends because of boredom.

7. Neither of the men chosen to lead the campaign wanted to devote _____ time to fund-raising.

8. Everyone named an Outstanding Mother of the Year had _____ own opinion about the ceremony.

9. Each of the brothers has won an athletic scholarship to the college of _____ choice.

10. I am beginning to enjoy my exercise class; _____ helps me relax.

EXERCISE 3

MORE ON MAKING PRONOUNS AND ANTECEDENTS AGREE

Write the appropriate pronoun in the blank in each of the following sentences. Look carefully for the antecedent before you choose the pronoun.

1. Bring home anything from Perfect Pizzas; _____ will taste good to me.

2. At the women's basketball tournament, one of the players hurt _____ back.

3. Every Saturday, Lennie and Geraldo take _____ cars to the car wash.

4. One of my antique cups is cracked so badly that _____ cannot be repaired.

5. All of my aunts gave me _____ version of the family feud that has been going on for years.

6. Everyone in the management program wore _____ best dress to the graduation dinner dance.

7. Ray cleaned his house thoroughly because he wanted everything to look _____ best for the visitors.

8. I think somebody from the men's soccer team left _____ cleats behind.

9. Nothing at the movies looked as if _____ would appeal to a teenage audience.

10. Either of the men could have given _____ seat to the elderly lady.

COLLECTIVE NOUNS AND THEIR PRONOUNS

Collective nouns refer to more than one person or thing. See the examples in the Infobox in Chapter 21, page 412.

Most of the time, collective nouns take a singular pronoun.

> collective noun   singular pronoun
>
> The **team** that was ahead in the playoffs lost **its** home game.

> collective noun   singular pronoun
>
> The **corporation** changed **its** policy on parental leave.

Collective nouns are usually singular because the group is losing a game or changing a policy *as one*, as a unit. Collective nouns take a plural pronoun only when the members of the group are acting individually, not as a unit.

> The **class** picked up **their** class rings this morning. (The members of the class pick up their own rings, individually.)

| **EXERCISE** **4** | **MAKING PRONOUNS AND ANTECEDENTS AGREE: COLLECTIVE NOUNS** |

Circle the correct pronoun in parentheses in each of the following sentences.

1. The computer company has a reputation for being extremely generous to (their/its) employees.

2. Skyward Airlines was involved in a campaign to change (their/its) image.

3. The flock of sheep enters the barn to have (their/its) coats shorn.

4. After the singer left the stage, the audience expressed (their/its) disappointment with boos and shouts.

5. Two of the teams were selling candy to raise money for (their/its) equipment.

6. The family lost (their/its) home in a fire last week.

7. I loved working at The Castle Company because (it/they) gave me such a generous package of benefits.

8. The club made a list of (its/their) responsibilities.

9. The general was worried that the army would not be able to hold (their/its) position.

10. The gang began to fall apart when the members started finding other things to do with (its/their) time.

| **EXERCISE** **5** | **EDITING A PARAGRAPH FOR ERRORS OF PRONOUN–ANTECEDENT AGREEMENT** |

Read the following paragraph carefully, looking for errors in agreement of pronouns and their antecedents. Cross out any pronouns that do not agree with their antecedents and write the correct pronoun above. There are five pronouns that need to be corrected.

ALONG THESE LINES/Pearson Education Canada

The Paper Company is a great place to work. The managers are firm but friendly in their relations with the employees, and working conditions are pleasant. The company has designed their policies to motivate employees, not to intimidate them. Everybody in the workplace knows they will be treated fairly. The Paper Company is not only considerate of workers; it is concerned for the environment. All the products are made of recycled paper. Thus, each of the items made for sale contributes their part to conservation. Workers and managers can feel good, knowing that he or she can help the planet. I wish everyone in this country would do their part, just as The Paper Company does.

EXERCISE 6

WRITING SENTENCES WITH PRONOUN–ANTECEDENT AGREEMENT

With a partner or with a group, write a sentence for each of the following pairs of words, using each pair as a pronoun and its antecedent. The first pair is done for you.

1. students . . . their

   sentence: Students who have children have to plan their time carefully.

2. council . . . its

   sentence: _____

3. anyone . . . his or her

   sentence: _____

4. celebrities . . . they

   sentence: _____

5. complaining . . . it

   sentence: _____

6. neither . . . her

   sentence: _____

7. each . . . his or her

    sentence: _____

    _____

8. Canada . . . it

    sentence: _____

    _____

9. movies and popular music . . . they

    sentence: _____

    _____

10. credit card debt . . . it

    sentence: _____

    _____

PRONOUNS AND THEIR ANTECEDENTS: BEING CLEAR

Remember that pronouns are words that replace or refer to other words, and those other words that are replaced or referred to are called antecedents.

Make sure that a pronoun has one clear antecedent. Your writing will be vague and confusing if a pronoun appears to refer to more than one antecedent or if it doesn't have any specific antecedent to refer to. In grammar, such confusing language is called a problem with **reference of pronouns**.

Two or More Antecedents

When the pronoun could refer to more than one thing, the sentence can become confusing or silly. The following are examples of unclear reference.

> Jim told his father that his bike had been stolen. (Whose bike was stolen? Jim's? His father's?)

> She put the cake on the table, took off her apron, pulled up a chair, and began to eat it. (What did she eat? The cake? The table? Her apron? The chair?)

If there is no one clear antecedent, you must rewrite the sentence to make the reference clear. Sometimes the rewritten sentence may seem repetitive, but a little repetition is better than a lot of confusion.

> **unclear:** Jim told his father that his bike had been stolen.

> **clear:** Jim told his father that Jim's bike had been stolen.

> **clear:** Jim told his father that his father's bike had been stolen.

> **clear:** Jim told his father, "My bike has been stolen."

unclear: She put the cake on the table, took off her apron, pulled up a chair, and began to eat it.

clear: She put the cake on the table, took off her apron, pulled up a chair, and began to eat the cake.

No Clear Antecedent

Sometimes the problem is a little more tricky. Can you spot what's wrong with this sentence?

unclear: Bill decided to take a part-time job, which worried his parents. (What worried Bill's parents? His decision to work part time? Or the job itself?)

Be very careful with the pronoun *which*. If there is any chance that using *which* will confuse the reader, rewrite the sentence and get rid of *which*.

clear: Bill's parents were worried about the kind of part-time job he chose.

clear: Bill's decision to work part time worried his parents.

Sometimes, a pronoun has nothing to refer to; it has no antecedent.

When Bill got to the train station, they said the train was going to be late. (Who said the train was going to be late? The ticket agents? Strangers that Bill met on the tracks?)

Maria has always loved medicine and has decided that's what she wants to be. (What does "that" refer to? The only word it could refer to is "medicine," but Maria certainly doesn't want to be "a medicine.")

If a pronoun lacks an antecedent, add an antecedent or get rid of the pronoun.

add an antecedent: When Bill got to the train station and asked the ticket agents about the schedule, they said the train was going to be late.

get rid of the pronoun: Maria has always loved medicine and has decided she wants to be a physician.

Note: To check for clear reference of pronouns, underline any pronoun that may not be clear. Then try to draw a line from that pronoun to its antecedent. Are there two or more possible antecedents? Is there no antecedent? In either case, you need to rewrite.

ALONG THESE LINES/Pearson Education Canada

EXERCISE 7	REWRITING SENTENCES FOR CLEAR REFERENCE OF PRONOUNS

Rewrite the following sentences so that the pronouns have clear references. You may add, take out, or change words.

1. Oscar told Victor that he had a bad temper.

2. The service at the The Island Rooster Restaurant was terrible; he was slow to bring our menus and forgot to take our orders.

3. I was offered a position at Express Service, which pleased me.

4. I loved my visit to Halifax; they are so friendly and warm.

5. My father is a computer systems analyst, but I am not interested in it.

6. Parents often fight with adolescent children because they are stubborn and inflexible.

7. The supervisor told the assistant that his office would be moved to a new location.

8. The car crossed the median and hit a truck, but it wasn't badly damaged.

9. They never told me about the fine print when I signed a lease for my apartment.

10. Don finally made a sale, which encouraged him.

<table>
<tr><td>EXERCISE
8</td><td>**EDITING A PARAGRAPH FOR ERRORS IN PRONOUN AGREEMENT AND REFERENCE**</td></tr>
</table>

Correct any errors in pronoun agreement or reference in the following paragraph. Write your corrections above the lines. There are six errors.

The food at Casa Taco is good, but the real attraction is the atmosphere. They are so friendly that a visit to the restaurant can seem like a family reunion. From the cashier to the counter staff, everybody does their best to make the customers feel special. For example, the people behind the counter know my order before I tell them, and they often tease me about being adventurous and trying new items. In addition, the lady at the cash register always has a smile and a joke for me. The good feeling spreads to all the customers. Nobody loses their temper or raises their voice over an incorrect order or a long wait. Even if the restaurant is crowded, the crowd never loses their patience. Casa Taco treats each customer like a special person and invites them into a special place.

CHAPTER 23
Using Pronouns Correctly: Consistency and Case

MAKING PRONOUNS CONSISTENT

When you write, you write from a point of view, and each point of view requires certain pronouns. If you write from the first-person point of view, you use the pronoun *I* (singular) or *we* (plural). If you write from the second-person point of view, you use the pronoun *you*, whether your subject is singular or plural. (Keep in mind that there is no such word as "youse," often used in error as the second-person plural.) If you write from the third-person point of view, you use the pronouns *he*, *she*, or *it* (singular) or *they* (plural).

Different kinds of writing may require different points of view. When you are writing a set of directions, for example, you might use the second person (*you*) point of view. For an essay about your childhood, you might use the first person (*I*) point of view.

Whatever point of view you use, use **consistency** in choosing pronouns. That is, you shouldn't shift person without some good reason.

> **not consistent:** Every time I go shopping on Boxing Day, parking lots are so crowded **you** have to drive around for hours, looking for a parking space.

> **consistent:** Every time I go shopping on Boxing Day, parking lots are so crowded I have to drive around for hours, looking for a parking space.

EXERCISE 1	CONSISTENCY IN PRONOUNS

Correct any inconsistency in point of view in the following sentences. Cross out the incorrect pronoun and write the correct one above it.

1. Breakfast is a meal on the run because I am always late for work and you never have time to cook a big breakfast.

2. After the students are seated in the classroom, the professor circulates an attendance sheet for you to sign.

3. Motorists should use caution when merging on the highway; if they don't check blind spots, you can be hit by another driver.

4. At my doctor's office, patients can wait for an hour before the doctor is ready to see you.

5. The law students filed into the auditorium, nervously waiting for the proctors to enter and give you the three-hour exam.

6. They were irritated by his conversation because you couldn't get a word into his endless chatter.

7. When we drove into Manitoba, the snow was coming down so heavily you could barely see the road.

8. In the college cafeteria, students sit at long tables, socialize with their friends, or do your homework.

9. Every time I visit my sister's house, you know she's been cleaning and polishing all day.

10. The last time I contacted my cellphone provider, I thought the staff was so rude that you swore you'd switch to another provider the next day.

EXERCISE 2

CORRECTING SENTENCES WITH CONSISTENCY PROBLEMS

Rewrite the following sentences, correcting any errors with consistency of pronouns. To make the corrections, you may have to change, add, or take out words.

1. You could tell the atmosphere was tense when we walked in and saw our friends sitting in silence.

   rewritten: _____

   _____

2. My grandmother's house was a favourite with all the grandchildren; you knew you would always have fun there.

   rewritten: _____

   _____

3. A supervisor can gain respect if you treat all the workers fairly and communicate openly.

   rewritten: _____

   _____

ALONG THESE LINES/Pearson Education Canada

4. Students who are just starting college can be overwhelmed by the reading assignments; you are not used to reading so much so quickly.

   rewritten: _____

   _____

5. The best part about my public speaking class is that you can relax when someone else is giving a speech.

   rewritten: _____

   _____

6. I can't ask Miguel to help me because he'll talk your ear off about self-reliance.

   rewritten: _____

   _____

7. It doesn't matter how politely I try to explain my situation; she'll get angry with you every time.

   rewritten: _____

   _____

8. Students who miss the test can take a make-up test only after the instructor decides you have a valid excuse.

   rewritten: _____

   _____

9. The worst thing about my job at the restaurant is that you have to spend hours on your feet.

   rewritten: _____

   _____

10. If a worker genuinely cares about a pleasant work environment, you shouldn't gossip with co-workers.

    rewritten: _____

    _____

CHOOSING THE CASE OF PRONOUNS

Pronouns have forms that show number and person, and they also have forms that show **case**. Following is a list of three cases of pronouns.

singular pronouns

	subjective case	objective case	possessive case
1st person	I	me	my
2nd person	you	you	your
3rd person	he, she, it	him, her, it	his, her, its

plural pronouns

1st person	we	us	our
2nd person	you	you	your
3rd person	they	them	their

The rules for choosing the case of pronouns are simple:

1. When a pronoun is used as a subject, use the subjective case.
2. When a pronoun is used as the object of a verb or the object of a preposition, use the objective case.
3. When a pronoun is used to show ownership, use the possessive case.

pronouns used as subjects:

She calls the office once a week.

Sylvia wrote the letter, and **we** revised it

pronouns used as objects:

Ernestine called **him** yesterday.

He gave all his money to **me**.

pronouns used to show possession:

I'm worried about **my** grade in French.

The nightclub has lost **its** popularity.

Problems Choosing Pronoun Case

One time when you need to be careful in choosing case is when the pronoun is part of a related group of words. If the pronoun is part of a related group of words, isolate the pronoun. Next, try out the pronoun choices. Then decide which pronoun is correct and write the correct sentence. For example, which of these sentences is correct?

Aunt Sophie planned a big dinner for Tom and **I**.

or

Aunt Sophie planned a big dinner for Tom and **me**.

Step 1: Isolate the pronoun. Eliminate the related words *Tom and*.

Step 2: Try each case:

Aunt Sophie planned a big dinner for **I**.

or

Aunt Sophie planned a big dinner for **me**.

Step 3: The correct sentence is

Aunt Sophie planned a big dinner for Tom and **me**.

The pronoun acts as an object, so it takes the objective case.

Try working through the steps once more, to be sure that you understand this principle. Which of the following sentences is correct?

Last week, **me** and my friend took a ride on the new commuter train.

or

Last week, I and my friend took a ride on the new commuter train.

Step 1: Isolate the pronoun. Eliminate the related words *and my friend.*

Step 2: Try each case:

Last week, **me** took a ride on the new commuter train.

or

Last week, I took a ride on the new commuter train.

Step 3: The correct sentence is

Last week, I and my friend took a ride on the new commuter train.

The pronoun acts as a subject, so it takes the subjective case.
    Note: You can also write it this way:

Last week, my friend and I took a ride on the new commuter train.

Common Errors with Pronoun Case

Be careful to avoid these common errors:

1. *Between* **is a preposition.** The pronouns that follow it are objects of the preposition: between *us*, between *them*, between *you and me*. It is *never correct* to write *between you and I.*

   examples:

   not this: The plans for the surprise party must be kept secret between you and I.

   but this: The plans for the surprise party must be kept secret between you and me.

2. **Never use** *myself* **as a replacement for** *I* **or** *me.*

   examples:

   not this: My father and myself want to thank you for this honour.

   but this: My father and I want to thank you for this honour.

   not this: She thought the prize should be awarded to Arthur and myself.

   but this: She thought the prize should be awarded to Arthur and me.

   The correct use of pronouns ending in *-self* or *-selves* is for emphasis (*I myself loved the movie*) or as reflexive verbs (*They congratulated themselves*).

3. **The possessive pronoun** *its* **has no apostrophe.** Remember that the equivalent possessive pronouns are *my, your, her, their,* etc., and none of those has an apostrophe. *It's* is used only as the contraction of *it is.*

   example:

   not this: The car held it's value.

   but this: The car held its value.

4. Pronouns that complete comparisons can be in the subjective, objective, or possessive case.

subjective: Christa speaks better than I.

objective: The comment hurt Manny more than **her**.

possessive: My car is as fast as **his**.

To decide on the correct pronoun, add the words that complete the comparison and say them aloud:

Christa speaks better than I (speak).

The comment hurt Manny more than (the comment hurt) **her**.

My car is as fast as **his** (car is).

Note that the pronoun you choose can change the meaning.

The comment hurt Manny more than (the comment hurt) **her**.

versus

The comment hurt Manny more than **she** (hurt Manny).

EXERCISE **3**	**CHOOSING THE RIGHT CASE OF PRONOUN**

Circle the correct pronoun in parentheses in each of the following sentences.

1. The elephant escaped when the trainer left (its/it's) cage open.

2. Though my brother is my family's favourite, I am smarter than (he/him).

3. When the neighbour couldn't get an answer, he kept calling Carla and (they/them) all night.

4. Without a guidebook, Mr. Martinez and (she/her) were lost in the big city.

5. I promise not to mention what we discussed; our conversation will be strictly between you and (I/me).

6. The nominating committee selected two applicants from out of town and (me/myself) as finalists for the position.

7. My pickup truck is twelve years old; it's on (it's/its) last legs.

8. His comments about the proposal were unfairly critical of my staff and (myself/me).

9. The security officer and (we/us) looked all over for the missing car.

10. The job was a wonderful opportunity; it was a new beginning for (me/I) and him.

EXERCISE 4

MORE ON CHOOSING THE RIGHT CASE OF PRONOUN

Circle the correct pronoun in parentheses in each of the following sentences.

1. After I met Frank at my sister's house, life began to change for (me/I) and him.

2. Before breakfast, Sylvia and (she/her) went out for an early morning run.

3. Dr. Leah Gupta is a dedicated researcher, but Dr. Andrew McKenna is just as committed as (she/her).

4. Marty is a much better listener than (he/him).

5. My husband planned a big surprise for the children and (I/me).

6. Even though you both speak French, your accent is different than (him/his).

7. James and I visited the old hockey arena, but it didn't have any of (its/it's) former magic.

8. I spent the whole afternoon looking for Tim and (she/her), but they must have gone out of town.

9. My grandfather's will left a small sum of money to be divided between my sister and (me/myself).

10. Officer Lee and (he/him) are looking into suspicious activity at the waterfront.

EXERCISE 5

WRITING YOUR OWN TEXT ON PRONOUN CASE

With a partner or with a group, write two sentences that could be used as examples for each of the following rules. The first is done for you.

Rule 1: When a pronoun is used as a subject, use the subjective case.

examples: He complained about the noise in the street.

Tired and hungry, they stopped for lunch.

Rule 2: When a pronoun is used as the object of a verb or the object of a preposition, use the objective case.

examples: _____

_____

Rule 3: When a pronoun is used to show ownership, use the possessive case.

examples: _____

_____

Rule 4: When a pronoun is part of a related group of words, isolate the pronoun to choose the case. (For examples, write two sentences in which the pronoun is part of a related group of words.)

examples: _____

_____

EXERCISE

6

EDITING A PARAGRAPH FOR ERRORS IN PRONOUN CONSISTENCY AND CASE

Correct any errors in pronoun consistency or case in the following paragraph. Write your corrections above the lines. There are seven errors.

I love to go to the Downtown Flea Market because there are so many things you can do and buy there. My brother and me often spend a whole Saturday afternoon at the market, snacking on the many varieties of ethnic food, listening to the music, and watching the performers. My favourite place for shopping is the used furniture area; I am always looking for an old lamp or a framed poster for my room. My brother loves the Greek market; he says it's pastry is the best in the city. We both like to sit and listen to the music. Each weekend, a different group plays, and some of the music is excellent. My friend Dave takes his girlfriend to hear the groups every Friday night. Dave and her like to catch all the new talent. Even my best friend Carlos, who plays a guitar in a local band, says some of the performers are as good as him. In addition, the market has street entertainers. Little children can visit a friendly clown and get your faces painted, and street dancers crowd the sidewalks, making dramatic moves to the sounds of a portable DVD player. I think anyone can spend a pleasant afternoon at the flea market. It's been the highlight of many days for myself.

CHAPTER 24
Punctuation

You probably know a good deal about punctuation. In fact, you probably know most of the rules so well that you punctuate your writing automatically, without having to think about the rules. Nevertheless, there are times when every writer has to stop and think, "Do I put a comma here?" or "Should I capitalize this word?" The following review of the basic rules of punctuation can help you answer such questions.

THE PERIOD

Periods are used two ways.

1. Use a period to mark the end of a sentence that makes a statement.

We invited him to dinner at our house.

When Richard spoke, no one paid attention.

2. Use a period after abbreviations.

Mr. Ryan

James Wing, Sr.

10:00 p.m.

Note: If a sentence ends with a period marking an abbreviation, do not add a second period.

THE QUESTION MARK

Use a **question mark** after a direct question.

Aren't polar bears adorable?

Do you have car insurance?

If a question is not a direct question, it does not get a question mark.

They asked if I thought polar bears were adorable.

She questioned whether I had car insurance.

ALONG THESE LINES/Pearson Education Canada

EXERCISE 1	PUNCTUATING WITH PERIODS AND QUESTION MARKS

Add any missing periods and question marks to each of the following sentences.

1. My grandmother offered me some cookies and iced tea, and she tried to get me to eat a sandwich too

2. When did Nadia start working at the credit card company

3. Felicia thinks Mr Johannsen is a great math teacher

4. Manny is not sure whether his father has auto insurance

5. Is Drew bringing his guitar

6. Lorene will try to get there at 3:30 pm, but she may be a little late

7. Gurpreet wanted to know when the movie started

8. My girlfriend asked me if I was taking a break from studying

9. I wonder why he is always twenty minutes late for class

10. How much more orange juice is in the refrigerator

THE COMMA

There are four main ways to use a **comma**, as well as other, less important ways. *Memorize the four main ways.* If you can learn and understand these four rules, you will be more confident and correct in your punctuation. That is, you will use a comma only when you have a reason to do so; you will not be scattering commas in your sentences simply because you think a comma might fit, as many writers do.

The four main ways to use a comma are as a lister, a linker, an introducer, or an inserter (use two commas).

1. **Lister.** Commas support items in a series. These items can be words, phrases, or clauses.

   comma between words in a list:

   The most popular colours for business suits are navy blue, charcoal gray, and black.

   comma between phrases in a list:

   I wanted a house on a quiet street, in a friendly neighbourhood, and near a school.

   comma between clauses in a list:

   Last week he graduated from college, he found the woman of his dreams, and he won the lottery.

   Note: In a list, the comma before *and* is optional, but most writers use it. We recommend using this comma because in some sentences it avoids ambiguity.

2. **Linker.** A comma and a coordinating conjunction link two independent clauses. Remember from Chapter 13 that the coordinating conjunctions

ALONG THESE LINES/Pearson Education Canada

are *for, and, nor, but, or, yet, so* (use the acronym FANBOYS to remember). The comma goes in front of the coordinating conjunction.

> I have to get to work on time, or I'll get into trouble with my boss.
>
> The movie was long, but the audience loved the action.

3. **Introducer.** Put a comma after introductory words, phrases, or clauses in a sentence.

comma after an introductory word:

> No, I can't afford that car.
>
> Dad, give me some help with the dishes.

comma after an introductory phrase:

> By the way, the meeting was changed from noon to one o'clock.
>
> In the long run, you'll be better off without him.
>
> Before the anniversary party, my father bought my mother a necklace.

comma after an introductory clause:

> If you call home, your parents will be pleased.
>
> When the phone rings, I am always in the shower.

4. **Inserter.** When words or phrases that are *not* necessary are inserted into a sentence, put a comma on *both* sides of the inserted material.

> The game, unfortunately, was rained out.
>
> My test score, believe it or not, was the highest in the class.
>
> Potato chips, my favourite snack food, taste better when they're fresh.
>
> James, caught in the middle of the argument, tried to keep the peace.

Using commas as inserters requires that you decide what is essential to the meaning of the sentence and what is not essential.

If you do not need material in a sentence, put commas around the material. If you do need material in a sentence, do not put commas around the material.

For example, consider this sentence:

> The girl who called me was selling magazine subscriptions.

Do you need the words "who called me" to understand the meaning of the sentence? To answer this question, write the sentence without these words:

> The girl was selling magazine subscriptions.

Reading the shorter sentence, you might ask, "Which girl?" If so, the words *who called me* are essential to the sentence. Therefore you *do not* put commas around them.

> **correct:** The girl who called me was selling magazine subscriptions.

Remember that the proper name of a person, place, or thing is often sufficient to identify it. Therefore, any information that follows a proper name is usually inserted material; it gets commas on both sides.

> Mixmaster Coffee, which has free Wireless access, is my favourite place to pass the time.
>
> Sam Harris, the man who won the marathon, lives on my block.

However, if there is more than one of the person, place, or thing, the information is essential.

The Mixmaster Coffee which is near my house has free Wireless access. (There is another Mixmaster Coffee that is not near your house and that may or may not have free Wireless access.)

The Sam Harris who won the marathon lives on my block. (There might be another Sam Harris, so you want to identify which Sam Harris you are referring to.)

Note: Sometimes, the material that is needed in a sentence is called **essential** (or restrictive), and the material that is not needed is called **nonessential** (or nonrestrictive).

Remember the four main ways to use a comma—as a *lister*, *linker*, *introducer*, or *inserter*—and you'll solve many of your problems using punctuation.

EXERCISE

2

PUNCTUATING WITH COMMAS: THE FOUR MAIN WAYS

Add commas only where they are needed in the following sentences. Do not add any other punctuation, and do not change any existing punctuation. Some of the sentences do not need commas.

1. Whether you like it or not you have to get up early tomorrow.

2. Skiing snowboarding and surfing all demand tremendous agility and fitness.

3. I was forced to call the emergency towing service and wait two hours for help.

4. The two-storey house by the lake is the most attractive one in the neighbourhood.

5. Chicken Delights the only restaurant in my neighbourhood is always crowded on a Saturday night.

6. No you can't get a bus to the city on Saturdays unless you are prepared to leave early.

7. Dripping wet and miserable I crouched under a huge tree until the rain stopped.

8. Nick got a job right after college for he had spent his final year making contacts and sending applications.

9. I wanted to look professional for my job interview so I wore a conservative suit.

10. Cleaning the kitchen is a chore because I have to scrub the sink wipe the counters empty the garbage and wash the floor.

Other Ways to Use a Comma

There are other places to use a comma. Reviewing these uses will help you feel more confident as a writer.

1. **Use commas with quotations.** Use a comma to set off direct quotations from the rest of the sentence.

   My father told me, "Money doesn't grow on trees."

   "Let's split the bill," Raymond said.

   He wrote, "I'll never love again."

   Note that the comma that introduces the quotation goes before the quotation marks. But once the quotation has begun, commas or periods generally go inside the quotation marks.

2. **Use commas with dates and addresses.** Use commas between the items in dates and locations or addresses.

   August 5, 1986, is Guraj's date of birth.

   We lived in Fernie, British Columbia, before we moved to Manitoba.

   Notice the comma after the year in the date and the comma after the province in the address. These commas are needed when you write a date or address within a sentence.

3. **Use commas for numbers.** Use commas in numbers of one thousand or larger.

   The price of equipment was $1,293.

   In SI style, which is now more commonly used in Canada, numerals of four digits have no separator (1293), and a space rather than a comma is used in numerals of five digits or more (563 000). Ask your instructor which method is preferred in your course.

4. **Use commas for clarity.** Put a comma when you need it to make something clear.

   Whatever you did, did the trick.

   I don't like to dress up, but in this job I have to, to get ahead.

EXERCISE **3**	**PUNCTUATION: OTHER WAYS TO USE A COMMA**

Use commas wherever they are needed in the following sentences. Do not add any other punctuation, and do not change any existing punctuation.

1. Mr. Chen used to say "Every cloud has a silver lining."

2. My best friend was born on January 29 1976 in Mississauga Ontario.

3. "I would never borrow your car without asking first" my little brother asserted.

4. She bit into the apple and mumbled "This is the best apple I've ever tasted."

5. I graduated from Deerfield High School on June 19 1995 and started my first real job on June 19 1996 in the same town.

6. The repairs on my truck cost me $2392.

7. The Reilly mansion across town is selling for $359000.

8. He ordered a sandwich, and she a drink.

9. On April 30 1996 my father warned me "Don't forget to mail your income tax forms."

10. "Nothing exciting ever happens around here" my cousin complained.

EXERCISE 4

PUNCTUATING WITH COMMAS: A COMPREHENSIVE EXERCISE

Put commas wherever they are needed in the following sentences. Do not add any other punctuation, and do not change any existing punctuation. Some of the sentences do not need commas.

1. I wanted a fabric with grey white and navy in it but I had to settle for one with grey and white.

2. He was born on July 15 1970 in a small town in Quebec.

3. I am sure Jeffrey that you are not telling me the whole story.

4. The family wanted to spend a quiet weekend at home but wound up doing errands all over town.

5. My favourite novel *Surfacing* is set in northern Ontario.

6. She devoted an entire day to cleaning the kitchen cabinets reorganizing the pantry shelves and scrubbing the hall floor.

7. The man who wrote you is a friend of mine.

8. Whether David likes it or not he has to work overtime again.

9. "Get out your notebooks" the teacher said.

10. Honestly I can't say which is a better buy.

11. I tried to reason with her I tried to warn her I even tried to frighten her but she was determined to proceed with her plans.

12. Pizza Pronto my favourite restaurant is going out of business.

13. We can call him tomorrow or stop by his house.

14. For the third time the child whispered "Mommy I want to go home now."

15. People who have never seen the ocean are not prepared for its beauty.

16. My sister is in two important ways the opposite of my mother.

17. In two important ways my sister is the opposite of my mother.

18. The visitors were friendly and polite yet they seemed a little shy.

19. If you lose lose with style and class.

20. The car in the garage doesn't belong to me nor do I have permission to borrow it.

THE APOSTROPHE

Use the **apostrophe** two ways.

1. Use an apostrophe in contractions to show that letters have been omitted.

do not = don't
I will = I'll
is not = isn't
she would = she'd
will not = won't

Also use the apostrophe to show that numbers have been omitted:

the summer of 2003 = the summer of '03

2. Use an apostrophe to show possession. If a word does not end in *s*, show ownership by adding an apostrophe and *s*.

the ring belonging to Jill = Jill's ring
the wallet belonging to somebody = somebody's wallet
the books that are owned by my father = my father's books

If two people jointly own something, put the *'s* on the last person's name.

Gillian and Mike own a house = Gillian and Mike's house

If two people each own something, put the *'s* on each person's name

Gillian and Mike each own a house = Gillian's and Mike's houses

If a word already ends in *s* and you want to show ownership, just add an apostrophe.

the dog owned by two boys = the boys' dog
the toys belonging to two cats = the cats' toys
the house belonging to Ms. Jones = Ms. Jones' house

Caution: Be careful with apostrophes. These words, the possessive pronouns, do not take apostrophes: *his, hers, theirs, ours, yours, its.*

not this: The pencils were their's.

but this: The pencils were theirs.

not this: The steak lost it's flavour.

but this: The steak lost its flavour.

ALONG THESE LINES/Pearson Education Canada

EXERCISE 5	PUNCTUATING WITH APOSTROPHES

Add apostrophes where they are needed in the following sentences. Some sentences do not need apostrophes.

1. I'm sure Morris intentions were good.
2. That movie sure doesnt live up to its reputation.
3. I love my cousins, but I disagree with their political views.
4. I was sure that the items recovered in the police raid would turn out to be ours.
5. I was delighted by Sioux Narrows natural beauty.
6. Professor Lyons is an expert in the field of childrens rights.
7. She had lost the womens hockey jerseys.
8. I know shes not interested in aerobics.
9. Theyll take the train to Jim and Davids house.
10. I can give the boys advice, but the problem is still theirs.

THE SEMICOLON

There are two ways to use **semicolons**.

1. Use a semicolon to join two independent clauses.

Michael loved his old Camaro; he worked on it every weekend.

The situation was hopeless; I couldn't do anything.

Note: If the independent clauses are joined by a conjunctive adverb, you still need a semicolon. You will also need a comma after the conjunctive adverb if the conjunctive adverb is more than one syllable long.

He was fluent in Spanish; consequently, he was the perfect companion for our trip to Venezuela.

I called the hotline for twenty minutes; then I called another number.

2. Use semicolons to separate items in a list that contains commas. Adding semicolons will make the list easier to read.

The contestants came from Kenora, Ontario; Brandon, Manitoba; and Estevan, Saskatchewan.

The new officers of the club will be Althea Bethell, president; François Rivière, vice-president; Ricardo Perez, secretary; and Lou Phillips, treasurer.

THE COLON

A **colon** is used at the end of a complete statement. It introduces a list or an explanation.

colon introduces a list: When I went grocery shopping, I picked up a few things: milk, eggs, and coffee.

colon introduces an explanation: The room was a mess: dirty clothes were piled on the chairs, wet towels were thrown on the floor, and an empty pizza box was tossed in the closet.

Remember that the colon comes after a complete statement. What comes after the colon explains or describes what came before the colon. Look once more at the two examples, and you'll see the point.

When I went grocery shopping, I picked up a few things: milk, eggs, and coffee. (The words after the colon, *milk, eggs, and coffee*, explain what few things I picked up.)

The room was a mess: dirty clothes were piled on the chairs, wet towels were thrown on the floor, and an empty pizza box was tossed in the closet. (In this sentence, all the words after the colon describe what the mess was like.)

Some people use a colon every time they put a list in a sentence, but this is not a good rule to follow. Instead, remember that a colon, even one that introduces a list, must come after a complete statement.

not this: When I go to the beach, I always bring: suntan lotion, a big towel, and a cooler with iced tea.

but this: When I go to the beach, I always bring my supplies: suntan lotion, a big towel, and a cooler with iced tea.

A colon may also introduce quotations (whether short and integrated into the sentence or long and set off from the text).

As early as 1961, historian W. L. Morton, in his book *The Canadian Identity*, observed the true nature of this country: "Not life, liberty, and the pursuit of happiness, but peace, order, and good government are what the national government of Canada guarantees."

EXERCISE 6	USING SEMICOLONS AND COLONS

Add semicolons and colons where they are needed to each sentence below. You might have to change a comma to a semicolon.

1. Eileen picked me up at the train station then she drove me to my sister's house.

2. Every Thanksgiving, we have the same meal roast turkey, stuffing, cranberry sauce, and pumpkin pie.

3. You should bring a jacket to the game otherwise, you're going to get cold.

4. When I started working at the restaurant, I had to be trained in customer relations, menu selections, and financial procedures.

5. Last night the Athletic League voted for Greg Patel, president, Lisa Tobin, vice president, Graham Pritchard, second vice president, and Daisy Fiero, treasurer.

6. You can keep an eye on the baby, meanwhile, I'll call the doctor about the baby's fever.

7. If you're going to the bakery bring me some bagels, a loaf of whole grain bread and some cinnamon buns.

8. Frank arrived at nine he's always prompt.

9. You can pick up a bath mat at Wal-Mart, and don't forget your son's goodies a wooden puzzle and a small stuffed animal.

10. I would never eat Brussels sprouts the very thought of it makes me sick.

THE EXCLAMATION MARK

The **exclamation mark** is used at the end of sentences that express strong emotion.

> **appropriate:** You've won the lottery!
>
> **inappropriate:** We had a great time! ("Great" already implies excitement.)

Be careful not to overuse the exclamation mark. If your choice of words is descriptive and makes use of a good vocabulary, you should not have to rely on the exclamation point for emphasis.

THE DASH

Use a **dash** to interrupt a sentence; use a pair of dashes to set off words within a sentence. The dash is somewhat dramatic, so be careful not to overuse it. In word processing, show a dash clearly by using two or three hyphens, not just one.

> This is my last chance to warn him—and he'd better listen to my warning.
>
> That silly show—believe it or not—is number one in the ratings.

PARENTHESES

Use **parentheses** to enclose extra material and afterthoughts.

> I was sure that Ridgefield (the town I'd just visited) was not the place for me.

If your sentence includes a comma, make sure you place it after the second parenthesis:

> **not this:** She was accepted at that college, (her first choice) but her parents wanted her to go to a school closer to home.
>
> **but this:** She was accepted at that college (her first choice), but her parents wanted her to go to a school closer to home.

Note: Commas in pairs, dashes in pairs, and parentheses are all used as inserters. They set off material that interrupts the flow of the sentence. The least dramatic and smoothest way to insert material is to use commas.

THE HYPHEN

A **hyphen** joins two or more descriptive words that act as a single word.

> The old car had a souped-up engine.
>
> Bill was a smooth-talking charmer.

EXERCISE 7	PUNCTUATING WITH EXCLAMATION MARKS, DASHES, PARENTHESES, AND HYPHENS

Add any exclamation marks, dashes, parentheses, and hyphens that are needed in the sentences below. A colon or comma would also be appropriate in some sentences; however, for this exercise, choose from the punctuation indicated.

1. His plan for making a million dollars was the most lame brained scheme I'd ever heard.

2. The Carlton Gallery of Fine Art the place where I had my first job is located east of the river.

3. My son can't go anywhere without his collection of amusements one hundred Pokémon cards, five Bakugan toys, Lego figurines, and a grimy stuffed lamb.

4. Rosa could tell that the speaker was nervous he fidgeted with his notes, stumbled over his words, and blushed beet red.

5. Godzilla is at the window

6. Bring a raincoat, sweaters, thermal underwear, heavy socks it's going to be freezing cold out there.

7. Cocoa Forest the smallest town in Midland County is best known for its Victorian houses and restored town square.

8. Don't you ever speak to me like that again

9. There are two kinds of desserts desserts that are good for you, and desserts that taste good.

10. Stop

QUOTATION MARKS

Use **quotation marks** for direct quotes, for the titles of short works, and for other, special uses.

1. Put quotation marks around direct quotes—a speaker or writer's exact words.

> My mother told me, "There are plenty of fish in the sea."
>
> "I'm never going there again," said Irene.
>
> "I'd like to buy you dinner," Peter said, "but I'm out of cash."
>
> My best friend wrote, "Stay away from that guy. He will break your heart."

Look carefully at the preceding examples. Notice that a comma is used to introduce a direct quote, and that, at the end of the quotation, the comma or period goes inside the quotation marks.

My mother told me, "There are plenty of fish in the sea."

Notice how direct quotes of more than one sentence are punctuated. If the quote is written in one unit, quotation marks go before the first quoted word and after the last quoted word.

My best friend warned me, "Stay away from that guy. He will break your heart."

But if the quote is not written as one unit, the punctuation changes.

"Stay away from that guy," my best friend wrote. "He will break your heart."

Caution: Do *not* put quotation marks around indirect quotations.

indirect quotation: He asked if he could come with us.
direct quotation: He asked, "Can I come with you?"

indirect quotation: She said that she wanted more time.
direct quotation: "I want more time," she said.

2. **Put quotation marks around the titles of short works.** If you are writing the title of a chapter, a short story, an essay, a newspaper or magazine article, an episode of a television series, a poem, or a song, use quotation marks.

In Grade Eight, we read Robert Frost's poem "The Road Not Taken."
My little sister has learned to sing "Itsy Bitsy Spider."

However, if you are writing the title of a longer work such as a book, movie, magazine, play, television show, or record album, put the title in italics.

Last night I saw an old movie, *Stand by Me.*
I read an article called "Campus Crime" in *Maclean's* magazine.

If you are handwriting or do not have access to italics, underline the titles of long works.

3. **There are other, special uses of quotation marks.** You can use quotation marks around special words in a sentence.

When you said "never," did you mean it?
People from Nova Scotia pronounce "boy" differently than I do.

(Words used in this way may also be put in italics, as we do in this book.)

If you are using a quote within a quote, use single quotation marks.

My brother complained, "Every time we get in trouble, Mom has to say 'I told you so.' "

Kyle said, "Linda has a way of saying 'Excuse me' that is really very rude."

ALONG THESE LINES/Pearson Education Education Canada

CAPITAL LETTERS

There are ten main situations in which you **capitalize**.

1. Capitalize the first word of every sentence.

Yesterday we saw our first soccer game.

2. Capitalize the first word in a direct quotation if the word begins a sentence.

My aunt said, "This is a gift for your birthday."

"Have some birthday cake," my aunt said, "and have some more ice cream."

(Notice that the second section of this quote does not begin with a capital letter because it does not begin a sentence.)

3. Capitalize the names of people.

Nancy Perez and Frank Scarpitti came to see me at the store.
I asked Mother to feed my cat.

Do not capitalize words like *mother, father,* or *aunt* if you put a possessive in front of them.

I asked my mother to feed my cat.

4. Capitalize people's titles.

I was a patient of Dr. Woo.
He has to see Dean Singh.

Don't capitalize when the title is not connected to a name.

I was a patient of that doctor.
He has to see the dean.

5. Always capitalize nationalities, religions, races, months, days of the week, documents, organizations, holidays, and historical events or periods.

In high school, we never studied the Korean War, just the Second World War.
The Polish-Canadian Club will hold a picnic on Labour Day.

Use small letters for the seasons.

I love fall because I love to watch the leaves change colour.

6. Capitalize the names of particular places.

We used to hold our annual meetings at Northside Auditorium in Montreal, Quebec, but this year we are meeting at Riverview Theatre in London, Ontario.

Use small letters if a particular place is not named.

We are looking for an auditorium we can rent for our meeting.

7. Use capital letters for geographic locations.

Jim was determined to find a good job in the West.

But use small letters for geographic directions.

To get to my house, you have to drive west on the freeway.

8. Capitalize the names of specific products.

I always drink Diet Pepsi for lunch.

But use small letters for a general type of product.

I always drink a diet cola for lunch.

9. Capitalize the names of specific school courses.

I have to take Child Psychology next term.

But use small letters for a general academic subject.

My adviser told me to take a psychology course.

10. Capitalize the first and last words in the titles of long or short works, and capitalize all other significant words in the titles. Significant words include nouns, pronouns, verbs, adjectives, adverbs, and some conjunctions (but not the coordinating conjunctions), and usually don't include prepositions.

I've always wanted to read The Old Man and the Sea.

Whenever we go to see a musical, my uncle sings "Don't Cry for Me,

Argentina" in the car.

Remember that the titles of long works, like books, should be italicized (underlined in handwritten work); the titles of short ones, like songs, are quoted.

| EXERCISE **8** | **PUNCTUATING WITH QUOTATION MARKS, ITALICS OR UNDERLINING, AND CAPITAL LETTERS** |

Add any missing quotation marks, underlining (italics), and capital letters to the sentences below.

1. Don't ever call me again, the repairman said, unless it's an emergency.

2. No one expected Home Alone to be such a popular movie, but it broke all box office records at the Sunset mall theatre.

3. James, you should be careful what you wish for, my aunt said, because you may get it.

4. That old word jock is mistakenly applied to anyone who likes sports.

5. My sisters all attended Broward Community college, but I'm going to a community college in the maritimes.

6. When I was growing up, my favourite television show was Thundercats, but now I love to watch old movies like It's a wonderful life or citizen kane.

7. Yesterday I tried to buy tickets for the concert at the coral beach amphitheatre, but the man at the ticket office said, we're sold out.

8. You always say I'm sorry when you never mean it, my boyfriend complained.

9. I told uncle Phil to be on time, but my uncle is a procrastinator.

10. Next semester I'm taking courses in public speaking, business, and economics; I've already taken the seminar course called preparing for a business career.

NUMBERS

1. Spell out numbers that are written as one or two words.

Alice mailed **two hundred** brochures.

I spent **ninety** dollars on car repairs.

2. Use the numbers themselves if it takes more than two words to spell them out.

We looked through **243** old photographs.

The sticker price was **$10,397.99**.

(Another accepted style, often used in scientific and business writing, is to write out the numbers one to nine and use numerals for numbers ten or larger.)

3. Also use numbers to write dates, times, and addresses.

We live at 24 Cambridge Street.

They were married on April 3, 1993.

ABBREVIATIONS

Although you should spell out most words rather than abbreviate them, you may use common **abbreviations** like *Mr., Mrs., Ms., Jr., Sr.,* and *Dr.* when they are used with a proper name. Abbreviations may also be used for references to time, and for organizations widely known by initials.

The moderator asked Ms. Steinem to comment.

The bus left at 5:00 p.m., and the trip took two hours.

He works for CIBC.

Note: It has become more common for periods not to be used in abbreviations of three letters or more. You would write B.C., but FAQ.

You should spell out the names of places, months, days of the week, courses of study, and words referring to parts of a book.

not this: I missed the last class, so I never got the notes for Chap. Three.

but this: I missed the last class, so I never got the notes for Chapter Three.

not this: He lives on Chestnut Street in Winnipeg, MB.

but this: He lives on Chestnut Street in Winnipeg, Manitoba.

not this: Pete missed his trig. test.

but this: Pete missed his trigonometry test.

| **EXERCISE 9** | **USING NUMBERS AND ABBREVIATIONS** |

Correct any errors in the use of numbers or abbreviations in the following sentences. Some sentences may not need corrections.

1. We are looking for Thomas Pittman, Jr., the man who wrote the editorial in today's paper.

2. My mother was born in Prince Albert, Sask., the youngest of 4 children, all girls.

3. The rent for the one-room apartment on Orchard St. was $1,250 a month.

4. I graduated from high school on June twenty-sixth, 2003, and I started my new job the following Mon.

5. The new biology prof. takes 2 weeks to return our test papers.

6. The answer to the psych. question is in Chap. 2 of the child psychology textbook.

7. The alarm went off at 7:00 a.m., so I had plenty of time to get ready for the flight to Calgary, Alta.

8. Dr. Chen found seventeen new specimens of a rare tropical insect; she will study them in her research facility at the Charter Chemical Co.

9. I sorted through three hundred and fifty photographs before I came across the one of our old house on Empire Ave. in Thunder Bay, Ont.

10. Mario missed his econ. class last Wed. because he fell and twisted his ankle about fifty m from the classroom building.

| **EXERCISE 10** | **A COMPREHENSIVE EXERCISE ON PUNCTUATION AND MECHANICS** |

Add any missing punctuation to the following sentences. Correct any errors in capitalization and in use of numbers or abbreviations.

1. My sister had a hard time meeting her three boys demands for attention but she did her best.

2. The people at the store were extremely helpful furthermore they were willing to handle special orders.

3. Making a roux which is a classic French technique is taught in cooking 101.

4. Every time I study with you she said I get good grades on my tests.

5. Parents should be willing to listen children should be willing to talk and both groups should be open to new ideas if families are going to live in harmony.

6. Repairing the damages caused by the fire cost three hundred and fifty-seven dollars.

7. My little sister walks around singing her favourite hannah montana song Lily do you want to know a secret all day in her squeaky little girl voice.

8. Dont forget to pick up the food we need for the picnic hamburgers hot dogs potato salad and corn.

9. No one told Jose about the job opening so he didn't apply for the position.

10. Leo was born in Fredericton NB on June 3 1968 and he grew up in a nearby town.

11. Christina Ruggiero who always sends me a birthday card is a considerate and thoughtful person.

12. We were sure that rain or shine he would be there.

13. I'm sorry dad that I was late for James farewell dinner.

14. Unless you replace those worn out tires you cant drive safely on rain slicked roads.

15. Philip asked Is there a shortcut to the warehouse

16. Philip asked if there was a shortcut to the warehouse

17. When he was in high school he took english courses but at Jackson college he is taking communication courses.

18. The girl running across the ice slipped and fell then she grabbed at a fence post and pulled herself up.

19. Bolton Furniture has kept its reputation for quality merchandise at a reasonable price thus its been able to survive in hard times.

20. I'm thinking of writing a book called how to manage your time but I never seem to have time to write it.

APPENDIX A
Grammar for ESL Students

NOUNS AND ARTICLES

A **noun** names a person, place, or thing. There are count nouns and noncount nouns.

> **Count nouns** refer to persons, places, or things that can be counted: three *doughnuts*, two *computers*, five *pencils*

> **Noncount nouns** refer to things that can't be counted: *medicine, housework, mail*

Here are some more examples of count and noncount nouns:

count	noncount
rumour	gossip
violin	music
school	intelligence
suitcase	luggage

One way to remember the difference between count and noncount nouns is to put the word *much* in front of the noun. For example, if you can say *much luggage*, then *luggage* is a noncount noun.

EXERCISE 1

IDENTIFYING COUNT AND NONCOUNT NOUNS

Write count or noncount next to each word below.

1. _____ sailboat

2. _____ button

3. _____ time

4. _____ sympathy

5. _____ clock

6. _____ health

7. _____ food

8. _____ milk

9. _____ banana

10. _____ tree

ALONG THESE LINES/Pearson Education Canada

Using Articles with Nouns

Articles point out nouns. Articles are either **indefinite** (*a, an*) or **definite** (*the*). There are several rules for using these articles:

- Use *a* in front of consonant sounds and use *an* before vowel sounds:

a card	an orange
a radio	an answer
a button	an entrance
a house	an hour
a nightmare	an uncle
a BLT	an MBA

Notice that *hour* takes *an* because you pronounce it with a vowel sound as though it were *our*, but *house* takes *a* because you pronounce it with the consonant sound *h*. Also, notice that the indefinite article for an abbreviation is based on whether the first letter is pronounced as a consonant (the *bee* in BLT) or as a vowel (the *em* in MBA).

- Use *a* or *an* in front of singular count nouns whose specific identity is not known to the reader (*a* or *an* means "*any* one").

   I ate **an egg**.
   James planted **a tree**.

- Do not use *a* or *an* with most noncount nouns:

   not this: Selena filled the tank with ~~a~~ **gasoline**.
   but this: Selena filled the tank with **gasoline**.

- Use *the* before both singular and plural count nouns whose specific identify is known to the reader:

   The dress with the beads on it is my party dress.
   Most of **the movies** I rent are science fiction films.

- Do not use *the* before plural count nouns if the specific identity is not known.
   Movies made in Canada are becoming more popular.
   He saw **horses** in the open pasture.

- Use *the* before noncount nouns only when they are specifically identified:

   not this: I need ~~the~~ **help**. (Whose help? What help? The noncount noun *help* is not specifically identified.)
   but this: I need **the help** of a good plumber. (Now *help* is specifically identified.)

   not this: Kindness of the people who took me in was remarkable. (The noncount noun *kindness* is being specifically identified, so you need *the*.)
   but this: The kindness of the people who took me in was remarkable.

EXERCISE **2**	USING *A* OR *AN*

Put *a* or *an* in the spaces where it is needed. Some sentences are correct as they are.

1. Mrs. Verinsky took us to _____ movie.

2. I need to buy _____ furniture for my new house.

3. My son was eating _____ orange.

4. My brother is studying _____ medicine and taking _____ course in anatomy.

5. Keith had _____ accident on Wednesday.

6. I can bring _____ coffee and _____ ice cream to Joe's birthday party.

7. Jimmy took me to _____ concert and _____ exhibition of famous racing cars.

8. All she wants is _____ respect.

9. Mark was carrying _____ umbrella with _____ hole in it.

10. Joanna has _____ confidence and _____ sense of humour.

EXERCISE 3

USING *THE*

Write *the* in the spaces where it is needed. Some sentences are correct as they are.

1. Larry missed _____ dinners his mother used to make.

2. Eventually, you will develop _____ patience to succeed in _____ child psychology.

3. I have always wanted to swim in _____ ocean.

4. I haven't had _____ luck that I need to win the lottery.

5. Stephanie goes to _____ supermarket near her house because that store has _____ best selection of _____ organic produce.

6. _____ newspapers in _____ garage need to be recycled.

7. Because of _____ hard work of _____ volunteers at our community garage sale, we made $500 for _____ community garden.

8. Getting a good job takes _____ determination and _____ hard work.

9. Some children watch _____ television after school instead of doing their homework.

10. Tom cleaned out _____ trash in _____ back yard but left _____ dead leaves under _____ porch for another day.

EXERCISE 4

CORRECTING A PARAGRAPH WITH ERRORS IN ARTICLES

Correct the errors with *a*, *an*, or *the* in the following paragraph. You may need to add, change, or eliminate articles. Write the corrections in the space above the errors. There are eleven errors.

When I was twelve years old, I had a dog like no other dog in the world. This dog had the intelligence and the courage, and he also had a crazy streak in his personality. His name was Buzzy, and he was the border collie.

On farms of England and Scotland, border collies are used to herd sheep, and these dogs love to chase anything that moves. They are full of the energy and have stamina of much larger dogs. Buzzy loved to run, and he could chase and herd almost any animal. I remember when he herded five ducks into a quacking group and pushed them into a pond. He was always looking for a opportunity to run and play. If he couldn't find anything to herd, he loved to play the fetch. He would retrieve a old tennis ball for a hour. He ran as fast as the bullet.

NOUNS OR PRONOUNS USED AS SUBJECTS

A noun or a **pronoun** (a word that takes the place of a noun) is the subject of each sentence or dependent clause. Be sure that all sentences or dependent clauses have a subject:

> **not this:** Drives to work every day.
> **but this:** **He** drives to work every day.

> **not this:** My sister is pleased when gets a compliment.
> **but this:** My sister is pleased when **she** gets a compliment.

Be careful not to *repeat* the subject:

> **not this:** The police officer ~~she~~ said I was speeding.
> **but this:** The police officer said I was speeding.

> **not this:** The car that I needed ~~it~~ was a sportscar.
> **but this:** The car that I needed was a sportscar.

EXERCISE 5

CORRECTING ERRORS WITH SUBJECTS

Correct any errors with subjects in the sentences below. Write your corrections above the errors.

1. Anthony he never gets up when hears the alarm clock.

2. In the summer, my car it often gets overheated.

3. Action movies with a good soundtrack they are the best.

4. After a long day, is difficult to concentrate on homework.

5. Sweatshirts are warm in winter; are also very comfortable.

6. My friend Inez she likes to walk in all kinds of weather.

7. Yesterday, the right rear tire on my truck it was flat.

8. Always comes to visit on New Year's Day and brings a special gift.

9. Whenever sees a coupon in the newspaper, he cuts it out.

10. The scariest part of the amusement park it was a haunted house.

VERBS

Necessary Verbs

Be sure that a **main verb** isn't missing from your sentences or dependent clauses.

not this: My boyfriend very ambitious

but this: My boyfriend **is** very ambitious.

not this: Sylvia cried when the hero in the movie.

but this: Sylvia cried when the hero in the movie **died**.

-s Endings

Be sure to put the -s on present-tense verbs in the third-person singular:

not this: He ~~run~~ in the park every morning.

but this: He **runs** in the park every morning.

not this: The concert ~~start~~ at 9:00 p.m.

but this: The concert **starts** at 9:00 p.m.

-ed Endings

Be sure to put an -ed ending on the past-participle form of a verb when necessary. There are three main forms of a verb:

present: Today I **walk**.

past: Yesterday I **walked**.

past participle: I **have walked**. He **has walked**.

The past-participle form is used after *were, was, had, has,* and *have*:

not this: He **has** ~~call~~ me every day this week.

but this: He **has called** me every day this week.

not this: My neighbour **was** ~~surprise~~ by the sudden storm.

but this: My neighbour **was surprised** by the sudden storm.

Caution: Do not add -ed endings to infinitives. An infinitive is the verb form that uses *to* plus the present form of the verb:

infinitives: to consider   to obey

not this: Dean wanted me **to** ~~considered~~ the proposal.

but this: Dean wanted me **to consider** the proposal.

not this: I taught my dog **to** ~~obeyed~~ commands.

but this: I taught my dog **to obey** commands.

ALONG THESE LINES/Pearson Education Canada

| EXERCISE **6** | CORRECTING ERRORS IN VERBS: NECESSARY VERBS, THIRD-PERSON PRESENT TENSE, PAST PARTICIPLES, AND INFINITIVES |

Correct any errors in verbs in the sentences below. Write your corrections above the lines. Some sentences do not need any corrections.

1. The letter was mail at the post office where my uncle work.

2. After I got divorced, I wanted to examining the good and bad points of moving to Alberta.

3. As a child, I was fascinating by dinosaurs and other prehistoric creatures.

4. Once a week, Lucy calls her family in Manila and tells them all her news.

5. Your new haircut look good on you; it make you look very handsome.

6. Laura had wrap all the gifts before the children arrived.

7. Two of the most generous neighbours in my building, Mike and Alice Hennessy, from the third floor.

8. Do not come to the dinner table unless you have wash your hands.

9. Good communication skills essential in any close relationship.

10. When Mrs. Simone need to relaxed, she lie on the couch and read a mystery novel.

| EXERCISE **7** | CORRECTING A PARAGRAPH WITH ERRORS IN NECESSARY VERBS, THIRD-PERSON PRESENT TENSE, PAST PARTICIPLES, AND INFINITIVES |

Correct the verb errors in the following paragraph. Write your corrections above the lines. There are seven errors.

Whenever we have a sale at the store where I work, we have to prepared for it for days. If the sale start on a Wednesday, for example, we work for hours on Monday and Tuesday, sorting the sale items and marking the merchandise with special sales tags. All this sorting and marking must be done after the store close, so the work continue late into the night. Then, at about 5:00 a.m. on Wednesday morning, the really hard work begins. We rush to put up the "Sale" signs, to displayed the marked-down items, and to be ready when the customers come in at 9:00. Before a sale begins, I have often earn as much as fifteen hours of overtime. A sale is fun for customers, but for salespeople it a hard way to make extra money.

ALONG THESE LINES/Pearson Education Canada

Two-Word Verbs

Two-word verbs contain a verb plus another word, either a preposition or an adverb. The meaning of each word by itself is different from the meaning the two words have when they are together. Look at this example:

> Sometimes Hamida **runs across** her sister at the park.

You might check *run* in the dictionary and find that it means "to move quickly." *Across* means "from one side to the other." But *run across* means something different:

> **not this:** Sometimes Hamida ~~moves quickly from one side to the other of~~ her sister at the park.

> **but this:** Sometimes Hamida **encounters** her sister at the park.

Sometimes, a word or words come between the words of a two-word verb:

> On Friday night, I **put** the garbage **out**; the sanitation department collects it early Saturday morning.

Here are some common two-word verbs:

ask out	Jamal wants to *ask* Teresa *out* for dinner.
break down	I hope my car doesn't *break down*.
call off	You can *call off* the party.
call on	I need to *call on* you for help.
come across	I often *come across* bargains at thrift shops.
drop in	I will *drop in* tomorrow to check on your progress.
drop off	My father will *drop* the package *off*.
fill in	You can *fill in* your name.
fill out	Danny has to *fill out* a complaint form.
hand in	We have to *hand in* our assignments.
hand out	I hope the theatre *hands out* free passes.
keep on	You must *keep on* practising your speech.
look into	Jonelle will *look into* the situation.
look over	Jake needs to *look* the plans *over*.
look up	I had to *look up* the street in the directory.
pick up	Tomorrow I *pick up* my first paycheque.
quiet down	The teacher told the class to *quiet down*.
run into	Nancy will *run into* Alan at the gym.
run out	The family has *run out* of money.
try on	Before you buy the shirt, *try* it *on*.
try out	She wants to *try* the lawnmower *out*.
turn on	*Turn* the television *on*.
turn down	Sal thinks Wayne should *turn* the job *down*.
turn up	Nick is sure to *turn up* uninvited.

EXERCISE 8

WRITING SENTENCES WITH TWO-WORD VERBS

Write a sentence for each of the following two-word verbs. Use the examples above as a guide, but consult a dictionary if you are not sure what the verbs mean.

1. call off _____

2. look up _____

3. keep on _____

4. fill out _____

5. run across _____

6. turn up _____

7. drop off _____

8. pick up _____

9. try out _____

10. ask out _____

Contractions and Verbs

Contractions often contain verbs you may not recognize in their shortened forms.

Affirmative Contractions	**Negative Contractions**
am = 'm (I'm)	am not = 'm not (I'm not)
is = 's (he's)	is not = isn't or 's not (he isn't or he's not)
are = 're (you're)	are not = aren't or 're not (you aren't or you're not)
was = XX (I was)	was not = wasn't (I wasn't)
were = XX (we were)	were not = weren't (we weren't)
have = 've (I've)	have not = haven't (I haven't or I've not)
has = 's (he's)	has not = hasn't or 's not (he hasn't or he's not)
had = 'd (he'd)	had not = hadn't (he hadn't)
will = 'll (they'll)	will not = won't (they won't)
would = 'd (I'd)	would not = wouldn't (I wouldn't)

The following verbs don't have contractions in the affirmative, but do in the negative:

cannot = can't	could not = couldn't	did not = didn't
do not = don't	does not = doesn't	
might not = mightn't	should not = shouldn't	

EXERCISE 9

CONTRACTIONS AND VERBS

In the space above each italicized contraction, write its long form. The first one is done for you.

She would
1. *She'd* let me know if she needed help.

2. *Alberto's* building a new house.

3. *Alberto's* built a new house.

4. *You'll* be sorry you missed the game.

5. The *car's* in the body shop for repairs.

6. On a rainy day, *I'm* likely to stay home and sleep.

7. *They'll* never sell their boat.

8. Do you think *you'd* like to visit Hong Kong?

9. *We've* proposed a good idea.

10. The neighbours *won't* turn down their television.

PREPOSITIONS

Prepositions are little words such as *with, for, of, around,* or *near.* (For more examples, see the Infobox in Chapter 12 on page 309.) Some prepositions can be confusing; these are the ones that show time and place.

Prepositions That Show Time

Use *at* to show a specific or precise time:

> I will call you **at** 7:30 p.m.
>
> The movie starts **at** midnight.

Use *on* with a specific day or date:

> The meeting is **on** Friday.
>
> Frances begins basic training **on** June 23.

Use *by* when you mean "no later than that time":

> Jean has to be at work **by** 8:00 a.m.
>
> We should be finished with the cleaning **by** 5:00 p.m.

Use *until* when you mean "continuing up to a time":

> Yesterday I slept **until** 10:00 a.m.
>
> The dentist cannot see me **until** tomorrow.

Use *in* when you refer to a specific time period (minutes, hours, days, months, years):

> I'll be with you **in** a minute.
>
> Nikela works **in** the morning. (You can also say **in** the afternoon, or **in** the evening, but **at** night.)

Use *during* when you refer to a continuing time period or within the time period:

> I fell asleep **during** his speech.
>
> My sister will study management **during** the summer.

ALONG THESE LINES/Pearson Education Canada

Use *for* to tell the length of a period of time:

> We have been married **for** two years.
>
> Wanda and Max cleaned the attic **for** three hours.

Use *since* to tell the starting time of an action:

> He has been calling **since** 9:00 a.m.
>
> We have been best friends **since** Grade Three.

Prepositions That Show Place

Use *in* to refer to a country, region, province, city, or neighbourhood:

> He studied **in** Ecuador.
>
> Mr. Etienne lives **in** St. Boniface.

Use *in* to refer to an enclosed space:

> He put the money **in** his wallet.
>
> Delia waited for me **in** the dining room.

Use *at* to refer to a specific address:

> The repair shop is **at** 7330 Glades Road.
>
> I live **at** 7520 Maple Lane.

Use *at* to refer to a corner or intersection:

> We went to a garage sale **at** the corner of Spring Street and High Park Avenue.
>
> The accident occurred **at** the intersection of Lakeshore Boulevard and Temple Road.

Use *on* to refer to a street or a block:

> Dr. Lopez lives **on** Hawthorne Street.
>
> Malcolm bought the biggest house **on** the block.

Use *on* to refer to a surface:

> Put the sandwiches **on** the table.
>
> There was a bright rug **on** the floor.

Use *off* to refer to a surface:

> Take the sandwiches **off** the table.
>
> She wiped the mud **off** the floor.

Use *into* and *out of* for small vehicles such as cars:

> Our dog leaped **into** the convertible.
>
> The children climbed **out of** the car.

Use *on* and *off* for large vehicles like planes, trains, buses, and boats:

> I was so seasick, I couldn't wait to get **off** the ship.
>
> I like to ride **on** the bus.

EXERCISE
10

CORRECTING ERRORS IN PREPOSITIONS

Correct any errors in prepositions in the following sentences. Write your corrections above the lines.

1. The dinner begins on 7:30 p.m. and will be over by 9:30 p.m.

2. I studied biology during two years until I changed my major to botany.

3. Come and see me on an hour, and we can talk about old times at Thunder Bay.

4. We got into the plane two hours before it left the runway.

5. The stack of mail in the table has been sitting there since a week.

6. The restaurant is at the corner of Victoria Avenue and Edward Street, but my house is farther down at River Drive.

7. I've been studying at my room since 4:00 p.m.

8. We walked to a sunny patio with bright wicker furniture in the tile floor.

9. Take my keys off the counter and put them on your backpack.

10. How long have you lived on 5545 Hammond Lane?

APPENDIX B
The Research Process

RESEARCH IN DAILY LIFE

During your college experience, you will no doubt use research techniques in your coursework as well as in your daily life. Even if you have not yet written a formal paper involving research, you probably have already employed various research techniques to solve problems or make crucial decisions. For example, deciding about what college to attend and learning about financial aid opportunities may have involved contacting professionals and taking careful notes. Similarly, if you are also a parent and have investigated community daycare options or family insurance plans, you are well aware of the importance of thorough research. Asking key questions and organizing your findings are research skills that can serve you well in college and in life.

USING RESEARCH TO STRENGTHEN ESSAYS

Many of the writing assignments you have completed thus far have probably been based on your own experiences, observations, or opinions. By writing regularly, you now know the importance of purpose, audience, organization, supporting details, and revision in producing a polished, final version of an essay. By appreciating the basics of effective writing, you can also recognize how essays can be strengthened through research. This appendix introduces you to the research process and explains how a student writer can strengthen his or her original essay by smoothly incorporating supporting material from outside sources.

AN EXAMPLE OF AN ESSAY WITHOUT RESEARCH

The following outline and short essay about dog-rescue groups are based solely on the writer's own experience and knowledge about dog-rescue operations. The writer's thesis is that such groups perform a humane service by rescuing homeless dogs and carefully matching potential adopters with suitable pets. (Later you will see how the writer smoothly incorporated information from five sources into an outline, draft, and final version of the essay.)

An Outline without Research

Here is the outline of an essay without research. You may notice that it is in the same form as the outlines you viewed in Chapter 11, "Writing an Essay."

ALONG THESE LINES/Pearson Education Canada

An Outline for an Essay without Research

I.   Dog-rescue organizations perform a humane service by saving homeless dogs and matching responsible adopters with a devoted new family member.

II. Dog-rescue volunteers play several roles.
   A. Some volunteers are "spotters" who look for specific breeds at local shelters.
   B. Experienced rescue volunteers may become coordinators and arrange assistance from various sources.
   C. Volunteers work with national organizations such as Save-A-Pet, which maintains a database of adoptable dogs from rescue groups throughout Canada and the United States.
   D. Volunteers assist at dog-rescue "Adoption Days" hosted by shelters and pet supply chains such as Pet Valu and PetSmart.

III. Rescue groups provide important information and benefits for prospective adopters.
   A. By viewing a rescue group's website, potential adopters can read about a dog's age, temperament, adoption fee, and any special medical conditions.
   B. If a potential adopter does not find a suitable dog, he or she can still complete an online application.
   C. On an application, a potential adopter can list his or her preferences for the age, sex, and size of the dog.
   D. Although some dogs are puppies rescued from abusive situations, most are adult dogs already socialized and housebroken.

IV. Careful screening often results in a successful adoption.
   A. Rescue groups routinely conduct home visits to check the living conditions and the neighbourhood.
   B. The applicant must have access to veterinary care.
   C. The applicant must agree to return the dog to the rescue organization if he or she can no longer care for the animal.
   D. A foster parent can fully inform the adoptive parent about potential adjustment problems.
   E. Careful attention to such details leads to a winning adoption process.

V.   Rescue groups not only provide care for homeless dogs, but also remind us of the joy made possible by compassionate adoption.

An Essay without Research

The following essay, written from the outline you have just reviewed, contains no research from outside sources; it is based solely on the writer's own knowledge and experience. As you read it, you will notice how the points in the outline have been developed through the use of specific details, effective sentence combining, and key transitions. You may also notice that some of the original words and phrases in the outline have been changed for better style.

The Humane Work of Dog-Rescue Groups

Although Canada and the United States are generally regarded as countries that love and pamper their pets, animal shelters are often filled to capacity with dogs that have been abandoned, abused, or surrendered by their owners. Sadly, some shelters routinely euthanize healthy dogs if no one claims or adopts them after a grace period ranging from just days to a few weeks. Fortunately, however, many shelters work closely with dog-rescue organizations that find loving, temporary homes where foster parents can provide care and, if necessary, rehabilitation. Staffed by dedicated volunteers, rescue groups perform a humane service by saving homeless dogs and enabling responsible adopters to gain a devoted new family member.

From rescuing retired greyhounds to saving mini "mutts," dog-rescue volunteers play several roles. For example, they often serve as "spotters" at local shelters, looking for specific dogs that can be fostered by individuals who specialize in specific breeds such as boxers and golden retrievers. Experienced volunteers may become coordinators who arrange for assistance from a variety of sources, including local veterinarians, groomers, transporters, and website designers. Many rescue groups work closely with organizations such as Save-A-Pet, whose website publishes a comprehensive list of adoptable rescue dogs throughout Canada and the United States. On weekends, rescue volunteers can be seen helping out during "Adoption Days" sponsored by shelters and retailers such as Pet Valu and PetSmart.

Rescue groups provide both crucial information and welcome benefits for potential adopters. When one becomes interested in a specific dog on a rescue group's website, he or she can read about the animal's medical needs, age, temperament, and adoption fee. Even if he or she does not spot a suitable dog but remains interested in adopting one from rescue, he or she can fill out an application and list preferences regarding a dog's age, sex, and size. Although rescue groups occasionally receive puppies and young dogs that have been picked up during police raids of abusive puppy mills and backyard breeders, the majority of dogs available for adoption are older ones. Any pet owner who has experienced the aggravation of sleepless nights and numerous housetraining "accidents" can appreciate the benefits of adopting an older, socialized, and housebroken dog.

Although the adoption process may take several weeks or even months to find the best match, careful screening improves the chances for a successful adoption. Rescue groups routinely conduct home visits of prospective dog owners to see if both the living conditions and the neighbourhood will be suitable for the dog's size, temperament, and exercise needs. In addition, the applicant must have access to veterinary care and agree to return the dog to the rescue organization if he or she can no longer properly care for it. A foster parent can fully inform the adoptive parent about a dog's potential adjustment problems because the animal's behaviour has been observed over a period of weeks—if not months—in a home setting. Careful attention to such details leads to a winning adoption process.

However a dog finds its way to a rescue group—by an owner surrender, a good Samaritan, or even by a police raid of an illegal breeding operation—it will have an opportunity to live out the rest of its life free from harm and neglect. Not only do rescue groups provide care for homeless dogs, but they also remind us of the joy made possible by compassion, commitment, and unconditional love.

FINDING RESEARCH TO STRENGTHEN ESSAYS

Locating Material in Your Library

The Library Catalogue If you decide to use research to strengthen an essay, you can take advantage of a number of options. Your public or college library probably has an online catalogue system that lists all of the library's books and major holdings. You can search the catalogue by a keyword related to your subject, or, if you already have information about authors who deal with your subject, you can search by an author's last name or the title of an author's book. An online catalogue can provide you with a list of sources, the call number of each source (the number that will help you find the book on the library shelves), and information regarding the availability of the source. The catalogue can tell you which location has a copy of the book you want. Be sure to take advantage of any "Help" menu the system provides as well as any orientation offered at your library.

Popular Periodical Indexes Libraries commonly subscribe to several index services that provide access to complete articles (called "full-text" articles) from periodicals (magazines, journals, and newspapers). Some of the most widely used periodical indexes include the following: *EBSCOhost*, *InfoTrac*, *LexisNexis*, *NewsBank*, *ProQuest*, and *WilsonWeb*.

Always preview articles carefully to see if they contain useful information for your research essay. Scan articles online, and print copies of the pages that will be useful for highlighting and note taking later. Also copy the first and last page of the article; these pages include information you will need for giving credit to the author and the source of the article. Be sure to ask your instructor if he or she will require copies of entire articles or just the pages you used in your essay.

Internet Search Engines You are probably very familiar with searching the Internet to obtain information. Your browser gives you access to institutions, organizations, and publications as well as libraries around the world through the World Wide Web. Unfortunately, the highly changeable nature of the Internet means that some links posted on websites may be unavailable, and students will have to conduct searches carefully. Also, outdated information may remain posted on a website indefinitely, so students need to be cautious about using statistics or expert opinions that are several years old.

Checking for Validity of Sources

The writer of the dog-rescue essay decided to strengthen his paper by adding material from outside sources. The instructor required students to incorporate information from at least one print publication (magazine, newspaper, or book) and two valid electronic (online) sources. While a traditional research paper involves a more comprehensive use of outside sources and a lengthier planning and research process, a short essay can often be enhanced by adding relevant material from experts. Regardless of the scope of any research assignment, the sources used must be valid.

The student began his Internet search by typing the key phrase "dog rescue organizations" into the Google search function. This initial search resulted in a list of several hundred potential sources. After consulting with his instructor about the validity of his sources, the student was able to narrow his list to several dozen suitable sources.

Although the Internet and popular search engines are valuable tools to use for research, students are often tempted to use information from a website without checking for accuracy or validity. Students should check the author's credentials, such as educational background and professional experience, and other significant connections. In addition, students should locate any information about the background of the company or individuals responsible for a website. For example, if a student is investigating dog-rescue groups, the words of a veterinarian or background information from a nonprofit organization such as the Canadian Federation of Humane Societies can generally be considered reliable. Because the veterinarian and the nonprofit group are experienced and have no financial ties to the selling of dogs, their information is more valid than opinions from a pet shop owner, who makes money selling pets, or from a chat room popular with pet owners, who may know very little about dog-rescue groups.

Print sources need to be evaluated just as carefully. For example, a brochure advertising quick or foolproof dog-training programs would not be as reliable as an article from a magazine endorsed by the Canadian Society for the Prevention of Cruelty to Animals (CSPCA). Many colleges offer library orientations that include suggestions for determining the validity of a website's information and of a print source's reliability.

If you have any doubt about a source's validity, check with your instructor or seek advice from a librarian. At the very least, see if an article lists the title or credentials of the author. If you have found an unsigned article, see if the organization responsible for the material lists its history and/or purpose. Also check for the publication date of the article, the original place of publication, the tone of the article (i.e. Does it avoid slang? Does it appear serious?), and the proper use of statistics and expert opinion. Using valid sources will lend credibility to your work.

INCORPORATING AND ACKNOWLEDGING YOUR SOURCES

Gathering and Organizing Sources

Once you have previewed your potential sources and have selected the ones best suited for your topic, you will need printouts of any online article (or at least the necessary pages) for highlighting and note taking. If you are using a book or a magazine in its original form, you need to photocopy the relevant pages. To keep track of all the sources you are using, you should staple or paper-clip the pages of each source and label each one clearly.

If you have narrowed your search to several sources (for example, three magazine articles, two newspaper articles, and one book), you could organize your sources alphabetically by the authors' last names. If an article does not list its author, you can use the first major word of the title in place of the author's last name. Then you can label your sources as Source #1, Source #2, and so forth. This type of labelling will be useful for you later as you develop an outline that includes references to your sources.

Your instructor may want to see a preliminary list of your potential sources, and he or she may also require that your notes from sources be written on note cards. Other instructors may encourage you to use your computer for note taking. Be sure you follow your instructor's specific guidelines and directions.

Taking Notes and Acknowledging Your Sources

When you take notes from one of your sources and use the information in your paper, you must acknowledge the source. This acknowledgment is called **documentation** because you are documenting, or giving credit to, the author and the work that provided the information. When you provide documentation within a research essay, you are using what is called **internal citation**. "Citation" means "giving credit," and "internal" means "inside," or "within," the paper. At the end of your essay, you list all the sources you cited within the paper. This list is called the **Works Cited** in MLA and the **References** in APA (see below). The list of works cited is on a separate page from the rest of the essay, and it is the last numbered page of the essay.

Avoiding Plagiarism

Plagiarism occurs when you use a source's words or ideas and fail to give proper credit to the author and/or source of the work. Even if you **paraphrase** (state someone else's ideas in your own wording; see Chapter 2), you must give credit to the original source.

Whether you summarize material from an outside source, quote directly from it, or even paraphrase from it, you must acknowledge the source. Failure to do so is a form of academic theft. Depending on departmental or college policy, the penalties for plagiarism can be severe, ranging from receiving a failing grade on the plagiarized paper or failing a course to expulsion. Some departments now use special software programs to check all student papers for plagiarism, and it is simply not worth the risk to submit research assignments without proper documentation.

Options for Acknowledging Your Sources

The Modern Language Association (**MLA**) system of documentation is used in English and the humanities. Psychology and social sciences use the American Psychological Association (**APA**) system of documentation. Be sure to follow your instructor's directions regarding documentation requirements for your research assignments. There are many handbooks available that contain both MLA and APA styles of documentation, and many writing courses require that students purchase a handbook. You may want to check with your instructor to see which handbook is used in your program.

Over the next several pages, you will see how MLA and APA documentation is used for summarizing, paraphrasing, and directly quoting information from sources. You will also see how books, periodicals, and electronic sources should be listed on a Works Cited or References page that conforms to MLA or APA guidelines.

Internal ("In-Text") Citation: MLA (2003) and APA Format

When using internal citation, you have several options for incorporating and giving credit to the source of your information. If you use a combination of techniques, your paper will read more smoothly. The following examples of summarizing, directly quoting, paraphrasing, and combining a direct quote and paraphrasing will provide you with sufficient documentation options as you draft your essay. Notice that authors, years, and page numbers (depending on the system) appear in parentheses, and this form is called **parenthetical documentation**.

ALONG THESE LINES/Pearson Education Canada

A Summary of an Entire Book

MLA

The book <u>One at a Time: A Week in an American Animal Shelter</u> describes the fate of seventy-five animals who passed through a local shelter in Northern California over a seven-day period (Leigh and Geyer).

APA

The book *One at a Time: A Week in an American Animal Shelter* describes the fate of seventy-five animals who passed through a local shelter in Northern California over a seven-day period (Leigh & Geyer, 2003).

Note: No page numbers are included in the in-text citation because the *entire* work is summarized. In MLA format, you will notice that the title of the book is underlined. MLA format also accepts italics for titles if the formatting is clear. You can ask your instructor whether you should use underlining or italics when using MLA format. In APA format, the title of the book is in italics, and major words are capitalized (i.e. not conjunctions, articles, and short prepositions of three letters or fewer), as well as proper nouns and the first letter in the title and subtitle. APA in-text citation uses an ampersand (&) and a comma before the year of publication.

A Direct Quotation

MLA

According to Leigh and Geyer, "The safest and most reliable identification is provided by a combination of an ID tag, which is easily visible, and a microchip, which is permanent" (2).

APA

According to Leigh and Geyer, "The safest and most reliable identification is provided by a combination of an ID tag, which is easily visible, and a microchip, which is permanent" (2003, p. 2).

Note: If you introduce the author in the sentence that quotes from his or her work, you do not have to include the author's name in parentheses at the end of the quoted material. APA citations include the year of publication, and 'p.' to represent the page from which the quotation was taken. Notice that the period for the sentence goes after the final parenthesis. When multiple authors are referred to in the sentence, write out *and* instead of using the ampersand as in in-text citations.

A Paraphrase

MLA

A clearly marked ID tag, along with a permanent microchip, provides an animal with the best and safest means of identification (Leigh and Geyer 2).

APA

A clearly marked ID tag, along with a permanent microchip, provides an animal with the best and safest means of identification (Leigh & Geyer, 2003, p. 2).

A Source Quoted in Another Author's Work

MLA

Kathy Nicklas-Varraso, author of <u>What to Expect from Breed Rescue</u>, notes that adopters will "most often get an adult whose chewing phase, housebreaking phase, and general puppy wildness are gone" (qtd. in Mohr).

APA

Kathy Nicklas-Varraso, author of *What to Expect From Breed Rescue*, notes that adopters will "most often get an adult whose chewing phase, housebreaking phase, and general puppy wildness are gone" (as cited in Mohr, n.d.).

Note: Nicklas-Varraso is the author being quoted; her comment was found in an online magazine article by Mohr. Mohr is the source that the student writer found. Therefore, Mohr is the source cited in parentheses. No page numbers are cited when the article comes from an online magazine. No date was associated with the article, so APA uses "n.d." instead of a year.

A Combination of a Direct Quotation and a Paraphrase

MLA   Leigh and Geyer emphasize that the best means of identification for an animal is "provided by a combination of an ID tag, which is easily visible, and a microchip, which is permanent" (2).

APA   Leigh and Geyer emphasize that the best means of identification for an animal is "provided by a combination of an ID tag, which is easily visible, and a microchip, which is permanent" (2003, p. 2).

A Source with an Unknown Author

MLA   As the article "The Rules of Local Zoning Boards" notes, many counties prohibit businesses from operating out of garages in residential communities (C1).

APA   As the article "The Rules of Local Zoning Boards" notes, many counties prohibit businesses from operating out of garages in residential communities (2004, p. C1).

or

MLA   Many counties prohibit businesses from operating out of garages in residential communities ("Rules" C1).

APA   Many counties prohibit businesses from operating out of garages in residential communities ("Rules," 2004, p. C1).

Note: In MLA and APA format, if no author is provided for a source, you can introduce the full title of the work in the sentence or place an abbreviation of the title in parentheses at the end of the information being cited. When your source is a newspaper article, as in the examples above, give the section of the newspaper and the page number, as in C1, which stands for section C, page 1. In MLA format, article titles are placed within quotation marks; publication titles such as books or periodicals are underlined. Similarly, in APA format, article titles are in quotation marks; however, publication titles are in italics rather than underlined, and the year is included in the citation.

Signal Phrases

In some of the above examples, **signal phrases** are used to introduce quoted or paraphrased material. Signal phrases such as "Leigh and Geyer emphasize," "According to Leigh and Geyer," "Kathy Nicklas-Varraso notes," and "As the article 'The Rules of Local Zoning Boards' notes" are phrases that enable you to lead smoothly into documented information. Here are some of the more commonly used signal phrases, using *Smith* as the author:

According to Smith,	Smith reports that
As Smith notes,	Smith claims that
Smith suggests that	Smith points out that
Smith emphasizes that	Smith contends that

Works Cited and References List: MLA and APA Format

The **Works Cited** (MLA) and **References** (APA) list of sources contain only the works you cited in your paper. This alphabetized list starts on a separately numbered page after the essay itself. The following sample entries represent some of the most commonly used sources. Entries should be **double-spaced,** and the second and subsequent lines of each entry should be **indented five spaces.** Double-spacing should also be used between each entry.

BOOKS

Book by One Author

MLA

MacDonald, Cheryl Emily. <u>Pets to Remember</u>. Canmore: Altitude Publishing, 2006.

APA

MacDonald, C. E. (2006). *Pets to remember.* Canmore: Altitude Publishing.

Note: Canmore is the place of publication, Altitude Publishing is the publisher, and 2006 is the year of publication. Short forms of the publisher's name should be used, so "Inc.," "Co.," and "Press" can be omitted. Note that book titles in APA format are in sentence case; that is, only proper names and the first letter of the title and subtitle are capitalized. Book titles are usually underlined in MLA format, italicized in APA format.

Book by Two Authors

MLA

Leigh, Diane, and Marilee Geyer. <u>One at a Time: A Week in an American Animal Shelter</u>. Santa Cruz: No Voice Unheard, 2003.

APA

Leigh, D., & Geyer, M. (2003). *One at a time: A week in an American animal shelter.* Santa Cruz: No Voice Unheard.

Note: In MLA format, when two or three authors are listed, the name of the first author is listed last name first, and the other authors are listed in regular order. If there are more than three authors, the name of the first author is listed last name first and followed by the Latin phrase *et al.,* which means "and others." In APA format, when up to and including six authors are named, list all the authors, using an ampersand (&) before the final author's name. If more than six authors are named, list all six, then replace additional authors' names with "et al." For both MLA and APA, et al. is not italicized, and a period is placed after "al." but not after "et."

Short Work in an Anthology

MLA

Belloc, Hillaire. "Letter from Canada." <u>The Very Richness of That Past: Canada through the Eyes of Foreign Writers</u>. Ed. Greg Gatenby. Toronto: Vintage Canada, 1995. 49–53.

APA

Belloc, H. (1995). Letter from Canada. In G. Gatenby (Ed.), *The very richness of that past: Canada through the eyes of foreign writers* (pp. 49–53). Toronto: Vintage Canada.

Note: An anthology is a book-length collection of short works such as articles, essays, poems, or short stories. It usually has at least one editor who compiles and organizes all of the short works, which are written by different authors. When you are citing from an anthology in MLA format, begin with the author of the short work and its title; then provide the name of the anthology and its editor. Continue with the place of publication, the publisher, and the year of publication. At the end of the entry, list the page numbers of the short work. The formatting of the entry in APA format is slightly different, including the order of information and the capitalization.

Introduction from a Book

MLA

Niedzviecki, Hal. Introduction. <u>We Want Some Too: Underground Desire and the Reinvention of Mass Culture</u>. By Niedzviecki. Toronto: Penguin Books, 2000. i–xvi.

APA

Niedzviecki, H. (2000). Introduction. In H. Niedzviecki, *We want some too: Underground desire and the reinvention of mass culture* (pp. i–xvi). Toronto: Penguin Books.

Note: Sometimes a book will contain an introduction, preface, or foreword written by someone other than the author of the book. When citing from such introductory material in MLA, begin with the author of this material, followed by the word *Introduction* (or *Preface* or *Foreword*) not enclosed in quotation marks or italicized or underlined, the name of the book, the author of the book (if different from the author of the piece, write in full as *By John Smith*), place of publication, publisher, date of publication, and page numbers of the introduction, which will be in small Roman numerals. For APA format, remember that the title of the book is in italics, and that only the proper nouns and first letter of the title and subtitle are capitalized.

Dictionary or Encyclopedia

MLA

"Luxate." <u>Nelson Canadian Dictionary of the English Language</u>. 2nd ed. Toronto: ITP Nelson, 1997.

APA

Harkness, J., Friend, D., Keefer, J., Liebman, D., & Sutherland, F. (Eds.). (1997). *Nelson Canadian dictionary of the English language* (2nd ed.). Toronto: ITP Nelson.

Note: "Luxate" is the word you defined by using this dictionary. APA format does not include the word you defined.

PERIODICALS

Periodicals are newspapers, magazines, and scholarly journals.

Newspaper Article

MLA

Weidner, Johanna. "A Great Outing for Fido: Dog Park Visits." <u>Guelph Mercury</u> 19 Jan. 2008: C2.

APA

Weidner, J. (2008, January 19). A great outing for Fido: Dog park visits. *Guelph Mercury*, p. C2.

Note: In MLA Works Cited listings, all months except May, June, and July are abbreviated. Months are not abbreviated in APA format. C2 refers to the section (C) and page number (2) of the article. Note that all key words in periodical titles are capitalized in both MLA and APA formats.

ALONG THESE LINES/Pearson Education Canada

Newspaper Editorial

MLA

"Reality Check, of a Sort." Editorial. <u>Edmonton Journal</u> 10 June 2008: A16.

APA

Reality check, of a sort. [Editorial]. (2008, June 10). *Edmonton Journal*, p. A16.

Note: Newspaper editorials do not list an author.

Magazine Article (from a Monthly or Bimonthly Publication)

MLA

Weder, Adele. "A Nip and Tuck." <u>Canadian Architect</u> Apr. 2008: 32–36.

APA

Weder, A. (2008, April). A nip and tuck. *Canadian Architect*, 32–36.

Note: "32–36" refers to the page numbers of the magazine where the article is found.

Magazine Article (from a Weekly Publication)

MLA

Taylor, Peter Shawn. "Licensed to Whup Ass." <u>Maclean's</u> 16 June 2008: 20–21.

APA

Taylor, P. S. (2008, June 16). Licensed to whup ass. *Maclean's*, 20–21.

Journal Article

MLA

Kirby, Dale. "Change and Challenge: Ontario's Collaborative Baccalaureate Nursing Programs." <u>Canadian Journal of Higher Education</u> 37.2 (2007): 29–48.

APA

Kirby, D. (2007). Change and challenge: Ontario's collaborative baccalaureate nursing programs. *Canadian Journal of Higher Education*, 37(2), 29–48.

Note: The number 37 is the volume number, 2 is the issue number, and 2007 is the year of publication. In APA, the volume number is italicized but not the issue number.

ELECTRONIC SOURCES

Electronic sources can include professional websites, online periodicals, works from subscription services (such as NewsBank), and even emails.

When you list a website as one of your sources, you should include as many of the following items as you can find on the site (the order will vary depending on whether you are using MLA or APA):

1. Author or group author's name
2. Title of the site or item
3. Date of publication or date of latest update
4. The company or organization that sponsors the website (if it is different from the group author)
5. Date you accessed the website
6. URL (list it with angle brackets for MLA)

Entire Website

MLA

Canadian Federation of Humane Societies. Home page. 13 June 2008
<http://cfhs.ca/>.

APA

(In text): The Canadian Federation of Humane Societies provides information
about protecting your pets in hot summer weather (http://cfhs.ca/).

Note: In this example, the sponsoring organization—the Canadian Federation of Humane Societies—is also the group author of the site, so it is not repeated. Occasionally, the URL address will appear on its own line because word processing programs will not split the site's address when slashes are used. You should not allow your wordprocessing program to hyphenate a URL, because the hyphen could be mistaken as part of the web address. In APA, if you are citing an entire website, give the address in the text of your essay rather than including it in the reference list.

Article or Short Work from a Website

MLA

Mohr, Lori. "Adopting from a Breed Rescue Group." Animal Forum.com.
13 June 2008 <http://www.animalforum.com/dbreedrescue.htm>.

APA

Mohr, L. (n.d.). Adopting from a breed rescue group. Retrieved June 13,
2008, from Animal Forum.com website: http://www.animalforum.com/
dbreedrescue.htm

Note: In this example, the name of the author is known; however, often the name might not be given. If the name of the author is not given, use the name of the sponsoring organization (e.g. Animal Forum) instead. Include a publication date if possible, and don't forget to include the date you accessed the article (i.e. June 13, 2008). Page numbers are not listed for online articles because different printers will affect the page numbering of the printed article. However, the exception to this rule is that if an article is contained within a PDF file, the page numbers can be listed because the numbers will be consistent regardless of the system used. Notice that in MLA format you use angle brackets around the URL and end with a period, and in APA format you don't use angle brackets and there is no final period after the URL.

Article from an Online Magazine

MLA

Woolf, Norma Bennett. "Getting Involved in Purebred Rescue." Dog Owner's
Guide 18 May 2005. 20 June 2008 <http://www.canismajor.com/dog/
rescinv.html>.

APA

Woolf, N. B. (2005, May 18). Getting involved in purebred rescue. *Dog Owner's
Guide.* Retrieved June 20, 2008, from http://www.canismajor.com/dog/
rescinv.html

Email

MLA

Stuckey, Rachel. "Information for Project Meeting." Email to the author. 28 May
2008.

APA

(In text): Rachel Stuckey (personal communication, May 28, 2008) proposed
solutions for the editorial queries in the author's text.

Note: In APA format, email should not be included in the References list. However, do provide an in-text citation (see above).

OTHER SOURCES: NON-PRINT

Personal Interview

 Sauer, Lara. Personal interview. 6 June 2008.

APA As with email, personal correspondence such as an interview is documented only in the text (see in "Email" above).

Radio or Television Program

MLA "Parents Again." W-FIVE. Narr. Sandie Rinaldo. CTV. CTVglobemedia. 16 Feb. 2008.

APA Fox, M. (Producer). (2008, February 16). Parents again [Television broadcast]. In Fox (Producer), *W-FIVE*. Toronto: CTVglobemedia.

Note: In this listing, "Narr." refers to the narrator of the program, and "CTV" refers to the network. The date is the date of the broadcast. Note the different information required for APA citations.

Incorporating Research into Your Outline

After you have compiled all of your notes from your sources, you need to determine what information you will use and where it best fits into your essay. The best way to do this is to work with your original outline before you draft a research version of your essay. Here again is the outline for the dog-rescue essay, but it is a bit different from the outline on page 464. This version now includes references to sources; key information from these sources will be the research that strengthens the essay.

Notice that the headings "Introduction" and "Conclusion" have been added to the outline. In this version, the writer wanted to include some relevant research in both the introductory and concluding paragraphs as well as in the body paragraphs, so he or she expanded the outline. By placing research references in the outline, the student writer will know where the new information will be included when he or she prepares the drafts and final version of the research essay.

Note: The references to the added research appear in bold print so that you can compare this outline with the previous one without research on page 464.

An Outline for an Essay with Research

    I.   Introduction
        A. Every year, more than 100,000 dogs and cats are euthanized at animal shelters and pounds across Canada. **See MacDonald, source #2.**
        B. Some shelters euthanize animals routinely. **See Leigh and Geyer, source #1.**
        C. Some shelters work with rescue groups.

        Thesis Statement: Dog-rescue organizations perform a humane service by saving homeless dogs and matching responsible adopters with a devoted new family member.

II.   Dog-rescue volunteers play several roles.
    A.   Some volunteers are "spotters" who look for specific breeds at local shelters.
    B.   Experienced rescue volunteers may become coordinators and arrange assistance from various sources. **See Woolf, source #5.**
    C.   Volunteers work with national organizations such as Save-A-Pet, which maintains a database of adoptable dogs from rescue groups throughout Canada and the United States.
    D.   Volunteers assist at dog-rescue "Adoption Days" hosted by pet supply chains such as Pet Valu and PetSmart.

III. Rescue groups provide important information and benefits for prospective adopters.
    A.   By viewing a rescue group's website, potential adopters can read about a dog's age, temperament, adoption fee, and any special medical conditions.
    B.   If a potential adopter does not find a suitable dog, he or she can still complete an online application.
    C.   On an application, a potential adopter can list his or her preferences for the age, sex, and size of the dog.
    D.   Although some dogs are puppies rescued from abusive situations, most are adult dogs already socialized and housebroken. **See Nicklas-Varraso in Mohr, source #3.**

IV.   Careful screening often results in a successful adoption.
    A.   Rescue groups routinely conduct home visits to check the living conditions and the neighbourhood.
    B.   The applicant must have access to veterinary care.
    C.   The applicant must agree to return the dog to the rescue organization if he or she can no longer care for the animal.
    D.   A foster parent can fully inform the adoptive parent about potential adjustment problems.
    E.   Careful attention to such details leads to a winning adoption process.

V.   Conclusion
    A.   Rescue groups provide an opportunity for a dog to live out the rest of its life free from harm and neglect.
    B.   We should "embrace nonlethal strategies" to show we are a humane society. See **Toronto Humane Society, source #4.**

Concluding Statement: Rescue groups not only provide care for homeless dogs, but also remind us of the joy made possible by compassionate adoption.

A Draft of an Essay with Research

The following is a rough version of the original essay on dog-rescue groups; it has been strengthened with some material from outside sources. (The material is underlined so that you can spot it easily.) The marginal annotations will alert you to (1) places where the information is directly quoted or paraphrased, and (2) places where revisions are necessary to achieve a better style. Note that this essay is being prepared using MLA documentation.

ALONG THESE LINES/Pearson Education Canada

The Humane Work of Dog-Rescue Groups

Although Canada and the United States are generally regarded as countries that love and pamper their pets, animal shelters are often filled to capacity with dogs that have been abandoned, abused, or surrendered by their owners. <u>Every year, more than 100,000 dogs and cats are euthanized at animal shelters and pounds across Canada (MacDonald).</u> Sadly, some shelters routinely euthanize healthy animals if no one claims or adopts them after a grace period ranging from just days to a few weeks. <u>Dogs such as these have only "about a fifty percent chance of getting out alive" (Leigh and Geyer viii).</u> Fortunately, however, many shelters work closely with dog-rescue organizations that find loving, temporary homes where foster parents can provide care and, if necessary, rehabilitation. Staffed by dedicated volunteers, rescue groups perform a humane service by saving homeless dogs and enabling responsible adopters to gain a devoted new family member.

From rescuing retired greyhounds to saving mini "mutts," dog-rescue volunteers play several roles. For example, they often serve as "spotters" at local shelters, looking for specific dogs that can be fostered by individuals who specialize in specific breeds such as boxers and golden retrievers. Experienced volunteers may become coordinators who arrange for assistance from a variety of sources, including local veterinarians, groomers, transporters, and website designers. <u>Norma Bennett Woolf writes for the online magazine, Dog Owner's Guide. Woolf states, "There's always room for more foster homes, fund-raisers, dog spotters, kennels, public relations workers, and trainers."</u> Many rescue groups work closely with national organizations such as Save-A-Pet, whose website publishes a comprehensive list of adoptable rescue dogs throughout Canada and the United States. On weekends, rescue volunteers can be seen helping out during "Adoption Days" sponsored by shelters and retailers such as Pet Valu and PetSmart.

Rescue groups provide both crucial information and welcome benefits for potential adopters. When one becomes interested in a specific dog on a rescue group's website, he or she can read about the animal's medical needs, age, temperament, and adoption fee. Even if he or she does not spot a suitable dog but remains interested in adopting one from rescue, he or she can fill out an application and list preferences regarding a dog's age, sex, and size. Although rescue groups occasionally receive puppies and young dogs that have been picked up during police raids of abusive puppy mills and backyard breeders, the majority of dogs available for adoption are older ones. Kathy Nicklas-Varraso wrote <u>What to Expect from Breed Rescue. This writer says, "You'll most often get an adult whose chewing phase, housebreaking phase, and general puppy wildness are gone" (qtd. in Mohr).</u> Any pet owner who has experienced the aggravation of sleepless nights and numerous housetraining "accidents" can appreciate the benefits of adopting an older, socialized, and housebroken dog.

Although the adoption process may take several weeks or even months to find the best match, careful screening improves the chances

Margin notes

statistic and paraphrased statement from website, author given

direct quotation from the preface of a book with two authors

direct quotation from an online magazine; sentence combining needed; magazine title should retain underlining in final version

a source quoted in another author's work; needs to be more smoothly blended

for a successful adoption. Rescue groups routinely conduct home visits of prospective dog owners to see if both the living conditions and the neighbourhood will be suitable for the dog's size, temperament, and exercise needs. In addition, the applicant must have access to veterinary care and agree to return the dog to the rescue organization if he or she can no longer properly care for it. A foster parent can fully inform the adoptive parent about a dog's potential adjustment problems because the animal's behaviour has been observed over a period of weeks—if not months—in a home setting. Nicklas-Varraso states, "Borderline pets are offered for adoption within strict guidelines, such as no other pets or fenced yards only" (qtd. in Mohr). Careful attention to such details leads to a winning adoption process.

direct quote; needs a transition

However a dog finds its way to a rescue group—by an owner surrender, a good Samaritan, or even by a police raid of an illegal breeding operation—it will have an opportunity to live out the rest of its life free from harm and neglect. "Some of our animals have been here for a long time, but no matter how long it takes, they stay with us until the day they are adopted" (Toronto Humane Society). Not only do rescue groups provide care for homeless dogs, but they also remind us of the joy made possible by compassion, commitment, and unconditional love.

direct quotation from a website; no author, no publication date

Note: A Works Cited page will be included in the final version of this essay.

PREPARING THE FINAL VERSION OF AN ESSAY WITH RESEARCH

Making Final Changes and Refinements

The final version of the research essay includes the refinements suggested in the margins of the previous draft. You will notice that the final essay reflects proper MLA documentation and page numbering format. Other improvements relate to the style of the essay. Changes from the previous draft include the following:

- The title has been changed to be more descriptive and appealing.
- Information from sources has been more smoothly blended by combining sentences and using signal phrases.
- An awkward repetition of "he or she" has been changed to the more specific term "a potential adopter" in the third paragraph.
- The word "humane" has been added in the last paragraph to reinforce the idea of compassionate care for animals.
- To conform to MLA format, the writer has placed his name, his instructor's name, the course title, and the date in the upper left-hand corner of the first page.
- Again following MLA guidelines, the writer has placed his last name and page number in the upper right-hand corner of each page of the essay.
- A Works Cited page, in proper MLA format, is included and appears as the last page of the essay.

ALONG THESE LINES/Pearson Education Canada

Roberts 1

Jason Roberts

Professor Alvarez

English 100

7 December 2008

Crusading for Canines: Dog-Rescue

Groups and Winning Adoptions

Although Canada and the United States are generally regarded as countries that love and pamper their pets, animal shelters are often filled to capacity with dogs that have been abandoned, abused, or surrendered by their owners. Every year, more than 100,000 dogs and cats are euthanized at animal shelters and pounds across Canada (MacDonald). Sadly, some shelters routinely euthanize healthy animals if no one claims or adopts them after a grace period ranging from just days to a few weeks. Dogs such as these have only "about a fifty percent chance of getting out alive" (Leigh and Geyer viii). Fortunately, however, many shelters work closely with dog-rescue organizations that find loving, temporary homes where foster parents can provide care and, if necessary, rehabilitation. Staffed by dedicated volunteers, rescue groups perform a humane service by saving homeless dogs and enabling responsible adopters to gain a devoted new family member.

From rescuing retired greyhounds to saving mini "mutts," dog-rescue volunteers play several roles. For example, they often serve as "spotters" at local shelters, looking for specific dogs that can be fostered by individuals who specialize in specific breeds such as boxers and golden retrievers. Experienced volunteers may become coordinators who arrange for assistance from a variety of sources, including local veterinarians, groomers, transporters, and website designers. As Norma Bennett Woolf suggests in the online magazine <u>Dog Owner's Guide</u>, "There's always room for more foster homes, fund-raisers, dog-spotters, kennels, public relations workers, and trainers." Many rescue groups work closely with national organizations such as Save-A-Pet, whose website publishes a comprehensive list of adoptable rescue dogs throughout Canada and the United States. On weekends, rescue volunteers can be seen helping out during "Adoption Days" sponsored by shelters and retailers such as Pet Valu and PetSmart.

    Rescue groups provide both crucial information and welcome benefits for potential adopters. When one becomes interested in a specific dog on a rescue group's website, he or she can read about the animal's medical needs, age, temperament, and adoption fee. Even if a potential adopter does not spot a suitable dog but remains interested in adopting one from rescue, he or she can fill out an application and list preferences regarding a dog's age, sex, and size. Although rescue groups occasionally receive puppies and young dogs that have been picked up during police raids of abusive puppy mills and backyard breeders, the majority of dogs available for adoption are older ones. Kathy Nicklas-Varraso, author of <u>What to Expect from Breed Rescue</u>, notes that adopters will "most often get an adult whose chewing phase, housebreaking phase, and general puppy wildness are gone" (qtd. in Mohr). Any pet owner who has experienced the aggravation of sleepless nights and numerous housetraining "accidents" can appreciate the benefits of adopting an older, socialized, and housebroken dog.

Roberts 3

Although the adoption process may take several weeks or even months to find the best match, careful screening improves the chances for a successful adoption. Rescue groups routinely conduct home visits of prospective dog owners to see if both the living conditions and the neighbourhood will be suitable for the dog's size, temperament, and exercise needs. In addition, the applicant must have access to veterinary care and agree to return the dog to the rescue organization if he or she can no longer properly care for it. A foster parent can fully inform the adoptive parent about a dog's potential adjustment problems because the animal's behaviour has been observed over a period of weeks—if not months—in a home setting. Nicklas-Varraso stresses that the "borderline pets are offered for adoption within strict guidelines, such as no other pets or fenced yards only" (qtd. in Mohr). Careful attention to such details leads to a winning adoption process.

However a dog finds its way to a rescue group—by an owner surrender, a good Samaritan, or even by a police raid of an illegal breeding operation—it will have an opportunity to live out the rest of its life free from harm and neglect. "Some of our animals have been here for a long time, but no matter how long it takes, they stay with us until the day they are adopted" (Toronto Humane Society). Not only do rescue groups provide humane care for homeless dogs, but they also remind us of the joy made possible by compassion, commitment, and unconditional love.

Roberts 4

Works Cited

Leigh, Diane, and Marilee Geyer. Preface. <u>One at a Time: A Week in an</u>

<u>American Animal Shelter</u>. By Leigh and Geyer. Santa Cruz: No Voice

Unheard, 2003. vii–viii.

MacDonald, Shelagh. "Can We Save Them All?" In <u>Animal Welfare in Focus</u>.

Spring 2004. Canadian Federation of Humane Societies. 25 June 2008

<http://cfhs.ca/info/can_we_save_them_all/>.

Mohr, Lori. "Adopting from a Breed Rescue Group." <u>Animal Forum.com</u>.

13 June 2008 <http://www.animalforum.com/dbreedrescue.htm>.

Toronto Humane Society. "News and Events: Keeping You Up to Date."

25 June 2008 <http://www.torontohumanesociety.com/newsandevents/

default.asp>.

Woolf, Norma Bennett. "Getting Involved in Purebred Rescue." <u>Dog Owner's</u>

<u>Guide</u> 18 May 2005. 20 June 2008 <http://www.canismajor.com/dog/

rescinv.html>.

CREDITS

ALONG THESE LINES/Pearson Education Canada